THI
ST. MARY'S
ST. MARY'S

ADVANCES
IN THE PSYCHOLOGY
OF HUMAN INTELLIGENCE

Volume 2

ADVANCES IN THE PSYCHOLOGY OF HUMAN INTELLIGENCE

Volume 2

Edited by

Robert J. Sternberg

Yale University

LEA LAWRENCE ERLBAUM ASSOCIATES, PUBLISHERS
1984   Hillsdale, New Jersey   London

Copyright © 1984 by Lawrence Erlbaum Associates, Inc.
All rights reserved. No part of this book may be reproduced in
any form, by photostat, microform, retrieval system, or any other
means, without the prior written permission of the publisher.

Lawrence Erlbaum Associates, Inc., Publishers
365 Broadway
Hillsdale, New Jersey 07642

ISBN   0-89859-287-9
ISSN   0278-2359

Printed in the United States of America

10   9   8   7   6   5   4   3   2   1

Contents

Preface   ix

Introduction
Robert J. Sternberg

1. **The Emperor's New Clothes: The "New Look" In Intelligence Research**   1
   Daniel P. Keating
   Roots of Contemporary Intelligence Research   3
   Componential Approaches to Intelligence   16
   Implications for Theory and Practice   36

2. **The Topography Of Ability And Learning Correlations**   47
   Richard E. Snow, Patrick C. Kyllonen and
   Brachia Marshalek
   Background   48
   The Study of Correlational Structure   50
   Reanalyses of Ability Organization   65
   Reanalysis of Ability-Learning Relationships   75
   Summary and General Discussion   88

3. **Reasoning As a Central Intellective Ability**   105
    Lance J. Rips
    Introduction   105
    Characteristics of A Theory of Reasoning   107
    Is There a Case Against Reasoning?   113
    The ANDS Model of Deductive Reasoning   123
    Adequacy Issues   131
    Principle Themes   142

4. **Deductions About Induction: Analyses Of Developmental
    And Individual Differences**   149
    Susan R. Goldman and James W. Pellegrino
    Introduction and Overview   149
    Cognitive Components of Analogy Solution   151
    Cognitive Components of Classification Solution   169
    Developmental Changes in Inductive Reasoning   171
    Individual Differences in Inductive Reasoning   179
    Multitask Performance Analysis-Unities in Inductive
        Reasoning   189
    Conclusions and Future Directions   193

5. **Analogical Thinking And Human Intelligence**   199
    Keith J. Holyoak
    Introduction   199
    A Theoretical Framework for Analogical Thinking   202
    Experimental Studies of Analogical Problem Solving   213
    Analogical Aspects of Intelligence   223

6. **A Cognitive Analysis of Mathematical Problem-Solving
    Ability**   231
    *Richard E. Mayer, Jill H. Larkin, and
    Joseph B. Kadane*
    Introduction   231
    Linguistic and Factual Knowledge are Needed for
        Translation   236
    Schematic Knowledge is Needed for Understanding   242
    Strategic Knowledge is Needed for Planning   253
    Algorithmic Knowledge is Needed for Problem
        Execution   265
    Implications   269

7. **Factors Affecting Individual Differences in Learning Ability**   275
   Lauren B. Resnick and Robert Neches
   Introduction   275
   Inventing an Efficient Procedure for Simple Addition   278
   Constructing Procedures on the Basis of Schematic
      Knowledge   288
   A Learning Episode From Genevan Research   302
   The Sources of Individual Differences   308
   Conclusion   319

8. **An Analysis Of Hierarchical Classification**   325
   Ellen M. Markman and Maureen A. Callanan
   Introduction   325
   What Counts as Evidence for Hierarchical Organization   328
   Research on the Development of Classification   331
   Collections Versus Classes as Hierarchical Organization   347
   Conclusion   360

9. **Why Some People Are Better Readers Than Others:
   A Process and Storage Account**   367
   Meredyth Daneman
   Scope of the Theory   367
   Evidence for the Theory   368
   By-Products of the Theory   379

Author Index   385

Subject Index   389

Preface

During the past decade, we have witnessed a remarkable resurgence of interest in the psychology of human intelligence. In the late 1960s, research in the field of intelligence seemed to have gone into at least partial remission. But today a large number of investigators are pursuing active research programs concerning human intelligence.

The rapid expansion of the field of intelligence convinced me of the need for a *Handbook of Human Intelligence*—a volume that would help guide research on intelligence during the next decade or so. But a handbook cannot keep up with a rapidly advancing field, and it was for this reason that I decided that there was also a need for a series of volumes to complement the handbook—in essence, to continue the work that I hope the handbook has initiated. This series of volumes is intended to mark significant advances in the psychology of human intelligence.

Advances in the Psychology of Human Intelligence, of which this is the second volume, contains articles by leaders in the field that document the progress that is being made toward understanding human intelligence. This series does not attempt to achieve the encyclopedic coverage of a handbook, but it can keep up with, and, I hope, lead the field in a way that no single, one-time volume could. Thus, the Advances series complements the handbook in its documentation and guidance of developments in research on human intelligence.

The concept of intelligence explored in this and subsequent volumes is broadly conceived. All volumes include contributions both by individuals whose research is clearly identified with the mainstream of research on intelligence and by individuals whose research may not be so identified but yet has an important bearing on our understanding of intelligence. Although contributors always rep-

resent a diversity of substantive and methodological foci, they share a serious-
ness of commitment and contribution to research on intelligence, broadly
defined.

The present volume reflects the diversity of approaches and substantive contributions that characterized Volume 1, and that will characterize future volumes.
The present volume contains chapters dealing with information-processing components and the context in which they operate (Keating), the structure of human
abilities and the role of learning in these abilities (Snow, Kyllonen, &
Marshalek), the relation between deductive reasoning and intelligence (Rips),
the relation between inductive reasoning and intelligence (Goldman & Pellegrino), the role of analogical problem solving in intelligence (Holyoak), mathematical abilities (Mayer, Larkin, & Kadane), learning abilities (Resnick & Neches), the development of hierarchical classification abilities (Markman &
Callanan), and reading abilities (Daneman). I believe that these contributions
represent some of the most exciting new developments in the study of human
intelligence.

Although this volume can certainly be read and understood in its own right, it
is intended to be cumulative with respect to Volume 1 of the series in its
contribution to the understanding of human intelligence. Volume 1, published in
1982, contained chapters in related but distinct areas from the chapters found in
Volume 2. These areas were attention (Hunt & Lansman), choice reaction time
(Jensen), reading (Frederiksen), spatial visualization (Cooper; Pellegrino &
Kail), number ability (Gelman), reasoning abilities and their development
(Sternberg), and complex problem solving (Chi, Glaser, & Rees; Polson &
Jeffries). I believe that those who follow the volumes in this series will find
themselves up-to-date on many of the most recent and noteworthy developments
in the psychology of human intelligence.

Robert J. Sternberg

Introduction

Robert J. Sternberg
Yale University

This volume attempts to achieve broad coverage of the kinds of research being done today under the rubric of human intelligence. But as is almost inevitably the case in a book of its kind, the selection of authors is biased. To the extent that there is such a bias, it is unabashedly toward the selection of authors whose work represents information-processing approaches to intelligence. In order to introduce the kinds of questions these approaches, and the chapters based on them, deal with, I have chosen a single key theoretical question that I believe each chapter addresses in a particularly apt way. I raise each of the questions here and discuss briefly how each given chapter addresses the questions I have selected. I wish to emphasize that the choice of questions is mine and that the authors of the chapters might not view their own contributions in the same light as I do. Nevertheless, I believe that my own perspective might provide at least a minimal unifying backdrop for the contributions of the various authors in the volume.

1. *What is the relationship, if any, between externally oriented, "contextual" approaches, and internally oriented, "processing" approaches to intelligence?* There are many ways of dividing up the styles and approaches of intelligence researchers. One of the clearest divisions is between those who emphasize the relationship of the individual to her or his external world, and those who emphasize the relationship of the individual to his or her internal world. In the past, there has been practically no interface between the two kinds of approaches. Contextual theorists have often scoffed at what they perceive as the triviality of the kinds of problems processing theorists address; processing theorists have often scoffed at what they have perceived as the lack of rigor and concern with mechanism that characterize contextual theorists. In a truly new

and exciting synthesis, **Keating** attempts to integrate externally- and internally-oriented approaches, and to show how they can be placed within a single framework. In so doing, Keating makes what I perceive to be a new and much needed synthetic contribution to what have been in the past, two disparate approaches and literatures.

2. *Can a structural model of intelligence be attained through techniques other than factor analysis?*   For most of the century, research on intelligence was dominated by a single method of latent-structure analysis, namely, factor analysis. The central issue in the field of intelligence was the structure of intelligence, and factor analysis was the only widely available data-analytic technique for exploring this structure. When information-processing research began to increase in popularity, the "baby was thrown out with the bath." Valid concerns about the inferences one could draw from exploratory factor analyses led researchers to other techniques of data analysis, but also led them away from dealing with questions of structure. **Snow, Kyllonen,** and **Marshalek** have taken a fresh approach to the concept of structure, using as a point of departure Guttman's radex model, but employing multidimensional scaling techniques rather than factor analysis as their primary method of data analysis. The result has been a fascinating, new picture of how abilities interrelate and seem to generate the behaviors that produce the correlations we obtain between intelligence tests (as well as tests of aptitudes and achievements). Their chapter represents the first serious and broad-ranging attempt to apply multidimensional scaling analysis to the structural analysis of abilities, and the attempt is manifestly successful in revealing insights that classical factor-analytic techniques seem to have hidden.

3. *What is the relationship of deductive reasoning ability to intelligence?*   It is by now an historical curiosity that when the term *reasoning* has been used in the literature on intelligence, it has much more often than not referred to "inductive" reasoning. Few theories or tests of intelligence deal with deductive reasoning at all. As a result, there is a large psychometric literature on inductive reasoning skills, but only a meager one on deductive reasoning skills. Perhaps the reason for this differential derives back to the factorial theory of Thurstone. Whereas Thurstone was able to obtain a stable inductive reasoning factor, he was not able to obtain a stable deductive reasoning factor. **Rips's** chapter represents a bold attempt to bring deductive reasoning back into intelligence. Rips's approach is clearly that of information processing rather than of psychometrics, but it succeeds in pointing out general mechanisms of deductive reasoning that are certain to be an integral part of any intelligent functioning system. Rips's model is more than a model of deductive reasoning; it is a model of how deductive reasoning is conducted and of how it relates to mental structures and processes in general. It thus succeeds in bringing back together two entities—deductive reasoning and intelligence—that, curiously, have rarely been studied in tandem.

4. *Is it possible to go beyond task analyses of inductive reasoning and to form an integrated, coherent theory of the phenomenon?* Information-processing research on inductive reasoning and its relationship to intellectual functioning has been very much in vogue in recent years. Readers of this literature, however, are often left with an uncomfortable feeling that the research is more oriented toward models of performance on specific tasks rather than toward general theories incorporating large numbers of inductive tasks. **Goldman** and **Pellegrino's** chapter goes a considerable way toward rectifying this imbalance. Not only does the chapter present what I believe to be the most comprehensive and clear overview of differential, developmental, and cognitive research on inductive reasoning, but it also makes the rare contribution of placing this work into an overall framework for understanding induction as it occurs across tasks. The authors transcend task specificity, and manage to unify a literature that has been notable for its scattered and task-specific quality.

5. *What is the relationship between analogical reasoning and analogical problem solving?* Although both are based on the concept of analogy, the literatures on analogical reasoning and analogical problem solving have grown up almost independently of each other. In general, analogical-reasoning items deal with problems of the form $A : B :: C : D_i$, where the subject's task is to select one from among several answer options (D_i). Analogical problem-solving items present one with a problem situation of some kind, from which one is expected at some later time to show transfer to an analogous problem situation. The fact that there is an analogy is sometimes pointed out, but more often than not left to the problem solver to figure out. **Holyoak's** chapter represents one of the first serious attempts to integrate accounts of analogical reasoning and problem solving under a general theoretical framework that could potentially account for both. Although his emphasis is clearly upon problem solving, he discusses issues of reasoning as well, and perhaps for the first time anywhere, relates the literature on analogical problem solving to the construct of intelligence. The chapter thus makes a unique joint contribution to what have been two literatures, those on analogical reasoning and analogical problem solving.

6. *Is it possible to apply componential forms of analysis to problem solving in algebra word problems?* Investigators using componential forms of analysis— analyses that decompose task performance into elementary information processes of one or more kinds—have had what I consider to be dramatic success in decomposition of tasks whose internal structures are very clearly delineated. Few attempts have been made, however, to apply such forms of analysis to less structured, more educationally relevant kinds of problems. **Mayer, Larkin,** and **Kadane** are among the few investigators who have made the plunge, and decomposed very complex performance into elementary constituents. In particular, they have shown that it is as possible to understand elementary information processes and strategies in algebra problems such as those found in school texts

and in the real world as it is possible to understand structured task problems through componential task decomposition. This chapter makes the exceedingly important contribution of showing that techniques widely used in the laboratory not only have potential applicability to more complex problems, but that with ingenuity and careful experimental technique, these techniques actually are applicable to complex problem solving. These authors not only talk about ecological relevance—they demonstrate it.

7. *What is the relationship between learning ability and intelligence?*   One of the most time-honored questions in the field of intelligence is that of how learning ability relates to intelligence. Perhaps no issue has proven as intractable, however. The large bulk of the literature in this area consists of disappointingly low correlations between scores on learning tasks and scores on intelligence tests. Using an approach to learning that is very different from the traditional approaches, **Resnick** and **Neches** have made a compelling case for the close relationship between learning and intelligence. By examining complex learning tasks rather than simple ones, and by building models that do justice to the complexity of the learning tasks and the processes involved in performing them, these authors have identified connections between learning and intelligence that have, for the most part, completely eluded past investigators. Their chapter thus makes a major contribution toward integrating two constructs that always seemed closely related, but whose relations seemed to defy empirical analysis.

8. *How can "Piagetian" hierarchical classification skills, and the categorical knowledge upon which they draw, be understood within an information-processing framework?*   Over the past several years, it has become fashionable for researchers to use information-processing techniques to study Piagetian types of tasks. Such research has at times seemed very task oriented, however, seeking to characterize processing on one task or another in a way that is complementary to, but not clearly integrable with, Piagetian analysis. **Markman** and **Callanan** go beyond mere "alternative analysis," and propose a synthesis that I believe incorporates Piagetian and information-processing approaches and insights into a single framework. Rather than serving as a stalking horse or a straw man, Piagetian analysis of task performance is richly integrated into a higher-order framework that also incorporates information-processing analyses. This is one of the few such analyses that goes beyond analysis of individual tasks, and for which the whole of the integration between forms of analysis is, I believe, clearly better than the sum of its parts.

9. *What storage and retrieval processes account for individual differences in reading skills?*   Attempts to understand sources of individual differences in reading skill have generally foundered on tasks that are either so close to standard reading that any correlations obtained between them and reading comprehension

have seemed less than impressive, or on tasks that are so far away from reading that they have yielded correlations that fail to impress for their lack of magnitude. Using an ingenious technique for measuring active functional working memory capacity, **Daneman** has offered a penetrating analysis that is not quite like anything which has been proposed in the past. In particular, **Daneman** has created a memory-span task that is conceptually quite distinct from standard reading comprehension tasks, but that yields correlations with reading comprehension measures that are almost astoundingly high. Moreover, these correlations are simple ones: They are not boosted up either by the entry of many variables or by the elusive chance variance that plagues multiple regression research. The proposed approach to theory and measurement seems to offer an extremely productive way of studying individual differences in reading skills.

In conclusion, the chapters in this book represent a diversity of problems and perspectives within the information-processing framework. I believe they do indeed describe significant "advances in the psychology of human intelligence" as studied from a multiplicity of viewpoints.

1

The Emperor's New Clothes: The "New Look" in Intelligence Research

Daniel P. Keating
*University of Maryland,
Baltimore County*

There can be little doubt about the existence of a resurgent interest in human intelligence research. The introduction of a new journal with considerable vitality and diversity, the explosion of research programs with direct or indirect ties to the resurgence, a special issue of *American Psychologist* (October 1981), and many other indicators are convincing proof. The current level of activity would have been difficult to predict not too many years ago, when traditional "intelligence" research had been relegated to the back rooms of scientific psychology, with some eager to usher it out the back door. In a short time, the perception of the field has changed dramatically, with more researchers taking up the "new" questions, or at least looking at longstanding questions in a new way, and with an anticipation of breakthroughs in our understanding.

The research that my colleagues and I have pursued over the last several years was sparked by this sense of renewed vigor and fits squarely into this resurgence (Ford & Keating, 1981; Keating & Bobbitt, 1978; Keating, Keniston, Manis, & Bobbitt, 1980; Keating, List, & Merriman, 1983; Manis, Keating, & Morrison, 1980). A major goal of this chapter will be to describe the logic of that research program, which has focused on the development of basic cognitive skills and their relationship to complex cognitive functioning.

But more is needed at this time than a straightforward summary of research goals, attempts, successes, and failures. At a deeper theoretical level, the suspicion grows that we are merely recreating with more sophisticated experimental and analytic tools the same fundamentally flawed quasi-scientific belief systems (Gould, 1981, Blum, 1978) that nearly led to the abandonment of these important questions in an earlier period. Primary sources of this problem are the unwillingness to abandon explicitly discredited assumptions about "intelligence," most importantly that *it* is a thing that exists in the head of the person, and that that should be our exclusive or principal arena for searching out answers as to *its* nature and development. Some corollaries are that *it* is connected in some direct although not fully understood way with standardized test scores; that whatever *it* is, we who study it formally have the primary right to define it, and hence usually wind up having more of it than other groups that differ on the basis of education, social class, race, sex, or a combination of these; and, finally, the implicit sense that differences in how much of *it* one has adequately explain the differences among people in their social status (power, wealth, occupation)—and that this is inevitable or desirable or both.

It would be unreasonable and wrong to argue that the set of corollaries above represents the thinking of all or even most of the researchers currently working on these questions; indeed, many would find more than one part of that set repugnant. The point I wish to make is much simpler: To the extent that our current work is constrained by a set of unexamined assumptions, such as those just described, our efforts will be misguided and our most interesting and important questions will not be addressed. Merely to reject the onerous conclusions is insufficient; theoretical rigor demands a thoughtful examination of the sources of the question.

Thus a second major goal of this chapter will be to consider seriously the unexamined assumptions of human intelligence research. To what degree do these assumptions determine the research that is done and the conclusions that are drawn? It is not easy to say. Space considerations render it even more difficult here. Two caveats make it at least possible. First, I will draw on my own research within three distinct theoretical perspectives (psychometric, Piagetian, and componential), not because they represent the best or most representative research from each approach, but rather because the theoretical direction may be more coherent. Second, the analysis will cover only highlights of the terrain. A more complex set of arguments and analyses remains a promissory note.

It will be the contention of these analyses that in most respects the nature of our questions about human intelligence has been fundamentally distorted by the continuing failure to place such questions in their social, historical, and political context because of the belief that such contextual issues are irrelevant, unnecessary, or unscientific. Substantive theoretical and practical progress in the understanding of human intelligence requires different questions to be addressed and different levels and methods of analysis to be used. Thus a third focus of the chapter, and a recurring theme of this approach, will be the consideration of what validity criteria for theories of intelligence are defensible. Given this analysis and these criteria, what are the promising directions for theory, research, and practice that would lead to advances in our understanding of human intelligence?

ROOTS OF CONTEMPORARY INTELLIGENCE RESEARCH

Measurement of Individual Differences

Virtually every history of human intelligence research places the formal beginning at the turn of the 20th century, with the work in France of Binet and his colleagues. Their systematic attempt to identify individual differences in "intelligence" that were of practical educational importance was clearly the first successful and the most influential one. It is instructive to note, however, that Binet's understanding of intelligence was quite pragmatic, and substantially different from the subsequent use of that construct in the United States (Gould, 1981).

Perhaps the most significant perspective, which changed markedly with the import of the Binet-Simon scales across the Atlantic, first by Goddard (1913) and then more memorably by Terman (1917), was Binet's notion of intelligence as modifiable and thus his binding together of the process of assessment with that of intervention. For Binet (1909), this was the only sensible reason for which a practical scale of intelligence could be used (Gould, 1981):

> If we do nothing, if we don't intervene actively and usefully, he will continue to lose time . . . and will finally become discouraged. The situation is very serious for him, and . . . it is a serious question for us and for all of society. . . . It is in this practical sense, *the only one accessible to us,* that we say that the intelligence of these children has been increased (through special instruction) [pp. 100–104].

The attraction of the Binet approach for American psychologists lay less in its potential for identifying educational problems and thus closely guiding instructional interventions and more in the possibility of generating a scale to arrange the population hierarchically in terms of a fixed (and typically inborn) characteristic termed "intelligence." The theoretical guide was Galton (1884) rather than Binet, especially for Terman. Given these prescientific predilections, it is not surprising that strong assumptions about the ability of the scales to identify accurately the most important aspects of human cognitive functioning were easily "confirmed" by weak and inadequate empirical findings. It is somewhat more surprising (and clearly more disconcerting) to see how many of these early assumptions, which have been successfully challenged in numerous critiques (Blum, 1978; Gould, 1981; Kamin, 1974; Sternberg, 1977), remain influential in current theorizing.

The American versions of intelligence tests were used to do more than grind theoretical axes, of course. Indeed, the explosion of test development and application occurred soon after their introduction into the United States, spurred considerably by the group "intelligence" tests of World War I. Within educational psychology, research on tests virtually replaced the study of learning and acquiring school skills by the mid-1920s, a trend that has begun to turn around only in the last few years (Farnham-Diggory & Nelson, in press).

The practical applications thus tended to focus on the social function of *selection* rather than on educational intervention. That this function fit rather neatly within the emergence of an increasingly hierarchized industrial economy (Braverman 1974) was not lost on the early test developers, including Terman (1919):

> The evolution of modern industrial organization together with the mechanization of processes by machinery is making possible the larger and larger utilization of inferior mentality. One man with ability to think and plan guides the labor of ten or twenty laborers, who do what they are told to do and have little need for resource-fulness or initiative [p. 276].

Scarr (1981) has recently discussed this difference between the use of assessment for selection rather than diagnosis, and notes that the latter is more obviously in the best interests of the child than the former. She notes, however, that "Institutions function to sort and select children into different tracks, both in the child's interests and in those of the institution as it relates to the larger society [p. 1160]." Even a cursory historical review would, I argue, indicate persuasively whose interests are typically served by this arrangement—and it is clearly not the children's (Bowles & Gintis, 1976). Whether or not one agrees with that evaluation, it is important, as Scarr argues, that the *use* of assessment of individual differences be seriously debated, and that its function for the institutions of society is at least as important in that debate as its function on behalf of the individual being assessed.

A commonplace distinction that is often advanced in response to the critique outlined here is that between the use and abuse of intelligence or aptitude tests. Critics are assumed to assert either that there are no individual differences in the skills assessed by psychometric tests or that they are irrelevant for educational decision making, both of which are easy to refute (or ridicule). The crucial questions, of course, have to do with the interpretation we place upon such observed differences, and what consequences there are for the individual and for the society of the typical use (not abuse) of mass testing. In an idealized version of reality, the use of standardized tests solely for the diagnostic and educational intervention benefits to the individual can be contemplated, but an analysis of what actually transpires in the use of testing and how it fits into the social context is more to the point.

Certainly it is the case that wide ranges of individual differences in the skills assessed by psychometric tests do exist, that these differences have considerable educational importance, and that the use of such tests sometimes benefits the education of individual students. This is perhaps illustrated most obviously in the case of developmentally precocious, or "gifted," children and youth (Keating, 1976; Stanley, Keating, & Fox, 1974). The diagnostic value of standardized tests that reveal that some students are performing several grades or more above their current educational placement is considerable. There can be no doubt that substantial numbers of children are poorly served by an educational system that fails to take account of their actual developmental level (Keating, 1980a).

Having recognized and demonstrated the reality of wide individual differences in development and their obvious educational relevance, we are confronted with the central dilemma of theory and practice. How are we to interpret and deal with these differences? On the one hand are, using Gould's (1981) term, the biological determinists. This position, and its variants, regards psychometric variance, either group or individual, as principally reflective of biological variation (Jensen, 1980). From this perspective, general intelligence (g) and factors of ability are more or less permanent characteristics of individuals, and test scores are reasonably good approximations of these characteristics. The logical application of test score information, therefore, is principally in terms of selection, of choosing the right kind of education or training to match each child's ability. Establishment of the 11+ examinations in England embodied this perspective most explicitly.

Although this position has fewer adherents than previously, at least in its purest hereditarian form, the key assumptions underlying it continue to be persuasive. First and foremost is the assumption that g, or at least some combination of abilities, does exist as a real characteristic within the individual. The basis of this assumption is typically fourfold: 1) everyday experience with "bright" and "dull" people; 2) factor-analytic findings; 3) association of test scores with important real world variables, especially class, education, and occupation; and 4) the variance per se in test scores, given apparently equivalent environments of those being tested. We can dismiss easily with the first of these, since what is bright and what is dull is too easily defined by the self-interested perspective of the observer. As but one published example, Bramel & Friend (1981) point out in a critique of the Hawthorne experiments that the researchers (Elton Mayo and Fritz Roethlisberger) replaced a worker in their experimental group, who had "gone Bolshevik" and was successfully persuading other workers that the study was a ruse to reduce piece rates, with one who was more cooperative and enthusiastic, and who goaded the other workers to increase their output. Which worker was bright and which dull would need to be argued in terms of one's analysis of capital/labor conflicts, not in terms of everyday experience, nor in terms of "objective" criteria of job performance such as productivity or supervisor's ratings.

Factor-analytic evidence seems at first glance far more objective, and indeed it has served as the basis for scientific investigation of human abilities for many years. Although differing in style and to some extent substance, the recent critiques of Sternberg (1977) and Gould (1981) are adequate to disabuse one's belief in the inherent reality of factors derived from test score matrices as factors or vectors of "mind." Two critiques are the most telling. Which factors one derives, and the way in which they are related to each other, are fundamentally arbitrary phenomena. The range and diversity of subjects included in the analysis, the variety of tasks administered to them, the procedures by which factors are extracted, the number of factors to be extracted, and the type of rotation (if any) of the factors, are *all* ultimately arbitrary decisions of the researcher—not to mention the interpretation placed on the factor structure once it is obtained. It should not be surprising then that merely to list all the factor models of intelligence that have been proposed would be a formidable task. Some of these models may be more plausible or more heuristically valuable than others, but precisely because the analysis is fundamentally arbitrary, none of them can through this method be proved "right" and competitors "wrong." Second, factors are twice-removed abstractions: First, as the test scores themselves are indicators of a presumed (but not demonstrated) underlying real ability variance; and subsequently as mathematical (that is, correlational) patterns of those abstractions. Thus, though superficially more appealing, psychometric factors are no more capable revealing the nature of intelligence than is everyday experience. As Thurstone (1947) warned: "The explanatory nature of factor analysis is often not understood. Factor analysis is useful . . . in those domains where basic and fruitful concepts are essentially lacking [p. 56]."

The greatest weight of construct validity evidence for the existence of abilities as individual characteristics of the person is usually founded upon the relationships between test scores and levels of education, occupational success, social class, or some combination of these. Certainly, evidence of this kind is statistically compelling. Although the raw correlations among these variables differ somewhat from study to study, the degree of relationship is typically moderate to strong, and always in the same direction—with higher test scores associated with higher levels of education, greater occupational success (measured in a variety of ways), and higher social class standing.[1] Given that this set of relationships conforms to the prevailing meritocratic ideology, it is relatively easy to pass over a serious consideration of the *causal* connections among the variables. Large-scale attempts to locate sources of these relationships have not been notably successful in isolating them, when other variables are appropriately partialed out (Jencks, Bartlett, Corcoran, Crouse, Eaglesfield, Jackson, McClelland, Mueser, Olneck, Schwartz, Ward, & Williams, 1979). Social structural analyses (Bowles & Gintis, 1976) have suggested that the assumptions underlying the meritocratic ideology need to be seriously challenged, and the danger of uncritically inferring that the "predictive" correlations of IQ or other test score data are indicative of a

---

[1]For purposes of this discussion, I use social class in the quantitative (i.e. lower to upper) sense, because that is how it is employed in the analysis described here. The more productive class analyses are those which explore historically the social relationships *between* classes (e.g., Braverman 1974).

separable, individual *causal* variable becomes clear. More reasonably, such data describe a *copredictive* system, within which a belief in any one as the causal mechanism must remain, at least for now, an assumption. The meritocratic reality is thus a social construction and legitimation (Berger & Luckmann, 1966), not based on objective proof.

Pursuing a different set of assumptions for a moment reveals a sharply contrasting construction of reality. If we view all psychometric test data as achievement indices, we avoid unfounded inferences regarding them as signs of underlying internal characteristics or traits of the individual. For purposes of maximized educational benefit to the individual, it is the developmental level with respect to a particular content or skill domain that is central, rather than the average developmental level (Keating, 1980a). With this perspective, the theoretical inclination is to look for explanations of cognitive skill or ability in the person-environment interactions rather than to seek entities within the head of the subject.

This perspective is clearly more difficult and complex to pursue, and even when arguing for some variant of this position, the search for intelligence "entities" can often reassert itself. In an otherwise perceptive commentary on the necessity of including within theories of human intelligence a recognition of the cognitive actor's scripts, plans, and goals, Schank (1980) nevertheless completes his analysis by suggesting that to get to the core of an individual's intelligence, we should place the individual in a totally novel situation that requires the discovery and solution of a problem posed so that the subject cannot "rely on any prior cultural information [p. 12]!" The lure of a physicalist explanation is a strong one, which is sometimes not deflected even by the awareness that a key feature of human cognitive activity is that it *is* purposeful and goal directed (Schank, 1980).

A major obstacle in moving toward more integrated and less psychologized theories of intelligence is precisely the complexity introduced with the admission of cultural and historical forces into such explanations. A certain rigor of internal validity is necessarily jeopardized by the admission of these external validity criteria (Campbell & Stanley, 1963). A striking example of this is the critical reaction to Jensen's (1980) arguments rejecting the claims of bias in mental testing. His definition of bias is essentially that tests are not biased if they neither over- nor underpredict the educational or job performance of some group (defined by race, sex, ethnicity, or class) compared to some other group. His summary of the evidence is that psychometrically sound tests are generally not biased in this way, and thus are valid indicators of underlying ability.

It is difficult to find any seams in the evidence Jensen produces. But the focus of the argument is entirely *within* the copredictive system described earlier. To conclude that tests are indeed valid and unbiased assessments of the abilities needed on the job or in school, the argument must assume the validity and unbiased nature of the criteria, that is, educational and occupational success. If variables external to the correlational system (such as culture or social structure) affect both the predictors *and* the criteria in similar ways, which is plausible or even likely, then the logic of Jensen's argument rests on evidence for its internal validity but on uncritical assumptions for its external validity.

Three main supports of the prevailing belief in intelligence as an internal characteristic of individuals—everyday experience of "more" and "less" intelligent people, factor analytic evidence, and the predictive validity of tests—can thus be seen as fundamentally flawed. But what of the pervasive variance in test scores, in which there is often enough common variance to require the admission of at least an empirical *g* factor (Keating, 1979a)? Is not the evidence of this type so overwhelming that we are compelled to agree with Scarr's assertion (1981): "I do not believe that any child can be made into any adult, and it is hopelessly silly for us to pretend that this is so [p. 1160]."? Certainly if the refutation of the prevailing view of intelligence required the denial or dismissal of the fact of individual differences, then the argument would fail on this point alone. Even excluding cases of identifiable organic damage, the variance in test performance is demonstrably large, and the conclusion that some children are intrinsically more intelligent than others seems unavoidable.

But once again we need to beware of obvious conclusions; they can reveal more about belief systems than about reality. Underlying the use of intelligence score variance per se as a demonstration of intrinsic individual differences in intelligence is the crucial assumption of equivalent cognitive socialization among children being tested. If IQ tests are indeed global cultural achievement tests, then the attribution of score differences to individual levels of intelligence rather than to cultural or socialization differences is gratuitous. How legitimate is a concern over the status of this assumption?

In the case of group differences, the presumption of cultural or socialization differences is a strong one, and no adequate dismissals of their importance exist. Two frequent arguments intended to diminish the importance of such differences can be noted. The first is by reference to "culture-free" or "culture-fair" intelligence tests, which attempt to minimize cultural differences by eliminating as much verbal, educational, or representational pictorial content as possible from the items. On most tests, group differences are accentuated rather than attenuated, supporting intrinsic intelligence rather than culture as the prime explanation. But this is a peculiar (and narrowly "psychological") view of culture. It is just as logical a priori to argue that such items devoid of content and obvious context represent the pinnacle of acculturation to a formalized and abstract mode of thinking, and some cross-cultural evidence supports this reasoning (Sharp, Cole, & Lave, 1979). Items that on their face may seem culture-fair because they are devoid of obvious cultural content may well be the most culturally loaded items.

A second approach is to examine some specific socialization hypothesis and to find it inadequate to explain the observed difference. A recent example of this approach is a study by Benbow & Stanley (1980), in which they examined a

proposed source of the difference between eighth-grade boys and girls on difficult mathematics tests. The observed difference was a disproportionately small
number of girls among the high scorers in several large samples. Formal mathematics instruction was essentially equivalent for these students (as a required
subject through this grade level); therefore the authors correctly ruled this out as
a potential socialization explanation. (It had initially been advanced to account
for similar differences at the end of senior high school.) But from this evidence
they then inferred the likely inadequacy of socialization explanations to account
for such large differences. Given that we do not know what aspects of socialization are central to the development of skill in mathematical reasoning, and given
that we do know that there are large socialization differences in general between
boys and girls, the elimination of one socialization variable is insufficient for the
implicit elimination of such explanations in general in favor of biology-based
accounts.

The crucial assumption of ''more or less equal'' socialization experiences for
most children requires more detailed and validated theories of the environment
and of individual development within them than are now available. Lacking
direct evidence of biological mechanisms, biological determinists should in fact
be as interested as environmentalists in the refinement of theories about the
socialization of cognition because the refutation of inadequate theories as the
primary (though indirect) evidence of biological mechanisms is a weak reed
indeed. In the case of group differences, the assumption of equivalence is, as
noted, especially unwarranted. Consider the educational system alone, within
which racial preference as an *official* policy of many states is still quite recent,
and de facto bias continues to flourish, notably in the massive per pupil expendi-
ture differentials of urban compared to suburban school districts within the same
state. That such differentials are often class based as well as racially biased
(Bowles & Gintis, 1976) merely supports the argument that speculations about
the underlying characteristics of children of environments different from test
writers, test givers, and test theorists are unsupportable in the absence of social
and political analysis.

But what of the differences that are observed among children from more
similar environments, within race and social class, or even within families?
Although there are individual differences in test scores among children from
similar environments, several observations preclude rapid acceptance of the
equivalent socialization assumption. First, it is precisely those cases when all
other things are equal that the predictive validity of the tests is shown to be of
lesser magnitude (Jencks et al., 1979); when relevant and measurable background variables are partialled out, the correlations of scores with educational
and occupational success are markedly attenuated. Even though the score differences remain, their importance *apart* from the context in which they are
predictive is questionable. Second, lacking validated theories of cognitive development (Keating, 1979a), we cannot be certain that we know and can measure

the relevant socialization variables that would justify the equivalence assumption. Most of the background socialization variables that are measured tend to be global aggregates (parental education and occupation, one or two working parents, and so on) that are closely associated with class differences and may miss the important features of the children's interaction with their surroundings. Thus, when social class is removed, the correlations of test scores with the "socialization" variables is reduced artifactually, leading to the erroneous conclusion that important individual differences can be observed even in homogeneous environments. When more detailed observations of actual developmental interactions are made (e.g., Block & Block, 1979; Scarr, 1981; Sigel, in press), the evidence strongly suggests that important socialization influences occur at the level of individual interactions. Interestingly, some of the more important interactions for cognitive development may not be cognitive themselves, but rather influence seemingly "noncognitive" areas as motivation, adjustment to adult demands, or ego resiliency. Even equating for obvious cognitive socialization experiences, which we cannot yet do, will therefore be insufficient, because test, school, and job performance are all affected by a range of socialization experiences outside the traditional intellective domain. The mere observation of individual differences in test scores within homogeneous populations adds little to the validity of the construct of intelligence as a characteristic within the person because: a) the predictive value of scores to real world criteria is markedly attenuated with the removal of measured socialization variables; b) the correlations of scores with socialization variables *within* social class are artifactually low because the aggregate nature of the variables makes them surrogates for social class in the first place; and c) when more interactive developmental observations are made, the role of socialization is seen to be more important, both in cognitive and noncognitive influences that can affect performance in each of the domains of interest.

The traditional psychometric conceptualization of intelligence and mental abilities is thus fatally flawed, if the difficulties outlined here cannot be overcome. Admittedly, it is difficult to speak of the refutation of a specific psychometric theory of intelligence. There are in reality many competing theories and models, but all of them rest upon enough common assumptions and conclusions that serious problems with the general structure of the argument affect each of them. The central core of the psychometric perspective is that intelligence and abilities are in fact things-in-the-person, and that assessments can be validly designed that tap them and reveal their structure. Often these assumptions are implicit, but sometimes explicit: "There is such a thing as intelligence. . . . We believe that it is a collection of things that go together much of the time [Sternberg, 1979, pp. 42–45]."

These are no mere semantic quibbles. Rather, the conceptualization of g, intelligence, or mental abilities as "things-in-persons" (rather than as observations of human actions in particular contexts) has dramatic effects both on theory and practice, and is properly seen both as a theoretical hangover of the hereditarian presumptions of the early test theorists and as a major support for meritocratic ideology. After considering some more recent perspectives on these same questions, I will return to the effects on theory and practice of common conceptualizations of intelligence.

To reiterate, this summary critique of prevailing interpretations of test score data does not, and does not need to, deny the observations of significant individual differences in the scores nor their educational relevance (Keating, 1976, 1980a). It does point out, however, that inferences about internal mental structures from test scores rest upon beliefs and assumptions that have not been validated and do not withstand critical scrutiny.

Developmental Structuralism: Piaget

Although psychometric theorists as well as Piaget have been interested in mental structures, Piaget (1950) differed from and critiqued the former on two grounds: He had a more explicit concern with *how* children think, with cognitive operations, with processes rather than products of thought; consequently he emphasized the importance of tracing the development of thinking within the child. For many years, Piaget had little influence on American psychologists of any kind, including intelligence theorists, for a variety of reasons (Brainerd, 1978; Gruber & Voneche, 1980). First, Piaget was primarily an epistemologist rather than a psychologist; he turned to developmental psychology principally as a means of answering epistemological questions (Piaget, 1970). Second, his version of structuralist arguments spoke more to continental modes of discourse, and to the French structuralist tradition in particular, than to the questions that occupied American psychologists at that time (Piaget, 1968).

Despite these difficulties, Piaget's perspective eventually gained a substantial following here, and in fact became the predominant theory for cognitive developmentalists during the 1970s (Sigel, 1981). Admittedly, it was often a distorted or even unrecognizable simplification of his position that was influential, but it nevertheless focused developmental psychologists' attention and energy on a number of crucial questions that had been submerged for some time. In particular, the issues of cognitive operations, of the coherence of thought, of qualitative shifts in the structures of thought with development, and indeed, of the nature of intelligence, received and continue to receive far more detailed treatment than in the decades preceding Piaget's influence in America. Although many would now argue that his theoretical reach exceeded his grasp (Brainerd, 1978; Keating, 1980b), few would dispute the centrality and ingenuity of the questions he raised (Siegler, 1978; Keating, 1979b). It was the promise of Piaget's theory to address these fundamental issues more effectively than either psychometric or behavioral/learning approaches that attracted and sustained the efforts of numerous researchers. Brainerd (1978) offers a comprehensive review and critique of these efforts.

The aspect of Piaget's theory that has received the most critical attention is the claim that cognitive operations of individuals are interrelated through cognitive structures, that these structures change qualitatively with development, that these stages of cognitive development are best described logico-mathematically, and that these logico-mathematical structures are in an important sense real organizing features of thought rather than mere theoretical abstractions (Piaget, 1970, p. 23fn). It is entirely reasonable that this set of assertions should be the most thoroughly investigated, because it represents the core of his theory. This core was embedded in a complex network of metatheoretical statements and heuristically valuable metaphors (Brainerd, 1978), but constructs such as organization and adaptation, assimilation and accommodation, equilibration, and the individual's active construction of mental structures, only have theoretical vitality as they relate to this core. Notably, it was only this theoretical core for which Piaget or his collaborators offered empirical evidence, although the evidence was typically illustrative and confirmatory rather than an attempt to demonstrate validity relative to competing formulations.

The earliest non-Genevan tests of the theory were generally supportive. The paradigmatic study of that period used the series of interesting tasks developed in Piaget's laboratory, but administered them more in accordance with the accepted standards of Western psychological research, including larger and more representative sample sizes and more standardized task administration procedures. In general the sequences of task accomplishment replicated the initial findings of Piaget and his collaborators who used an informal clinical method to obtain their results. Indeed, replications of task sequence findings, especially within the concrete operational stage, became for a while a virtual cottage (or thesis!) industry in the United States.

It was not until the mid-1970s that there developed much of a critical literature on Piaget's theory, but this wave of revisionism seems to have been both rapid and effective in undermining some of its main supports. The criticism forms around three major lines of argument: The tenuous connection between the theoretical claims and the evidence presented on their behalf; the focus on competence (that is, logical structural) explanations of task performance with minimal attention to other factors that may invalidate the competence inference; and the inability to discriminate empirically between Piagetian and psychometric measurement methods and results. Only a brief review of these concerns will be presented here, because they have been examined in detail elsewhere (Brainerd, 1978; Keating, 1980b).

As a competence theory of the structure of mental operations, how is the theory to be validated? Several criteria seem crucial: 1) tasks that require similar or identical operations should be solved (or not) consistently by the same individual; 2) tasks whose logical components are in theory prior to the logical components of other tasks should be easier, that is, task performance should occur in the same sequence on all occasions; and 3) the means or rules by which the logical operations are inferred from the task performance should be explicit and consistent. Serious problems arise in the application of each of these criteria to the evidence supportive of the theory. Although the broad sequences laid out by Piaget are generally observed, they do not hold up well when the tasks are altered in even minor ways. Further, the sequences are more easily observed over broad age ranges and levels of task difficulty than in narrower ranges, although there is no a priori reason to assume that the narrow rather than broad *logical* sequences are less important to the theory (Flavell, 1982a). One reason for this could be measurement error, but in many cases measurement error has been used to explain away negative results and ignored in the case of positve results, although error is of course random (Keating, 1980b). The evidence, then, that stages defined by logical structures are identifiable (Flavell, 1982a,b), is not convincing.

In any case, replicable task performance sequences would not be convincing by themselves, because task difficulty is defined by more than its logical components. Exegesis of the Piagetian literature in fact fails to reveal an unambiguous interpretation of the precise connection between task performances and presumably underlying logical competence (Ennis, 1975; Keating, 1980b). Osherson (1975) argued persuasively that several different logical competence theories could equally well generate the same task performance predictions as Piaget's theory, and that on the basis of experimental evidence there existed no clear way of distinguishing among the structural models. To paraphrase Ennis (1975), the experimental evidence is thus probably irrelevant to the proof or disproof of the theory, but to the extent that it is relevant, it is not particularly supportive.

A more influential critique is embodied in what can be called the performance factor approach. The paradigmatic study here is to select some aspect of performance that may be related to doing well on some frequently used Piagetian task, but that is (or seems to be) unrelated to its logical requirements. By manipulating that component in the presentation of the task (that is, making it easier or harder, although typically the former), the researcher attempts to show that the task difficulty is significantly altered. If successful, the task is not only dislodged from its logical sequence, but also it is demonstrated that logical competence is only one, and perhaps not the most important factor in the task performance. That this undermines the use of task performance data to establish a theory of logical competence is obvious.

The prototypic research program of this type is summarized by Trabasso (1975). He and his colleagues investigated transitive inference problems of the type widely used in Piagetian research (variants of "If A is greater than B, and B is greater than C, which is greater, A or C?"). They hypothesized that young children, who find this type of task quite difficult, might be having trouble with something other than the logical inference that is required, specifically the memory demands of the task. (In the standard paradigm, there are usually five rather than three terms to the problem, and it is represented by a physical analogue, such as different colored sticks.) Prior to testing for the accuracy of the logical inference (the key structural question), they asked the young children to answer questions about the premises (that is, "Which is larger, A or B?"—which had of course been presented directly). They found that many children failed this part of the task, and thus did not have access in memory to the information in the premises that would make the logical inference possible in the first place. In a training study, they then did repetitions of presenting the premises and asking questions about them until the children demonstrated mastery of them. When the crucial logical inference questions were then asked, large majorities of children who had previously failed the task now passed it, which presumably they could not have done without having the logical competence to do so. A countercritique is that by repetition of the premises, the logical requirements of the task were eliminated; the subjects might now be simply reading off a spatial array (Trabasso, 1975). If true, however, that necessarily implies that the task was not a reliable indicator of logical structure in the first instance, because there is no way to guarantee that older children and adults are not spontaneously using a spatial strategy rather than a logical one (Keating & Caramazza, 1975).

If the first wave of Piaget-inspired research was dedicated to demonstrating what children could *not* do in support of illustrative task sequences, then the second wave of revisionist research has been dedicated to demonstrating what children *could* do with a little help on nonlogical or performance factors. Supplanting the old cottage industry with a new one, this research paradigm has amply demonstrated the important role of performance factors in numerous Piagetian tasks, from conservation to class inclusion to transitive inference to proportional reasoning and beyond. Indeed, simple demonstrations of the influence of performance factors on these tasks have no doubt outlived their usefulness as theoretical critiques (Keating, 1980b; Sigel, 1981).

Another way of conceptualizing the core theoretical contribution of Piagetian theory is to view it as an alternative approach to assessment of intelligence, superior to psychometric approaches in its focus on qualitative change, on reasoning about novel situations rather than repetition of learned information, and on more realistic tasks (Kuhn, 1979). Whether or not those claims can be justified, a prior condition is whether Piagetian assessment can be empirically discriminated from psychometric assessment; if not, its utility as an alternative assessment approach is clearly limited. Simple correlational assessments (e.g., Keating, 1975; Keating & Schaefer, 1975) suggested considerable overlap of the Piagetian and psychometric domains, although a review of the literature reveals a pattern of conflicting results (Keating, 1980b). Factor-analytic studies seemed to suggest that they could be separated into "operational" and "psychometric" intelligence. But in cases of the clearest separation of factors, the results were confounded by the failure to factor age out of the Piagetian task performance, although it was partialled out of the psychometric scores because they were already age graded (Keating, 1979a, 1980b; Humphreys, 1980). In those cases, chronological age loaded heavily on the Piagetian factor and negligibly on the psychometric factor. Thus, even at an empirical level, the distinction is hard to maintain.

The combined weight of these criticisms has removed Piaget's theory from its central position in the study of the development of intelligence (Sigel, 1981), at least in its explicit formulation. Given the range of problems that he worked on and the depth of his theoretical contribution, however, it is likely that his influence will be considerable and helpful for some time to come. One of the more interesting recent developments that rests squarely on the work of Piaget is Siegler's (1978, 1981) rule assessment approach. Rather than positing logical structures as the core of cognitive development, Siegler describes underlying rules or strategies for problem solving—essentially a pared down version of Piaget's theory without the structural assertions.

Siegler (1978) identified a number of tasks in which the rules, empirically derived, might be expected to operate. Across many of these tasks, the evidence is persuasive that relatively unambiguous descriptions of rules can be extracted from children's task performance. To infer that they are somehow central to cognitive development generally rather than interesting performance descriptions, however, requires somewhat more compelling evidence. Specifically, is rule assessment valid for a range of tasks beyond the discrete and bounded ones (e.g., balance beams) from which it is derived? And are rules generalized within individuals, such that they tend to use the same level of rules on different tasks? Initial evidence on both these questions is not supportive. In applying the approach to a more continuous-variable problem—time, speed and distance—Siegler & Richards (1979) found a substantially larger number of subjects to be unclassifiable by the rule system. More problematic is the finding that rule use between concepts within individuals was not at all consistent (Siegler, 1981). Even though less theory-bound than Piaget's approach, the centrality of these rules or strategies in explaining "what develops" seems questionable.

In most respects, however, Siegler's approach responds to the major critiques of the inadequacy of Piagetian theory. It examines rules as one component of performance on cognitive tasks, but does not rule out other possible components. Additionally, it attempts to manipulate the selected component through training to estimate its actual contribution to the main task (Siegler, 1978). These are key features of a more general *componential* approach.

Before turning our attention to that componential approach, however, consider the similarity of the bases for rejecting psychometric and Piagetian theories, despite the obvious differences between them. Although in principle Piaget advanced as a key feature of his theory the individual's interaction with the environment as central to the construction of cognitive structures, the actual working out of the theory suggests a much stronger maturational component (Sigel, 1981). This may be attributed to the focus on the child's actions upon the physical environment, and on principally physical tasks: Because the physical environment is essentially uniform (gravity, displacement, and so on), the internal maturational components would take precedence. The effect of this emphasis, in any case, was to generate a new but not fundamentally different search for entities in the head of the child, albeit "operational" rather than factor structures. In other words, Piaget's theory gave rise to yet another version of reification, even though the initial intent may have been otherwise. This is Vygotsky's (1978) fundamental critique of the Piagetian approach: It focused on the individual's construction of (idealized) internal mental structures and failed to recognize the significance of *social interaction* to the individual's construction of cognitive reality—and thus underestimated the essentially social nature of all human cognitive activity (Wertsch, 1981).

In retrospect, it is ironic that the most telling criticisms of Piaget's theory have come from researchers operating from an information-processing framework, given that Piaget criticized psychometrics for *its* focus on products rather than processes. We can now consider whether the "new look" in intelligence research, the wedding of the descriptive data of the psychometric approach with the hoped-for explanatory power of the information-processing framework, provides a better understanding of the perennial unanswered questions about the nature and development of human intelligence.

COMPONENTIAL APPROACHES TO INTELLIGENCE

Theoretical Background

Simultaneous with the explosion of Piagetian research in the United States was a resurgence of interest in cognitive structures and operations from a substantially different perspective, that of adult experimental psychology. Beginning in the mid-1960s, and spurred by Neisser's (1967) early summary and prospectus for this approach, researchers explored a long series of topics whose organizing feature was a concern with the actual, on-line cognitive activity of the individual. This "information-processing" framework provided the impetus for the development of sophisticated experimental tasks and techniques to investigate various aspects of human cognition, although it is clear that there is no single information-processing theory that guides these efforts. The currently favored rubric is in fact cognitive science, which incorporates information processing with a number of other fields such as artificial intelligence and cognitive research in the brain sciences.

As Cronbach (1957) noted some time ago, the amount of useful discourse between psychologists attuned to experimental approaches, of which cognitive science is currently the most central, and those favoring correlational approaches, which traditionally includes those who study human intelligence defined psychometrically, has been pitifully small. With the rapid development of information-processing experimental techniques, this breach made progressively less sense. Correlational research had generated a tremendous amount of descriptive findings relating observed individual differences to each other, but with little or no explanatory power, as argued above. And although experimental approaches to cognitive processing seemed initially self-sufficient, problems of external validity soon became apparent here as well. A full critique of validity problems within this experimental paradigm is beyond the scope of this chapter. Suffice it to say that the dangers of developing an isolated laboratory psychology in which features of cognitive processing identified there bear no obvious nor explored connection with the cognitive activities of humans in everyday life, and in which the identification of cognitive processes is isomorphc with the tasks in which they are "discovered," are major ones that have not been overcome (Newell, 1973).

The theoretical complementarity of correlational and experimental approaches to human cognitive activity, in particular as represented by information processing and the measurement of intelligence, was soon noted and employed (Carroll, 1976; Hunt, 1978). The strength of the psychometric approach lies in its ability to explore the relationships among different estimates of performance on complex tasks, but it is incapable of understanding or explaining the nature of these relationships within a measurement system. The strength of the experimental approach is in its ability to explore in a relatively unambiguous and nonarbitrary fashion the underlying mechanisms of cognitive activity, but from the experimental evidence alone it is not possible to tell whether the identified features of the processing system have any general validity or are merely uninteresting epiphenomena of a particular task or technique. In retrospect, the joining of these two approaches was inevitable; whether the joint product lives up to expectations is what we need now to consider (Keating, 1980c).

Given that it makes sense to apply information-processing analytic techniques to an understanding of individual differences in measured cognitive abilities, there are still some important questions in how this enterprise should proceed. The logical goal of all these attempts is to identify the components of the cognitive processing system that are the sources of individual difference variance in complex cognitive skills such as those measured on psychometric tests, or, by proxy, those needed for academic or occupational success. Thus a general term for all such efforts is componential approaches to intelligence. Pellegrino & Glaser (1979) made a further division within this, however, between what they called a "cognitive correlates" approach and a "cognitive components" approach, and suggested componential analysis be reserved for the latter. The former can be characterized as more of a "bottom-up" analysis: If individual differences in complex cognitive skills are due largely or partly to identifiable aspects of the cognitive processing system, such as short-term memory efficiency, long-term memory retrieval, organization of the semantic network, problem-solving strategies, and the like, then experimental techniques can be used to isolate parameters of these processing features and used to explain the target variance (Carroll, 1976, 1981; Hunt, 1978; Keating, 1979a).

This can be contrasted with a more "top-down" approach, in which the test item is taken as a complex task in its own right, and the goal of the analysis is to decompose it through a task analysis. Through this task decomposition, identifiable components of the processing actually engaged in by individuals when working on complex problems can, it is hoped, be isolated. Sternberg (1977, 1981a) and his colleagues have conducted the most sophisticated and extensive research from this perspective, using regression analysis to contrast different processing models of the same task. From these contrasts, best-fit models are used to estimate the most important features of processing on these tasks. If both of these approaches are sound ones and can fulfill the theoretical promise of the joint application of psychometric and experimental analyses, then the "top-down" and "bottom-up" results ought, at some point, to converge more than metaphorically (Keating, 1979a, 1980b; Sternberg, 1981b). To examine the prospects of validational efforts, we can consider first the cognitive components analyses and then the cognitive correlates approach.

Cognitive Components of Mental Abilities

The focus of this critique is the analysis of Sternberg's (1977, 1980a, 1981a, and references therein) componential approach. Only the most central points will be noted, and those briefly; for a more detailed treatment see Pellegrino & Lyon (1979) or Keating (1980d). What are the major threats to the validity of findings using Sternberg's approach? The four major concerns are reliability of the components, generalizability across analyses of different tasks, interpretation of identified components, and overall coherence of the theory.

How reliable are the components identified in componential analysis? If we pose the question in terms of the replicability of the regression analyses, the answer is that they are fairly reliable. In the analysis of analogical reasoning items, for example, some components are consistently related to the criterion variance, whereas others are consistently unrelated. A continuing controversy, however, is whether the differences between the best-fit regression model and other (rejected) models are substantial enough to be replicable, but there has been some support even for the replicability of these differences, even though they may be small. With a reasonable set of criteria for component reliability, it is clear that this is probably less problematic for this approach compared to the standards of the field in general (Sternberg, 1980b).

Whether or not the components, even though reliable within analyses of same or similar tasks, are sufficiently generalizable to be theoretically helpful is more problematic. Several related kinds of generalization need to be demonstrated. First, are the components meaningful for tasks other than those that generated them in the first place? Within different kinds of analogical reasoning, different components have been more or less important in different studies, and the connection of, say, mapping within the task as presented for experimental purposes to mapping as (or if) it occurs in the solution of "real" analogy problems, remains to be demonstrated. Second, Pellegrino and Lyon (1979) note that it is easier to generate researchable models for intelligence test items that can easily be analyzed into discrete pieces of information or solution steps. Whether it would work for other kinds of intellectual functioning is unclear. Note the similarity of this problem to that confronting Siegler's (1978) rule-assessment paradigm. Certainly it makes heuristic sense to concentrate on more easily analyzed problems in the development of a new methodology, but it is also legitimate to wonder at what point selection for heuristic purposes becomes definitional for the theory. In other words, if intelligence becomes what intelligence tests measure, does cognition become what cognitive scientists model?

A related question about generalizability is whether the contexts in which components are identified are too constrained, such that the transfer of explanation to the same skills in other contexts is compromised. In the initial analogical reasoning work (Sternberg, 1977), the clearest models emerged for the "people-piece" analogies, in which the same very limited set of information was continually repeated, but was progressively noisier for geometric and verbal analogies. In a similar vein, Bobbitt (1979) presented geometric matrix problems that varied systematically across three levels of stimulus complexity and three levels of rule difficulty. When these were presented in item blocks of ascending levels of difficulty (simple-easy to complex-hard, nine blocks in all), subjects performed in a predictable fashion that could be easily modeled with good reliability. But when the same items were presented randomly, so that a particular problem type could not be anticipated, the reaction times and errors were far noisier and less reliable. Taken together, these findings suggest that the identification of cognitive components may depend in crucial ways upon the regularity of information-in-context. One reason for this is that real world problem solving depends heavily on deciphering what the problem space is and what parameters are relevant (Schank, 1980), whereas cognitive modeling proceeds easily (and perhaps *only*) when those sources of ambiguity and lack of definition are removed. If so, the range of such cognitive models will be highly constricted.

Even if the problems of reliability and generalizability could be adequately resolved, there would remain the necessity of tying together the results with an unambiguous theoretical interpretation. With a substantial amount of solid empirical data to work from, some of these concerns might be reduced in importance, but on the basis of preliminary interpretations, it seems likely to be controversial. This is identical to the problem of interpreting factor structures.

Two examples suffice to illustrate the difficulty. In the analogical reasoning studies, the components most consistently related to the criterion performance were called *encoding* and *preparation-response*. The former was the amount of time the subject spent on the precuing part of the task, which was under the subject's control. Paradoxically, individuals with the better test scores spent a longer time encoding the cue information, when logically the expectation would be that they are more efficient extractors of relevant information and thus should encode more rapidly and efficiently. The apparent paradox is resolved into a simple "jangle" fallacy if we call the component *study time,* and consider the likely possibility that the higher scoring subjects were doing more than merely encoding the representational elements of the information—that they were in fact carrying out some preliminary solution steps. The longer this preparation, the shorter the response time when the full task came up, the point at which they were instructed to solve as quickly as possible. The second component, preparation-response, was not actually modeled directly, but was instead the intercept of the regression slope—the total response time not otherwise analyzed into components. This measure of unanalyzed reaction time has been found to have substantial correlations with test performance in other research paradigms as well, and defies simple interpretation. It may include such processing components as preparation and response, but it can obviously be influenced by such factors as the subject's vigilance, concentration, or sheer willingness to work on the task. Because the component is an ambiguous conglomerate of residual reaction time, tying it to particular cognitive process(es) goes beyond the definitional power of the method.

It should be noted that these criticisms arise from the application of a set of strict but not unreasonable validity criteria, and that the problems examined here are not restricted to this approach alone. In response to some of these concerns, Sternberg (1980a,b) has argued that the approach is still in a formative stage and is realtively better off than some others in dealing with validity issues. He has also suggested some major modifications in the theory. Principally this has entailed the addition of metacomponents that involve the individual's more active learning, transfer, and control processes, and the recognition that these may need to be studied in tasks where performance is not already entrenched (Sternberg, 1980a, 1981c). Whereas it is clear that these topics require greater attention, it is less clear in what meaningful sense acquisition, retention, transfer, and monitoring can be understood as components in the original sense of the term. If by component we mean nothing other than "something that may differ between skilled and unskilled performers," then the theoretical structure that relates components to each other becomes superfluous and we can speak merely of a list of potentially important variables (Keating, 1980d). Given that many of these problems are held in common with the correlates approach, we should consider that perspective before proceeding to a summary evaluation.

Cognitive Correlates of Individual and Developmental Differences in Mental Abilities

Much of the work that can be conveniently gathered under this heading has been reviewed by Carroll (1976, 1981; Carroll & Maxwell, 1979) and will be alluded to here only occasionally. As Carroll and Maxwell note (1979), most of these studies have examined straightforwardly the relationship between an experimentally derived parameter, which is believed to represent an isolated feature of the cognitive processing system, and some test score or scores. Also, most of the research has been conducted with adults (e.g., Hunt, 1978; Chiang & Atkinson, 1976; Hogaboam & Pellegrino, 1978). This last point is potentially quite significant, especially if the relationships between experimental parameters of processing and measured mental ability change as a function of development. It does, in fact, seem likely that different sources of processing variance make more or less of a contribution to performance on complex tasks as a function of developmental level (Keating, 1979a). It is precisely this relationship of underlying cognitive components to performance on complex cognitive tasks, studied developmentally, that has been the focus of our research program. Before turning to the results of that research program, it is instructive to consider what we have seen as the primary validity requirements of this approach. The substantive review will follow from this as an examination of whether progress has been made in meeting the key construct validity requirements.

The first of these has already been noted, and that is that a theory of intelligence must be developmental (Keating, 1979a). The explanations of individual differences in complex cognitive skills will almost certainly vary with developmental level. Even if this were not the case, a full picture of intellectual functioning is not possible without a clear idea of its history and context (Piaget, 1950; Vygotsky, 1978).

Second, the connection between the experimentally derived parameters and the underlying processes of structures they are presumed to represent must be theoretically specific. The major advantage of the information-processing perspective is its commitment to a task analysis that is as nonarbitrary and unambiguous as possible. This advantage is lost when the rationale for a particular parameter/process identification is not explicit and defensible. As Chi (1978) and others have argued, this is often the most difficult and controversial step in the research.

Third, there must be converging estimates of parameters from substantially different tasks. Even well defended logical inferences in the preceding step can not guarantee that a particular cognitive component is accurately represented in a particular parameter. Elimination of the suspicion of task specificity (Newell, 1973) through converging evidence from different tasks is needed to make the inferences adequately robust.

Fourth, it is necessary to demonstrate that the cognitive components are capable of accounting for more variance in tasks where the theoretical connection is stronger. Speed of mental rotation, for example, ought reasonably to explain more variance on spatial ability tests than on vocabulary tests. The convergent and discriminant validity evidence called for in these last two steps are important to protect against the possibility that confounding factors, such as global reaction time differences, will yield artifactually positive results.

Fifth, an adequate number of trials are needed to establish the internal consistency reliability of the parameters, which can be estimated in a number of ways (Stanley, 1971). Sixth, adequately large sample sizes must be used in order to insure reasonable stability for the correlational inferences. A brief consideration of these requirements reveals that a research program that attempts to respond to the mandates of experimental, differential, and developmental methodologies simultaneously confronts serious problems. Multiplying trials per task by tasks per parameter by parameters per ability generates a substantial amount of experimental time per subject in even the least complicated instances, and the further requirement of substantial sample sizes both within and across age only adds complexity. It should not be surprising to learn, then, that in the series of studies we have conducted each is flawed in some way, although they can also be seen as successive approximations to more conclusive construct validity studies. Of course, the centrality of some validity requirements became apparent only through the progress of the research itself.

The initial study (Keating & Bobbitt, 1978) was essentially exploratory, designed primarily to establish if possible the broad outlines of the connections between cognitive processing parameters and mental abilities at several ages. We examined three different cognitive processing parameters: Speed of decision making, indexed by choice reaction time minus simple reaction time (C–SRT); short-term memory efficiency, indexed by slope of reaction time across memory set size—one, three, or five digits—using the now standard S. Sternberg (1969) paradigm; and efficiency of access to name codes, indexed by reaction time differences under name and physical identity instructions (NIPI) in a same/different letter comparison task, using a card sorting variant of the task described by Posner, Boies, Eichelman, and Taylor (1969). As indicated, the intent was that each parameter represent as purely as possible its theoretical processing analogue; thus we constructed parameters employing the subtraction method. The criterion variable in this first study was Raven's (1960) Progressive Matrices, which as a presumed measure of g could not provide discriminant validity evidence. We had 20 subjects at each of three ages (9–, 13–, and 17–year-olds), and therefore used analysis of variance (ANOVA) of high versus low scorers rather than the preferred direct correlational analysis.

Despite (or perhaps because of) these limitations, the initial results were quite encouraging. In this ANOVA design, effects of the processing variable would show up as an interaction between ability and/or age and experimental condition.

Age interacted significantly with condition in two cases (choice reaction time and name code retrieval), and ability level interacted significantly also in two cases (name code retrieval and short-term memory scanning). Thus basic cognitive processing differences were implicated in both individual and developmental differences. In short-term memory scanning there was also a tantalizingly close ($p < .07$) three-way interaction among age, ability, and memory set size, in the direction that the high-scoring 9–year-olds' slope looked quite similar to the adolescent groups, whereas the lower scoring children were less efficient, that is, had higher slopes. The (questionable) regression analyses with Raven's matrices scores as the criterion necessarily conformed to these findings fairly closely, with something between 15% and 30% of the ability variance accounted for by the cognitive processing parameters. We viewed these results as consistent and encouraging.

Relative to the construct validity requirements described above, however, there were substantial gaps in this study. Given the obtained relationships between the experimental parameters with test scores and age, we wondered if they indicated real connections between processing and ability differences, or might in fact be merely task-specific correlations. Because of the danger of task specificity in studying processing/ability relationships, we decided to focus next on that question. We first performed a post hoc analysis of the connections between theoretically similar and dissimilar stages in the processing sequence from the data in the original study, and did not find disconfirming evidence; but we were dissatisfied with the confounded nature of that analysis (Keating & Bobbitt, 1978).

Accordingly, we decided to explore the memory scanning data further, and designed a multitrait, multimethod study (Campbell & Fiske, 1959) to examine both the generalizability of the scanning process across tasks and the replicability of the nearly significant interaction of age, ability, and experimental condition. This was of particular interest at the time because Chi (1977) had reviewed a number of studies of developmental differences in speed of short-term memory scanning and had concluded that they could not be found replicably. In a study with college undergraduates, Chiang and Atkinson (1976) had found evidence for the validity of scanning across tasks in a study similar to ours but had not found evidence for connections between this processing variance and ability as measured by the Scholastic Aptitude Tests. We hoped that the results from a convergent-discriminant validity study might serve to clarify this somewhat confused situation.

The design of the study was to examine the search process in two different tasks (Keating, Keniston, Manis, & Bobbitt, 1980), memory scanning and visual scanning. The memory scanning task was identical to that in the first study. The visual scanning simply reversed the order of stimulus presentation: The subjects first saw the individual target digit, and were then presented with an array of one, three, or five digits and asked if it contained the target. From each task for each subject we calculated a slope (the search-processing parameter) and an intercept from the best-fit regression of reaction time across (memory or visual) set size. The theoretical expectation was for high within-process, across-task correlations (slope-slope and intercept-intercept) relative to across-process, within- or between-task correlations (the four slope-intercept r's). We did observe this, average $r = .53$ for the former and .12 for the latter, a significant difference between the two average correlations. There was an even larger difference when we corrected the correlations for attenuation due to parameter unreliability (which we calculated from trial block intercorrelations), .92 versus .14. Thus the search-processing parameter seemed robust across these two tasks, with the caveat that much of the positive correlation stemmed from the intercepts rather than the slopes.

We also found significant effects for age (9–, 11–, 13–, and 15–year-olds) in both memory and visual search, although we had not found this effect in the first study. Contrary to expectation, we found *no* ability effect, nor a hint of the intriguing three-way interaction (age, ability, experimental condition) of the first study. We speculated that this was due to the use of a different ability measure, because we had in this instance used the California Test of Mental Maturity rather than Raven's matrices, in the hope of exploring specific rather than general processing/ability connections. The absence of any ability/processing relationships precluded these analyses. Our confidence in identifying the existence of this processing parameter was enhanced, but the connections between it and individual or developmental differences was far from clarified.

Although promising, the inconclusive nature of these results led us to pursue the central question in two different directions. First, it seemed that a finer grained analysis of the role of attention and its allocation within a particular task was called for, because up to this point we had made some strong assumptions that a stages-of-processing approach was appropriate for investigating individual and developmental differences, without having explored it directly (Manis, Keating, & Morrison, 1980). Second, we had focused on isolating cognitive processing components as opposed to structural or organizational components, and Chi's (1978) study rendered that assumption questionable. Thus we decided to explore both processing and structural components in the same study in order to examine their relative contributions to performance on a complex cognitive task (Ford & Keating, 1981). Such direct comparisons are needed as well to reduce the confounding inherent in univariate investigations of multivariate phenomena (Keating, 1979a).

We examined the allocation of processing capacity in a primary-secondary task design modeled after the work of Posner and Boies (1971) and Posner and Klein (1972). The logic of this design is that it permits the specification of points during processing where more attentional effort is being utilized. This is shown through interference in the performance of a constant secondary task that is presented at key points during different stages of the primary task.

In this study, the primary task was letter-match decision under name and physical identity conditions, although in contrast to Keating & Bobbitt (1978), the letters were presented in sequence, with an 1100 msec delay between the first and second letter. While viewing the letters in a tachistoscope, subjects were randomly presented with an audible tone through earphones, to which they responded with a button push (secondary task). The auditory probes occurred at five positions hypothesized to correspond to particular stages of processing of the primary task: probe 1—alerting (500 msec after warning signal); probe 2 and 3—early encoding of the first letter (150 and 300 msec after first letter onset); probe 4—later encoding (500 msec after first letter onset); and probe 5—responding (250 msec after second letter onset). The data of interest involve the degree of interference in reaction time to the auditory probe relative to a baseline reaction time, as a function of different stages of processing, and specifically whether attentional allocation varied as a function of development. The results confirmed that capacity allocation did change as a function of stage of processing (as indexed by increases in auditory probe reaction time), and that this capacity allocation changed as a function of age, observed as an age by stage of processing interaction.

The pattern of these results is shown in Figure 1.1. The difference score is the increase in reaction time to the auditory probe as it occurred at various points in the processing of the primary task. The second graders had significantly greater interference than sixth graders or adults at each position, and sixth graders showed more interference than adults at probes 4 and 5, later encoding and responding.

The evidence for the utility of the stages of processing approach, and for the developmental relevance of specifically processing-based variables, was important, although it did not indicate what the developmental mechanisms might be nor what contribution the kind of capacity allocation we identified would make to complex problem solving or other cognitive skills. We speculated that the connection might reside in an understanding of automaticity, because the process showing the least developmental differences might be expected to be the first to become automatic (alerting and early encoding vs. later encoding and responding). Direct investigations of this connection are necessary to examine this post hoc speculation.

The process investigated in the next study to be described (Ford & Keating, 1981) proved harder to capture in on-line processing: long-term memory (LTM) retrieval. We selected this process for two reasons. First, it was an obviously theoretically important cognitive process for many complex tasks. Second, because LTM *structure* had been characterized in several different organizational models, it was possible to design a study that explored simultaneously the role of two different aspects of cognitive functioning process and structure in a relevant complex task, vocabulary knowledge. This contrast of different sources of variance was an attempt to implement the requirement that models should be multi-

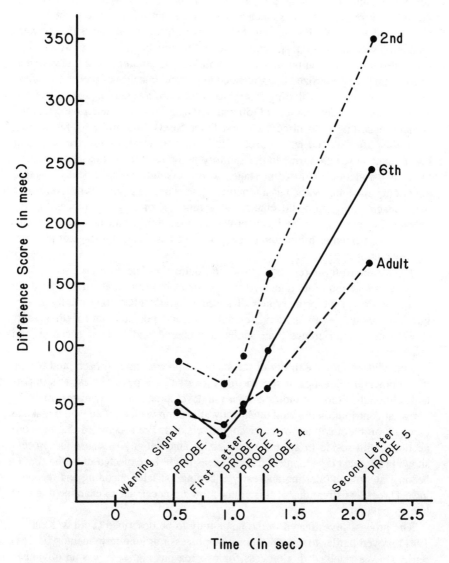

FIG. 1.1.   Mean difference scores, in msec, of the three age groups in Manis, Keating, & Morrison (1980).

variate because the world clearly is (Keating, 1979a). Because semantic retrieval from a long-term store is one of the hardest areas in which to separate structural and processing features of the cognitive system, we attempted to define these variables in contrast to each other, and to make our assumptions as explicit as possible.

The processing variable, LTM retrieval, was defined analogously to short-term memory search, in that we examined subjects' reaction time to respond whether or not a particular word belonged to a just-named category as a function of the salience of that word to the category. If the given category is *bird,* for example, the response time for *robin* is faster than for *turkey;* robin is a better exemplar of a bird than a turkey is. We reasoned that a slope of reaction time across association strength would yield a relatively pure parameter of LTM retrieval, because the other processes involved (encoding, decision, response) ought not to fluctuate much as a function of association strength, once the item's meaning had been accessed.

Although the logic is similar to that of the S. Sternberg (1969) short-term memory search paradigm, there is a major obstacle: Memory set size is already an interval if not a rational scale. For the dimension of association strength (of words to categories), an empirical scale has to be developed, and any one approach will be inadequate. To construct the scale, we obtained two kinds of evidence from fourth and eighth graders and college undergraduates: Production frequency data ("Name the first six birds . . . musical instruments . . . etc. that come to mind"), and direct ratings of association strength. Interestingly, for correlations of the production frequencies and ratings of category-word pairs, the results indicated striking consistency both within and across-age and within- and between-methods of measurement: The median of all correlations was about .9.

We used the production frequency and direct ratings data in two ways: First, to construct a scale of association strength so that in the verification task (that is, reaction times to indicate category membership of low, medium, and high association strength words) the values would be as similar as possible for all age groups; and second, to calculate four variables for each subject on how typical or atypical his/her memory organization was, relative to the total group—two variables each from the individual's production frequency data and ratings. From each subject's production frequency data, we calculated the sum of the ranks of group frequencies of the words generated, as well as the number generated that were in the top ten ranks for each category. We then calculated for each word rating for each subject a standard (z) score difference from the group rating, which we summed both as regular and absolute values. These four measures provided substantially theoretically different ways of tapping into systematic atypicality of individual's LTM organizational structures.

The targeted criterion variable was a vocabulary test appropriate for each age group. We also included a Raven's matrices test for purposes of discriminant validity, since LTM retrieval is logically more connected with vocabulary recall than with the on-line nonverbal problem solving of the matrices.

We did find significant age differences both in the LTM retrieval and organizational parameters, although more clearly in the former than in the latter. There was a substantial and monotonic decrease in the slope of retrieval reaction time from fourth grade through eighth grade to the college sample; for the fourth–eighth grade difference, in fact, the 95% confidence intervals were non-overlapping. By contrast, the organizational parameter yielded a nonmonotonic increase in typicality, such that individual fourth graders on average gave less typical responses, but the eighth graders gave more typical responses than adults, although not by much. The 95% confidence intervals of all three groups overlapped considerably in this instance.

Results of the individual differences analysis were interesting in several respects, and are shown in Table 1.1. For the fourth and eighth graders, the LTM retrieval parameters (both true and false response slopes) were substantially related to verbal ability and to Raven's matrices scores. The directions of all correlations were in the theoretically predicted direction, although the retrieval/verbal ability correlations did not significantly exceed the retrieval/Raven's matrices correlations, as we had expected. For adults, the retrieval/verbal ability correlations were not significant. (Raven's matrices scores were not available for the adults.) Of the twelve LTM organizational parameter/verbal ability correlations (four in each age group), only two were signifi-

TABLE 1.1
Intercorrelations of LTM Retrieval and Organization Scores
And Cognitive Ability for Each Age Group

	Cognitive Ability				
	Verbal Ability Test			Raven's SPM	
	4th Grade	8th Grade	Adult	4th Grade	8th Grade
LTM retrieval efficiency:					
Slope (true words)	-.59***	-.50**	-.08	-.39*	-.35*
Slope (false words).............	-.66***	-.66***	.14	-.49**	-.41*
LTM organization typicality:					
Production score no. 1 (sum of ranks)	.06	.37*	.06	-.48*	.01
Production score no. 2 (no. top 10s)	-.09	-.10	.00	.42*	-.01
Rating score no. 1 (mean z score)	-.27	-.20	-.10	-.01	-.41*
Rating score no. 2 (mean absolute z score)	-.42*	-.29	-.23	.02	.27

Note: N = 24 for each age group. Adults did not take the SPM - See Raven (1960)
*p < .05.
**p < .01.
***p < .001.

cant, and those in opposite directions. Highly typical responses were associated with higher test scores in one case (fourth grade, rating score 2) but with lower scores in the other (eighth grade, production score 1). The moderately strong connection in the younger samples between processing variance and measured ability was thus contrasted with the absence of any connection between LTM structural variance and test scores, highlighting the importance of process variables. The lack of a processing/ability connection for adults is consistent with other findings (Hogaboam & Pellegrino, 1978), and suggests again the importance of a developmental analysis.

We considered these results to be quite promising. A finer grained analysis had demonstrated the utility of a stages-of-processing approach for examining developmental differences (Manis, Keating, & Morrison, 1980). A contrasting analysis of the roles of cognitive processing and structural variables in complex cognitive functioning highlighted the former, particularly for children (Ford & Keating, 1981). Each of the reported studies contributed to answering some specific construct validity concern, but each left open a number of plausible alternatives to the conclusion that complex cognitive skills could be successfully explained by identifiable and measurable components.

On the strength of these results and analyses, Judith List, William Merriman and I designed and conducted a large-scale convergent/discriminant construct validity study to incorporate as many of the criteria listed earlier as possible (Keating, List, & Merriman, 1983). We obtained a large enough sample size to justify correlational analyses, including factor analysis: N = 60 at each of three ages, fourth and eighth grade and adults. We decided to examine convergent and discriminant validity by contrasting two clearly distinct domains, verbal and spatial ability, and indexed each psychometrically with both individual and group tests for each subject. As parameters to represent the retrieval processes theoretically related to verbal ability, we selected two that are from different tasks but represent a similar process: the NIPI variable, which is related to name code accessing (Keating & Bobbitt, 1978) and the LTM semantic retrieval slope of reaction time across association strength (Ford & Keating, 1981). For the spatial ability processing analogues, we examined speed of mental rotation of two quite different kinds of stimulus materials, alphabetic letters and schematic facial profiles. Given the negative results of Ford & Keating (1981) on the organizational or structural components of LTM retrieval, we decided against adding variables from that level of analysis. But we did examine the possible operation of strategic or control processing in one of the tasks from each of verbal and spatial processing. For the former, we presented the letter-match (NIPI) task under two conditions, simultaneous and sequential presentation. We hypothesized that with the advance information on one of the letters, subjects could strategically generate an image of the possibly correct match(es) before the second letter came up. This should reduce the NIPI difference, because under physical identity instructions a straight physical match is always possible, whereas under name identity instructions there should be greater facilitation with the reduced uncertainty in having encoded the first letter prior to second letter presentation. In spatial processing, we added an advance information task to the letter-rotation procedure, by indicating with an arrow where the top of the letter would be before each trial. (The subject's judgment is whether the letter appears in normal or mirror image.) In both cases, the strategy variable was defined as the *reduction* in the RT differences (NIPI or slope across degrees of rotation) in the advance information compared to the standard presentation.

Thus the design called for an examination of two ability domains, verbal and spatial, in terms of eight possible cognitive components: Semantic retrieval and name code access (in standard and delayed presentation) as basic processing variables relevant to the verbal domain; simultaneous vs. sequential NIPI as a strategy variable in the verbal domain; letter rotation (in standard and advance information presentation) and facial rotation as basic processing variables relevant to the spatial domain; and advance position information on letter rotation compared to the standard condition as a strategy variable in the spatial domain. The convergent-discriminant validity predictions followed from this arrangement of variables, although the domain specificity of the strategy variables was not crucial. One might, in fact, expect them to correlate with each other as meta-componential (!) control processes, and to predict each ability score equally well. One practical constraint should be noted before proceeding to the results. The complexity and duration of the experimental tasks overwhelmed the fourth graders, who were not able to complete all of them. Thus the full validity data are available only for the eighth graders and adults; data obtained from the fourth graders will not be discussed further here.

The results are too complicated to be reported fully, but the major conclusions are clear enough to be conveyed through some of the key findings. For convergence of the similar-process parameters from different tasks, the results were modest for eighth graders, with an average $r = .31$ for the three spatial rotation processing parameters, and $r = .23$ for the three retrieval processing parameters, compared to an average $r = .08$ for the nine divergent-process correlations. Contrasting these figures suggests that the convergence is in the right direction, but it is clearly not impressive. An interesting way of exploring the degree of convergence is to consider each parameter as an "item" of an information-processing "test." Using the Spearman-Brown prophecy formula (Stanley, 1971), the reliability of the spatial processing test is .57, of the retrieval processing test .47, and of the divergent processing test .44. The contrast is not compelling.

For the adults, the convergence is minimal, with an average $r = .17$ for the spatial processing parameters, $r = .13$ for the retrieval processing parameters, and $r = .10$ for the divergent-process correlations. Besides the fact that the tasks are superficially more different from each other than in the earlier study where substantial parameter convergence was obtained (Keating, Keniston, Manis, &

Bobbitt, 1980), another reason for lack of convergence here is that these analyses included *no* intercept data, but only difference or slope parameters, which theoretically represent more isolated processing variance. It should be noted that within-parameter realiabilities estimated from odd-even trial intercorrelations were reasonable for the parameters examined here, so correction for attenuation does not alter the general trend of the results.

Were the processing parameters consistently related to the ability variance in these samples? Even if the parameters did not converge as predicted, which could result from an inaccurate task analysis, the processing/ability connections could still be observed. We constructed two within-age standard scores for each subject for the verbal and spatial ability tests, and used them as criteria in a series of regression analyses. For each regression, we first entered as a group the three cognitive processing variables theoretically relevant to the criterion, followed by the three that were theoretically less related, also as a group. For the eighth graders, the verbal ability composite was significantly predicted by the retrieval processing variables, $R = .46$ ($p < .004$); the addition of the spatial rotation variables adds to this only slightly, $R = .53$. The spatial ability composite was not predicted significantly by the spatial rotation variables, $R = .19$; the addition of the retrieval processing variables did not change this, $R = .22$. For the adults, however, the exact opposite pattern obtained, with one curious exception. On the verbal ability criterion, the retrieval processing variables were not significant predictors, $R = .12$. Note that this finding with its companion for the eighth graders is an accurate replication of the findings of Ford & Keating (1981). But when the spatial processing variables are added in, the prediction is significant, $R = .37$ ($p < .01$). Thus the theoretically relevant processing variables failed to predict the criterion, whereas the irrelevant ones did predict significantly. Given the results so far, we could argue that this last finding is a random fluctuation, that the replication of the retrieval processing/verbal ability correlations demonstrates the robustness of that relationship, and that the failure in the spatial domain was due to inappropriate processing and/or test variables. For the adults' spatial ability criterion, however, the spatial rotation variables *do* predict significantly, $R = .45$ ($p < .005$). Adding the retrieval processing variables adds a little, $R = .52$. An examination of the zero-order correlations does not change the picture in any significant way and will not be treated here. Also, the strategy variables were unrelated to either criterion or to each other.

Even a sympathetic critic would be hard pressed to find compelling construct validity evidence in this pattern of results. Compared to standard procedures used in other similar studies, these investigations were conducted with at least equal rigor. Internal evidence from secondary analyses (parameter reliabilities, error rates, test norms, and so on) revealed no anomalous findings and it is thus unlikely that the results can be explained away as artifacts. The unavoidable conclusion seems to be that when key construct validity requirements are adhered to (which is rarely), the evidence for cognitive processing/mental ability relationships is inconclusive at best, or, more fairly, disconfirming. Less comprehensive studies of this relationship, such as those in the series that led to the last one reported, can give misleading indications of positive results, at least partly *because* of the limitations placed on them by not considering certain central issues.

We have of course speculated about the particular pattern of findings in this and prior studies, in addition to drawing the general negative inference regarding construct validity. We suspect that at least three factors can be seen as having a role in the positive results that were obtained. First, the notion of automaticity may prove to be an important one, as noted earlier. It is probably not coincidental that the most interesting correlations are found among children and younger adolescents rather than among older adolescents or adults. When a cognitive process becomes fully routinized, we can probably learn little from it as a source of understanding how a complex task is performed. It is interesting to note that Vygotsky (1978), writing in the early 1930s, anticipated this in some detail:

> In psychology we often meet with processes that have already died away, that is, processes that have gone through a very long stage of historical development and have become fossilized. These fossilized forms of behavior are most easily found in the so-called automated or mechanized psychological processes which, owing to their ancient origins, are now being repeated for the millionth time and have become mechanized. They have lost their original appearance, and their outer appearance tells us nothing whatsoever about their internal nature. Their automatic character creates great difficulty for psychological analysis [pp. 63–64].

The understanding of human information processing may be possible through an analysis of process-in-formation, which cross-sectional, correlational studies do not allow.

Second, the correlations are more likely to be positive and significant when there is a close similarity in the actual content of the tasks. In semantic category verification, for example, the subject is given a category (that is, a word like *bird*) and asked to decide quickly if it goes with another word (that is, the exemplar *robin*). This is similar in many respects to what one actually does on many vocabulary test items. As noted, the ability criteria in the Keating, List, & Merriman (1983) study were constructed from a battery of age-appropriate individual and group ability tests. An examination of them following the anomalous spatial processing/ability connection for adults revealed a stronger similarity in the content of the processing and ability tasks the adults performed, compared to the eighth graders. Note that this after-the-fact similarity was only obvious because we were looking for it, given the empirical finding. This raises the suspicion that we may often have been comparing two different ways of measuring virtually identical skills, rather than exploring the theoretical relationship between two independently defined variables.

Third, the fact that the most consistent finding in this series of studies was the connection of semantic retrieval and verbal ability deserves some thought. All things considered, it is probably noteworthy that these tasks have the most obvious meaning connected with them. Not only are the stimulus materials drawn from natural language, but the cognitive activity of searching for and using words is hard to decontextualize totally. Compared to deciding whether two letters are physically identical or whether a rotated letter is in normal or mirror image, with which we have little or no common experience, retrieving word meaning is, in a word, meaningful.

Could we design a series of studies, given these considerations, that would yield a pattern of results conforming more closely to the theoretical assumptions of componential analysis? By selecting experimental and psychometric tasks that are more similar, by systematically varying such things as difficulty level and meaningfulness, and by considerable fine-tuning, one could almost certainly generate such a pattern of findings. But consider the theoretical value of such results. Their interpretability is entirely compromised for precisely the same reason that factor analytic evidence is an unreliable guide to mental structures: The tautology of presumed internal entities and the carefully structured tasks used to discover and "prove" their existence.

Summary and Evaluation of Componential and Correlates Approaches

A critical reading of the literature on componential approaches to intelligence, conceptualized either as "top-down" components or as "bottom-up" correlates, reveals some fundamental problems. One view of these problems is that they result from an ultimately productive integration of theories of intelligence, which is in a formative stage characterized by fits and starts. This evolutionary view (although not a good metaphor because as used here it suggests progression, not a necessary component of biological evolution) is explicitly advocated by Sternberg (1981b), who sees a successful integration of correlationally based structural theories and experimentally based processing theories in the offing.

Although the evidence to date does not compel one to accept a different view, I contend that it is persuasive enough to argue that such an integration is unlikely if not impossible. The problems of reliability, replicability, generalizability, theoretical specificity, and range of explanations considered in the preceding sections are more than technical obstacles to be overcome through more research and refined methodology. Instead, I would now argue that they are the natural consequences of fundamental misconceptions about the nature and development of human intelligence. Most of the misconceptions are not due to the irrelevance of the topics that have been studied; surely, cognitive processes such as search, retrieval, encoding, monitoring and so on must play a role in human cognitive activity.[2] Rather, they result more from topics *not* included in our investigations from this perspective.

What, then, is missing from our analyses that leads to such fundamental problems? Basically, it is that we have typically failed to attend to the context in which intellectual functioning occurs and to the context in which theorizing proceeds. For the individual cognitive actor, context encompasses such key (and complicated!) constructs as development, meaningfulness, goals, motivation, and culture. For the theorist, it encompasses a variety of topics normally studied by sociologists of science, such as the role of social science theories in the maintenance of social control (Karier, 1976; Poulantzas, 1978) or the social class of those who can engage professionally in theory construction (Bramel & Friend, 1981).

If such considerations are vital to our understanding of these important questions, why have they been downplayed or ignored, even at a point when researchers are taking a "new look" at intelligence? A full answer to that question would require a detailed analysis not possible here, but a broad outline of that analysis would include two general points.

First, there is a consistent tendency to reduce the problem of human intelligence to an entity in the head of the person. This is clearly seen in the work of the early test theorists and factorists, whose hereditarian bias led them to an easy conclusion that some central, biological core was differentially distributed among populations. To us, the crudity of Galton's (1884) racist and elitist conclusions about a physiologically based distribution of natural abilities, drawn incidentally *prior* to the existence of any empirical data, is obvious, but the underlying assumption of a discoverable physical entity has been hard to overcome. Psychology has yet to deal with its "physics envy." Certainly it is no accident that the American interpretation of Piaget focused on the internal stages and structures as the only important feature of his genetic epistemology, to the exclusion of other aspects that could be developed, such as a fuller working through of the biological metaphor or deeper exploration of the notion of the individual as constructor of cognitive reality. This focus was not inconsistent with Piaget's own emphasis, as I have argued, but it nonetheless fit most neatly into psychology's cognitive predilections as a *maturational* theory (Sigel, 1981).

---

[2]A different critique not developed here would raise the issue of how social forces determine the reigning metahpors of social science research, and thus the kind of topics investigated. A productive line of inquiry would be the value of human information-processing analyses to a potential (or ongoing) deskilling of cognitive activity analogous to the deskilling of crafts (Braverman 1974). Is there a structural analogy between Taylor's time-motion studies, the analysis of craft skills, and their transfer to assembly line machine production on the one hand, and, on the other, information-processing analysis, the construction of information transfer and decision systems, and the embedding of these in computers? For management, the benefits of centralized control of so-called mental as well as manual labor seem obvious, as does the impact on white collar workers as in the past on their blue collar counterparts.

The "new look" in intelligence research also fits too comfortably within this pattern. Peering through the fancy new garments woven from components, rules, and metacomponents, we can see the older but no wiser figure, g. Openly proclaimed by Galton, Spearman, Burt, and others, then rejected as too simplistic to explain human intellectual functioning, it is staging a comeback in its new guise as the hardware of human information processing. There is much time but little metaphorical distance between brain size (Broca, 1861) and computer capacity as explanations of individual or group differences.

Tying such constructs as cognitive processing, strategies, rules, monitoring, task analysis, and so on, to psychometrically measured abilities is doubly unfortunate: First, because the correlational structures are in fact evanescent, and thus the research efforts will go unrewarded in the search for explanations; second, because in embedding them in this structure of pseudoexplanation, they are themselves reified and risk losing their heuristic value. Naming a parameter with a processing label no more guarantees it to be a description of actual cognitive activity than naming a test IQ makes it a real assessment of intellectual capacity.

Besides the ideology of intelligence as a thing-in-a-person that constrains psychology's ability to deal with the broader, contextual issues of human intelligence, a second reason is the structure of the discipline itself. To contend, for example, that an understanding of the nature and development of human intelligence would focus on the individual's internalization of external social relationships (Vygotsky, 1978) brings into the picture topics such as culture and its historical roots, the nature of the social structure, material conflicts between classes in the society, and so on. They are inseparable from human social relationships. Investigations of human intelligence predicated upon these issues do not fit easily within disciplinary boundaries. That the structures to support the development of a social science that does not respect disciplinary boundaries do not now exist is stating the obvious, and the construction of such a social science is not only a challenging intellectual task but a formidable political one as well.

There is a more explicit political issue that constrains psychological investigations of human intelligence. Admitting such contextual issues into the realm of debate challenges directly the myth of scientific neutrality. It is easier to conduct research on human intelligence when it can be seen as neutral, nonpolitical, nonideological science (Carroll & Horn, 1981; Jensen, 1980). Of course, it never has been nor could be neutral, nonpolitical, and nonideological because it is intimately intertwined with and inseparable from social structures. One of the ingenious "catch-22's" of contemporary social science is that pointing out the clear ideological components of supposedly neutral science is regarded as ideological, hence unscientific and dismissable; whereas ignoring the ideological components is regarded as taking a neutral stance, hence scientific and serious.

Recognizing and refuting not only the critically unexamined core of conventional wisdom about human intelligence but also the obstacles to that critical examination that stem from the social structures of social science research, are major steps toward improved theory and practice. But refutation is only the first step: It clears the field of unnecessary obstacles, but without progress in our understanding of the important and real phenomena involved, the result is nihilistic. We need to consider how to proceed in a productive fashion.

IMPLICATIONS FOR THEORY AND PRACTICE

A critique of extant theories of intelligence can proceed quite straightforwardly, but the specification in detail of where one goes from here is much more complex. Numerous issues and ideas suddenly become possible lines of pursuit within a novel framework, but which ones are likely to be fruitful and important is nearly impossible to project. Such predictions are usually pointless anyway; directions only become clear through pursuing the work itself. Instead, I will propose what seem to me reasonable underpinnings of such an enterprise and invite interested parties to join the dialogue.

One central idea is a recognition of the thorough interdependence of theory and practice in this (and other) domains. It has become commonplace to lament the artificial divisions between basic and applied social science, or even to argue that they are not really different at all. Despite this, many continue to conceive of the theorist/researcher's role as the arbiter of what is worthwhile or important science, even though the researcher may have little contact with the everyday use of the constructs developed, whereas the practitioner's role is to learn from this wisdom and decipher how to use it. Some in fact see an evolving role for professional interpreters of scientific wisdom for those in the trenches, sort of a scientist/practitioner middle-person (not an outlandish idea given the existing chasm between theory and practice). The threats to the quality of both theory and practice from this artificial division are serious (Morrison, Lord, & Keating, in press). Whereas uninformed and disorganized practice is as likely to be harmful as helpful, it is equally true that theories must be explored through practical applications before they can be considered valid. The discussion that follows will attempt to reflect this perspective. The two organizing themes for examining where we go from here are development and social change—and if the former seems more like theory and the latter more like practice, the fault will be mine, for surely we need a practice of human development and a theory of social change as much as the reverse.

Development

The currently most promising perspective for understanding the nature and development of human intellectual functioning is to be found in the work of L. S. Vygotsky (1962, 1978). Although he died nearly 50 years ago, his ideas have only slowly penetrated American psychological thinking from their Soviet origins, and to date that penetration has been relatively superficial. Many more American psychologists are familiar with the work of his student, A. R. Luria, although Luria and his colleagues viewed Vygotsky's work as the source of the most important organizing ideas (Wertsch, 1981). The ideas of Vygotsky that have received some attention, such as self-regulation (Copeland, in press; Kendall & Hollon, 1980) or zones of potential development (Brown & French, 1979), are only partial reflections of the depth of the analysis. A full explanation of Vygotsky's perspective is not possible here; see Wertsch's (1981) helpful summary and analysis, and of course, Vygotsky (1962, 1978). The key explanatory construct for Vygotsky was *development,* which he used very broadly. To understand human activity, he argued, one must know its historical (that is, developmental) roots. There are four critical levels of analysis of development, and each must be understood in reference to the others. For readers familiar with marxist analysis, the historical materialist approach inherent in Vygotsky's analysis will be apparent.

The first important history is evolutionary history. Without this, we can not hope to understand the initial material base of human cognitive activity, the biological human organism. Of particular interest, of course, are investigations of the specific evolutionary history of *Homo sapiens.* One central feature of the evolution of humans from this perspective is the concept of intelligent *mediation* of human activity, through tools and tool use as means of production and through signs and sign systems as a means of socially organizing production. Wertsch (1981) cites a key passage from Engels' *Dialectics of nature:*

> When after thousands of years of struggle the differentiation of hand from foot, and erect gait, were finally established, man became distinct from the monkey and the basis was laid for the development of the brain that has since made the gulf between man and monkey an unbridgeable one. The specialization of the hand—this implies the *tool,* and the tool implies specific human activity, the transforming reaction of man on nature, production [p. 24].

A consequence of this understanding is a challenge to the sharp division of mental and manual labor (Braverman, 1974; Poulantzas, 1978). Modes of production based on the separation of conception from execution thus confront human intellectual functioning in a fundamental way, and engender resentment among those subject to it (Bramel & Friend, 1981; Braverman, 1974). Recall the commentary by Terman (p. 4) for a clear indication of the ideological support for the subjugation of "inferior mentality."

Although understanding the evolutionary history is important, it will not tell us all, or most, of what we need to know about human intelligence. Specifically, we need to avoid the simple applications of physiological analogies that lead to recurring versions of biological determinism. Gould (1981) presents a strong series of arguments that human intelligence is better understood as biological potential expressed most clearly in the flexibility of the organism:

> Why should human behavioral ranges be so broad, when anatomical ranges are generally narrower? . . . Consider first of all the probable adaptive reasons for evolving such a large brain. Human uniqueness lies in the flexibility of what our brain can do. . . . Secondly, we must be wary of granting too much power to natural selection by viewing all capacities of our brain as direct adaptations. I do not doubt that natural selection acted in building our oversized brains . . . (but not) all major capacities must arise as direct products of natural selection. These additional capacities are ineluctable consequences of structural design, not direct adaptations. . . . The idea that natural selection should have worked for flexibility in human evolution is not an ad hoc notion born in hope, but an implication of neoteny (in which rates of development slow down, retaining juvenile features) as a fundamental process in our evolution. Humans are learning animals [pp. 331–33].

This flexibility is expressed through the second level of analysis in Vygotsky's approach, the cultural-historical. Through the use of sign systems, humans learn to control or regulate not only their own behavior through mediational processes, but also develop means of transmitting what has been learned through time: thus culture and history. Vygotsky's interest in semiotics and in the influence of signs (particularly language) on thought stems from this observation. To understand the processes of thought and their development in the child, it is necessary to understand the actual nature of *social* interactions, which are the external relationships the child will internalize. Even seemingly basic concepts such as space and time are not, therefore, derived or constructed naturally from an unchanging physical reality, but arise instead through an internalization of the historically determined external social interactions that give them meaning (Poulantzas, 1978). This also highlights the importance of cross-cultural research in which development is investigated with respect to the culture and society in which it takes place, and not just in reference to Western standards (Sharp, Cole, & Lave, 1979; Wertsch, 1981).

It is the history of these internalizations that are the core of the individual's development. This is the third level of analysis, ontogenesis. Under this heading, Vygotsky considers a number of topics that are more familiar to developmental psychologists, including self-regulation, inner speech, zones of potential development, and others.

In the fourth level of developmental analysis, microgenesis, we find the most easily adaptable guidelines for carrying out research with children. Microgenesis refers to short-term changes of the individual that capture longer term transitions of developmental significance. It is in such short-term studies that one might hope to see the importance of various components to the acquisition of specific cognitive skills. This is a counter to the study of already fossilized mechanisms; one seeks to observe the building up of an intellectual skill before it has become (or as it becomes) mechanized.

An interesting example of the joining of a microgenetic, acquisition-focused perspective with a sophisticated use of information-processing methodology is seen in a study by Manis (1981). He presented a series of words, which varied in readability (e.g., *tassel* vs. *trough*), to normal and disabled readers (fifth and sixth grades). They learned to pronounce them and to identify them with a corresponding picture. As expected, the normal readers were faster and more accurate in the first session on all words. He then examined them on three subsequent occasions. Although the accuracy on all words and the speed on regular (that is, readable) words improved rapidly for the disabled readers, the automaticity on the difficult words remained poor. Thus, one special difficulty poor readers may be having is in the rapid decoding of irregularly pronounced words. The important lesson from this study is that this specific problem area, decoding irregular words, was identified through looking carefully at the process of acquiring new material *as it was becoming automatized.* It suggests that there is considerable promise for detailed studies of cognitive components of important skills *when* they are examined in the course of acquisition, that is, microgenetically.

To see if in fact the identified process is of major importance, it would of course be necessary to carry the observation into a practical application. This suggests an expanded notion of how we should proceed toward developing valid theories of cognitive development, which would include contextual validation. A brief outline might resemble the following:

1. A task or skill is selected for analysis. From the perspective argued here, it makes sense to select cognitive skills that are important in their own right for analysis, such as reading, arithmetic, critical thinking, and so on (Farnham-Diggory & Nelson, in press). Although more difficult to model than tasks designed specifically to test models, such as tower of Hanoi (Klahr, 1978) or balance beam (Siegler, 1978), the poor record of generalizability of cognitive components suggests that we work directly on problems we wish to know something about.

2. Because it is not normally possible to examine all cognitive components of a complex skill simultaneously, some component or subset is selected for analysis (such as decoding irregular words).

3. In one or more controlled studies, it is demonstrated that the selected component plays (or does not play) an apparent role in the performance of the target skill. A casual perusal of the cognitive and developmental journals indicates that this phase comprises a majority, and perhaps an overwhelming one, of the studies reported (for example, Keating & Bobbitt, 1978; Keating, Keniston,

Manis, & Bobbitt, 1980; Ford & Keating, 1981; and others). What should logically be the beginning of the validity process is frequently mistaken for the end!

4. Through a variety of interventions, there is an attempt to induce the component in the performance of the child. The point here is to see *if* the child can perform the identified process (for example, remembering premises of transitive inference problems).

5. If the learners can do the component, does it help on the target task? Young children can apparently learn metacognitive techniques relatively easily, but it rarely has much of an impact on their ability to use them spontaneously (Cavanaugh & Perlmutter, 1982). When the addition of the component fails to influence the main task, it is of little interest, and some lower level of analysis needs to be repeated. (Those readers who feel compelled may now construct flow-charts.)

6. Does it help on anything besides the main task from which it was derived? That is, is there any transfer to other closely related tasks? Distantly related tasks? In an interesting study, Siegler (1978) carried through an investigation of the balance-beam problem to the level of discovering that a combination of encoding training ("Count the weights and measure the distance") and feedback on a number of trials improved the sophistication of the rules the children were using—but only on the balance beam. Without the transfer study, the suspicion lingers that what we learned was that if you tell children fairly explicitly how to do a particular problem, they can learn it. Were there related changes where we might have expected them, on other proportional reasoning problems for example? In other words, what developed?

7. Even if transfer is demonstrated across tasks, we would still need to know if the changes implied by the research are robust across contexts as well as across tasks. Can the component change be implemented in practice? Reading the historical literature of the field (e.g., Farnham-Diggory & Nelson, in press) yields an uncomfortable feeling of rediscovering the wheel. Why? If, as argued, the various histories are interdependent, and if ontogenesis is the history of the internalizations of external social relationships, then it follows that if potentially beneficial developmental ideas are not translated into practice, thus becoming available as external relationships, they cannot be "real" ontogenetically. This extension of the validity process into the realm of practice is thus a theoretical as well as a practical necessity. Otherwise the only material reality of the science is the ink in journals and on resumés.

Social Change

The historical materialist perspective described here (in barest outline) is not the only one from which concerns about positive developmental practices arise. Analysts arguing from a traditional positivist perspective (well represented, for example, in the *American Psychologist* special issue on testing, October 1981) often argue for substantive reforms in practices affecting intellectual development. The Head Start programs are a noteworthy example of such positive influences in the realm of educational intervention. What, then, is different or better about the perspective outlined here?

In essence, it is that it seeks to understand in depth the role that educational and developmental theory and practice play in the broad social formation. Understanding the source of abuses of psychometric assessment, for example, may lead to improved practice. But without a concomitant exploration of the material and ideological effects of mass testing within the social structure (Karier, 1976; Bowles & Gintis, 1976), more basic problems will not be addressed. Even discounting the role of intelligence testing in the 1924 Immigration Restriction Act, or in support of racist stereotypes, or as the basis of "eugenic" involuntary sterilization, as historical aberrations (and more—if as defenders argue there's a baby in here worth saving, it rests in remarkably dirty bath water!), the *intended* use of testing to sort and select for institutional purposes—that is, to maintain a societal hierarchy—requires a serious social and political analysis.

Such an analysis of the uses of cognitive assessment would lead to several conclusions. As indicated earlier, I do not think it would lead to the abandonment of assessment. But it would argue for fundamental changes in its function. Most importantly, recognizing the contextual and developmental nature of human intelligence, it would view failures as those of the social system and not of the individual. As the examples of Cuba and Nicaragua show, illiteracy of peasant populations is readily reversed in the context of social structural transformations and the associated cultural changes. Is urban illiteracy and school failure in the United States any less systemic in nature? It is hard to see how it is different.

Properly understood and in the appropriate context, careful cognitive assessment is not only useful but also desirable. Two examples suffice. Assessment as a close companion of instruction and intervention can assist the developmental process substantially. As Binet argued long ago, the purpose of intellectual assessment is to see how to modify intellectual functioning. This consciously guided cognitive socialization works best (and perhaps only) when the connection is a close one; the benefits are not reaped through infrequent group testing leading to large-scale educational tracking. Second, results can and have been used as indices of some known physiological abnormalities, such as Down's syndrome, PKU, lead toxicity, and so on.

But assessment as an index of problems is of little use if not as a spur to deal seriously with all aspects of those problems, including social structural aspects. The expansive hopes for the support of human development of the 1960s, however naive, formed a better practice of human development than the withdrawal of help from nutritional, environmental protection, and educational programs for poor and handicapped children, which is the emerging practice of the 1980s (Cordes, 1982). Having argued successfully for developmental needs in another time is neither comfort nor guidance for the present. We need to understand much more clearly what social forces permitted the limited gains in support of programs to assist children's development in that earlier period, as well as the social forces leading to their current evisceration (Keating, 1982; Papagiannis, Klees, & Bickel, 1982). This alone is cause for sober reflection; it is to be hoped that the product of that reflection is a more extensive and substantive theory and practice in the future.

REFERENCES

Benbow, C. P. & Stanley, J. C. Sex differences in mathematical ability: Fact or artifact? *Science,* 1980, *210,* 1262–1264.

Berger, P. L. & Luckmann, T. *The social construction of reality.* Garden City, N.Y.: Doubleday, 1966.

Binet, A. *Les isées modernes sur les enfants.* Paris: Flammarion, 1909. (1973 edition; cited in Gould, 1981.)

Block, J. H. & Block, J. The role of ego-control and ego-resiliency in the organization of behavior. In W. A. Collins (Ed.), *Minnesota symposia on child psychology* (Vol. 13). Hillsdale, N.J.: Lawrence Erlbaum Associates, 1979.

Blum, J. M. *Pseudoscience and mental ability.* New York: Monthly Review Press, 1978.

Bobbitt, B. L. *An information processing analysis of matrix problem solving.* Unpublished doctoral dissertation, University of Minnesota, 1979.

Bowles, S. & Gintis, H. *Schooling in capitalist America.* New York: Basic Books, 1976.

Brainerd, C. J. *Piaget's theory of intelligence.* Englewood Cliffs, N.J.: Prentice-Hall, 1978.

Bramel, D. & Friend, R. Hawthorne, the myth of the docile worker, and class bias in psychology. *American Psychologist,* 1981, *36,* 867–878.

Braverman, H. *Labor and monopoly capital: The degradation of labor in the 20th Century.* New York: Monthly Review Press, 1974.

Broca, P. Sur le volume et la forme du cerveau suivant les individus et suivant les races. *Bulletin Société d'Anthropologie Paris,* 1861, *2,* 139–207, 301–321, 441–446. (Cited in Gould, 1981.)

Brown, A. L. & French, L. A. The zone of potential development: Implications for intelligence testing in the year 2000. *Intelligence,* 1979, *3,* 255–273.

Campbell, D. T. & Fiske, D. W. Convergent and discriminant validation by the multitrait-multi-method matrix. *Psychological Bulletin,* 1959, *56,* 81–105.

Campbell, D. T. & Stanley, J. C. Experimental and quasi-experimental designs for research. In N. L. Gage (Ed.), *Handbook of research on teaching.* Chicago: Rand McNally, 1963.

Carroll, J. B. Psychometric tests as cognitive tasks: A new "structure of intellect." In L. B. Resnick (Ed.), *The nature of intelligence.* Hillsdale, N.J.: Lawrence Erlbaum Associates, 1976.

Carroll, J. B. Ability and task difficulty in cognitive psychology. *Educational Researcher,* 1981, *10,* 11–21.

Carroll, J. B. & Horn, J. L. On the scientific basis of ability testing. *American Psychologist* 1981, *36,* 1012–1020.

Carroll, J. B. & Maxwell, S. E. Individual differences in cognitive abilities. *Annual Review of Psychology,* 1979, *30,* 603–640.

Cavanaugh, J. C. & Perlmutter, M. Metamemory: A critical examination. *Child Development,* 1982, *53,* 11–28.

Chi, M. T. H. Age differences in the speed of processing: A critique. *Developmental Psychology,* 1977, *13,* 543–544.

Chi, M. T. H. Knowledge structures and memory development. In R. S. Siegler (Ed.), *Children's thinking: What develops?* Hillsdale, N.J.: Lawrence Erlbaum Associates, 1978.

Chiang, A. & Atkinson, R. C. Individual differences and interrelationships among a select set of cognitive skills. *Memory and Cognition,* 1976, *4,* 661–672.

Copeland, A. P. Children's talking to themselves: Its developmental significance, function, and therapeutic promise. In P. C. Kendall (Ed.), *Advances in cognitive-behavioral research and theory* (Vol. 2). New York: Academic Press, in press.

Cordes, C. Children seek voice on Capitol Hill. *APA Monitor,* 1982, *13,* 16–17.

Cronbach, L. J. The two disciplines of scientific psychology. *American Psychologist,* 1957, *12,* 671–684.

Ennis, R. H. Children's ability to handle Piaget's propositional logic: A conceptual critique. *Review of Educational Research,* 1975, *45,* 1–41.

Farnham-Diggory, S. & Nelson, B. Cognitive analyses of basic school tasks. In F. Morrison, C. Lord, & D. Keating (Eds.), *Applied developmental psychology* (Vol. 1). New York: Academic Press, in press.

Flavell, J. H. Structures, stages, and sequences in cognitive development. In W. A. Collins (Ed.), *Minnesota symposia on child psychology* (Vol. 15). Hillsdale, N.J.: Lawrence Erlbaum Associates, 1982. (a)

Flavell, J. H. On cognitive development. *Child Development,* 1982, *53,* 1–10. (b)

Ford, M. E. & Keating, D. P. Developmental and individual differences in long-term memory retrieval: Process and organization. *Child Development,* 1981, *52,* 234–241.

Galton, F. *Hereditary genius.* New York: Appleton, 1884.

Goddard, H. H. The Binet tets in relation to immigration. *Journal of Psycho-Asthenics,* 1913, *18,* 105–107.

Gould, S. J. *The mismeasure of man.* New York: Norton, 1981.

Gruber, H. E. & Voneche, J. J. (Eds.). *The essential Piaget.* New York: Basic Books, 1980.

Hogaboam, T. W. & Pellegrino, J. W. Hunting for individual differences in cognitive processes: Verbal ability and semantic processing of pictures and words. *Memory and Cognition,* 1978, *6,* 189–193.

Humphreys, L. G. Methinks they do protest too much. *Intelligence,* 1980, *4,* 179–183.

Hunt, E. B. Mechanics of verbal ability. *Psychological Review,* 1978, *85,* 109–130.

Jencks, C., Bartlett, S., Corcoran, M., Crouse, J., Eaglesfield, D., Jackson, G., McClelland, K., Mueser, P., Olneck, M., Schwartz, J., Ward, S., & Williams, J. *Who gets ahead? The determinants of economic success in America.* New York: Basic Books, 1979.

Jensen, A. R. *Bias in mental testing.* New York: Free Press, 1980.

Kamin, L. J. *The science and politics of IQ.* HIllsdale, N.J.: Lawrence Erlbaum Associates, 1974.

Karier, C. Testing for order and control in the corporate liberal state. In N. Block & G. Dworkin (Eds.), *The IQ controversy.* New York: Pantheon, 1976.

Keating, D. P. Precocious cognitive development at the level of formal operations. *Child Development,* 1975, *46,* 476–480.

Keating, D. P. (Ed.). *Intellectual talent: Research and development.* Baltimore: Johns Hopkins University Press, 1976.

Keating, D. P. Toward a multivariate life span theory of intelligence. In D. Kuhn (Ed.), *Intellectual development beyond childhood.* San Francisco: Jossey-Bass, 1979. (a)

Keating, D. P. Piaget on knowing how versus knowing that. (Review of *Success and understanding* by Jean Piaget.) *Contemporary Psychology,* 1979, *24,* 688–689. (b)

Keating, D. P. Four faces of creativity: The continuing plight of the intellectually underserved. *Gifted Child Quarterly,* 1980, *24,* 56–61. (a)

Keating, D. P. Thinking processes in adolescence. In J. Adelson (Ed.), *Handbook of adolescent psychology.* New York: Wiley, 1980. (b)

Keating, D. P. Intelligence: Born again or dying out? (Review of *Human intelligence,* R. J. Sternberg & D. K. Detterman, Eds.), *Contemporary Psychology,* 1980, *25,* 608–609. (c)

Keating, D. P. Sternberg's sketchy theory: Defining details desired. *Behavioral and Brain Sciences*, 1980, *3*, 595–596. (d)

Keating, D. P. *On the necessity of a political economy of human development*. Comments on a symposium, "Report of the SRCD Congressional Science Fellows." Southeastern Conference on Human Development, Baltimore, April 1982.

Keating, D. P. & Bobbitt, B. L. Individual and developmental differences in cognitive-processing components of mental ability. *Child Development*, 1978, *49*, 155–167.

Keating, D. P. & Caramazza, A. Effects of age and ability on syllogistic reasoning in early adolescence. *Developmental Psychology*, 1975, *11*, 837–842.

Keating, D. P., Keniston, A. H., Manis, F. R., & Bobbitt, B. L. Development of the search-processing parameter. *Child Development*, 1980, *51*, 39–44.

Keating, D. P., List, J. A., & Merriman, W. E. Cognitive processing and cognitive ability: A multivariate validity investigation. 1983. Paper presented at the Biennial Meeting of the Society for Research in Child Development, Detroit, Michigan.

Keating, D. P. & Schaefer, R. A. Ability and sex differences in the acquisition of formal operations. *Developmental Psychology*, 1975, *11*, 531–532.

Kendall, P. W. & Hollon, S. D. Assessing self-referent speech: Methods in the measurement of self-statements. In P. C. Kendall & S. D. Hollon (Eds.), *Cognitive-behavioral interventions: Assessment methods*. New York: Academic Press, 1980.

Klahr, D. Goal formation, planning, and learning by pre-school problem solvers or: "My socks are in the dryer." In R. S. Siegler (Ed.), *Children's thinking: What develops?* Hillsdale, N.J.: Lawrence Erlbaum Associates, 1978.

Kuhn, D. The significance of Piaget's formal operations stage in education. *Journal of Education*, 1979, *161*, 34–50.

Manis, F. R. *Word knowledge and the development of word identification skills in normal and disabled readers*. Unpublished doctoral dissertation, University of Minnesota, 1981.

Manis, F. R., Keating, D. P., & Morrison, F. J. Developmental differences in the allocation of processing capacity. *Journal of Experimental Child Psychology*, 1980, *29*, 156–169.

Morrison, F. J., Lord, C. A., & Keating, D. P. (Eds.). *Applied developmental psychology* (Vol. 1). New York: Academic Press, in press.

Neisser, U. *Cognitive psychology*. New York: Meredith, 1967.

Newell, A. You can't play 20 questions with nature and win: Projective comments on papers on this symposium. In W. G. Chase (Ed.), *Visual information processing*. New York: Academic Press, 1973.

Osherson, D. N. *Logical abilities in children*. Vol. 3: *Reasoning in adolescence: Deductive inference*. Hillsdale, N.J.: Lawrence Erlbaum Associates, 1975.

Papagiannis, G. J., Klees, S. J., Bickel, R. N. Toward a political economy of educational innovation. *Review of Educational Research*, 1982, *52*, 245–290.

Pellegrino, J. W. & Glaser, R. Cognitive components and correlates in the analysis of individual differences. *Intelligence*, 1979, *3*, 187–214.

Pellegrino, J. W. & Lyon, D. R. The components of a componential analysis. *Intelligence*, 1979, *3*, 169–186.

Piaget, J. *The psychology of intelligence*. London: Routledge & Kegan Paul, 1950.

Piaget, J. *Le structuralisme*. Paris: Presses Universitaires de France, 1968.

Piaget, J. *Genetic epistemology*. New York: Columbia University Press, 1970.

Posner, M. I. & Boies, S. J. Components of attention. *Psychological Review*, 1971, *78*, 391–408.

Posner, M. I., Boies, S. J., Eichelman, W. H., & Taylor, R. L. Retention of visual and name codes of single letters. *Journal of Experimental Psychology Monograph*, 1969, *79*, 1–16.

Posner, M. I. & Klein, R. M. On the functions of consciousness. In S. Kornblum (Ed.), *Attention and performance*. (Vol. 4). New York: Academic Press, 1972.

Poulantzas, N. *State, power, socialism*. London: New Left Books, 1978.

Raven, J. C. *Guide to the standard progressive matrices.* London: Lewis, 1960.

Scarr, S. Testing *for* children. *American Psychologist,* 1981, *36,* 1159–1166.

Schank, R. C. How much intelligence is there in artificial intelligence? *Intelligence,* 1980, *4,* 1–14.

Sharp, D., Cole, M., & Lave, C. Education and cognitive development: The evidence from experimental research. *Monographs of the Society for Research in Child Development,* 1979, *44* (Serial No. 178).

Siegler, R. S. The origins of scientific reasoning. In R. S. Siegler (Ed.), *Children's thinking: What develops?* Hillsdale, N.J.: Lawrence Erlbaum Associates, 1978.

Siegler, R. S. Developmental sequences within and between concepts. *Monographs of the Society for Research in Child Development,* 1981, *46* (Serial No. 189).

Siegler, R. S. & Richards, D. D. Development of time, speed, and distance concepts. *Developmental Psychology,* 1979, *15,* 288–298.

Sigel, I. E. Child development research in learning and cognition in the 1980s: Continuities and discontinuities from the 1970s. *Merrill-Palmer Quarterly,* 1981, *27,* 347–371.

Sigel, I. E. Relationships between parents' distancing strategies and children's cognitive performance. In L. Laosa & I. E. Sigel (Eds.), *Families as learning environments for children.* New York: Plenum, in press.

Stanley, J. C. Reliability. In R. Thorndike (Ed.), *Educational Measurement* (2nd ed.). Washington, D.C.: American Council on Education, 1971.

Stanley, J. C., Keating, D. P., & Fox, L. H. (Eds.). *Mathematical talent: Discovery, description, and development.* Baltimore: Johns Hopkins University Press, 1974.

Sternberg, R. J. *Intelligence, information processing, and analogical reasoning: The componential analysis of human abilities.* Hillsdale, N.J.: Lawrence Erlbaum Associates, 1977.

Sternberg, R. J. Stalking the IQ quark. *Psychology Today,* 1979, *13,* 42–54.

Sternberg, R. J. Sketch of a componential subtheory of human intelligence. *Behavioral and Brain Sciences,* 1980, *3,* 573–584. (a)

Sternberg, R. J. Componentman as vice-president: A reply to Pellegrino & Lyon's analysis of "The components of a componential analysis." *Intelligence,* 1980, *4,* 83–95. (b)

Sternberg, R. J. Testing and cognitive psychology. *American Psychologist,* 1981, *36,* 1181–1189. (a)

Sternberg, R. J. The evolution of theories of intelligence. *Intelligence,* 1981, *5,* 209–230. (b)

Sternberg, R. J. Intelligence and nonentrenchment. *Journal of Educational Psychology,* 1981, *73,* 1–16. (c)

Sternberg, S. The discovery of stages: Extension of Donders' method. *Acta Psychologica,* 1969, *30,* 276–315.

Terman, L. M. *The Stanford revision and extension of the Binet-Simon scale for measuring intelligence.* Baltimore: Warwick & York, 1917.

Terman, L. M. *The intelligence of school children.* Boston: Houghton Mifflin, 1919.

Thurstone, L. L. *Multiple factor analysis.* Chicago: University of Chicago Press, 1947.

Trabasso, T. Representation, memory, and reasoning: How do we make transitive inferences? In A. D. Pick (Ed.), *Minnesota symposia on child psychology* (Vol. 9). Minneapolis: University of Minnesota Press, 1975.

Vygotsky, L. S. *Thought and language.* Cambridge, Mass.: MIT Press, 1962.

Vygotsky, L. S. *Mind and society.* Cambridge, Mass.: Harvard University Press, 1978.

Wertsch, J. V. *The concept of activity in Soviet psychology.* Armonk, N.Y.: M. E. Sharpe, 1981.

2 The Topography of Ability and Learning Correlations

Richard E. Snow
Patrick C. Kyllonen[1]
Brachia Marshalek
Stanford University

The understanding of human mental abilities, their organization, and their relation to learning and problem-solving is a central goal for cognitive psychology today. But if new research toward this goal is to incorporate and build upon existing evidence, it needs convenient and theoretically suggestive ways to represent this evidence as a starting point. In particular, the accumulated correlational evidence on individual differences in cognitive aptitude for learning needs to be organized into a theoretical map that will be useful in guiding experimental analyses aimed at identifying underlying process and content structures that might account for such individual differences (Snow, 1980a). Such a map could help investigators choose appropriate reference ability constructs for use in the external validation of process measures derived from laboratory tasks (Sternberg, 1977). The map might also suggest the most direct ways to proceed in attempting to extend process models built for particular tasks across families of related cognitive and learning tasks. And, of course, the regular, replicated features of correlational structure for such tasks are among the important facts that new theories of intelligence must explain.

The purpose of the present chapter is to propose such a map, to demonstrate its fit with existing correlational evidence, and to study its interpretive implications. Its uses in guiding new research are suggested.

---

[1]Now at Air Force Human Resources Laboratory, Brooks Air Force Base, San Antonio, Texas.

BACKGROUND

Throughout this century, the correlational study of intelligence was greatly aided by the development of the mathematical methods now referred to, generically, as factor analysis. These methods provided several competing models of ability organization, because the methods and the theorists who developed and used them differed in key ways. Although learning measures were brought explicitly into the factor-analytic tradition only rarely, it was implicitly assumed all along that intelligence was learning ability; to reach an agreed-upon understanding of the organization of intellectual ability differences was, at least in part, to understand learning differences.

Spearman's (1904, 1923, 1927) notion of a general factor grew out of correlations among educational achievement tests, when the Galton-McKeen Cattell approach to elementary process measurement failed. His theory of a general mental ability factor underlying all cognitive and learning performances, and special factors unique to each task, was then transformed into a hierarchical ability organization with several tiers of major and minor group factors between the general and specific levels (see Vernon, 1950, 1969). The hierarchical model was the product of one style of factor-analytic method. R. B. Cattell (1963, 1971; see also Horn, 1976), followed with oblique rotational methods to produce the variation on the hierarchical model known as the theory of fluid and crystallized intelligence. The theory was then extended to account for the evident role of abilities in learning; simply put, it was assumed that fluid intelligence was invested in learning, particularly complex school learning, to produce crystallized intelligence and achievement (for further discussion see Snow, 1982). Various more localized learning aids and proficiencies were also provided thereby.

The principal competing model arose from Thurstone's (1938) method of rotation to simple structure, to identify parallel primary abilities. Thurstone and his coworkers contended that complex cognitive and learning performances were the result of various combinations of these primary factors. Allison (1960), Stake (1961), and some others, then applied the Thurstonian model to look for primary ability-learning correlations. And Guilford (1967), in extending the list of primary abilities to over 120, also attempted to connect some of them theoretically to one or another kind of learning.

But the way one thinks about the organization of abilities and their role in learning must be at least partly determined by the techniques used to analyze the interrelationships. It is comforting when different methods yield comparable interpretations and challenging when they do not. Most comparative analyses of ability organization and most attempts to understand ability-learning relations, however, have been conducted *within* the factor-analytic tradition. Other, rather different methods of analyzing the structure of interrelations among measures, such as multidimensional scaling and various hierarchical clustering techniques, have been only rarely applied. Thus it seems important to study these other methods in this connection; their results may corroborate one or another conception of ability and learning organization derived from factor analysis, or they may suggest new and different structural hypotheses of use in guiding process-analytic research. In particular, multidimensional scaling maintains attention on the continuous space represented by correlation matrices, in addition to its partition into distinct areas or units. Even though factor methods also operate on continuous dimensions, typical usage focuses primarily on the distinct factor units. Multidimensional scaling, then, may suggest interpretations of abilities that go beyond the traditional view that factors are the basic conceptual units for theory building.

Factors have been interpreted theoretically as identifying basic traits, but they can also be interpreted as classification principles—convenient labels for regions in a more continuous space. And modern versions of the sampling theory of Thomson (1919, 1939; see Humphreys, 1971, 1979) or the transfer theory of Ferguson (1954, 1956; see Snow, 1982) also provide alternative interpretations of ability-learning relations that seem compatible both with a continuous space analysis of correlations and with information-processing theories of particular tasks.

Only Guttman (1954, 1965, 1970) has studied this possibility programmatically. He applied one form of nonmetric multidimensional scaling to develop his radex model as an alternative to Thurstone's factor model. But his pioneering efforts have not been pursued systematically. The present chapter follows Guttman's lead by applying nonmetric scaling to reanalyses of ability and learning matrices that had originally been designed and analyzed along Thurstonian lines. Because the hierarchical view of ability organization has come to be regarded as the most parsimonious and popular factor model today (Cronbach & Snow, 1977; Snow, 1978), and because the hierarchical and radex models have been shown to be conformable (Marshalek, 1977; Marshalek, Lohman, & Snow, 1982), it would be helpful if Thurstone-style analyses of ability and learning could be subsumed under those models. Also, because the Cattell-Horn theory seems closest to an integrated view of ability and learning differences(Snow, 1982), special interest attaches in these reanalyses to the fluid-crystallized distinction. The ultimate aim is a framework for what we here call ''response-sampling'' theories of ability and learning, based on a new version of Guttman's radex model.

Since the work reported here was planned and carried out, Sternberg (1981a) has characterized the hierarchical and primary ability models as Stage IIa and Stage IIb theories in the evolution of correlational theories of intelligence. In Sternberg's view, Guttman's radex model is a Stage III theory that merges the two previous theories and represents a kind of end point to correlational theory evolution. We see the hierarchical and radex models as alternative representations of the same topographic structure that also, we agree, incorporates the

Thurstone view. We argue that this structure is not an end point for correlational theories but rather the best starting point for theories of intelligence that aim to integrate facts arising from experimentally based process analyses with the correlational evidence. This chapter elaborates that view.

THE STUDY OF CORRELATIONAL STRUCTURE

The methods of factor analysis impose, in one way or another, a metric and usually linear structure on correlation matrices that reduces the number of dimensions needed to account for the original correlations and tests certain kinds of hypotheses about the nature of these dimensions. Most factor-analytic methods are well known and described in the vast literature that was accumulated over this century; we need not review that literature here. Useful introductions and reviews have been provided recently by Korth (1975a, 1975b) and Mulaik (1975); the latter includes some discussion of Guttman's radex notions in relation to factor analysis of learning matrices, a point to which we return later in this chapter.

One major alternative to factor analysis is multidimensional scaling, as long argued by Guttman (1954, 1965). Other alternatives are provided by various hierarchical clustering schemes, of which the most useful appears to be the additive tree method (Sattath & Tversky, 1977). These techniques differ from factor analysis in important ways. Except for Guttman's work, these methods were mainly designed for representing psychological similarity or distance among stimulus objects, not particularly for the analysis of test intercorrelations. Similarity data are usually obtained by asking people to judge directly the similarity or dissimilarity of two stimuli (e.g., words, forms, colors), though indirect similarity measures are sometimes obtained by examining the degree to which two stimuli are confused. The scaling techniques yield spatial or planar representations and the clustering techniques yield various hierarchical cluster or tree representations of the stimulus objects, each designed to reveal aspects of the underlying structure of the similarity data. They are based on different underlying models of similarity and hence lead to different interpretations. The spatial model, which locates objects in a continuous euclidean space, emphasizes the continuous dimensions of similarity, whereas the tree model, which subsumes objects within discrete clusters, emphasizes the unique and common features of objects and groups of objects. For some kinds of stimulus objects, one model may be more appropriate than the other (Pruzansky, Tversky, & Carroll, in press). In other cases, the two models may complement one another and reveal different aspects of the data structure. Each model can be expected to complement the representation provided by the factor model.

A detailed methodological comparison of the spatial, tree, and factor models, using some of the same data sets discussed in the present chapter, is provided by Kyllonen, Marshalek, and Snow (1982). Discussion here centers on the multidimensional scaling results because these seem closest to providing an integrated framework for further research.

Multidimensional Scaling of Task Intercorrelations

The aim of any multidimensional scaling is to find a geometric configuration of points in n–dimensional space in which the interpoint distances best correspond to the similarities of the objects scaled. Nonmetric multidimensional scaling methods were developed independently by Shepard (1962) and Kruskal (1964a, 1964b) and by Guttman (1965). It was Guttman who demonstrated the value of the approach to the study of ability organization by reanalyzing parts of the mental test intercorrelation matrices reported by Thurstone (1938) and Thurstone and Thurstone (1941).

Nonmetric multidimensional scaling uses only rank order information from the original correlation matrix. Thus, the degree to which the final solution is satisfactory can be determined by assuming not a linear but a monotone relationship between the original correlations and recovered distances in the configuration. "Stress" is the term used to quantify violations of the monotonicity assumption in the final configuration, and hence is an inverse measure of goodness-of-fit. Percentage of variance accounted for is normally not used to determine degree of fit, as in factor analysis, because a linear relationship between correlations and recovered distances is not assumed. Although the nonmetric scaling methods discard information about the metric properties of the relations between tasks, it can be demonstrated that ordinal information is sufficient to produce a tightly constrained solution.

The advantages of the nonmetric over the metric approach to studying similarity relations were noted by Guttman (1968) and Shepard (1962). First, fewer restrictions in the nonmetric approach permit a satisfactory solution in a smaller dimensional space. Usually, only two or three dimensions are used. Second, specialized metric algorithms may be difficult to defend for some problems because they may involve unwarranted assumptions. Finally, greater generalizability and easier replication are generally permitted by the nonmetric approach because nonmetric scaling is unaffected by any monotone transformation of the data (e.g., scaling solutions for the correlation matrix and for the squared correlation matrix would be identical). For a general review of the assumptions, properties, and techniques of nonmetric multidimensional scaling, see Shepard (1962), Kruskal (1964a, 1964b), Shepard, Romney, and Nerlove (1972), and Kruskal and Wish (1978).

Interpretation of Task Similarity

In the present case, the objects we seek to represent are cognitive performance tasks and the measures of similarity are the correlations among scored performances on the tasks. A high correlation is taken to suggest close psychological similarity between two tasks; a low correlation requires careful thinking because such correlations are indirect and incomplete measures of intertask similarity. Their interpretation for theoretical purposes has often been left implicit and unclear. Several obvious and not so obvious points need to be kept in mind at once. These are discussed briefly in the following sections.

Scoring System Similarity.   Task intercorrelations depend on the scored task performances, so the interpretation of similarity depends on the scoring systems applied. Scores based on item response latencies may reflect quite a different sort of task similarity than scores based on the correctness of item or trial performance, for example, and either sort of similarity may be quite different from subjective ratings of item, trial, or task similarity. Use of a common scoring system across all tasks to be compared reduces the problem of interpretation, but this is often impossible. Various paradigmatic cognitive tasks to be intercorrelated may require different operationalization, theoretically, as for example in Rose's (1980) work on information-processing abilities. The correlation of ability and learning task performance also usually involves correlation across different scoring systems.

Summary Score Similarity.   It is usually the case also that performance scores must be summed or averaged across multiple observations. Because ability has usually been defined as a person's successful dominance over task requirements or demands, the number of items correct or the number of trials to successful completion has usually been the summary score selected. But it is important to note that any task or performance characteristics that lead to similar summary scores for two tasks will contribute to this sense of task similarity. Two tasks that have similar time limit conditions, or that afford similar attack strategies, may be quite dissimilar in item content. Also, similar total scores may be composed of quite dissimilar item or trial response patterns. Summary scores can contain variance due to learning, adaptation, and strategy shifting within the task that would not be observable in performance on any one item or trial. Thus, it is the summary or total performance score selected, under whatever task conditions are set, that determines the aspect of similarity displayed by task intercorrelations. The task comparison is limited to this aspect of similarity. An interpretation at the level of item performance may often be insufficient to account for performance task similarity at the level of summary scores.

Variant and Invariant Similarity.   In typical usage and as used here, task intercorrelations depend on comparisons between individuals. They display the degree to which two tasks rank order some sample of persons similarly. Thus, those cognitive functions required for task performance that do not lead to differences in performance between individuals (e.g., aspects of performance that require the same amount of time for all individuals, or that all individuals execute successfully or unsuccessfully) do not influence task intercorrelations. These can be called *invariant* aspects as opposed to the *variant* aspects of performance—the cognitive functions that *do* lead to individual differences in task performance. The similarity displayed in task intercorrelations can be interpreted only in terms of variant similarity. Thus, a theory of intelligence based only on task intercorrelations must be incomplete. A comprehensive theory of intelligence must account for both the invariants and the variants in performance. But such a theory *must* at least account for the variants and the correlations between them; it is this aspect of theory construction that correlational analysis of task similarity seeks to inform. It should be noted also, for it is often forgotten, that what is found to be variant or invariant in cognitive tasks depends on the sample of tasks and the sample of persons studied. Variant aspects of performance can become invariant in some samples, and vice versa.

Sign and Sample Similarity.   The sampling view just noted begs the distinction between sign and sample interpretations of cognitive performance similarity. As suggested above, summary test scores, and factors based on them, have often been thought of as signs indicating the presence of underlying or latent traits. But nothing in the structure of cognitive tasks, or the administration or scoring systems used, or in the analysis of correlations between the resulting scores, inherently requires that task similarity be interpreted as signs of latent traits. An alternative interpretation of test scores as samples of cognitive processes and contents, and of correlations as indicating the similarity or overlap of such samples, is equally justifiable.

The factor-sign-trait line of reasoning may not be particularly troublesome if "trait" is read as "variable," or if a definition of "trait" such as Cronbach's (1970) is maintained:

> A *trait* is best described as the probability that one will react in a defined way in response to a defined class of situations. . . . The trait postulate is threefold:
> • Behavior is consistent; a person tends to show the same habitual reaction over a range of similar situations.
> • People vary in the degree or frequency of any type of behavior.
> • Personalities have some stability [p. 560].

Unfortunately, as applied in the study of intelligence, factor-sign-trait interpretation too often imply to the public's mind, and to some investigators, the discovery of singular fundamental entities, even if descriptions such as "functional unities" are used. The term "trait" was borrowed by early theorists from biology, where it still often refers to hereditary, permanent, and physically based characteristics. It is a treacherous term, even when the original definition is relaxed and redirected for the purposes of psychological theory, because it is inevitably associated in a triumvirate with the terms "factor" and "entity."

Factor analyses can suggest explanatory constructs to account for observed task similarity, as can multidimensional scaling, or additive tree analysis or other clustering methods. Some such constructs *may* reflect traits, as originally defined; that is a question for further research. But none of these methods necessarily yields trait structures. There are other interpretations, such as the response sampling view, to be considered and, especially in the case of the multidimensional scaling methods, there are other kinds of correlational structure to be discovered.

Response Sampling and Similarity.   It is useful here to consider in more detail the response sampling view of cognitive performance similarity between tasks, because it seems more compatible with the information-processing theories of intelligence now emanating from experimental analyses of cognitive tasks and because it has always been a viable, if neglected, alternative. An individual's cognitive system can be considered a very large bank of cognitive processing skills and chunks of organized knowledge from which samples are drawn according to the demands of particular cognitive tasks. As Humphreys (1971) phrased this view,

> Intelligence is defined as the entire repertoire of acquired skills, knowledge, learning sets, and generalization tendencies considered intellectual in nature that are available at any one period of time. An intelligence test contains items that sample the totality of such acquisitions. Intelligence so defined is not an entity such as Spearman's 'mental energy.' Instead the definition suggests the Thomson 'multiple-bonds' approach . . . . [with] one important difference. . . . It is not essential that the person whose intelligence is measured has acquired a specific response to each stimulus or set of stimuli presented. Learning sets and generalization tendencies were introduced in the definition to preclude critical interpretations of this type [p. 32].

The bits and pieces of response residing in this bank or repertoire can be thought of as S–R bonds, information-processing components, schemata, plans, learning sets, generalization tendencies, knowledge structures in a semantic network, productions in a production system, or all of these. Some theoretically neutral term could be adopted to simplify reference to the contents of the bank, but provisionally we use the term "response components," or simply "components," even though this usage may stretch the definition Sternberg (1977) intends; it is the case that the same term has been used by Guttman (1954) to describe differences in complexity among tests.

Here, such components are assumed to have one or another of the properties of these other constructs; a component is applied when appropriate stimulus conditions for its application exist, and its application results either in an observable response or in a change in the cognitive system in which it resides. Successful performance of any cognitive task requires the application of some subset of these components, and the application needs to be organized in some appropriate way. Such an organization can be called an assembly of components. Tasks differ in the components and assemblies they call forth. Individuals differ in how well the components and assemblies they can produce match the demands of the task at hand. By performing successfully, individuals demonstrate that the objective task requirements are well matched by the component assemblies they can produce. Individuals performing poorly demonstrate a poorer match, or some degree of mismatch, between the demands of the task and the assemblies of components they can assemble.

Individual differences can be both intra- and inter-individual, in this view. Response sampling theory implies that intelligence is defined idiosyncratically, to some degree; the contents of the bank will differ across time within and between persons, as will the component assemblies called forth. Both the intra- and the inter-individual differences can arise from several sources. Individuals can differ in the speed or efficiency with which a particular sampled response component is executed, in the sequence in which an assembly of components is executed, in the types of components included in the assembly, or in the organization and reorganization, over time, items, or trials, of the assembly as a whole. These different sources have been referred to as parameter, sequence, route, and summation or strategy differences, respectively (see Snow, 1978, 1981). Sternberg (1977) has advanced a similar set of distinctions with other terminology.

Now consider two tasks judged similar because the performance ordering of individuals on each produces high correlation between them. They can be said to require similar samples of response components or component assemblies, or similar changes in such assemblies over time. In contrast, two tasks judged dissimilar because they do not correlate can be said to require quite different samples of response components or assemblies, or changes over time. This view loosens considerably the traditional factor-sign-trait interpretation of task intercorrelation. When two tests are found to correlate highly and consistently, the traditional interpretation tends to close off further analytic research on internal validation; the investigator interprets the two tests as "tapping the same latent trait" or "measuring the same thing" and pursues further demonstrations of construct validity in the relations of the tests, or a factor combining them, to external criteria. In the response sampling view, high correlation suggests an overlap of the response samples required by the two tests and the next step is to identify the variant response components and component assemblies that are common to the two.

From this point, an investigator might adopt the componential analysis approach developed by Sternberg (1977, 1979, 1981a, 1981b) or the related experimental approaches of Pellegrino and Glaser (1980) or Frederiksen (1980), for example. Such analyses seek to identify the variant and invariant response components involved in performance on a particular task and to build internally valid componential models of such tasks. Attempts are then made to validate identified components externally by correlating their measures with external tasks. The project of which the present chapter is a part is also based on such research.

But we differ in emphasis. Because our research is ultimately aimed at a theory of aptitude and achievement relationships in worldly human performance, we place heavier emphasis than have other researchers on task similarity observed in the structure of correlations across large ranges of tasks, many of which have been shown to have practical correlates. We aim to map such patterns to focus analytic research more directly on task similarity in *total scores,* interpreted as composed of *similar response samples* of *variant* components and *assemblies* of such components, to account for individual differences. The *invariant* components of *item* performance, which have been the focus of much prior research, are regarded as secondary in importance; it is the total score correlations that are of worldly significance (see Snow 1980a).

Types of Structure

Task similarity, as restrictively defined above, can be studied in large collections of tasks by analyzing the matrix of intertask correlations using any of a number of methods, as noted. The aim is to discover orderly and interpretable correlational structures as an aid to understanding human ability organization. It must be kept in mind that the sorts of structures discovered in this way are built on between-task, across-person relationships; they are not at this stage interpreted as representing or modeling within-person cognitive structures, though at a later stage they can be translated into implications about within-person structures.

We concentrate here on a comparison of the types of correlational structure so far obtained from factor analysis and nonmetric multidimensional scaling of mental test intercorrelations. It is argued that the structure obtained from nonmetric scaling encompasses that obtained from factor analysis; that the hierarchical factor model and the radex model derived therefrom are directly parallel in their implications; and that the most important implication for further theory and research concerns a continuum of apparent processing complexity in a revised radex model of ability organization. For a detailed discussion of the justification for this view, see Marshalek (1977) and Marshalek, Lohman, and Snow (in press). Only some of the points of that discussion are elaborated here.

Simplex, Circumplex, and Radex. Guttman's (1954, 1965, 1970) radex model originated in his work with factor analysis, but gained its main support from his nonmetric scaling analyses of portions of the Thurstone data. In any radex, or "radial expansion of complexity," two orderings of tasks appear simultaneously; one ordering suggests a simplex structure, the other suggests a circumplex structure. Because the task intercorrelations are subject to measurement and sampling errors, the orderings actually observed are rough approximations and should technically be referred to as quasi-simplex and quasi-circumplex structures. We here follow the common practice of using the simpler terminology and thus of not distinguishing between the formal mathematic models of such structures and the approximate patterns in empirical data.

Guttman (1954) observed that ability tests within a test content area tended to form a straight line array when scaled according to their intercorrelations:

> Within all tests of the same kind, say of numerical ability, differences will be in degree. We shall see that addition, subtraction, multiplication, and division differ among themselves largely in the degree of their complexity. Such a set of variables will be called a *simplex*. It possesses a simple order of complexity. The tests can be arranged in a simple rank order from least complex to most complex [p. 260].

He also noted (Guttman, 1954) that tests of comparable complexity that are sampled from different content areas tended to form a circular array when scaled:

> Correspondingly, all tests of the same degree of complexity will differ among themselves only in the kind of ability they define. We shall postulate a law of order here too, but one which is not from "least" to "most" in any sense. It is an order which has no beginning and no end, namely, a circular order. A set of variables obeying such a law will be called a *circumplex,* to designate a circular order of complexity [p. 260].

The covariation of the simplex and circumplex structures forms a radex—a disc in two-dimensional space or a sphere in three dimensions, with triangular or conic areas containing verbal, numerical, and figural-spatial test contents, for example.

In Guttman's (1954) earliest formulation of the radex model, complexity was interpreted as a continuum in which tests differed in the number of performance components they required; more complex tests required the same components as simpler tests, plus additional components. Thus, complexity was a direct function of the number of performance components the test sampled. Guttman predicted that complex tests would fall on the periphery of the radex because complexity could result from many different combinations of various components; he assumed, in other words, that complex tests would have fewer components in common with each other than would simple tests, and thus would show lower intercorrelations than would simpler tests. After his scaling reanalysis of some of Thurstone's data, however, he remarked (Guttman, 1965):

> When first discussing the radex for intelligence tests some dozen years ago, I hypothesized it would express a radial expansion of complexity; simplicity would be in the center and expand outwardly with complexity. Complex tests in different areas would tend to be less correlated with each other because they go off in different directions of complexity. The present data show that quite the opposite may be true. . . . [p. 34].

Instead of a radial expansion of complexity, then, the radex seemed to represent a radial expansion of simplicity. The failure of his initial prediction apparently led Guttman to abandon the earlier ideas about a complexity continuum in favor of distinctions between analytic vs. achievement tests, or rule-inferring vs. rule-applying vs. achievement tests (see Schlesinger & Guttman, 1969, Guttman, 1970). The failure, however, actually supports another view of the complexity continuum, to which we will return later in this chapter.

Factors and Hierarchical Factor Models.   Factors and hierarchical organizations of factors appear to provide a type of correlational structure that differs from the sort of structure comprising the radex model. But factors are simply mathematical axes constructed and placed according to one or another set of rules to fit clusters of tests that intercorrelate highly. Factors are dimensions, not just discrete test clusters, but researchers usually interpret them as representing clusters, especially at the primary factor level, where Thurstone and Guilford chose to operate. In multidimensional scaling, where the points representing highly intercorrelated tests would cluster closely together spatially, including such a factor axis would produce a factor point roughly in the middle of the points for the tests the factor loaded. (In a system of orthogonal factors, however, some factor points would fall somewhat outside the clusters of tests they loaded.) Thus factors at this level can be thought of as classification principles for the test points they encompass. Of course, they can also be interpreted as source traits governing the distance between test points, or as the assembly of common components sampled by the tests, as noted earlier.

Hierarchical factor structures are obtained by allowing primary factors to correlate (via oblique rotation, for example). Factoring these factors through however many tiers it takes to reach a single "general" factor provides higher order factors that can be converted through the application of other sets of rules (Schmid & Leiman, 1957; Wherry, 1959) into orthogonal hierarchical structures. Snow (1978) has discussed the advantages of such structures. At the top of such hierarchies is "general" ability or "G"—a broad factor that accounts for performance in a great variety of intellectual tasks. It would be preferable if such a factor were simply called "broad" or "central" to the matrix, but "general" has been common usage even though it promises too much. Tests that correlate highly with this factor, in a representative battery, are "complex" tests, requiring abstract problem-solving analysis and rule inferring. At the next or major group level are crystallized ability (G_c), representing verbal comprehension and mathematical and other knowledge tests, fluid ability (G_f), representing complex nonverbal and analytic reasoning tests, and visualization ability (G_v) representing various spatial tests. Each of these subdivides imperfectly into narrower, more specific factors at the next lower, minor group level, where most of Thurstone's and Guildford's primary factors would be classed. At the lowest level are test-specific factors that usually show low correlations with one another and with other measures in the universe of ability and achievement tests.

It is important to note that the term "hierarchy" has two meanings. It is used to identify a graded series, in essentially the same way that Guttman (1954) used the term "simplex." It is also used to refer to a series of subsumptions as in nested or hierarchical experimental designs (Winer, 1962). If one constructs a logical hierarchy for ability factors, one is likely to depict it as a strictly nested or subsumption hierarchy (See Vernon, 1950; Humphreys, 1962). But the ability factor hierarchies commonly reported in the literature are empirical hierarchies (or better, quasi hierarchies), not logical ones. In the hierarchical factor structure just described, for example, quantitative ability at a lower level is usually found to be empirically connected to both G_c and G_f ability at a higher level (see Snow, 1978; Vernon, 1965). Also, it is not clear that G_v subsumes all of the more specific spatial abilities that have been identified (Lohman, 1979b). Thus, the hierarchical factor model is a rough, loosely organized, empirical quasi hierarchy; though it includes subsumptions, it is not strictly a hierarchical subsumption structure, but it does suggest a graded series.

Tests can be located using two main features of such an empirical factor hierarchy: the vertical or complexity dimension, from general to specific; and the horizontal or content facet, which at middle levels of the hierarchy is dominated by the distinction between spatial, numerical, and verbal content. In this view, the complexity dimension can be defined as a graded series of ability tests along a continuum according to their correlation with G. More complex tests (e.g., Raven Matrices, Verbal Analogies) show high correlation with G, whereas apparently simpler tests (Memory Span, Visual Memory, Perceptual Speed) show only low or small correlation with G.

At lower levels of the hierarchy, other facets may also determine the clustering among tests. But whereas tests can be classified on many other facets, causing a simple hierarchical model to break down (Humphreys, 1962), the complexity continuum and the content facet are more important than others studied to date in predicting the correlations among tests.

The Radex and Hierarchical Factor Models in Parallel.   A radex and a hierarchy are not mathematically identical as logical structures. But the radex and hierarchical *factor* models are parallel, both mathematically and empirically; the radex model turns out to be a scaling representation of the hierarchical factor model and the latter is a hierarchical factor representation of the radex.

As argued elsewhere (Marshalek, 1977; Marshalek, Lohman, & Snow, in press), the geometry of circles and spheres applies to a radex. Thus, the farther any point is from the center, the greater is its average distance from all other points (i.e., the lower is its average correlation with all other tests and thus with G). The closer any point is to the center, the smaller is its average distance from all other points (i.e., the higher is its average correlation with all other tests and thus with G). In a perfect radex, G appears in the center. The same geometry applies to the hierarchical factor model. G is constructed to be an axis at the center of a positive manifold of test vectors. With G removed, various group factor axes can be constructed consecutively to account for residual projections lying in different directions from G (or other previously constructed axes) toward the periphery of the manifold. G is reconstructed as the center of the manifold by allowing group factor axes to correlate.

Empirically, it is the case that complex tests that load G highly scale near the center of the radex, whereas simple tests with low loadings on G scale near the periphery of the radex and show their principal loadings on minor group or fairly specific factors in the hierarchy. Intermediate tests, loading primarily on intermediate factors in the hierarchy, scale in the intermediate regions of the radex.

Thus, the vertical dimension that runs from bottom to top in the hierarchical model parallels the continuum that runs from periphery to center along the simplex arrays of the radex model. The horizontal aspect in the hierarchical factor model parallels the content facet in the radex model. The vertical or simplex continuum seems to represent increasing apparent processing complexity of mental tests.

A Demonstration.   It may be objected that a hierarchical factor model, when typically drawn for print as a pure subsumption hierarchy, carries two implications that do not seem to fit the radex representation. First, it depicts the test variables on the lowest level as though they were permutable or exchangeable as equal measures of their group factors or the general factor; the radex shows ordering information that seems to be lost in the hierarchy. Second, the horizontal spread or content distinction of the hierarchical factor model does not fold back on itself as does the content circumplex in the radex model. But these implications only reflect the limitations of simplified printed illustrations.

Consider a hypothetical example in which 10 tests are intercorrelated such that nonmetric scaling analysis yields a propellerlike configuration in two dimensions, as shown in Figure 2.1a. Each letter stands for one of the ten test points. There are three categories of test content (A, B, and C). The subscripts indicate increasing apparent complexity along each of the simplex arrays. Test G, the most complex test, appears in the center of this simplified radex. If the matrix of intercorrelations that led to this scaling configuration is factored hierarchically, it will result in the factor pattern matrix shown in Figure 2.1b (where loading values are indicated as rank ordered within columns from lowest "0" to highest "4"). The solution yields a general factor G defined by tests G, A_3, B_3, and C_3, and three group or content factors A, B, and C, that would be equidistant from one another in the scaling, probably anchored near tests A_2, B_2, and C_2. But the typical depiction of the hierarchical factor results would be shown as in Figure 2.1c. The drawing can mislead one into thinking that tests within factors are

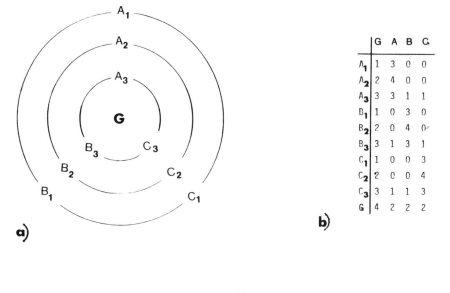

	G	A	B	C
A_1	1	3	0	0
A_2	2	4	0	0
A_3	3	3	1	1
B_1	1	0	3	0
B_2	2	0	4	0
B_3	3	1	3	1
C_1	1	0	0	3
C_2	2	0	0	4
C_3	3	1	1	3
G	4	2	2	2

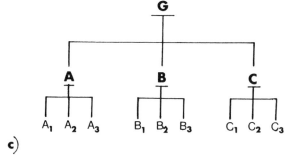

FIG. 2.1.   Hypothetical example of radex and hierarchical model parallelism: a) a radex scaling for ten tests; b) the associated hierarchical factor matrix; c) the associated hierarchical factor diagram.

permutable by suppressing the dimensional information that is actually in the factor solution in Figure 2.1b. Were the hierarchy constructed to retain the dimensional information that reflects correlation with G, as occurs in the additive tree clustering method for example (see Kyllonen, Marshalek, and Snow, 1982), then the ordering of tests would show the same pattern as retained in the scaling, where the tests are clearly not permutable. The drawing of Figure 2.1c further misleads by suggesting that two of the group factors, A and C, are more dissimilar from one another than either is from the third, B, and thus do not form a circumplex. However, in the scaling of Figure 2.1a *and* in the actual factor solution of Figure 2.1b, it is clear that each pair of group factors are equally similar. Again, the dimensional information that preserves distances has simply been omitted from the hierarchical illustration. The horizontal dimension of the hierarchical factor model *does* fold back on itself in the radex model.

Figure 2.1a and 2.1b also show how position in the simplex arrays translates into loadings on the general factor to suggest the vertical or complexity parallelism. But it may also be objected that the general factor in the hierarchical model and the complexity continuum in the radex model really only collapse all kinds of complexity into one; although each test in the array A_1, A_2, A_3, and G may be in some sense more complex than the tests that precede it, this need not be the same kind of complexity that increases across the array B_1, B_2, B_3, and G, and still a third kind of complexity may operate in the C array. Furthermore, neither the general factor nor the radex arrays help explicate in any detail the nature of such complexity.

This issue cannot be addressed in the abstract for it is at base an empirical question, deserving much further research. It is a question, this chapter argues, that provides one of the basic goals for a theory of intelligence. We advocate the radex model as a step in the right direction toward this goal precisely because it spreads complexity out for detailed examination in different regions of test content and because the nonmetric scaling approach stays close to the tests and primary correlations that most directly display it. Much of the rest of this chapter is devoted to demonstrating that the map provided by the radex model fits existing correlational data, yields many substantive hypotheses about the nature of complexity, and identifies arrays of concrete tasks to use in their study.

As an empirical demonstration of all this, Figure 2.2 reproduces a two-dimensional scaling solution reported previously by Marshalek (1977) and by Snow (1980a). It is based on a reference test battery administered to 241 high school students, a fairly representative sample of both tests and persons. Marshalek, Lohman, and Snow (in press) have given also the hierarchical factor solution for these data. The details on tests and procedure, and the basic correlation matrix, are available from Snow, Lohman, Marshalek, Yalow, and Webb (1977). Each point represents a test; points are coded for content as well as for three levels of apparent complexity, as defined by correlation with G. Test points that combine to define important factors are connected by solid lines and an adjacent bold face symbol identifies the factor (i.e., Fluid Intelligence, G_f; Crystallized Intelligence, G_c; Visualization, G_v; Memory Span, MS; Perceptual Speed, PS; Closure Speed, CS).

Apparently complex tests and clusters representing higher order factors scale near the center; apparently simpler tests and clusters representing lower order factors scale near the periphery. Snow (1980a) interpreted the centrality of G_f tests, particularly, as suggesting that such tasks involve to a greater degree the assembly and control processes needed to organize short-term adaptive strategies for solving novel problems. The simpler tests and factors seem based on simple

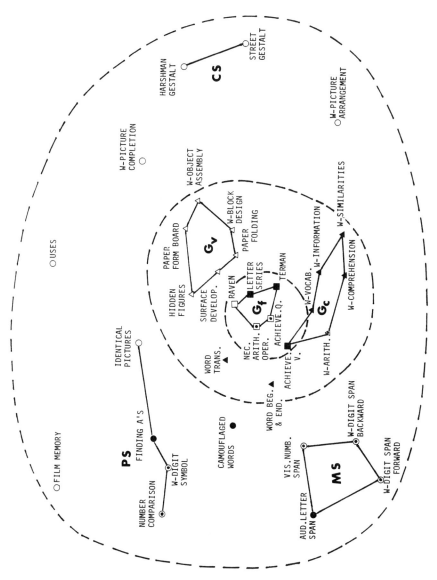

FIG. 2.2. Nonmetric scaling of ability test matrix for 241 high school students with factor clusters superimposed. Complex, intermediate, and simple tests are indicated as black (verbal), dotted (numerical), and white (figural-spatial) squares, triangles, and circles, respectively. (From Marshalek, Lohman, & Snow, in press)

items that are highly similar to one another, where speed is critical and automatic processing possible, with little need for adaptation of processing across items.

A dividing line could be drawn that separates the points into those representing figural-spatial content in the northeast region and verbal-numerical content in the southwest region. Snow (1980a) interpreted this pattern as suggesting a contrast between analogic and digital processing requirements. Guttman's (1965, 1970) three content wedges did not appear here perhaps because the numerical content area was inadequately sampled. Carroll (1980), in discussing the implications of Figure 2.2, also noted that a comparison of northwest and southeast points suggested a possible contrast between more automatic, rote processing and more creative, intuitive processing, respectively. Carroll also thought that a third dimension (rising from the paper) would represent the level of processing complexity that individuals could attain.

We shall revisit these and related hypotheses later. This first empirical demonstration suffices to show that a radex map is viable, and that it suggests hypotheses about cognitive processing variations associated with patterns of test similarity. But the radex of Figure 2.2 is somewhat distorted due to inadequate test sampling. There are some open spaces in the map, and numerical test sampling was limited as already noted. Marshalek, Lohman, and Snow (in press) also described the effect of limited sampling of persons on the radex resulting from this same test battery administered to 123 Stanford undergraduates. This restricted sampling had the effect of reducing variance in G_c tests, the kinds of ability most central to admission decisions, and thus distorting the radex in understandable, but troublesome ways. These observations make it clear that test and person sampling is an important consideration in bringing the results of such analyses from different studies into an integrated map.

Other Types of Structure.   Although this chapter concentrates on the radex structure as the best summary of test correlational evidence to date, it should not be concluded that no extensions or alternatives are possible. There may be other types of structure to be discovered. As Humphreys (1962) argued, the addition of test facets complicates the problem and may force major revisions in structural models as evidence accumulates. Also, continuing reanalysis of Guilford's (1967) Structure of Intellect Model, which includes Guttman's content facet but not the complexity continuum, may suggest extensions or complications. There is some evidence that the complexity continuum is reflected in the product x operation cells within the content areas of Guilford's model (Cronbach & Snow, 1977; Snow, 1978). There is also the possibility of hierarchical reorganization of some of Guilford's data (Guilford, 1982; Haynes, 1970; Lohman, 1979b). But there is also, at least hypothetically, a combination of radex and Guilford structures that could form a torus (see Varella, 1969).

REANALYSES OF ABILITY ORGANIZATION

Having shown that the radex model can incorporate the hierarchical factor model theoretically and also empirically in one fairly representative sample of persons and tests, our next step was to show that the radex structure appears and is interpretable in correlation matrices that are well-known for their support of a Thurstonian primary factor model as well as a hierarchical factor model. The data reported by Thurstone (1938) and Thurstone and Thurstone (1941) seemed the best candidates.

Thurstone's Primary Mental Abilities Matrix

Thurstone's (1938) study was the first major application of his then newly designed factor-analytic methods. The purpose of his analysis was to isolate the "primary mental abilities" presumed to comprise intelligent performance in a wide variety of situations. Thurstone chose the tasks for the battery so that verbal, numerical, and figural content were represented, and special emphasis was given to "measures of general intelligence." The subjects were college students. By applying the centroid factor method followed by rotation to simple structure, Thurstone isolated seven stable primary factors and two additional tentative factors. No general factor appeared, but Thurstone's methods were clearly not geared to produce one. Reanalyses of the 1938 matrix by Eysenck (1937), who used a hierarchical factor extraction procedure, and by Holzinger and Harman (1938), who used the bifactor method, did reveal a higher order general factor. Part of Thurstone's matrix was also reanalyzed by Guttman using his Smallest Space Analysis, a nonmetric multidimensional scaling, as noted above. Our aim was to reanalyze Thurstone's entire matrix using nonmetric scaling techniques.

Procedure.   Multidimensional scaling was applied to Thurstone's (1938) 57 × 57 tetrachoric correlation matrix using the KYST program (Kruskal, Young, & Seery, 1973). To avoid nonoptimal scaling solutions, we first obtained solutions for six dimensions and used as the starting configuration for each lower dimensional solution the configuration from the higher dimensional solution, collapsing over the last dimension. In our experience, this approach provides better starting configurations and results in better fits. We also used two different starting configurations at the highest (sixth) dimension: One generated by the metric TORSCA procedure (a part of the KYST program), the other generated randomly. In all our analyses, these two starting configurations resulted in similar final configurations and yielded essentially the same stress values, suggesting there were no local minima; obtained solutions were therefore considered opti-

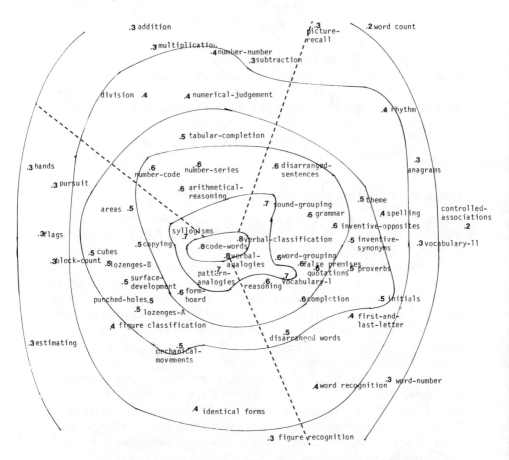

FIG. 2.3.   Nonmetric scaling of the Thurstone (1938) ability test matrix showing
G factor loadings. Dashed lines distinguish the content wedges. The position of *G*
loading numerals identifies the location of each test point.

mal. Here (and elsewhere in the chapter) we focus on the two-dimensional
solution (the plane representation), because it is simplest to interpret. In no case
did allowing a third dimension alter interpretations based on two dimensions or
add other significant hypotheses.

Both common factor analysis (with communalities in the diagonals) and principal components analysis (with unities in the diagonals) were also applied.
These analyses provided task loadings on the first (unrotated) factor or component and a varimax-rotated factor pattern matrix. Because there has been controversy over which method, principal components, or common factor, gives the
most appropriate estimates of task loadings on the general factor (*G*), we re-

gressed principal components loadings on common factor loadings and found them correlated almost perfectly (r = .9995), with zero intercept. The common factor loadings were thus used as the estimate of each task's *G* loading.

Results.   The first concern was whether the scaling representation provided the same information as the factor-analytic representation. We tested the degree to which the multidimensional scaling captured the general factor structure by representing both the scaling and factor-analytic solutions simultaneously. Figure 2.3 shows that tasks loading highest on *G* (i.e., the first principal factor) appeared in the center of the configuration. Tasks falling within the center circle showed *G* loadings of at least .8, those falling within the second of the series of concentric circles showed *G* loadings of at least .7, and so on, until all tasks fell within at least one circle (at .2). It is clear from Figure 2.3 that the scaling representation captures the general factor structure.

The same configuration can be assessed as to how it captures the structure of the rotated factor pattern matrix, i.e., the group factor structure. Figure 2.4 shows clusterings of tasks based on rotated factor loadings from our own re-analysis imposed on the scaling configuration, but we also tested other available analyses of the matrix (e.g., Eysenck, 1939; Holzinger & Harman, 1938; Zim-merman, 1953); all the patterns were similar. Tasks are clustered in Figure 2.4 on the basis of their highest group factor loading. Only those tasks that loaded highest on the Spatial Relations factor, for example, are clustered in the SR cluster. Figure 2.4 shows that the group factor structure was essentially captured by the multidimensional scaling solution. Tasks are grouped in the following factor clusters: Spatial Relations (SR), Numerical Skill (NS), Classification (C), Auditory (A), Word Fluency (WF), Verbal Comprehension (VC), and Memory (M). Two small reasoning clusters appear in the center of the radex; these appear similar to Thurstone's induction, or I factor, and another small reasoning factor he labeled D. If one were to adopt the Cattell-Horn language here, one would probably equate SR with G_v, VC with G_c, and the two reasoning factors together as parts of G_f.

Discussion.   It is clear that the nonmetric scaling captures the essential infor-mation from the factor analysis: the general factor and group factor structures. The most important question, however, is whether the similarity representations provide any additional information about the structural relationships among tasks not readily available from the factor analysis.

Figures 2.3 shows, in addition to the *G* circles, the three major distinctions in task content, indicated as wedges for verbal, figural, and numerical regions. This grouping provides a clear demonstration of the radex structure. Tasks differ simultaneously along the complexity continuum, as indicated by decreasing *G*

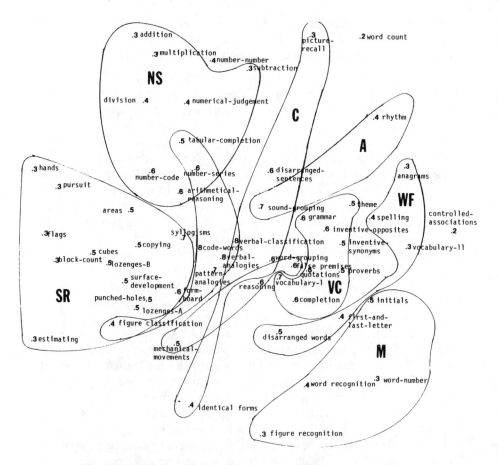

FIG. 2.4.   Nonmetric scaling of the Thurstone (1938) ability test matrix with factor clusters superimposed. The position of *G* loading numerals identifies the location of each test point.

loadings at positions farther from the center, and along the content facet, as indicated by their position in one or another wedge of the circumplex.

The meaning of the content facet is obvious, but it is not obvious what it means to say that tasks differ in complexity. One possibility is that one task includes all the components of another task plus some additional components, following Guttman's definition of complexity. The Numerical wedge in Figure 2.3 provides an illustration of how this definition might be used to interpret the array of tasks that, in Figure 2.4, are clustered together to form the NS factor. On the periphery are the basic computation tasks, Addition, Multiplication, and

Subtraction.[2] One contour closer to the center are tasks requiring combinations of these skills; Numerical Judgment, which requires quick estimation of various kinds of complex calculations; and Division (of seven place digits by one place digits), which combines the operations of multiplication, addition, and subtraction. Still closer to the center are tasks requiring some detection of patterns and relationships, in addition to combinations of computational skills. In these four tasks—Tabular Completion, Number Code, Number Series, and Arithmetical Reasoning—the subject is not told what computations to perform, but instead must decide which are the appropriate computations based on information in the problem. Thus, in the Numerical wedge, there is an ordering of tests along the complexity continuum, where increasing complexity is defined as the addition of components, that is captured empirically by the scaling solution.

However, task complexity is probably not this simple. Consider a numerical task consisting of items such as the following:

$$[(8 + 3) / (2 \times 11)] - (16 - 4) = ?$$

Such a task would require a combination of all the components involved in the basic computation tasks. However, it would likely not load as highly on G as some of the other complex tasks in the Numerical wedge, such as Number Series. As a further aspect of complexity, we hypothesize that tasks are complex as they require *assembly* and *control* processes. Assembly processes are likely to be involved, for example, when multiple hypothesis testing is required. Lists of hypotheses about the relations among elements in items of the task are generated and serve as plans for attacking the problem. A task such as Number Series seems to involve assembly processes. The solver tests different hypotheses about the relationships between the numbers in the series. These hypotheses are probably ordered by the likelihood of applying on each item; that is, they are not random hypotheses. It is likely that individuals differ in the appropriateness of the hypotheses they generate, in the order in which they test them, and in the degree to which the order is adapted during the process. The most proficient problem solvers probably test the most likely hypotheses first. An example of a control process would be an operation by which the solver keeps track of which hypotheses have been tested and which should be tested next. It is also likely that individuals differ in the degree to which they are able to keep track of what they have done, and what they should be doing next; they probably differ as well in the degree to which they catch errors as they make them.

Some complex mathematical problems tend also to be novel tasks, whereas

---

[2]Here and elsewhere space limitations do not permit including detailed descriptions of all tests. The interested reader can find such descriptions in the original sources.

others seem to be more similar to those faced in school learning, i.e., more familiar. The former would be expected to scale near G_f measures, the latter near G_c measures. But Thurstone's task sampling in the Numerical Wedge did not allow a check on this.

Other task arrangements within local regions of the configuration or across or around some circumplicial contours suggest hypotheses about the task differences in the operations of working memory. As one example, consider the memory tasks appearing in the southeast region of the configuration. The four tasks, Initials, Word Number, Word Recognition, and Figure Recognition, all lie roughly equidistant from the center of the radex; they all load similarly on G (.3 to .5). But the tasks are dissimilar with respect to content: Figure Recognition, which is a choice recall memory task consisting of figural stimuli, lies in the Visual wedge, and the other memory tasks, which do not use figural stimuli, lie in the Verbal wedge.

Furthermore, a process distinction is apparent. Tasks within the memory cluster can be ordered along a multiple choice vs. free recall dimension, Initials and Word Number are free recall (paired associates) memory tasks; Word Recognition and Figure Recognition are multiple choice memory tasks (requiring choice of the target figures from a larger list). This dimension can be extended beyond the memory cluster. Identical Forms, just to the left of the memory cluster, is a Perceptual Speed test requiring subjects to match a target figure with one of five alternative matching figures; perhaps such a task is the "purest" instance of multiple choice recognition, because memory demand is minimized and the choice aspect is all that is required. Continuing around the circumplex to its northeast pole, Picture Recall is a test in which subjects study a picture, then later recall its detailed features. The Word Count test, also appearing at this extreme free response pole, is a measure of one's ability to generate verbal material; it is simply a count of words used in a written description of a close friend. Other tasks such as Rhythm, Anagrams, Spelling, Controlled Associations, and Vocabulary II, appear to be positioned suggestively at intermediate points on this dimension, and all are at approximately the same low level of complexity. The dimension may capture some of the differences between directed memory search with abundant retrieval cues and multidirectional search in the absence of effective retrieval cues. This particular ordering of tests would be difficult if not impossible to detect in a factor analysis, because the ordering crosses a number of factors.

Thus, structures of task similarity revealed by nonmetric scaling, within the factor clusters in the example of the numerical task series, or across them in the example of the recognition-recall dimension, suggest ranges of tasks that may exhibit orderly changes in variant components and assemblies involved in performance. In either case, the scaling configuration brings out patterns in the data that are hidden or obscured in the results of factor analyses. Perhaps the most important distinction between the two techniques is that the radex scaling places each task, not only with respect to the major facets of content and level of complexity but also with respect to many other possible dimensions that may influence performance similarity simultaneously.

To summarize, then, the following conclusions and implications can be drawn: a) the nonmetric scaling captures both the general factor and the group factor structures; b) the resulting configuration of tests approximates the radex model in both its complexity and content facets; c) this suggests hypotheses about variations across ranges of tasks reflecting increasing processing complexity and the contrast between recognition and recall processes.

The Thurstone and Thurstone Matrix

Three years after the initial study, Thurstone and Thurstone (1941) repeated their factor analysis of a similar battery of 60 tests. The purposes of this analysis were: to replicate the 1938 study, to determine if the same factor structure found with a college-age sample would be obtained for eighth graders; to test whether factors could be purified by eliminating the factorially more complex tasks; and to determine if the Verbal Comprehension and Word Fluency factors could be more clearly subdivided. The 1941 battery thus differed from the 1938 battery; there were fewer visual-figural and numerical content tasks, and the tasks were considerably simpler, in keeping with the factor purity objective and the younger sample of persons. The primary factors the Thurstones obtained turned out to be more or less similar to those of 1938. Additionally, they were able to extract from the 1941 battery what they called a "second-order general factor" by factor analyzing the matrix of factor intercorrelations.

Procedure. We applied the KYST program to the 60×60 matrix following the procedures described in the previous section. As before, we also performed principal factor and principal component analyses.

Results. As with the 1938 matrix, we were interested first in determining the degree to which the scaling representation captured the general and group factor structures. Figure 2.5 shows that tasks with the highest G loadings appeared in the center of the configuration whereas tasks with lower G loadings fell progressively closer to the periphery—precisely the same results as for the previous analysis. Note, however, that for the 1941 matrix the "center," as defined by the central circle, is a bit off the true center of the configuration, and leaves complex tests such as letter series somewhat distant from the general factor for this matrix. This is due to the variation in point density at different regions in the configuration. There is a heavy clustering of points representing reading comprehension and vocabulary tasks in the southeast corner of the configuration.

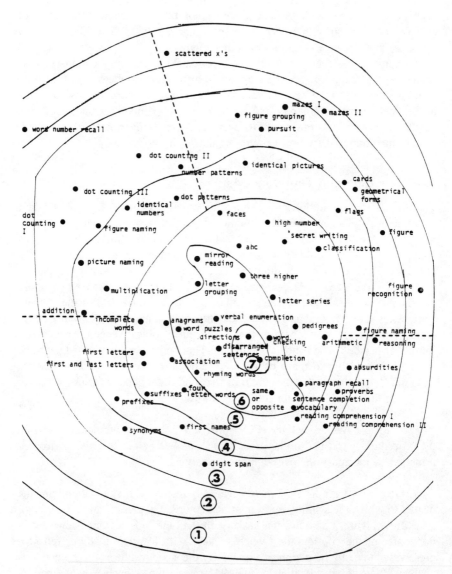

FIG. 2.5. Nonmetric scaling of the Thurstone and Thurstone (1941) ability test matrix showing *G* factor loadings for different contours. Dashed lines distinguish the content wedges.

Local densities of this sort will have the effect of shifting the "least-squares" center from the true center. Homogeneous distribution of points depends on representative sampling of tasks. In the 1941 study, tasks involving reading and sentence comprehension were overrepresented.

The radex representation here also captures a content distinction similar to that shown in the previous analysis. Verbal, Numerical, and Figural wedges are drawn into Figure 2.5. There is also a clear separation within the Verbal wedge between verbal fluency and verbal comprehension tasks. One of the Thurstone's goals was to determine if this type of separation of verbal-content tasks could be made. The plane representation confirms this further distinction, within the verbal region.

In Figure 2.6, we have again shown the original primary factor solution as clusters superimposed on the scaling solution of Figure 2.5. The Thurstones obtained ten such factors for the 1941 matrix. Among these were Verbal Comprehension (V), Word Fluency (W), Induction (I), Number (N), Space (S), and Perceptual Speed (P), as identified in Figure 2.6. Also obtained was a memory factor that in Figure 2.6 would be dispersed around the peripheral circumplex connecting Digit Span, First Names, Word-Number Recall, and Figure Classification. Three other unnamed factors are not identified in our figure. Again, the group factor structure is fairly neatly shown in the scaling.

Discussion.   The induction factor appears closest to the true center of the scaling and is probably also closest to what would be called G_f. The verbal cluster could probably be called G_c. Both the numerical and the memory factors are distributed because they were poorly represented in the Thurstone's task sampling. The memory tests, in particular, defined a weak factor. In the scaling, it would appear that the content difference among the four memory tests was the overriding influence.

One might attempt to construct hypothesized simplex structures within the Verbal, Word Fluency, and Perceptual Speed factor clusters from the scaling. But the points for Verbal and Word Fluency tests are closely packed, and a Perceptual Speed simplex would need to include points not contained in the factor cluster. Also note that the Space factor is fairly peripheral because complex spatial tests included in the 1938 matrix were excluded in 1941. It appears that the Thurstones focused their task sampling in 1941, based on the 1938 findings, to accomplish certain purposes. Yet the radex structure is only slightly distorted as a result.

Another point of interest concerns the relative importance of content vs. complex process aspects of task interrelationships in comparing the analyses of the 1938 and 1941 Thurstone data. Figure 2.3 displayed a clear content distinction for all but the center-most tests in the 1938 data. The interpretation would be that the content facet is important in determining task similarity for all but the most central tests, where some kind of processing similarity becomes more impor-

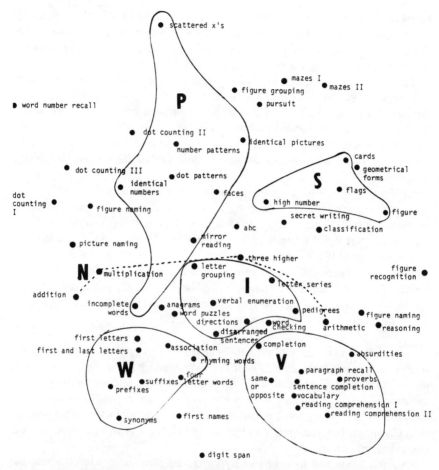

FIG. 2.6. Nonmetric scaling of the Thurstone and Thurstone (1941) ability test matrix with factor clusters superimposed.

tant than the content being processed. In the 1941 data, as scaled in Figure 2.5 however, the content distinction can be seen clearly in the configuration only for the more peripheral tasks, those with *G* loadings less than .5. For tasks with *G* loadings greater than .5, the importance of process seems to overwhelm the importance of content.

It is possible that this result reflects the different age and educational levels of each sample—college students for the 1938 battery, and eighth graders for the 1941 battery. The cognitive differentiation hypothesis (Anastasi, 1970; Ferguson, 1954, 1956; Garrett, 1946) suggests that the development of human intelligence involves a process of differentiation and specialization of abilities as a function of age and education, as well as other learning experience. One cannot adequately judge this hypothesis on the basis of the number of factors extracted for samples of different ages because this depends on many other conditions, including task and person sampling for different matrices. The basic structure of the scaling solutions, though also subject to distortion from sampling differences, may be less sensitive to this effect than the number of factors extracted. A comparison of Figures 2.3 and 2.5 suggests that the involvement of specialized knowledge structures in determining task similarity increases with age and education. Thus, for younger students the dominant source of individual differences may be in the processes of complex problem solving while, for older, more educated and more selected students, individual differences in knowledge structures may be more important.

In summary, the nonmetric scaling captures both the general factor and group factor structure, and displays the radex model, in the 1941 data as it did in the 1938 data. A comparison of the two analyses suggests, in addition, that differentiation of abilities with age and education may appear in scaling solutions as a relative prominence of process distinctions in younger samples, and of content distinctions in older samples, in the central regions of the radex.

REANALYSIS OF ABILITY-LEARNING RELATIONSHIPS

The conceptual link between intelligence and individual differences in learning is long standing. But solid empirical evidence about ability-learning relationships has been hard to come by, partly because serious methodological problems have attended the work. Glaser (1967) reviewed much of the older literature. Cronbach and Snow (1977) concentrated on the conceptual and methodological issues in their review, but singled out two studies, by Allison (1960) and Stake (1961), for extra attention. Both studies had carefully developed a matrix of learning measures, based on laboratory learning tasks, and related these measures to a large reference battery of ability tests. Cronbach and Snow (1977) concluded that:

> Considering all studies together, it appears that learning rates on closely similar tasks do correlate, whereas correlations among different tasks are usually rather low. Presumably 'narrow' factors influence performance on specific types of task. Task-specific factors limit the extent to which aptitudes can predict learning. But aptitude measures do correlate with learning to a greater extent than two independent learning scores correlate with each other. The unreliability of learning measures puts a ceiling on all such correlations. A concept of general mental ability is adequate to account for nearly all the correlations observed, except where a separate rote-memory factor is pertinent. Allison and Stake both found rote-memory tests related to rote learning, and forming factors rather distinct from conceptual tests and tasks [pp. 141–142].

Much of the past thinking and research on ability and learning, however, has been dominated by the factor-analytic approach and particularly the Thurstone model. Allison and Stake, for example, worked with Gulliksen (1961), who had been a Thurstone student. To reach their conclusion about the relation of general ability to conceptual learning, Cronbach and Snow (1977) had to ignore the factor-analytic results in favor of simple tallies of correlation coefficients. They did not consider the fluid-crystallized distinction directly. It is reasonable to expect that multidimensional scaling and clustering approaches might help further to sharpen the Cronbach-Snow conclusion and might bring out features of ability-learning structure not seen in the simple tallies of correlations or in the factor analyses.

The Allison Matrix

Allison developed a battery of 39 reference ability tests and a separate battery of 13 learning tasks. Both were administered to a sample of 315 Navy recruits. For each learning task, a rate parameter indicated the average rate of learning across trials for each individual and a curvature parameter distinguished between early learning (during the first half) and late learning (during the second half) of the task trials. It was expected that both task-specific and broader learning factors would appear and that some of these factors would reflect task process requirements (e.g., rote vs. relational learning), whereas others would reflect task content distinctions (e.g., verbal vs. figural stimuli).

Allison concluded that learning was multidimensional and that process and content distinctions in learning tasks corresponded to similar distinctions in cognitive tests. His interbattery factor analysis showed four corresponding factors between the reference battery and the learning task parameters. These were called: conceptual process; rote process; mechanical; and psychomotor. He did not look for the more general pattern detected by Cronbach and Snow (1977).

Our reanalysis sought to examine the general ability hypothesis more carefully. We identified those of Allison's reference tests that seemed to represent crystallized ability (G_c), fluid ability (G_f), and visualization ability (G_v), expecting to find differential relationships between learning task performance and these three ability constructs. It was hoped that these relationships would reflect task similarities not only in content but also in underlying psychological processes.

Procedure.   First, a principal components analysis was performed on the ability reference battery. Results confirmed Allison's finding that seven factors were sufficient. The Principal Factors method was then applied to the battery and seven factors were rotated by the varimax procedure. The first factors of the rotated solution were of primary interest in distinguishing G_f, G_c, and G_v tests.

Next, nonmetric multidimensional scaling (KYST) was performed on the ability reference matrix and on the combined ability-learning matrices. The results of these scaling analyses were interpretable but complicated, and the stress values for the ability-learning combination scalings were relatively high.

It was thus decided to form three ability composites for the G_c, G_f, and G_v constructs, based on a combination of the results for the ability test scaling and the factor analyses. A G_c cluster was formed with Sentence Completion, Vocabulary, the General Classification Test, and the Otis IQ test. A G_f cluster was formed with Mathematical Aptitude, Ship Destination, and the Armed Forces Qualification Test (AFQT). A G_v cluster was formed with Cards, Paper Folding, Paper Form Board, Mechanical Aptitude Test, and the Guilford-Zimmerman Test of Mechanical Knowledge.

To investigate the relationships between ability and learning performances, correlations between the G_c, G_f, and G_v construct composites and the learning parameters were then obtained. Allison had reported only the overall correlation matrix, and not the raw data; therefore, we computed the new correlation matrix, including the composites, by applying a variance-covariance matrix model. This new correlation matrix was completed separately for the learning rate measures and the learning curvature measures. These matrices were then submitted to nonmetric scaling again using the KYST program.

Results.   The scalings of the correlations among individual ability tests and learning task parameters showed complex G_c and G_f tests densely packed in a region below the center of the configuration; simpler ability tests and many of the learning task were scattered toward or on the periphery and covered approximately 270 degrees of the most peripheral circumplex. Some learning tasks scaled close in to the G_c and G_f clusters; these were principally the CIC plotting and Verbal Concept Formation tasks and to some extent the Spatial Concept Formation task, regardless of the learning parameter included. A separate G_v cluster was clearly identifiable and included the Meccano Assembly (rate parameter) and Breech Block (curvature parameter) learning tasks. A Perceptual Speed ability cluster was also distinguishable; a rate parameter from one of the Spatial Concept Formation tasks seemed proximal to it.

It was hoped that the reduced matrix using ability composites would simplify and clarify this picture. The intercorrelations among the three ability composites were: .87, .77, and .53 for G_f–G_c, G_f–G_v, and G_c–G_v, respectively. These high intercorrelations suggest that in Allison's sample a strong general factor runs through the ability test matrix; its presence impedes differentiation of special ability factors. Thus, most of the variance in each of the three construct factors can be accounted for by the other two factors; only 19%, 11%, and 33% of the variance is unique in G_c, G_f, and G_v respectively, and thereby free to correlate differentially with the learning task parameters. Given the relatively small proportion of unique variance brought to the learning situation through each ability construct, it is noteworthy that a differential pattern of correlations between

TABLE 2.1
Correlations Between Ability Composites and Learning-Task
Parameters for the Allison Reanalysis
(N = 315)

	Rate Parameter Correlations with			Curvature Parameter Correlations with		
	Gc	Gf	Gv	Gc	Gf	Gv
Rotary Pursuit	01	-01	-09	03	08	12
Sidewalk Maze	01	03	01	-03	-03	01
Breech Block	01	00	03	10	31	51
Word Code	12	07	08	17	14	03
Sonar	15	12	05	05	01	03
Spatial Concept Formation-I	15	14	13	26	31	25
Meccano Assembly	16	38	50	-01	02	15
Spatial Code	21	20	11	22	26	17
Knob Code	24	19	15	01	02	03
Verbal Concept Formation-I	31	26	18	42	38	23
Spatial Concept Formation-II	40	40	35	13	12	15
Combat Info Center Plotting	48	55	40	50	58	41
Verbal Concept Formation-II	54	41	29	49	40	18

Notes: $r = .11$ significant at .05 level.
The curvature parameter is reflected from that given by Allison (1960) to produce positive correlations.
Positive correlations indicate early learning for higher ability subjects.

abilities and learning task performances still appeared. Table 2.1 shows the correlations between each of the ability composites and the learning rate and curvature parameters. The learning tasks are rank ordered in the table from simple to complex according to the correlation of the rate parameter with G_c. In general, ability was most strongly related to performance on Verbal Concept Formation, Spatial Concept Formation, CIC Plotting, and Meccano Assembly tasks. Overall, G_c was the ability construct most strongly related to task performance, but its contribution varied with different tasks. G_c was clearly the most important predictor of performance in the two Verbal Concept Formation tasks, especially the version of the task (VCF-II) that cannot be solved by rote memorization. All abilities predicted performance in the Spatial Concept Formation tasks about equally. G_f best predicted performance on the CIC Plotting task, and G_v best predicted performance on the Meccano Assembly task.

The relationships between ability and the curvature parameter were generally consistent with those found for the rate parameter, although learning curvature was better predicted than learning rate, on average. For the curvature parameter, abilities correlated most highly with performance on the Verbal Concept Formation tasks, Spatial Concept Formation I, CIC Plotting, and the Breech Block tasks. As with the rate parameter, G_c best predicted Verbal Concept Formation performance, G_f best predicted Spatial Concept Formation-I and CIC Plotting performance, and G_v best predicted Meccano Assembly and Breech Block performance.

Figure 2.7a and 2.7b show the two-dimensional scaling solutions for the two matrices of learning parameters, including the ability composites. In both cases, the ability constructs appear on the left side of the configuration and the learning tasks fan out to the right. Learning tasks that correlate highest with each of the respective ability constructs in Table 2.1 are connected to that ability point by a dotted line in the figures. These scalings simplify the full scalings described previously (by reducing the fans connected to abilities from about 270 degrees of a full circle to the approximately 70 degrees shown in Figures 2.7a,b) but retain the same complex to simple ordering of the learning tasks.

Discussion.   One interpretation of the differential ability learning correlations would trace similar content across ability and learning measures. But content correspondence would have also predicted relations that did not obtain. For example, Spatial Code and the Spatial Concept Formation tasks all consisted of nonverbal content but were not best predicted by G_v. Those tasks correlated as highly or more highly with G_c or G_f. Most of these correlation differences are small in terms of percentages of variance, but some are appreciable, given this sample size. The scaling configurations in Figure 2.7a and b are suggestive of hypotheses other than simply that of content similarities.

Another line of interpretation would seek an account of both the simple to complex ordering of learning tasks and whatever differential correlation they show with ability composites simultaneously. This view is based on the fluid-crystallized ability distinction discussed by Snow (1981). Some of the tasks, such as CIC plotting, Meccano Assembly, and Breech Block Performance, are novel and appear to demand more flexible adaptation; they seem to require that the subject assemble new strategies for learning, some of which require spatial ability. G_f and/or G_v showed the highest correlations with these tasks. In other tasks, such as Knob Code, Word Code, Spatial Code, and the verbal and spatial concept formation tasks, a more familiar or traditional approach to learning seems to be called for; these tasks seem more similar to learning tasks that subjects might be expected to have experienced before and so could be approached by retrieving and adapting old strategies from memory rather than assembling new ones. G_c tended to correlate more highly with these tasks.

At the same time, the G_c correlations show a graded series of increasing complexity. A similar but not identical graded series of learning tasks is seen in their correlations with G_f. For G_v, however, the gradient changes more abruptly to reach high correlations. The suggestion is that learning tasks also differ along a complexity continuum and can be placed in a radex model; the learning com-

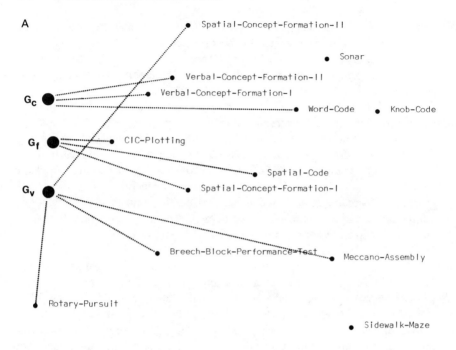

A

FIG. 2.7. Nonmetric scaling of the Allison (1960) learning task matrix with ability composites included: a) learning differences measured by the curvature parameter; b) learning differences measured by the rate parameter.

plexity continuum is smooth leading to G_c and G_f, both flat and then abruptly steep as learning tasks do or do not require G_v ability.

There are also some suggestive differences between the rate and curvature parameters. For Breech Block, G_v was associated with early vs. late learning but not with overall learning rate. For Mecanno Assembly, G_v was associated with both parameters but principally with rate. G_v ability apparently only provided a head start in the first task but was an aid throughout the second task. In the latter task G_c and G_f contribute to the prediction of overall rate but are not associated with early learning. The same pattern appears for G_c and G_f on Knob Code and to some extent on Spatial Concept Formation II. Such patterns again suggest that G_c acts as a more pervasive aid in learning whereas G_v applies as a special aid in some tasks. Many of the differences are small, because the general factor perceived by Cronbach and Snow (1977) is the overriding factor. But the differential trends show through enough to deserve further research.

The main conclusions and implications are as follows: a) laboratory learning

B

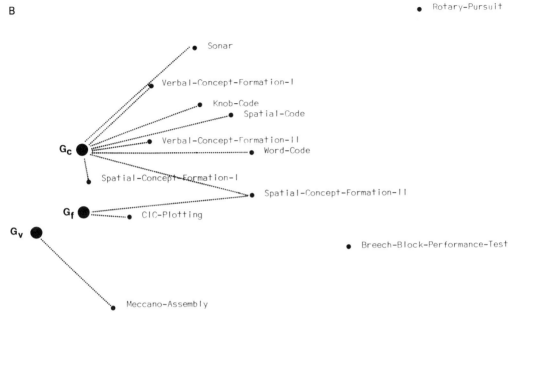

tasks can be placed into the radex map according to their correlations with ability tests; b) although a pervasive general factor runs through both ability and learning matrices, there are differential correlational patterns suggesting that complex familiar learning tasks correlate somewhat more with G_c, whereas complex novel learning tasks correlate somewhat more with G_f or G_v; c) a complexity continuum is apparent among learning tasks that appears as a smooth gradient with respect to G_c and G_f; d) G_v appears to be a special aid relevant only to some learning tasks and perhaps only to some stages of such tasks; e) the complexity gradient for G_v appears to change abruptly rather than smoothly.

The Stake Matrix

Stake (1961) also hypothesized that learning performance parameters would be correlated with intellectual abilities, but that a general learning ability factor distinct from a general intelligence factor would appear along with factors specific to learning. Further, he expected that school grades would contribute uniquely to the prediction of learning, that his learning parameters would be orthogonal to one another, and that content (verbal vs. nonverbal), process (relational vs. rote), and motivational factors could be extracted from measures of learning performance. His matrix contained 37 ability measures and 12 learning tasks, administered to 240 seventh graders.

Stake's most consistent finding was that both mental test and learning task performances reflectd a pervasive general ability factor. He also found that school grades did not contribute to the predictive validity of the aptitude tests in relation to learning. As for the proposed learning dimensions, only a separate numerical learning factor could be extracted. Stake concluded that no factors separated verbal vs. nonverbal, rote vs. relational, or high vs. low motivational learning tasks.

For the reanalysis, we hypothesized that by distinguishing G_f and G_c abilities, the relationships between ability and learning could be clarified. Beyond content similarities between tests and tasks, we expected differential correlation patterns suggestive of learning process distinctions. Some tasks should depend more on the fluid processes involved in adapting to novel learning conditions whereas others should depend more on applying previously acquired, crystallized learning skills and strategies.

Procedure.   As in the Allison reanalysis, principal components analysis was applied to the reference ability battery to determine the number of factors in that matrix. The principal factor method was then applied with four factors rotated orthogonally by the varimax procedure. Multidimensional scaling was then applied to the matrix of ability tests. Both the factor-analytic and the scaling solutions showed school grades to be clearly distinguishable from the other measures. Grades came from Social Studies, Language, Arithmetic, Reading, and Spelling classes. Another cluster was formed by measures of G_c, namely PMA Verbal-Words, PMA Reasoning-Words, Arithmetical Reasoning, the Otis IQ test, and the Stanford Achievement Test. A third cluster was formed by two tests of G_f or G_v, primarily PMA-Space and PMA-Figural-Reasoning. We were unable to separate G_f from G_v measures in this battery and thus refer to this cluster of tests as G_{fv} measures in the reanalysis. Ability composites were formed from tests in the three clusters (G_{fv}, G_c, and Grades) again by application of the variance-covariance method.

Multidimensional scaling was then performed on the ability test-learning task matrices and on the learning task matrices with only the G_c, G_{fv}, and Grades composites included from the ability matrix as before. Again the stress values for the individual test and task matrices reached relatively high values.

Results.   The scaling of individual ability tests and learning tasks provided a clear radex with G_{fv}, G_c, and the constituents of grades near the center, simpler tests and some learning tasks in the intermediate region, and the rest of the learning tasks in the periphery. But the structure was somewhat irregular as before, and seemed likely to be simplified without substantial distortion by relying on the scaling of the learning tasks with only the ability composites included.

Table 2.2 shows the relationship between each of the ability composites and the learning task performances for both the rate and curvature parameters. Again, learning tasks are ordered from simple to complex according to the correlations between rate parameters and G_c. For 10 of the 24 tasks, G_c best predicted performance; for 11 tasks, G_{fv} best predicted performance; for 2 tasks, Grades best predicted performance. The correlation of learning with Grades appeared almost entirely due to the strong relationship between Grades and G_c. With G_c partialed out, the contribution of Grades to learning performance prediction was eliminated in all but the Picture-Number task. On the other hand, G_{fv} contributed uniquely to learning-prediction for a number of tasks. In general, the ability composites better predicted learning performance as represented by the rate parameters rather than the curvature parameters.

TABLE 2.2
Correlations Between Ability Composites and
Learning-Task Parameters for the Stake Reanalysis
(N = 240)

	Rate Parameter Correlations with			Curvature Parameter Correlations with		
	Gc	Gfv	Grades	Gc	Gfv	Grades
Word Groups	24	29	18	21	24	14
Jungle Maze	33	15	08	31	13	07
Listening Comprehension II	35	39	25	12	06	-01
Word Memory I	36	48	38	28	36	25
Choice Board II	38	36	25	11	11	08
Listening Comprehension I	42	55	46	04	07	10
Figure-Shape Matching	45	37	28	35	30	22
Choice Board I	46	54	40	26	39	27
Picture Number Matching	49	48	49	24	26	34
Word Memory II	50	67	58	40	49	38
Number Pattern I	52	36	29	48	34	27
Number Pattern II	52	50	41	46	45	37

Notes: $r = .13$ significant at .05 level.
The rate and curvature parameters are reflected from that given by Stake's (1961) error and curvature parameters, respectively, to produce positive correlations. For curvature, positive correlations indicate early learning for higher ability students.

84

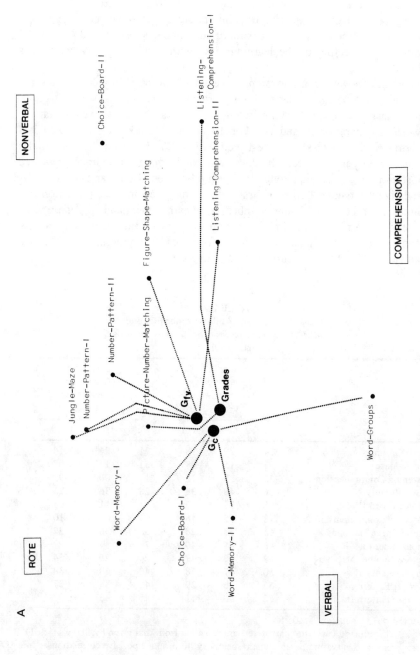

FIG. 2.8. Nonmetric scaling of the Stake (1961) learning task matrix with ability composites included: a) learning differences measured by the curvature parameter; b) learning differences measured by the rate parameter.

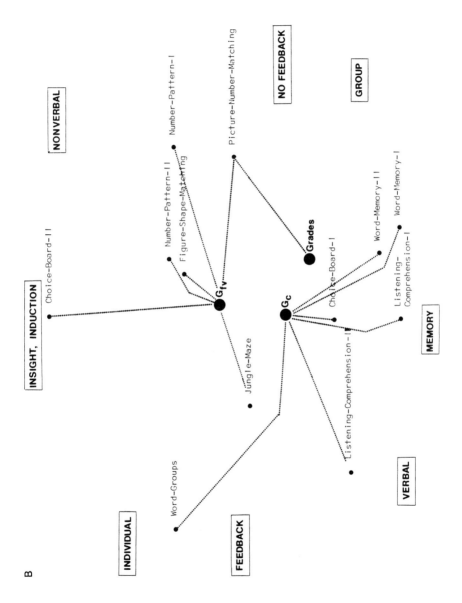

B

NONVERBAL

NO FEEDBACK

GROUP

INSIGHT, INDUCTION

Choice-Board-II

Number-Pattern-I

Picture-Number-Matching

Number-Pattern-II

Figure-Shape-Matching

G_{fv}

Grades

Word-Memory-II

Word-Memory-I

Choice-Board-I

Listening-Comprehension-I

G_c

Jungle-Maze

MEMORY

Listening-Comprehension-II

VERBAL

Word-Groups

INDIVIDUAL

FEEDBACK

85

Figure 2.8a shows the two-dimensional scaling representation for the curvature parameter. The three ability composites appear at the center of the configuration, with the learning tasks that relate to each composite radiating outward. Content (verbal vs. nonverbal) and process (rote vs. comprehension) axes are superimposed onto the configuration. The Word Memory tasks, Choice Board 1, and Jungle Maze fall on the rote end of the configuration; Choice Board II, the Listening Comprehension tasks, and the Number Pattern tasks fall toward the comprehension side of the process axis. Similarly, tasks line up on the content axis depending on whether the task consisted of verbal or nonverbal stimuli. The G_{fv} tasks tend toward the nonverbal side of the configuration.

Figure 2.8b shows the two-dimensional plot from the three-dimensional solution when task performance was measured by the rate parameter (again only two dimensions seemed interpretable). Presence-of-feedback and group vs. individual administration dimensions are imposed on the configuration along with the process (memory vs. insight or induction) and content (verbal vs. nonverbal) axes. Only one task, Listening Comprehension II, which involved no feedback, appears misplaced on the presence-of-feedback axis. The administration dimension captures the finding that, for those tasks that were administered in parallel form, once individually and once to a group (Number Pattern, Word Memory, and Listening Comprehension), the individually administered version (identified as I) always appears below and to the right of the group administered version (identified as II) in the configuration.

Discussion.   Stake's original analysis did not yield separate general factors for learning and ability. As Cronbach and Snow (1977) pointed out (see also Snow, 1978), Stake's raw correlations show that some ability tests correlated more highly with learning task performance than separate learning tasks correlated with each other. Here, ability composites, formed by combining similar tests, had even stronger relationships with learning task performance, lending further support to the conclusion that ability was related to learning in Stake's data. Further, the results of the multidimensional scaling show that the learning tasks encircle the ability tests, rather than falling together in a learning-task cluster.

Another conclusion drawn by Stake was that Grades did not add to the predictive validity of aptitude measures in predicting learning. This conclusion is confirmed here; only one task, Picture-Number Matching, correlated significantly with the Grades composite when general ability was partialled out. Thus, although Grades emerged as a separate factor, the relationship of the Grades factor to learning appears to be nothing more than the relationship between G_c and learning.

A third conclusion drawn by Stake was that content, process, and motivation dimensions could not be extracted from the learning task analysis. The multidimensional scaling, on the other hand, allowed content, process, knowledge-of-results, and group vs. individual administration dimensions to be detected.

Perhaps the most important finding of our reanalysis was that the picture of intelligence-learning relationships may be sharpened by dividing G into separate major group abilities. Table 2.2 and Figure 2.8a and b show that learning tasks relying more on the G_c abilities were, with one exception, verbal content tasks. The task performances best predicted by G_{fv} tended to be nonverbal tasks. However, as in the Allison reanalysis, more than content differences were captured. The tests that entered the G_c composite included arithmetic and picture memory tests—tests with nonverbal content, but presumed to tap crystallized knowledge. In general, learning tasks calling for crystallized mental skills were best predicted by the G_c composite and tasks requiring fluid-analytic skills were best predicted by the G_{fv} composite. Again, however, the correlation differences are relatively small, but some are noteworthy with this sample size.

As with the Allison data, there is also an apparent gradient of complexity in Stake's data. These tasks, then, could also be placed on the complexity continuum of the radex. The younger age sample used by Stake might account for the higher average correlations, relative to Allison's young adult sample. This might again support the hypothesis of cognitive differentiation with age and education that was suggested by the comparison of the Thurstone's two samples. But the two sorts of learning tasks used by Allison and Stake were rather different. Stake's tasks appear to be more similar to school tasks than do Allison's. Even so, the complexity gradients for G_c and G_{fv} in Stake's data do appear to differ somewhat. Unfortunately, the absence of a distinction between G_f and G_v here makes it difficult to examine these gradients in more detail, or to check the special learning aid character of G_v that appeared in Allison's data.

Again, then, the Stake reanalysis suggests that: a) ability and learning correlations fit the radex model; (b) learning tasks scale along complexity gradients leading to different major group factors somewhat differently; and c) the scaling representation can capture content and process distinctions built into the learning tasks.

SUMMARY AND GENERAL DISCUSSION

The reanalyses reported above are consistent in implying that a radex model fits cognitive ability test and learning task matrices, at least when tests, tasks, and persons are sampled more or less representatively. It was also shown that the hierarchical factor model of ability organization is mathematically and empirically consistent with the radex model, and that nonmetric multidimensional scaling can incorporate the results of past hierarchical or Thurstonian factor-analytic research into the same easily visualizable, comprehensible representation. The radex thus emerges as the most general theoretical model to date on both substantive and methodological grounds. It seems to provide a fairly comprehensible map of the correlational terrain that process theories of intelligence and learning must eventually cover (Snow 1980a).

This final section brings together observations and implications for further research and explores in more detail the interpretation and use of the suggested radex map. First, methodological issues are summarized. Then, substantive issues concerning the nature of task complexity, the fluid-crystallized distinction, and ability-learning relationships are examined. Idealized versions of the map are provided.

Methodological Summary

Reanalysis of existing correlational data on cognitive abilities and learning with alternative methods can make an important contribution to the construction of a theory of intelligence. It allows an opportunity to study and compare advantages and disadvantages of different methods in representing the correlational evidence any theory must explain. In particular, it helps to show the ways in which prior theorizing about abilities and learning may have been limited by choice of method. One main purpose in this chapter has been to demonstrate the application of the newer nonmetric multidimensional scaling techniques to the analysis of ability test and learning task correlation matrices that had previously been analyzed from a Thurstonian factor analytical perspective. In so doing, we were able to identify patterns of relationships both among ability tests and between them and learning tasks that had been overlooked in previous analyses. Nonmetric multidimensional scaling seems particularly well suited to further exploratory reanalyses of other ability and learning data available from the work of Thurstone, Guilford, and many others. Such further exploration can be expected to elaborate the picture presented in this chapter substantially. It also seems clear that future research on ability-learning relations will need to take a multimethod approach. No one method will be best in every instance. It can be recommended, however, that nonmetric scaling will most often be the approach that brings the results of all methods into clear relation to one another. Because it stays close to the original measures, requires minimal assumptions, and provides a simple spatial representation, it is the method of choice when only one method is used, in our view. Multidimensional scaling and factor analysis are best seen as complementary tools.

Nonetheless, the approach one takes in analyzing the structure of relationships among measures of ability or learning will influence one's theory of intelligence. Although factor analysis and multidimensional scaling provide much the same information, the scaling representation leads to more direct consideration of the transfer relations among tasks, and to the various dimensions or facets along which tasks can differ simultaneously. Transfer relations among tasks are presumed to be a function of intertask similarities in the sampling of response components. The multidimensional scaling configuration represents these relations by the physical euclidean distances between tasks. The closer two tasks are to one another, the more functional similarity presumably exists between them and therefore the greater the transfer relationship to be expected. Conversely, the farther two tests are from one another in the configuration, the less functional similarity there is, and the less the transfer relation to be expected. It seems natural to interpret these continuous distances in terms of similarities in response samplings for different tasks. Perhaps unintentionally, the typical factor analysis deemphasizes the continuous surface of transfer relations among tasks. The factor analyst is likely to describe tests that load highly on a particular factor as more or less "univocal" measures or signs of the underlying ability-trait-entity represented by the factor. Crisp divisions among factors are the result. In Thurstone's (1938) writings, especially, this flavor of factors as signs of the underlying intellectual capacities of the organism comes through.

The simultaneous multidimensional orderings of tasks provided by the scaling approach is also a distinctive strength relative to the factor analysis. We were able to detect, for example, simplicial orderings within factor clusters and circumplicial orderings across factor clusters, but also distinctions between recognition vs. recall, presence vs. absence of knowledge-of-results, and other orderings not captured by any previously reported factor analysis. The fact that cognitive tasks or objects in general can be shown to differ along many dimensions simultaneously, and that this ordering can be captured in a two- or three-dimensional scaling representation, is one of the most powerful features of nonmetric scaling, and may account for its popularity in several areas of experimental psychology. Factor analysis can be made to represent these same orderings, as long as the investigator has some hint of their importance beforehand. Because a priori dimension specification is not necessary with multidimensional scaling, the technique is especially valuable for exploratory purposes. Generally, multidimensional scaling seems to force a consideration of more aspects of task performance than does factor analysis.

Finally, the structures of task similarity we consider important to emphasize in the scaling configurations reported on this chapter will always be imperfect in empirical data. We believe that the radex model is presently the best way to think about cognitive task intercorrelations generally, but it is clear that dense task sampling in some particular region can distort the general radex and force that region to center stage, regardless of where it might have appeared in the scaling of more representative samples of tasks. This fact can actually be used to advantage as continuing research focuses on tasks in particular regions. Similarly, variations in person sampling from study to study can lead to variations in the radex representations obtained. Some of these variations may have important substantive interpretations, as the comparison of sample age and educational level between the two Thurstone studies suggested.

Between and Within Persons and Tasks

As stated in an introductory section of this chapter, the analysis of task similarity based on between-task, across-person correlations is limited to the discovery of structures representing summary score similarity expressed by the variant aspects of each task performance. Such similarity can be interpreted as reflecting commonality, or at least family resemblance, in the samples of response components, or component assemblies, or changes in such assemblies over time, that are called for by the correlated tasks. The correlational structures obtained in various ability and learning task matrices suggest task families or clusters, but also graded series of tasks or simplexes and other dimensional arrays of tasks, including circumplexes. Though derived from between-task, across-person correlations, it would be wrong to suppose that such structures say nothing about within-person or within-task structures. Certainly, simplex, circumplex, or radex structures are not themselves models of within-person or within-task structures. But these correlational structures provide hypotheses about the latter types of structure.

The response sampling view laid out earlier suggested that two highly correlated tasks require similar response component samples. Examination of the two tasks can suggest what aspects of task requirements are similar and, thus, hypotheses about the variant components or assemblies demanded within each task. Also, because individuals performing successfully on a task differ from individuals performing less successfully in how well the response sampling they can produce matches the demands of the task, such differences lead to hypotheses about the variant response components and assemblies residing within each individual. Comparisons between single pairs of tasks and pairs of persons are problematic, because a pair of objects can be similar or different in many characteristics. But this problem is reduced when large ranges of tasks can be studied and when multiples of tasks can be ordered systematically rather than simply paired or clustered.

When task scalings yield content distinctions they suggest that different variant response assemblies are required within persons to handle different kinds of task content, and that similar content requires similar response assemblies within persons; some persons possess them or can produce them and some do not or cannot. But the continuous character of the circumplex helps identify tasks with various mixtures of content requirements and thus various mixtures of response sampling. Componential experimental analysis of such ranges of tasks, rather than individual tasks in isolation, should increase the probability that the important variant components within persons are discovered.

The simplex orderings of tasks produce similar opportunities. As a range of tasks shows an orderly progression of increases or decreases in apparent complexity, they suggest a similar progressive change in the component assemblies required within individuals. Again, if increasing correlation with G across tasks can be thought of as a graded series of steps, one is more likely to isolate the within-person components that contribute to this increase by analyzing appropriately chosen pairs of tasks along the gradient of complexity than by studying isolated tasks.

The Radex Map

All cognitive tasks exist in a correlational network, referred to in the factor-analytic tradition as the positive manifold. The radex model provides a structure for that network that suggests how sets of tasks should be chosen for more intensive study so as to reach early solid payoff. It offers a guideline through the network in that sense.

Figure 2.9 has been constructed as an idealized radex showing some of the ability and learning tasks studied in this chapter. Tasks have been selected and placed in this idealized version based on the results of our various analyses and reanalyses, and on our intuitions. Some of our scalings were rotated or reflected so that the content wedges could be assigned a fixed location in the figure. We have not attempted to include all types of tests or all ability factors.

In the center of the radex is Raven Progressive Matrices, our choice as the best measure of G. Ranged immediately around this are highly complex tests which, though based on verbal, numerical or spatial-figural content, probably reflect the complex processes of general intelligence, or of G_c, G_f, and G_v, more than they reflect content differences. The rest of the radex is divided into content areas. In each, we have attempted to construct one or more simplex series of ability and learning tasks. There is only one simplex for the numerical domain, that obtained from Figure 2.3. However, learning tasks of comparable sorts can easily be constructed. In the verbal domain, there are two simplexes for ability tasks and one for learning tasks. Word fluency tasks stand at the simplest level, just outside the circle. In the spatial domain; similarly, there are two ability and one learning simplex, with closure speed tasks at the simplest level outside the circle. Memory span and perceptual speed tasks are placed at the simplest level in the upper left and right hand regions on the content distinctions they seem to straddle, respectively. One could argue with some of these task placements. Reading Comprehension, for example, appears at a relatively simple level here because Thurstone's fairly simple tasks scaled in this region. But of course more complex comprehension tasks could be constructed and placed closer to the center.

Our purpose in presenting this figure is to suggest that task analyses of the sort demonstrated by Carroll (1976), and by the experimental studies of an increasing number of cognitive psychologists, ought to address collections of tasks of this sort programmatically. It is not suggested that the tasks shown are the only tasks of interest; other radex collections could certainly be constructed from other scaling configurations. It is suggested, however, that systematic analysis of the

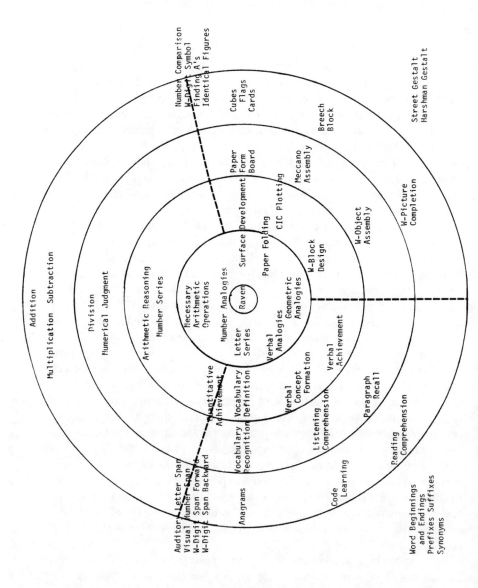

FIG. 2.9. Hypothetical radex map showing suggested ability and learning simplexes and the content circumplex.

relationships in some such map will provide the shortest route to a theory of intelligence.

The Complexity Continuum

We take the complexity continuum of the radex model to be the most important single feature of the correlational evidence on cognitive tasks amassed to date. The correlation of a task with G approximates the apparent complexity of its required cognitive operations. The simplex arrays of the radex model order tasks in graded series with respect to this increasing complexity, separately for different kinds of task content. Thus, understanding G means understanding these gradations of complexity, and the radex map provides a means of choosing tasks for study so as to optimize the research route toward the primary goal of a theory of intelligence, as suggested above.

In this last section, we try to sharpen some alternative hypotheses about the nature of complexity and summarize the implications derivable from the re-analyses reported in this chapter. We also propose an addition to the generalized radex map that emphasizes its topography. Some further suggestions for substantive and methodological studies are also given.

Complexity in Ability Tests. In his review of hierarchical theories of intelligence, Jensen (1970) stated the complexity hypothesis with respect to G and added an important qualification:

> This complexity continuum is not the same as difficulty *per se*. Repeating a series of 10 digits, for example, is a dificult task if judged by the percentage of the population who can do it, but in a more fundamental psychological sense it is a less complex task than answering the question: 'In what way are a banana and an orange alike?' An echo chamber or a tape recorder can repeat a 10–digit series, but a relatively complex computer would be required to 'infer' the correct superordinate category, given two subordinates, as in the banana-orange question [p. 147].

Guttman (1965) also added an important qualification in attempting to reconcile his earlier hypothesis about a radial expansion of complexity with the fact that complex tests scale in the center of the radex. He distinguished "analysis" and "achievement," noting that "complexity is not the same thing as analyticity (the distinction between being complex or simple is not the same as the distinction between analysis and achievement) [p. 34]."

We would agree that complexity is not just difficulty or analyticity, though these may be aspects of complexity. Because it is not just analytic tests, however, but also complex achievement tests that seem to scale towad the center of the radex, we consider complexity rather than analyticity, per se, as the more general concept. "Achievement" tests range from simple to complex just as do "ability" tests (Snow, 1980b).

The formal definition of a simplex provides one hypothesis about the nature of complexity, as noted earlier. As one steps in from task to task along any one simplex array in the radex, performance components are added; each task requires all of the components involved in the next simpler (more peripheral) task, plus additional components. In his formulation of the simplex, Guttman (1954) did not define these performance components substantively. Nonetheless, it is possible that more complex tasks differ from less complex tasks simply in the number of response components that must be assembled into a performance program to meet task demands. Some recent studies have demonstrated that objective manipulation of task components designed to increase complexity also increase correlation with G, in both the figural-spatial (Lohman, 1979a) and verbal content domains (Marshalek, 1981).

A second hypothesis is also possible, however; increases in apparent complexity from task to task may reflect the increased involvement of one or more centrally important components, rather than simply an increase in the number of components involved in performance. Such a component (or component assembly) might be identified as one reflecting Guttman's (1970) rule-inferring process or Spearman's (1927) eduction of relations and eduction of correlates, for example, or some of the components that Sternberg (1979) has found centrally involved in many kinds of reasoning tasks.

Another related possibility is that the speed of executing any given component differs from person to person and that this reaction time differential accumulates as the number of components involved in performance accumulates across tasks, or as the operation of some central component is more critical or more frequent in the performance program for a task. Jensen and Figueroa (1975) first noticed that the backward digit span task seemed always to be more highly correlated with G, i.e., more complex, than forward digit span. This appears also in our multidimensional scaling in Figure 2.2. Impressed by the apparent complexity difference in an apparently simple and homogeneous pair of tasks, Jensen (1981) has now gone on to posit a "speed of information processing" hypothesis that might operate as suggested above. He has developed a reaction time paradigm in which "the relationship of g loadings to differences in task complexity among tasks that are very homogeneous in terms of test format, content, and fundamental task requirements [pp. 40–41]" can be investigated. Initial studies suggest that rather high correlations with G can be obtained for reaction time parameters reflecting speed at increasing levels of task complexity (defined as uncertainty in his task). The highest correlations with G seem to come from a parameter reflecting intraindividual variability—higher oscillation relates to higher G (Jensen, 1982).

Still a fourth hypothesis can be studied. More complex tasks may require more involvement of executive assembly and control processes that organize and monitor the operation of response components assembled into a performance program for the task. In particular, complex tasks seem to require adaptation or strategy-shifting within and between items as task performance proceeds in a task, and between tasks. Kyllonen, Woltz, and Lohman (1981) have demonstrated that strategy shift models designed to reflect this sort of adaptation do indeed correlate with complex mental tests. Snow (1980a) has shown eye movement patterns during test performance that also seem to suggest this phenomenon and has discussed the hypothesis in more detail (Snow, 1981). It is tempting to relate these strategy-shifting differences to Jensen's intraindividual variability in reaction time, but this possibility has not been studied. Thus, increasing correlation with G, and increasing correlation among superficially different tasks as one moves up the complexity continuum, may reflect increasing variance due to executive, control, and adaptive functions. It may be that the response component assemblies for simple tasks on the periphery of the radex are more automatic and repetitive and thus less in need of item-to-item adaptation. Such specificity and automaticity would also account for the low correlations among tasks at the periphery of the radex (see also Sternberg, 1981a).

It is possible of course that increases in apparent processing complexity reflect some combination of all of these sources: more components, more central components, more adaptive or flexible organization of components, and more accumulated differences in associated reaction times. It is also possible that different sources of complexity operate and accumulate in different content regions of the radex.

Figure 2.10 has been constructed from our hypothetical scaling example in Figure 2.1 to suggest this. In the verbal or numerical domain, for example, a simplex progression might involve an orderly addition of components as one moved from task to task toward the center of the radex, much as Thurstone's numerical tasks displayed in Figures 2.3 and 2.4, and in our idealized Figure 2.9. Each task adds an additional component or an additional assembly of components. The process of assembly and reassembly is more complicated as there are more components, so there is more executive control involved, and a central reasoning component is also increasingly involved, perhaps at both a primary componential and an executive or metacomponential level. Because all the components differ parametrically in reaction time across persons, substantial reaction time differences also accumulate. In the figural-spatial domain, however, there is little or no progression. Tasks remain simple and separate until a certain component (e.g., three-dimensional visualization) is sampled by complex spatial tasks. This causes the need for executive processing also, and high correlation with other complex but nonspatial tests. Lohman (1979b) has conducted extensive reanalyses of figural and spatial test batteries, concluding that spatial abilities do not fit neatly into a hierarchical model, as do verbal and numerical abilities, so this example is not far fetched.

This simple hypothetical figure suggests the possible topography of the radex,

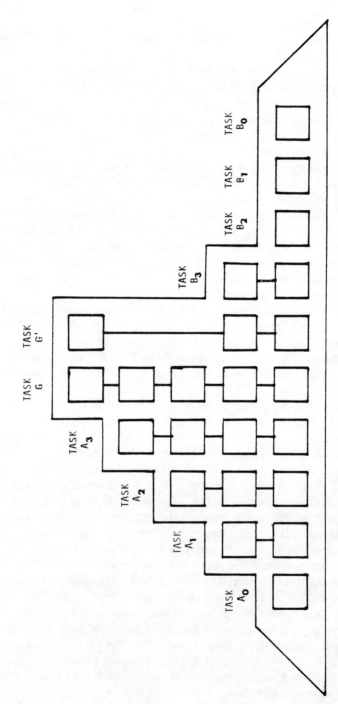

FIG. 2.10. Hypothetical cross section of the radex map showing the simplex progression of components in two content areas.

just as the circumplex contour lines drawn into Figures 2.2, 2.3, 2.5 and 2.9 suggest tiers or elevations associated with increasing correlation with G. It is perhaps the third dimension of the radex that Carroll (1980) had in mind; here, however, it is not a third dimension in the conventional scaling sense. Rather it is a theoretical, schematic cross section of the radex "mountain." In effect, complex ability tests and factors, such as G_c, G_f, and G_v scale in the upper highlands near the peak, various minor group factors scale somewhat further down the slope in various directions, and simple, specific abilities are scattered in the lowlands.

Complexity in Learning.   Learning tasks, like ability tests, should also scale along the slopes of the radex mountain. Tasks of the sort studied by Allison and Stake are likely to be simple or of intermediate complexity; only a few are complex, and our scaling results in Figures 2.7 and 2.8, as well as our larger scalings described in the text, are consistent with this expectation. Laboratory learning tasks often contain a kind of ceiling; they end in perfect or near-perfect performance if practice is extended far enough. Individual differences, if any, in late trials, are likely to reflect task-specific factors; early trials might show more complexity, in the sense of more components or more assembly, reassembly and executive control of components. Correlations for earlier trials with more complex ability tests should be higher than for later trials. Indeed, this is precisely what Fleishman's research has often shown with psychomotor learning tasks (see Fleishman, 1962, 1972; Fleishman & Hempel, 1954). Fleishman's learning trial interrelations typically displayed simplex form. Jones (1962) also has interpreted learning as a process of simplification because the simplex model seems to offer the best account of virtually all learning trial intercorrelations ever reported. One would expect, then, that as a task is learned, components are removed; that is, their contribution to variance is diminished. Scaling the earlier trials of such a task would place it nearer the center of the radex; scaling the later trials would move it toward the periphery. Cronbach and Snow (1977), however, have noted a misinterpretation of such data. Complex ability tests can correlate with early trials and not with late trials, not because abilities are involved early and not late, but because more able students do their cognitive organizational work faster or earlier in learning, whereas less able learners do their cognitive organizational work slower or later in learning; over trials then, correlations of learning gains with ability tests are in effect changing from positive to negative. It is of course possible that both interpretations are correct—more able learners may do their cognitive work earlier and may also involve more or different cognitive components in this work, than do less able learners.

Cronbach and Snow (1977) also showed that, in learning tasks of the sort represented by sequences of school lessons, complex abilities correlated with later as well as earlier performance. Unlike laboratory tasks, such learning tasks have no clear ceiling; completion leads to new tasks or stages that incorporate or call up new samples of components. The progressive stages of school mathematics learning is a good example, and these might parallel the quasi-simplicial relations among Thurstone's Numerical Factor tasks. For such series, learning may be better seen as a process of complex accumulation in the radex topography; more able learners stay ahead of less able learners in adding components and also perhaps in using more or different components in this process. Many complex learning tasks are of this character, and it is noteworthy that learning curve parameters in these sorts of tasks correlate highly with general abilities (see, e.g., Snow, Wescourt, & Collins, 1980). As learning becomes complex, higher correlations with complex ability tests should be expected; such tasks would be expected to scale more toward the center of the radex than would most laboratory tasks. Finally, school achievement tests that summarize the accumulation of much complex learning over long periods, correlate highly with G, and ultimately define G_c in radex scalings such as our Figure 2.2.

Further research might hope to distinguish different kinds of complexity, in both ability and learning tasks, by examining implications of the different mathematical models that can generate simplicial structures. There are at least six types of simplex models, according to Jöreskog (1970). Jones (1962) has demonstrated how one might think substantively about some alternative underlying models (see also Corballis, 1965; Mulaik, 1975).

Response Sampling and the Fluid-Crystallized Distinction

It follows that the distinction between fluid and crystallized ability is not merely a distinction between two fairly general factors, even though factor analysis represents it this way. In the more continuous space of the radex model, the distinction is better seen as reflecting the regional reference or sphere of relative influence of two aspects of cognitive functioning, or two kinds of response sampling. Clearly, the human cognitive system must somehow be geared to acquire, retain, and reuse concepts and procedures that will aid in new learning and problem-solving tasks. But the system must also be geared to adapt these previously crystallized concepts and procedures and to assemble new ones, because the new tasks to be faced may differ appreciably from those experienced in the past. Some tests or tasks are relatively familiar; some are relatively novel. The more novel the task, the more fluid and facile must be the adaptation process, if successful performance is to be achieved. The fluid and crystallized regions of the radex reflect this variation in emphasis between the demands of more novel and more familiar tests and tasks (see Snow, 1981).

It is superficial, we believe, to equate the crystallized-fluid distinction with a content-process or verbal-nonverbal distinction. There is a healthy tension today between process-oriented theories (see, e.g., Sternberg, 1981a) and content- or knowledge-oriented theories (see, e.g., Chi, Glaser, & Rees, 1981). But it is likely that both knowledge structures and process structures are involved in all task performances. There are now the beginnings of theories that show how they might integrate in both verbal (Marshalek, 1981; Sternberg & Powell, in press) and nonverbal (Lesgold, Feltovich, Glaser, & Wang, 1981) task domains.

Our scaling reanalyses of the Thurstone data show the fluid-crystallized distinction quite clearly, even though prior attempts at reanalyzing those data with other factor methods have not done so. The distinction appears also in our scalings of the Allison and Stake learning matrices. Our reading of the learning task descriptions provided by those authors suggests strongly that the fluid-crystallized distinction corresponds to the relative novelty vs. familiarity of the tasks used. Thus, the distinction applies to both ability tests and learning tasks and, along with the complexity continuum, allows both tests and tasks to be located in the same radex space.

Conclusion

The radex map implies a topography built of underlying cognitive and learning components sampled by the demands of particular tasks. The map organizes much correlational data on ability tests and learning tasks. Correlational research can continue to explore and elaborate the map. But it cannot alone distinguish and test the various process interpretations of cognitive organization and change noted above. The map can, however, guide analytic experiments of the sort designed by Sternberg (1977, 1979) to determine what components are being added or changed as one moves from task to task along the various complexity continua in the radex. Strategy-shift models of the sort studied by Snow (1980a, 1981) and Kyllonen, Woltz, and Lohman (1981) can be used to detect adaptive changes in component assemblies along these continua. And computer models of the sort designed by Anderson, Kline, and Beasley (1980) can suggest how this adaptive, additive process might work. A unification of correlational and experimental theories of intelligence and learning should be the result.

ACKNOWLEDGMENTS

The work reported in this chapter was partly supported by the Personnel and Training Research Programs, Office of Naval Research, under Contract No. N000014–79–C–0171 to Richard E. Snow. The views and conclusions contained in this document are those of the authors and should not be interpreted as necessarily representing the official policies, either expressed or implied, of the Office of Naval Research or the U.S. Government. Support for this work by a James McKeen Cattell Fund award to the senior author is also gratefully acknowledged.

REFERENCES

Allison, R. B., Jr. *Learning parameters and human abilities*. Unpublished doctoral dissertation, Educational Testing Service and Princeton University, Princeton, N.J., 1960.

Anastasi, A. On the formation of psychological traits. *American Psychologist*, 1970, *25*, 899–910.

Anderson, J. R., Kline, P. J., & Beasley, C. M. Complex learning processes. In R. E. Snow, P-A Federico & W. E. Montague (Eds.), *Aptitude, learning and instruction* (Vol. 1): *Cognitive process analyses of aptitude*. Hillsdale, N.J.: Lawrence Erlbaum Associates, 1980.

Carroll, J. B. Psychometric tests as cognitive tasks: A new "Structure of Intellect". In Resnick, L. B. (Ed.), *The nature of intelligence*. Hillsdale, N.J.: Lawrence Erlbaum Associates, 1976.

Carroll, J. B. Discussion: Aptitude processes, theory and the real world. In R. E. Snow, P-A Federico & W. E. Montague (Eds.), *Aptitude, learning, and instruction* (Vol. 1): *Cognitive process analyses of aptitude*. Hillsdale, N.J.: Lawrence Erlbaum Associates, 1980.

Cattell, R. B. Theory of fluid and crystallized intelligence: A critical experiment. *Journal of Educational Psychology*, 1963, *54*, 1–22.

Cattell, R. B. *Abilities: Their structure, growth, and action*. Boston: Houghton Mifflin, 1971.

Chi, M. T. H., Glaser, R., & Rees, E. Expertise in problem solving. In R. Sternberg (Ed.), *Advances in the psychology of human intelligence* (Vol. 1). Hillsdale, N.J.: Lawrence Erlbaum Associates, 1981.

Corballis, M. C. Practice and the simplex. *Psychological Review*, 1965, *72*, 339–406.

Cronbach, L. J. *Essentials of psychological testing*. New York: Harper and Row, 1970.

Cronbach, L. J. & Snow, R. E. *Aptitudes and instructional methods*. New York: Irvington, 1977.

Eysenck, H. J. Primary mental abilities. *British Journal of Educational Psychology*, 1939, *9*, 270–275.

Ferguson, G. A. On learning and human ability. *Canadian Journal of Psychology*, 1954, *8*, 95–112.

Ferguson, G. A. On transfer and the abilities of man. *Canadian Journal of Psychology*, 1956, *10*, 121–131.

Fleishman, E. A. The description and prediction of perceptual-motor skill learning. In R. Glaser (Ed.), *Training research and education*. Pittsburgh: University of Pittsburgh Press, 1962.

Fleishman, E. A. On the relation between abilities, learning, and human performance. *American Psychologist*, 1972, *11*, 1017–1032.

Fleishman, E. A. & Hempel, W. E., Jr. Changes in factor structure of a complex psychomotor test as a function of practice. *Psychometrika*, 1954, *19*, 239–252.

Frederiksen, J. R. Component skills in reading: Measurement of individual differences through chronometric analysis. In R. E. Snow, P-A Federico & W. E. Montague (Eds.), *Aptitude, learning, and instruction* (Vol. 1): *Cognitive process analyses of aptitude*. Hillsdale, N.J.: Lawrence Erlbaum Associates, 1980.

Garrett, H. E. A developmental theory of intelligence. *American Psychologist*, 1946, *1*, 372–378.

Glaser, R. Some implications of previous work on learning and individual differences. In R. M. Gagné (Ed.), *Learning and individual differences*. Columbus, Ohio: Merrill, 1967.

Guilford, J. P. *The nature of human intelligence*. New York: McGraw-Hill, 1967.

Guilford, J. P. Cognitive psychology's ambiguities: Some suggested remedies. *Psychological Review*, 1982, *89*, 48–59.

Gulliksen, H. A. Measurement of learning and mental abilities. *Psychometrika*, 1961, *26*, 93–107.

Guttman, L. A new approach to factor analysis: The radex. In P. F. Lazerfield (Ed.), *Mathematical thinking in the social sciences*. Glencoe, Ill.: Free Press, 1954.

Guttman, L. The structure of interrelations among intelligence tests. In *Proceedings of the 1964 invitational conference on testing problems*. Princeton, N.J.: Educational Testing Service, 1965.

Guttman, L. A general nonmetric technique for finding the smallest coordinate space for a configuration of points. *Psychometrika*, 1968, *33*, 469–506.

Guttman, L. Integration of test design and analysis. In *Proceedings of the 1969 conference on testing problems*. Princeton, N.J.: Educational Testing Service, 1970.

Haynes, J. R. Hierarchical analysis of factors in cognition. *American Educational Research Journal*, 1970, *7*, 55–68.

Holzinger, K. J. & Harman, H. H. Comparison of two factor analyses. *Psychometrika*, 1938, *3*, 45–60.

Horn, J. L. Human abilities: A review of research and theory in the early 1970s. *Annual Review of Psychology*, 1976, *27*, 437–485.

Humphreys, L. G. The organization of human abilities. *American Psychologist*, 1962, *17*, 475–483.

Humphreys, L. G. Theory of intelligence. In R. Cancra (Ed.), *Intelligence: Genetic and environmental influences*. New York: Grune & Stratton, 1971.

Humphreys, L. G. The construct of general intelligence. *Intelligence*, 1979, *3*, 105–120.

Jensen, A. R. Hierarchical theories of mental ability. In W. B. Dockrell (Ed.), *On Intelligence*. London: Methuen, 1970.

Jensen, A. R. The chronometry of intelligence. In R. J. Sternberg (Ed.), *Advances in the psychology of human intelligence* (Vol. 1). Hillsdale, N.J.: Lawrence Erlbaum Associates, 1982.

Jensen, A. R. & Figueroa, R. A. Forward and backward digit span interaction with race and IQ: Predictions from Jensen's theory. *Journal of Educational Psychology*, 1975, *67*, 882–893.

Jensen, A. R. *Test validity: g vs. the specificity doctrine*. Paper presented to the American Psychological Association, Los Angeles, August 1981.

Jones, M. B. Practice as a process of simplification. *Psychological Review*, 1962, *69*, 274–294.

Jöreskog, K. G. Estimation and testing of simplex models. *British Journal of Mathematical and Statistical Psychology*, 1970, *23*, 121–230.

Korth, B. Exploratory Factor Analysis. In D. J. Amick & H. J. Walberg (Eds.), *Introductory multivariate analysis*. Berkeley, Calif.: McCutchan, 1975. (a)

Korth, B. Rotations in Exploratory Factor Analysis. In D. J. Amick & H. J. Walberg (Eds.), *Introductory multivariate analysis*. Berkeley, Calif.: McCutchan, 1975. (b)

Kruskal, J. B. Multidimensional scaling by optimizing goodness of fit to a nonmetric hypothesis. *Psychometrika*, 1964, *29*, 1–27. (a)

Kruskal, J. B. Nonmetric multidimensional scaling: A numerical method. *Psychometrika*, 1964, *29*, 28–42. (b)

Kruskal, J. B. & Wish, M. *Multidimensional scaling*. Beverly Hills, Calif.: Sage, 1978.

Kruskal, J. B., Young, F. W., & Seery, J. B. *How to use KYST, a very flexible program to do multidimensional scaling and unfolding*. Unpublished paper, Bell Telephone Laboratories, 1973.

Kyllonen, P. C., Marshalek, B.,& Snow, R. E. *Spatial and tree representations of cognitive task interrelations*. Unpublished paper, School of Education, Stanford University, 1982.

Kyllonen, P. C., Woltz, D. J., & Lohman, D. F. *Models of strategy and strategy-shifting in spatial visualization performance* (Tech. Rep. No. 17). Stanford, Calif.: Aptitude Research Project, School of Education, Stanford University, 1981.

Lesgold, A. M., Feltovich, P., Glaser, R., & Wang, Y. *Radiological expertise*. Paper presented to the American Educational Research Association, Los Angeles, April 1981.

Lohman, D. F. *Spatial ability: Individual differences in speed and level* (Tech. Rep. No. 9). Stanford, Calif.: Aptitude Research Project, School of Education, Stanford University, 1979. (a)

Lohman, D. F. *Spatial ability: A review and reanalysis of the correlational literature* (Tech. Rep. No. 8). Stanford, Calif.: Aptitude Research Project, School of Education, Stanford University, 1979. (b)

Marshalek, B. *The complexity dimension in the radex and hierarchical models of intelligence*. Paper presented to the American Psychological Association, San Francisco, August 1977.

Marshalek, B. *Trait and process aspects of vocabulary knowledge and verbal ability* (Tech. Rep. No. 15). Stanford, Calif.: Aptitude Research Project, School of Education, Stanford, University, 1981.

Marshalek, B., Lohman, D. F., & Snow, R. The complexity continuum in the radex and hierarchical models of intelligence. *Intelligence,* in press.

Mulaik, S. A. Confirmatory factor analysis. In D. J. Amick and H. J. Walberg (Eds.), *Introductory multivariate analysis.* Berkeley, Calif.: McCutchan, 1975.

Pellegrino, J. W. & Glaser, R. Components of inductive reasoning. In R. E. Snow, P-A Federico, & W. E. Montague (Eds.), *Aptitude, learning, and instruction* (Vol. 1): *Cognitive process analyses of aptitude.* Hillsdale, N.J.: Lawrence Erlbaum Associates, 1980.

Pruzansky, S., Tversky, A., & Carroll, J. D. Spatial vs. tree representations of proximity data. *Psychometrika,* in press.

Rose, A. M. Information-processing abilities. In R. E. Snow, P. A. Federico, & W. E. Montague (Eds.), *Aptitude, learning, and instruction* (Vol. 1): *Cognitive process analyses of aptitude.* Hillsdale, N.J.: Lawrence Erlbaum Associates, 1980.

Sattath, S. & Tversky, A. Additive similarity trees. *Psychometrika,* 1977, *42,* 319–345.

Schlesinger, I. M. & Guttman, L. Smallest space analysis of intelligence and achievement tests. *Psychological Bulletin,* 1969, *71,* 95–100.

Schmid, J. & Leiman, J. The development of hierarchical factor solutions. *Psychometrika,* 1957, *22,* 53–61.

Shepard, R. N. The analysis of proximities: Multidimensional scaling with an unknown distance function (I & II). *Psychometrika,* 1962, *27,* 125–140 and 217–246.

Shepard, R. N. Representation of structure in similarity data: Problems and prospects. *Psychometrika,* 1974, *37,* 373–421.

Shepard, R. N., Romney, A. K., & Nerlove, S. B. (Eds.), *Multidimensional scaling: Theory and applications in the behavioral sciences* (Vol. 1). New York: Seminar Press, 1972.

Snow, R. E. Theory and method for research on aptitude processes. *Intelligence,* 1978, *2,* 225–278.

Snow, R. E. Aptitude processes. In R. E. Snow, P. A. Federico, & W. E. Montague (Eds.), *Aptitude, learning, and instruction* (Vol. 1): *Cognitive process analyses of aptitude.* Hillsdale, N.J.: Lawrence Erlbaum Associates, 1980. (a)

Snow, R. E. Aptitude and achievement. *New directions for testing and measurement,* 1980, *5,* 39–59. (b)

Snow, R. E. Toward a theory of aptitude for learning: I. Fluid and crystallized abilities and their correlates. In M. P. Friedman, J. P. Das, & N. O'Connor (Eds.), *Intelligence and learning.* New York: Plenum, 1981.

Snow, R. E. Education and intelligence. In R. J. Sternberg (Ed.), *Handbook of Human Intelligence.* New York: Cambridge University Press, 1982.

Snow, R. E., Lohman, D. F., Marshalek, B., Yalow, E., & Webb, N. *Correlational analyses of reference aptitude constructs* (Tech. Rep. No. 5). Stanford, Calif.: Aptitude Research Project, School of Education, Stanford University, 1977.

Snow, R. E., Wescourt, K., & Collins, J. *Individual differences in aptitude and learning from interactive computer-based instruction* (Tech. Rep. No. 10). Stanford, Calif.: Aptitude Research Project, School of Education, Stanford University, 1980.

Spearman, C. "General Intelligence": Objectively determined and measured. *American Journal of Psychology,* 1904, *15,* 201–292.

Spearman, C. *The nature of intelligence and the principles of cognition.* London: MacMillan, 1923.

Spearman, C. *The abilities of man.* New York: MacMillan, 1927.

Stake, R. E. Learning parameters, aptitudes, and achievement. *Psychometric Monographs,* 1961 (No. 9).

Sternberg, R. J. *Intelligence, information processing and analogical reasoning: The componential analysis of human abilities.* Hillsdale, N.J.: Lawrence Erlbaum Associates, 1977.

Sternberg, R. J. The nature of mental abilities. *American Psychologist,* 1979, *34,* 214–230.

Sternberg, R. J. The evolution of theories of intelligence. *Intelligence,* 1981, *5,* 209–230. (a)

Sternberg, R. J. Toward a unified componential theory of intelligence: I. Fluid ability. In M. P.

Friedman, J. P. Das, & N. O'Connor (Eds.), *Intelligence and Learning*. New York: Plenum, 1981. (b)

Sternberg, R. J. & Powell, J. S. Comprehending verbal comprehension. *American Psychologist,* in press.

Thomson, G. H. On the cause of hierarchical order among correlation coefficients. *Proceedings of the Royal Society,* A, 1919, *95.*

Thomson, G. H. *The factorial analysis of human ability.* London: University of London Press, 1939.

Thurstone, L. L. Primary mental abilities. *Psychometric Monographs,* 1938 (No. 1).

Thurstone, L. L. & Thurstone, T. G. Factorial studies of intelligence. *Psychometric Monographs,* 1941 (No. 2).

Varella, J. A. Elaboration of Guilford's SI model. *Psychological Review,* 1969, *76,* 332–336.

Vernon, P. E. *The structure of human abilities.* New York: Wiley, 1950.

Vernon, P. E. Ability factors and environmental influences. *American Psychologist,* 1965, *20,* 723–733.

Vernon, P. E. *Intelligence and cultural environment.* London: Methuen, 1969.

Wherry, R. J. Hierarchical factor solutions without rotations. *Psychometrika,* 1959, *24,* 45–51.

Winer, B. J. *Statistical principles in experimental design.* New York: McGraw-Hill, 1962.

Zimmerman, W. S. A revised orthogonal rotation solution for Thurstone's original primary mental abilities test battery. *Psychometrika,* 1953, *18,* 77–93.

3 Reasoning as a Central Intellective Ability

Lance J. Rips
Behavioral Sciences Department
University of Chicago

INTRODUCTION

There was a time when a theory of reasoning was a serious concern as part of a yet more general theory of mental structure. In L. L. Thurstone's 1938 account, *Primary mental abilities,* reasoning was singled out as an especially appropriate object of study, since one could ask, "How many reasoning abilities are there, and just what is each of them like? [p. 2]." Thurstone's program (and those of his followers) was to assemble pencil-and-paper tests that seemed to tap some aspect of reasoning: syllogism tests, series tests, analogies tests, arithmetic word problems, geometrical puzzles, classification problems, and so forth. The investigators administered the battery to a large group of subjects, correlated subjects' test scores for each pair of tests, and submitted the correlation matrix to factor analysis. The hope was that the revealed factors would "isolate and define more precisely primary abilities in the domain of reasoning" (Green, Guilford, Christensen, & Comrey, 1955, p. 135). Thurstone himself claimed to have identified at least two such reasoning components in his data: an "Inductive" factor most clearly represented in tests like Number Series ("Find the rule in the series below and fill in the blanks: 16, 20, —, 30, 36, 42, 49, —") and a "Deductive" factor associated with such tests as Nonsense Syllogisms ("Good or bad reasoning?: Red-haired persons have big feet. All june bugs have big feet. Therefore, some june bugs are red haired.").[1]

---

[1]Thurstone (1938) also identified a separate factor associated with arithmetic word problems; however, it is somewhat unclear whether he regarded this as a third type of reasoning ability.

But in the 1950s, this pleasing induction/deduction distinction began to splinter. Adkins and Lyerly (1952) suggested that there were at least three factors that were together responsible for induction: perception of abstract similarities, concept formation, and hypothesis verification. Green et al. (1953) also proposed dividing induction into three factors, but a different three, which they termed "eduction of perceptual relations," "eduction of conceptual relations," and "eduction of conceptual patterns." In addition, Green et al.'s analysis produced several other factors that they took to be related to reasoning: A "general reasoning" factor connected with arithmetic word problems, a "symbol substitution" factor responsible for numeric equations, and a factor for "eduction of correlates" having to do with completion-type analogies. In much the same way, recent studies of deduction have shown that what once seemed a unitary factor is more likely a composite of elementary abilities (e.g., Sternberg, 1980).

Partly because of conflicting results like these, nobody much believes these days that factor analysis will provide a royal road to a theory of reasoning. But the demise of this purely psychometric approach leaves us without any obvious candidates to fill the position it vacated. If factor analysis can't provide a framework for the psychology of reasoning, what will?

There appear to be two main reactions to this situation—one a kind of principled pessimism, the other a guarded optimism. According to the pessimistic alternative, no adequate theory of reasoning is possible. It may be, for example, that people are constituted in such a way that what we call reasoning is only a collection of ad hoc methods that are constructed on the fly to deal with particular tasks. Psychological laws of reasoning do not exist on this account, although for any given instance of reasoning we can come up with an explanation in terms of more specific cognitive mechanisms (e.g., retrieval and comparison operations) and more general problem-solving schemes (e.g., means-ends analysis). This position is consistent with opinions expressed recently by Newell (1980) and others.

The opposing view—the one I would like to defend—admits that although we don't have a theory of reasoning that is as embracing as the one Thurstone dreamed of, we do have prospects for a theory of deductive reasoning that at least meets some of the tests of adequacy. Theories of this type were introduced by Osherson (1974, 1975, 1976) in a series of monographs on children's logical abilities and related models have since been proposed by Braine (1978), Johnson-Laird (1975), and myself (Rips, 1983). These theories attempt to explain the mental goings on when subjects reason about propositional arguments, that is, arguments whose validity turns on sentence connectives such as *and, or, not, if . . . then . . . ,* and *neither . . . nor . . . .* Extensions of the theories have also been proposed for a fragment of predicate logic (Osherson, 1976), and for modal operators like *cause* (Osherson, 1975; Rips, 1983), *necessity,* and *obligation* (Osherson, 1976). The theories apply to tasks in which subjects evaluate the validity of arguments, produce conclusions to stated premises, and remember or judge the naturalness of proofs. According to the point of view represented by these theories, the reasons offered in support of the pessimistic view are incorrect, so that even if the above models should turn out to be empirically wrong, we should still keep looking for the right ones.

An adequate defense of the optimistic position requires several steps that set the agenda for this chapter. The basic theme begins with the idea that cognitive explanations of intelligent behavior presuppose a concept of reasoning that meets certain criteria. These requirements are set out in Section 1 under the headings of *centrality, generativity,* and *generality.* Section 2 examines the pessimistic view and tries to show that neither abstract problem-solving abilities nor task-specific strategies are likely to explain reasoning in a way that satisfies the cognitive requirements. By contrast, the third and fourth sections give some reasons to believe that the deduction models mentioned above can meet them, at least in principle. As a concrete example, I'll describe one such model that I've developed, the evidence that supports the model, and the prospects for extending it to a general theory. The conclusions reached in Sections 1 and 2 are applicable, I hope, to reasoning in the broadest sense, including probabilistic or plausible reasoning (e.g., Collins, 1978). I use "reasoning" and "inference" interchangeably to refer to this overall ability. Sections 3 and 4 concentrate on deduction as a special case. This reflects in part my greater familiarity with research on deduction, and in part the greater availability of deduction theories in both logic and psychology. However, I don't want to imply that no progress has been made in other areas of reasoning, and interested readers should consult Collins (1978), Nisbett and Ross (1980), and Pellegrino and Glaser (1980) for discussions of the psychology of nondemonstrative inference.

CHARACTERISTICS OF A THEORY OF REASONING

Reasoning has some unique aspects that distinguish it from related abilities, aspects that any adequate cognitive psychology must explain. One such aspect is that reasoning occupies a central position in our explanations of behavior, partly because these explanations are themselves instances of reasoning and presuppose like abilities on the part of those whose actions are being explained. Second, reasoning, like language, is productive, and this potential for creating and understanding arguments means that reasoning mechanisms must be extendable to a broad domain. A related point is that any successful theory of this kind must be general in accounting for subject differences and task differences of the usual sort. Taken together, these characteristics serve to eliminate as serious contenders certain views of reasoning and provide design features for a correct theory.

Centrality

Some cognitive processes are more fundamental than others in an explanation of mental phenomena. Keeping score in tennis is a cognitive process, but one that's less central than the arithmetic procedures on which it is based. Understanding the poem "An Ordinary Evening in New Haven" is less fundamental than the lexical, syntactic, and semantic abilities that are responsible for it. Learning to juggle is less essential than learning component skills like grasping or throwing. The centrality of a cognitive process is probably due to a combination of factors, as is the centrality of other actions or routines (Galambos & Rips, 1982). But very roughly speaking, a cognitive process C1 is more central than another C2, if an individual, a human cognizer, can do C1 without doing C2 but not C2 without C1. Obviously, someone can do basic arithmetic without thereby keeping score in tennis, since keeping score includes other factors such as knowledge of the rules of the game, perceptual recognition, and so on. It's more difficult, though maybe not impossible, to envision tennis score keeping without arithmetic, our mental architecture being what it is.[2]

The kind of centrality I have in mind is a matter of on-going processes, not of developmental or other preconditions. It may be, for example, that arithmetic skill develops within the context of particular sorts of counting tasks like keeping score in games or enumerating blocks in a pile. For all I know, these tasks may be the only ways arithmetic can be learned, so that score keeping or block counting are psychologically necessary precursors of math. But this kind of connection is not the one at issue in the rough definition above. Even if score keeping is a prerequisite in acquisition, it obviously need not be a part of what adults engage in when they perform some piece of arithmetic, and it is therefore not more central than arithmetic itself. The same goes for other enablements of a mental act. We may have to read the arithmetic problem or attend to some spoken instructions before we can begin the task. However, prerequisites like listening to instructions aren't in any ordinary sense part of actually performing arithmetic operations, though they may be important or even necessary concomitants. One could try to give cognitive centrality a more refined formulation, but this informal notion is all we need in the present context.

What I want to claim is that reasoning is cognitively central relative to many other mental processes, including important ones like perception and comprehension. The evidence for this comes from two main sources: theory in cognitive psychology and philosophical analyses of action. However, we can also gain some indirect support for this thesis from subjects' intuitive judgments about the nature of intelligence. The data come from a study by Sternberg, Conway,

---

[2]The notion of centrality is similar to the idea of "level generation" developed by Goldman (1970) in the context of a general theory of action. However, Goldman's relation depends on both causal and conventional properties of acts, whereas centrality is intended to capture only causal connections. Note too that a somewhat different notion of centrality might be developed in terms of closeness to primitive operations rather than in terms of process dependence, and this alternative might prove more useful for certain purposes. The goal of the present discussion is not to explore all of the factors that might affect centrality, but to describe one conception that is helpful in locating reasoning with respect to other mental activities.

Ketron, and Bernstein (1981). Subjects were asked to rate a large set of descriptions according to how characteristic each of them is of an ideally intelligent person. (The descriptions had been obtained from another group of subjects and included items like "is a source of good ideas," "studies hard," "accepts others for what they are," etc.) Factor analysis of the ratings revealed three main dimensions, which Sternberg et al. call "practical problem-solving ability," "verbal ability," and "social competence." The problem-solving dimension is the most important of these, accounting for 29% of the variance, compared to 10% for verbal ability and 7% for social competence. More important, the highest loading descriptions on the problem-solving factor were "reasons logically and well" and "identifies connections among ideas."

We needn't rely entirely on intuitions, however. Reasoning has come to occupy in cognitive psychology the theoretical position we would expect of a central ability. Chapters on reasoning in cognitive textbooks usually follow those on such topics as perception and comprehension; but the direction of the theory is the other way round, the latter topics being explained in terms of inference. For example, the standard theory about how I'm able to see that there's (say) a capital "A" in front of me is that I infer the object from perceptual fragments that have been sampled by my visual system. These fragments or features are compared to stored representations, and the evidence produced by this comparison is inductively combined with prior hunches and the like to yield the right decision that it's an "A." With more complex objects—for example, three-dimensional, partially obscured, or ambiguous ones—proportionally more work is done by the inference and decision mechanisms and proportionally less by raw features (see Fodor & Pylyshyn, 1981, and Ullman, 1980, for defense of this view). Although not everyone believes this story (Gibsonians, in particular, do not), it's reasonable to suppose that if there is any direct causal dependence between the two, it runs from perception to inference.

Similarly, theories of text comprehension require inferences to generate expectations about upcoming information and to knit new input with what has gone before. Understanding a sentence like *Susan is a Republican, but she's honest* forces an inference about the probable attitude of the speaker or writer toward Republicans (Lakoff, 1971). Likewise, the sequence *I walked into the room; the chandeliers sparkled brightly* doesn't explicitly mention, but leads us to infer, that the room contained chandeliers (Clark, 1975). Lakoff's point about the first of these examples was that the inference is involved in judgments about the very grammaticality of the original sentence. But whether or not inference is crucial to grammar, it does seem crucially involved in understanding: We would deny that someone had fully comprehended the sentence if he or she had missed the implication. True, comprehension can also affect inference in the sense that understanding of a reasoning problem is required for a correct response in any explicit test of reasoning ability. Furthermore, in a developmental context or in a logic classroom, understanding may lead to an improvement in inference skills.

But these enablements are quite different from the direct process dependence of comprehension on reasoning, and as already noted, centrality depends on the latter relation, not on precursors. Comprehension seems to play a minor role, if any, during the course of reasoning itself, whereas reasoning is a proper part of on-going comprehension.[3] (See Harris, 1981, and Warren, Nicholas, & Trabasso, 1979, for accounts of research on inference-making in text understanding.)

The same conclusion about the centrality of reasoning can be derived from analyses of practical thinking. Explaining why people perform given actions ordinarily means attributing to them a set of beliefs and goals. Adele bought the cake because she likes eating delicious things and believes that anything chocolate is delicious. Gary made a U-turn because he was in a hurry and thought a U-turn quicker than driving around the block. But as Davidson (1970) and Dennett (1971, 1981) have pointed out, interpretations of this kind presuppose more than a single belief. The propositions that we explicitly attribute to others must also be melded in a coherent way to other beliefs via inferential links. Adele's belief about chocolate serves to explain her behavior only if she also believes, among other things, that the cake in question is chocolate, and she is able to deduce that the cake is therefore delicious. In other words, we tend to rely on assumptions about people's inference abilities (among other abilities) as implicit parts of our account (though these assumptions are defaults that might be overridden if we find we are dealing with someone—perhaps, a 4–year–old—whose mental abilities are different from our own).

There are certainly limits to the amount of inferential power that we are willing to attribute even to normal adults (as Stich, 1981a, has emphasized in a critique of Dennett). Still, these assumptions about reasoning are quite resilient; for if we find that our explanations are false, we are much more apt to blame peripheral factors than to call into question a person's inference abilities. If Adele denies that the reason she bought the cake is that she believes chocolate delicious, we look for other possible reasons or for simple processing errors (e.g., she picked up the wrong parcel by mistake). We don't immediately doubt her ability to perform universal instantiation (i.e., to reason from *All chocolate things are delicious* and *This cake is chocolate* to *This cake is delicious*). If this is true, it tallies with the evidence from cognitive psychology in placing reasoning toward the center of our mental sphere. These action explanations are obviously

---

[3]There is a more general sense of "comprehension" in which comprehension really is involved in reasoning. This is the sense of seeing the relation among the parts of an entity. For instance, we might say that we've comprehended or understood the design of a cathedral, if we've come to appreciate its structural relations. Greeno (1977) has discussed some ways in which geometry theorem proving demands this kind of understanding. However, in the above discussion, "comprehension" is used to refer to the ordinary syntactic and semantic aspects of natural language processing.

informal, but at this juncture it appears likely that any more rigorous account of everyday behavior will also have to be formulated in terms of goals, beliefs, and inferential connections among them (Schank & Abelson, 1977).[4]

Unless these facts about cognition and behavior can somehow be explained away, a theory of reasoning must come to grips with the problem of how reasoning manages to occupy the place it does in the hierarchy of cognitive processes. In the same way that we would judge inadequate a theory of numerical ability that treated arithmetic skill on the same level as score keeping, we ought to reject a theory that failed to get straight the relation of inference to other mental acts. If reasoning comes out as cognitively dispensable relative to perception, comprehension, or choice, then something has gone seriously wrong. Because some of the theories discussed in Section 2 are on the verge of just this problem, we should keep this centrality consideration before us.

Generativity

A cognitive theory has the double task of: (a) discriminating the very large (probably infinite) class of inferences that humans assent to from the equally large class of those they don't; and (b) doing so within the limited capacities that humans have available. This productivity is what James (1890) took to distinguish reasoning "distinctly so called" from "that simpler kind of rational thinking which consists in the concrete objects of past experience merely suggesting each other [pp. 329–330]." To take a simple example, if you believe that sentence *S1* is true and also that *S2* is true, then you can infer that *S1 AND S2* is true; given this new sentence you can also infer that *S1 AND S1 AND S2* is true; this new sentence in turn permits yet another inference to *S1 AND S1 AND S1 AND S2;* and so forth. Of course, you wouldn't want to produce a stream of inferences of this trivial sort unless you had to (e.g., in support of some further theorem); nevertheless, the fact that these deductions can be made on demand is something that a cognitive theory must explain. The vast number of inferences puts a high premium on mental operations that cover as much ground as possible with minimum cognitive overhead; that is, we should prefer inference mechanisms that are relatively efficient, all other things being equal.

---

[4]Jennifer Church (1982) has pointed out that no self-respecting pessimist would take this as evidence that explanations of action depend on reasoning. Instead, they would see it as dependence on problem solving or some other process. I think this is right. However, what I am trying to establish is that these explanations are of a particular type. It may indeed be true that problem solving is required here, but it's problem solving of a very restrictive sort. In explaining actions, we don't ordinarily presuppose the ability to solve the Tower of Hanoi problem or a chess or cryptarithmetic puzzle, but we do presuppose the ability to perform modus ponens and universal instantiation. What I will argue later is that even if reasoning is a kind of problem solving, it nevertheless demands its own psychological theory.

The analogous problem in linguistics is well-known (e.g., Chomsky, 1957, 1965), and the analogy itself has been elaborated by Osherson (1976, Ch. 8). According to Chomsky (1965), grammatical competence includes the ability to interpret infinitely many sentences; therefore, "a generative grammar must be a system of rules that can iterate to generate an indefinitely large number of structures [p. 15]." The ability to iterate in the proper ways is equally required by a theory of reasoning, and indeed, this is no coincidence, given the mutual relevance of grammatical and logical description. Part of the inference potential of a sentence depends on its structural composition, and although there is considerable disagreement about the extent to which this "logical form" mirrors "grammatical form," it is uncontroversial that there are rule-governed relationships between the two.

This need for "generativity" in inference causes worry about the sorts of inference models that are restricted to arbitrary reasoning tasks, for example, categorical syllogisms (Erickson, 1974; Guyote & Sternberg, 1981; Johnson-Laird & Steedman, 1978; Revlis, 1975), conditional syllogisms (Rips & Marcus, 1977; Taplin & Staudenmayer, 1973), linear syllogisms (Clark, 1969; Huttenlocher, 1968; Sternberg, 1980), and the selection task (Johnson-Laird & Wason, 1970). An inference system that is specialized for dealing with categorical syllogisms, for instance, is an unlikely cognitive component, because categorical syllogisms themselves do not constitute a meaningful class, either with respect to current logical or psychological theory. Part of the attraction of categorical syllogisms to psychologists is that they form a neat factorial structure that invites experimentation. But this factorial simplicity has kept experimentalists from exploring related arguments that don't happen to share Aristotelian syllogistic form. There is nothing wrong with trying to explain subjects' responses to syllogisms; however, the models we posit ought to be extendable to a wider, more natural set of arguments.

Generality

The generativity requirement, just discussed, demands that inference mechanisms generalize over humanly solvable problems. However, we can also ask for generality of another sort, the sort provoked by Thurstone's question about the relation among reasoning abilities. Despite the inconsistent conclusions of the factor-analytic studies, these experiments did succeed in demonstrating that some reasoning tests are more similar than others. Performance on a number series test is more like that on letter series than on syllogisms, and scores on analogy tests are more like those of word classification problems than arithmetic word problems. A theory of inference should be in the business of accounting for these relationships.

One can also hope for generality over the range of strategies that subjects apply in solving a particular problem. Although individual differences may turn out to be uninteresting from the point of view of reasoning, it is also possible they will be helpful in deciding among rival models of group data. Moreover, the existence of individual differences in logical competence is pertinent to recent claims concerning universal rationality (see Cohen, 1981, and critiques of Cohen's position by Jepson, Krantz, & Nisbett, 1981, and Stich, 1981b). We will return to these issues in the fourth section, armed with some data on individual differences in deduction.

IS THERE A CASE AGAINST REASONING?

Simply stated, the pessimistic position is that there is no point in taking reasoning as an object of serious scientific study because no interesting generalizations are likely to emerge in doing so. This position is worth careful consideration, for it is not at all hard to find arguments to support it. In particular, a pessimist might point to the following facts: First, the tasks that psychologists have investigated under the heading of reasoning comprise anything but a homogeneous domain, consisting of everything from mental paper folding to cryptanalysis and from rearranging scrambled sentences to planning a nautical course. The chances are extremely slim that there is any high-level cognitive ability shared by just this set of problems. There is certainly nothing that distinguishes this set from the kinds of tasks studied by somewhat different methods in the problem-solving literature (indeed, logic problems and number series problems have been studied from both perspectives), and this suggests that we might profitably view reasoning as problem solving rather than an isolated domain of its own. In other words, just as we have viewed categorical syllogisms as a psychologically arbitrary set of problems that are best seen as part of a wider context, so reasoning problems as a whole may be more meaningfully seen from the perspective of the entire class of problem-solving tasks.

A second fact that appears to support the pessimistic claims is the well-known finding that the "content" of reasoning problems exerts a strong effect on subjects' solutions. As an example, take the conditional argument whose premises are $IF\ p,\ q$, and q, and whose conclusion is p (sometimes called "affirming the consequent"). This argument is invalid when IF is treated as the material conditional (i.e., true when the antecedent p is false or the consequent q is true). However, subjects' evaluation of the argument depends heavily on the propositions that are substituted for the variables p and q (Adams, 1980; Marcus & Rips, 1979; Rips & Marcus, 1977; Staudenmayer, 1975). For example, subjects are more likely to judge Argument (1) invalid, where the propositions describe an arbitrary arrangement of symbols on a card, than to judge Argument (2) invalid, where the propositions refer to a simple pinball-type device:

(1) If there is a B on the left side of the card, there is a 1 on the right side. There is a 1 on the right.

There is a B on the left.

(2) If the ball rolls left, then the red light flashes. The red light flashed.

The ball rolled left.

Similar results have been obtained in other sorts of conditional reasoning problems (e.g., Fillenbaum, 1978; Griggs & Cox, 1982; Legrenzi, 1970; Thistlethwaite, 1950; Wason & Johnson-Laird, 1972). There is also a long line of research concerning syllogism-like arguments based on controversial topics (e.g., "No man can be blamed for destroying anything that belongs to himself. The life that he destroys by suicide belongs to himself. Therefore, suicide is an act for which no man can be blamed."). Most of these experiments have shown at least a small tendency for subjects' evaluation of the arguments' validity to coincide with their belief in the truth of the conclusion (Feather, 1964; Gorden, 1953; Janis & Frick, 1943; Lefford, 1946; Morgan & Morton, 1944; Revlin & Leirer, 1978; Thouless, 1959). Such effects do not necessarily indicate irrationality on the subjects' part, since they may arise from quite reasonable pragmatic or strategic considerations.

However, content effects pose a problem for reasoning theory. In order to predict subjects' responses in standard inference tests, it looks as though the theory will have to take into account subjects' world knowledge, for example, their knowledge of pinball machines in Argument (2). This is, in fact, the main conclusion of Wason and Johnson-Laird's (1972) review of the psychology of reasoning:

> The emphasis which we have placed on content in reasoning shows that a purely formal, or syntactic, approach to it may suffer from severe limitations. . . . Only gradually did we realize that there was no existing formal calculus which correctly modelled our subjects' inferences, and second that no purely formal calculus would succeed. Content is crucial, and this suggests that any general theory of human reasoning must include an important semantic component [pp. 244–245].

Of course, formal logic too has a "semantic component" that specifies the relation between the elements of a language and their referents, but this kind of component is probably not what Wason and Johnson-Laird have in mind. Whereas the formal semantics of an argument is constrained by the argument's logical form, this new type of semantic component must go beyond logical form to take into account subjects' background beliefs about the topics introduced in the premises. The trouble is that a system that evaluates arguments on the basis of generic beliefs about such things as pinball machines—or, in other experiments, tropical fish, laws governing drinking, postal requirements, and what have you—makes it difficult to see how any consistent inference theory could be formulated. A theory of reasoning whose principles must be revised whenever we learn something new is hardly worth the bother. Such a system would be more a theory of fact retrieval than of reasoning.

Both the reasoning-as-problem-solving and the reasoning-as-fact-retrieval approaches hold out the promise that important new generalizations will result from viewing inference in these ways, and I think we can agree that these approaches may very well promote new insights. Weaknesses arise, however, when this is interpreted as a claim that problem solving or fact retrieval is all the theory one needs for reasoning. Such claims are precisely the pessimist's bill of fare, and they call for a closer look.

Reasoning as Problem Solving

One would be astonished if reasoning was psychologically unrelated to skill in mathematical puzzles, chess or go problems, anagrams, cryptarithmetic, and other tasks that have standardly been posed to subjects in problem-solving experiments (Greeno, 1978; Simon, 1978). Going a step further, one could view reasoning as simply another problem-solving activity, which differs from that in, say, chess puzzles only in relatively minor ways (e.g., number of steps in the solutions or the number of special-purpose strategies that one can bring to bear on them). If this is right, we might then look to theories of problem-solving for a unified account of this entire cognitive area. This view of reasoning as problem-solving has been forcefully argued by Newell (1980), and we can usefully examine his doctrines to see what light they shed on our understanding of inference.

Newell's basic goal is to provide a framework general enough to cover the gamut of subject strategies, both within and between experimental tasks—essentially the third of the criteria discussed in the previous section. On Newell's account, what provides this framework is the notion of a "problem space," which he defines as "a set of symbolic structures (the states of the space) and a set of operators over the space. Each operator takes a state as input and produces a state as output. . . . Sequences of operators define paths that thread their way through sequences of states [p. 697]." Problem-solving theory is the study of behavior explainable in terms of problem spaces. The idea of a problem space is illustrated most easily in a game like chess, since one can take the set of possible configurations of pieces on the board as the states and the legal moves in the game as the operators. In this light, the activity involved in planning a chess move consists in mentally performing legal moves from the current position and evaluating the resulting states.

However, the problem-space concept is applicable to any "symbolic goal-oriented activity," according to Newell, and to reasoning problems in particular. Suppose, for example, we take as the states of a reasoning problem space the set of propositions believed to be true at any particular moment. We can take as operators mental rules that produce new propositions on the basis of old ones— for example, a rule like modus ponens, which produces conclusion q from the premises *IF p, q,* and *p*. Thus, if at time t, we believe both that *Carrie is in Chicago* and that *if Carrie is in Chicago, Emily is in Rochester,* and if the rule of modus ponens is one of our mental operators, then we may come to hold at time t + 1 the three propositions *Carrie is in Chicago, If Carrie is in Chicago, Emily is in Rochester,* and *Emily is in Rochester.* Applying a sequence of operators in this way (tracing a path through the problem space) gives rise to a mental proof or derivation. Because many current models of reasoning characterize deduction in terms of internal proofs of this sort, the problem-space hypothesis is clearly compatible with these models and with the data they predict (see, e.g., Braine, 1978; Johnson-Laird, 1975; Newell & Simon, 1972, Part 3; Osherson, 1974, 1975, 1976; Rips, 1983). In particular, the model presented in the third section of this chapter is deeply indebted to problem-solving theory. A problem-space characterization can also be given to nonpropositional models of reasoning that employ internal diagrammatic symbols (e.g., Venn diagrams) so long as operations on the symbols can be broken down into a discrete series of states.

There is no doubt, then, that problem-solving theory is applicable to clear-cut reasoning tasks. The broad sweep of the problem-space hypothesis easily fulfills the generality criterion sketched above. And because it is obviously possible to design recursive procedures to explore the states in a problem space, this hypothesis also has the promise of meeting the generativity requirement as well. However, the extremely general nature of the problem-space concept may itself be cause for concern, since it could turn out that the concept is so abstract that it provides no insight at all into the nature of reasoning. There are really two problems here: One is that problem-solving theory glosses over some important distinctions that we need in explaining inference. The other is that the problem-space notion may itself be too loosely constrained to be empirically helpful.

Let's start with the first of these problems. As we've already seen, the problem-space concept can describe many different cognitive tasks. Not only can it characterize difficult problems like chess puzzles, but also such relatively low-level processes as item recognition in short-term memory (which is modeled by Newell, 1973, in a way that is entirely consistent with search in a state space). It follows that if we identify search in a problem space with reasoning, we are committed to viewing item recognition and similar cognitive nitty gritty as instances of reasoning, and this, I think, would be intuitively unacceptable to most cognitive psychologists. Proponents of the reasoning-as-problem-solving position are quite justified in pointing to both the miscellaneous character of traditional reasoning tasks and the extensive overlap of these tasks with those in the problem-solving area. Nevertheless, the haphazard sample of reasoning tests, though regrettable, does not imply that there is no stable population from which they have been drawn. The kind of overlap that obtains between reasoning tasks and tasks involving problem-space search is more likely subset to superset than coextension. For although these domains may be vague, there appear to be straightforward examples of problem-space search without reasoning. Item recognition is one such example. If this is true, then the problem-space hypothesis is, at best, an incomplete account of reasoning because we will need some explanation of how inference differs from noninferential search.

The problem becomes more acute when we consider the role that reasoning plays in explaining other cognitive activities. In discussing the centrality criterion, we noted that reasoning, but not (say) learning to play the ukulele, is a well-entrenched psychological concept, useful in accounting for many other mental processes. The problem-space hypothesis, however, is unable to explain this contrast between central and peripheral processes, since both could presumably be couched in terms of state-space search. What causes trouble for the reasoning-as-problem-solving idea is the asymmetry of explanations: Although reasoning may be helpful in accounting for how one learns the ukulele, no one would suggest an appeal to ukulele learning in accounting for reasoning. Thus, in addition to the notion of an abstract space, we need some more restrictive provisions that will enable us to see what's unique about reasoning among other mental events. These might be formulated as constraints on the components of the space; for example, allowing only operators that correspond to deductive or inductive rules. However, the job of determining which rules to count as deductive (or inductive) for purposes of the theory is not one that can be accomplished by the problem-space hypothesis alone.

The second difficulty for the claim that reasoning is nothing but search in a problem space concerns the problem-space concept itself. Because there are no constraints at all on either the states of the space or on the functions (operators) defined over them, one has trouble imagining any aspect of cognition that couldn't be represented in some way or other as search in a space. This lack of constraint leaves one with the uneasy feeling that the hypothesis has little empirical content. Newell (1980) is fully sensitive to this potential triviality problem, and he proposes five possible tests that could help confirm the psychological reality of problem spaces. These can be summarized as follows: (a) In certain novel situations, subjects' problem space should directly mirror the surface features of the problem statement. Thus, if subjects are using this space, one should be able to predict their solution behavior from the same surface features. (b) Subjects' behavior in recovering from mistakes should depend on the same space that predicts correct solutions. (c) Skills that subjects acquire in solving a problem should be predictable in terms of better methods of searching through the same problem space. (d) Subjects' knowledge about the topology of one space should transfer to similar ones. (e) The space for a given problem should predict individual subject's task strategy as derived from other ways of analyzing the task (in particular, flow-chart models of the solution).

I think these points help clarify the claims of the problem-space hypothesis but are, nevertheless, extremely weak tests of those claims. Newell himself questions whether Test (c) could ever be experimentally distinguishable from other hypotheses about learning to solve a problem, and Tests (b), (d), and (e) all suffer from similar difficulties. Predicting error patterns [Test (b)] in a principled way requires an independent characterization of these erroneous behaviors. However, evidence from preliminary trial-and-error is usually built into the problem space itself; we learn very little about the problem space if the subject just hands us the correct solution. Predicting transfer [Test (d)] requires an independent definition of problem similarity, which is also typically unavailable. The ability to predict flow-charts [Test (e)] seems to be guaranteed by the total freedom of the problem-space modeler to choose states and functions arbitrarily. It is only in Test (a) that we have a challenging hurdle for the problem-space hypothesis; in these novel settings we should be able to manipulate the features of the space experimentally and observe the effects on behavior. But as it turns out, the types of problems from which one can derive the space directly are exactly the sort of problems least likely to disconfirm the theory. These are puzzles like the Tower of Hanoi that dictate the possible moves to solution, so that subjects have little choice (short of refusing to take part in the study) but to conform to some type of problem-space description. Given three fixed pegs and three movable disks and the task of getting the disks from one peg to another, the subject is going to manipulate the disks. And given that he or she manipulates the disks, one can "explain" the behavior in terms of search in a problem space. In short, the problem-space hypothesis in this broad sense is too underspecified to do much serious scientific work.

I don't want to suggest that Newell or other problem-solving researchers have consciously adopted the view that reasoning is nothing but search in a problem space. In other psychological domains (parsing, object perception), they have been quite willing to accept more narrowly specified theories within the problem-space hypothesis (see, e.g., Newell & Simon, 1976). Furthermore, the problem-solving approach is a welcome corrective to the one-task-one-model situation that exists in the reasoning literature (and that Newell rightly criticizes). But the problem-space hypothesis is not sufficient for a theory of reasoning, and the missing parts of the theory are not (or are not yet) to be found in problem-solving research. (For further difficulties with Newell's approach within the framework of Artificial Intelligence, see the trenchant critique by Moore, 1982.)

Nor do I want to maintain that these difficulties are peculiar to problem-solving approaches. Even research programs that are explicitly devoted to reasoning can share the problem that the principles they describe are really applicable to a much broader range of cognitive abilities and hence tell us little about reasoning per se. This is true, I believe, of much of the recent work in cognitive-differential psychology (e.g., Pellegrino & Glaser, 1980; Sternberg, 1981). What these programs have produced are high-level generalizations coupled with specific analyses or flow-charts of individual tasks (usually the same tasks we've met before, e.g., syllogisms or number series). Sample generalizations are that inference takes place in the processing stages of encoding, combination, comparison, and response, each carried out by elementary cognitive components (Sternberg, 1981), and the idea that inductive reasoning is affected by rule complexity and ambiguity (Pellegrino & Glaser, 1980). However, these generalizations are probably equally appropriate to any rule-governed cognitive performance—item recognition, dichotic listening, phoneme monitoring, word or picture naming, lexical decision, letter matching, and other favorite tasks. These generalizations may be a useful framework for cognitive research, but they are not to be confused with a theory of reasoning.

Reasoning as Fact Retrieval

There are two forms of the thesis that reasoning consists of recalling memorized facts: a hardline and a softened approach. The hardline version maintains that the way people evaluate an argument is to see if its conclusion is true: Whenever the conclusion agrees with the subjects' preconceived beliefs, then they are willing to accept the argument as a good one. This approach, which casts subjects as mental opportunists of a sort, has been well encapsulated by Morgan and Morton (1944): "Our evidence will indicate that the only circumstance under which we can be relatively sure that the inferences of a person will be logical is when they lead to a conclusion which he has already accepted [p. 39]." This extreme view has less clout today than previously, but traces survive in some current writing. For example, Evans (1982a) concludes that various forms of response bias contribute more to subjects' performance on deductive tasks than does any underlying logical ability. Although Evans (1982b) does maintain that subjects possess rudimentary logical competence, this competence does not extend even as far as most categorical or conditional syllogisms (e.g., he suggests that "abstract conditional reasoning performance indicates no more than a superficial understanding of the sentence *If p then q,* and little evidence of any depth of reasoning [p. 231].") By contrast, the softened view places less emphasis on simple biases and preconceptions. On this view, what subjects retrieve is not the conclusion, but a mental representation of the topic of the argument—for example, sets of cards in Argument (1) and pinball machines in Argument (2). To decide whether the argument is valid, subjects perform tests on this representation in more or less the way that they might run an experiment. If the tests confirm the hypothesis-conclusion, then the argument is valid.

In its hardline form, the thesis that reasoning is fact retrieval suffers from an insurmountable problem: There are just not enough (memorized) conclusions to go around. The nemesis for this theory is the generativity of reasoning, because the number of arguments that we can handle outstrips the number of propositions that we can practically learn and store. Indeed, the psychological value of reasoning is precisely that it minimizes learning and storage, permitting us to arrive at propositions without having to memorize them. For example, consider the case of ordinary genealogical relations (Rips & Stubbs, 1980). In an extended family consisting of 20 members, there are a total of 190 kin relations between pairs of these individuals, of the sort *Agatha is the aunt of Helen, Helen is the cousin of Thomas,* and so on. Learning all 190 by rote would be a taxing memory feat; but luckily, this is unnecessary since the full set can be recovered by applying inference rules to a small subset of these relationships (e.g., the subset consisting of all relations of the form *X is the parent of Y*). We can deduce that Agatha is Helen's aunt by reasoning that X is the aunt of Y just in case there are two other individuals, Z and W, such that Z is the parent of X and W, and W is the parent of Y (provided, of course, that X is a woman), and verifying that these parent-of relations hold of Agatha and Helen's family. This can obviously mean enormous savings in learning and retention; but if reasoning really does play this economizing role, then reasoning can't simply amount to retrieval of stored propositions.

A pure reasoning-as-fact-retrieval hypothesis amounts to the assumption that all inferences are the result of a type of response bias. According to this view, if the conclusion of an argument is a proposition that subjects antecedently believe to be true, then they are prone to accept the corresponding argument as valid no matter what its form. Earlier results on content effects in syllogistic reasoning were sometimes explained in just this way (e.g., Janis & Frick, 1943; Lefford, 1946; Morgan & Morton, 1944), but response bias is probably not the end of the story. Recall the pinball example in Argument (2) that was used to illustrate content effects. Surely, subjects don't have prior beliefs in the proposition *The ball rolled left,* which happens to be the conclusion of this argument; hence, simple response bias won't suffice to explain why subjects accept it. Nor does the general topic of the argument, the pinball machine, itself seduce subjects into calling it valid; other arguments about the same device end up with fewer incorrect "valid" responses (e.g., compare (2) to: *If the ball rolls left, the red light flashes; The red light didn't flash; Therefore, the ball rolled left*). To be sure, prior beliefs are at work here, but not through mindless response bias.

This is, of course, not to deny that belief in the conclusion of an argument sometimes affects subjects' decisions. As already mentioned, the weight of evidence confirms a small trend in this direction (though see Henle & Michael, 1956), and there are plenty of other varieties of bias that one can bring into play in explaining reasoning data (Evans, 1982a, 1982b). Indeed, given a broad enough conception of response bias, one can find evidence for bias in most of the empirical findings in the area. For instance, Pollard (1982) maintains that acceptance of Argument (2) can be explained in terms of a kind of bias in which subjects are unable to retrieve a relevant counterexample (a case in which the red light flashes but the ball doesn't roll left). Something like this may be correct, but note that we are already pretty far removed from a simple notion of response bias of the sort developed in signal detection theory. Pollard's suggestion presupposes a cognitive system in which it makes sense to register counterexamples in assessing an argument, and it is most unlikely that such a system can be explicated purely in terms of response factors. In general, the project of constructing a theory of inference by enumerating response tendencies appears no more likely to get off the ground than the Skinnerian program of using response tendencies to explain language. The need for generativity dooms both programs from the start.

The softened form of the fact-retrieval hypothesis is much more credible, since it doesn't insist that all of the work in reasoning is based on the conclusion alone. On this view, what is retrieved in reasoning is a model of the argument's referents, where the correctness of the argument depends on the properties of the model (Johnson-Laird, 1982; Kahneman & Tversky, 1982). For example, in the case of Argument (2), one could construct a mental facsimile of the pinball machine and then determine the validity of the argument by internal simulation. That is, one performs a thought experiment with the imagined device to see whether, when the red light flashes, the ball always rolls left. The advantage of this simulation idea is that it accounts for content effects by building the content into the thought process itself. The constraints imposed by the pinball machine in (2) affect the acceptance of the conclusion because these constraints determine whether the conclusion is true in the internal simulation. Essentially the same idea has proved useful in Artificial Intelligence (AI) programs that answer questions about domains such as electronic circuits. Simulation of a circuit can often lead to quicker answers than more general forms of reasoning applied to the same data base (see, e.g., Brown & Burton, 1975).

But I think we should be careful about trading on a false analogy. AI question-answers of this type work by reading their answers off a real simulation of their referents, and they therefore require a good deal of special knowledge in order to make the simulation run. Certainly, we can reason about topic areas for which our knowledge is much too sketchy to support a full-blown simulation in the computer science sense. If reasoning required the detailed information necessary for a true simulation, we would once again be faced with the problem of explaining the generativity of our reasoning skills. This strongly suggests that the mental simulations in question must be fairly abstract. In the case of Argument (2), for example, a typical subject is unlikely to know enough about the inner workings of a pinball machine to be able to simulate its behavior fully. (de Kleer & Brown, 1981, show that detailed knowledge is required for mental simulation of even as simple a device as an electrical buzzer.) If the same argument were phrased in terms of a person's behavior (*If Susan married Larry* . . .) or political affairs (*If Britain attacks Norway* . . .), then even experts would be hard pressed to put together a working simulation. More likely, subjects have a few specific facts and rules of thumb that they make do under the conditions of the problem. But if this is the case, do "mental simulations" amount to anything more than the idea that these content-specific facts supplement the premises in reasoning about a related argument?

We reach a similarly skeptical view by noting that even true simulations are more supplements than substitutes for reasoning. A simulation—or, for that matter, actual experimentation with the object at issue—doesn't by itself decide the answer to a question or the validity of an argument. The simulation just runs. What are missing are rules for setting up the simulation in a way that is consistent with the question or premises and rules for interpreting the output as a possible answer or evaluation (Pylyshyn, 1980). In the same way, mental models and simulations may provide computational short-cuts in certain kinds of problems. They don't eliminate the necessity for reasoning about these problems; what they do is provide the reasoning mechanism with additional data.[5]

In short, a simulation heuristic leaves us with the task of explaining the underlying mechanisms that get us from the premises to the conclusion. Thus, both of the approaches examined above—fact retrieval and problem solving— beg the central psychological question about inference: What is the cognitive process that sanctions the conclusion of some arguments (i.e., the intuitively valid ones) but not others? The hypothesis that inference is search in a state space begs the question of why certain state-space transitions are valid and others not. The hypothesis that inference is retrieval of content-specific propositions or models begs the question of what mental authority governs the use of these facts. To provide a satisfactory answer to these questions, we need a specific reasoning theory, and describing such a theory for deductive reasoning is the task of the remainder of this chapter.

---

[5]Johnson-Laird's (1982) approach to mental models has processing implications that differ from those of Kahneman and Tversky (1982) or de Kleer and Brown (1981). When applied to categorical syllogisms, Johnson-Laird's models amount to mental tokens corresponding to elements of classes mentioned in the problem (Johnson-Laird & Steedman, 1978). These tokens are manipulated to determine whether any conclusions are valid, but they don't simulate the behavior of their referents. For this reason, the models are immune to the difficulties with mental simulations raised above. On the other hand, Johnson-Laird's proposal raises some interesting questions: What cognitive advantage could there be for reasoning in terms of tokens rather than directly in propositions? That is, if information is stored propositionally (as I think Johnson-Laird believes), then why should we need to recast it in a completely different form for purposes of reasoning? If all that is needed is a model of the propositions, why can't the propositions themselves serve as the model (as in Henkin's, 1949, completeness proof)?

THE ANDS MODEL OF DEDUCTIVE REASONING

So far, I have tried to argue that the pessimistic view is wrong on internal grounds. It seems unlikely that reasoning can be explained away on the basis of other types of mental processes. However, we can put together a more persuasive case against the pessimist by exhibiting a theory of reasoning that is psychologically valid. A number of proposals of the sort I am about to discuss have recently been advanced for deductive inference, and although there are some important differences among these theories, the differences are probably outweighed by their similarities. The cornerstone of all these proposals is the assumption that, in evaluating a deductive argument, people construct a mental proof or derivation, doing informally what logic students are taught to do formally. This comes down to applying a series of inference rules to the premises and conclusion of an argument in order to check whether the conclusion follows. The rules are intuitively obvious principles that bridge the cognitive distance within the argument, enabling one to see clearly why the argument is valid (if it is). In all of the current psychological models, these rules are of the so-called "natural deduction" type, first invented by Gentzen (1935/1969) and Jaskowski (1934), and now very commonly employed in introductory logic texts (e.g., Thomason, 1970). The basic feature of these rules is that they permit the conclusion to be derived directly from the premises, rather than from a set of primitive logical axioms.

The particular model to be considered here is called ANDS (short for A Natural Deduction Sytem) and has been implemented as a computer program written in LISP. In essence, ANDS consists of two components: The inference rules themselves, which exist as separate subroutines in the program; and a working memory that stores the steps in the proof. In addition, ANDS makes certain assumptions about the inference rules' accessibility that are helpful in accounting for subjects' deductive failures. The model comes up with a proof by first storing the premises and conclusion of an argument in working memory. The inference rules then scan these memory contents to determine whether any deductions are possible. If so, the procedures add the newly deduced propositions to memory; this updated configuration is scanned again; further deductions are made, and so on, until either a proof has been found or no more rules apply. In the first case, the argument is declared valid; in the second, it's declared invalid. Thus, almost all of the work is carried out by the inference rules, which decide whether deductions are possible, add propositions to memory, and keep the procedure moving toward a solution.

In the three parts of this section, ANDS is described by studying its performance on a sample proof. The first subsection introduces the example argument and sketches an intuitive explanation of why this argument is valid. In Subsection 2, this explanation is compared in a preliminary way to ANDS' derivation, so that we can get a feel for the way this derivation is expressed. The basic parts of the proof are the Subgoal Tree and the Assertion Tree, and these two tree structures are examined in turn in the context of the sample proof. In the third subsection, ANDS' inference rules are briefly described and are illustrated by showing how they construct the proof in our running example. (For more details on ANDS and its applications, see Rips, 1983.)

The Sample Argument

For concreteness, let's consider a fairly typical argument of the sort that we would like ANDS to be able to handle. The following one has the advantage of being reasonably straightforward and yet capable of illustrating most of ANDS' features.

(3) If Betty is in Little Rock or Phoebe is in Tucson, then Ellen is in Hammond. Phoebe is in Tucson, and Mary is in New Brunswick.

It's not true that if Ellen is in Hammond, then Phoebe is not in Tucson.

Before getting into the details of ANDS' proof, let's think about the meaning of this argument. The conclusion says that a certain conditional proposition is *not* true, namely:

(4) If Ellen is in Hammond, then Phoebe is not in Tucson.

In order to show that this conditional is false, we might try to prove its negation directly, but another reasonable strategy would be to assume temporarily that the conditional is true and see if this leads to a contradiction. If we can find such a contradiction, then by a reductio ad absurdum, the negation of the conditional must be right and the argument valid. So let's assume (4) and see what happens.

Looking back to (3), we notice that we're given the fact that *Phoebe is in Tucson* (in the second premise), and that this proposition contradicts the one in the consequent clause of (4), *Phoebe is not in Tucson.* We haven't quite got the contradiction yet because the last proposition is only embedded in (4). However, this gives us something to go on—if we can deduce this last portion of (4), we've got our contradiction and we're home free. At this point, it would be very nice if we knew that *Ellen is in Hammond,* because this proposition, together with (4), would give us the missing part of the contradiction by a simple modus ponens inference. We don't really know this, but we do see that this proposition is the consequent of the first premise in (3). Because of this premise, we can show that *Ellen is in Hammond* if we know that *Betty is in Little Rock or Phoebe is in Tucson.* To summarize: We want to produce a contradiction by showing that Phoebe is and is not in Tucson on the basis of (4) and the premises of (3). The "is" part is immediate. The "is not" part follows from *Ellen is in Hammond* [by

(4)] and *Ellen is in Hammond* follows from *Betty is in Little Rock or Phoebe is in Tucson* [by Premise 1 of (3)].

As it turns out, we know nothing at all about Betty, but we do know that Phoebe is in Tucson; this is just what the second premise tells us. So we're done: Phoebe is in Tucson; therefore, Ellen must be in Hammond. And because Ellen is in Hammond, Phoebe must not be in Tucson. This is the contradiction we've been looking for. Assumption (4), which led to this contradiction, must therefore be false, and its negation, the conclusion of Argument (3) is true.

There are other ways of describing why Argument (3) is valid, but the above explanation seems natural in that its steps are intuitively reasonable ones. The explanation may seem somewhat long-winded once we've grasped the essential features of the argument. But in fact, the validity of arguments like (3) is not obvious to subjects who have had no formal logic background (cf. Argument X in Table 2 below), and under these circumstances, the snappiest explanation or proof may not be the most helpful. In what follows, we compare this explanation to ANDS' own proof strategy.

The Shape of Proofs in Working Memory

ANDS' proofs are built up in working memory in the form of two interconnected tree structures, the Assertion and the Subgoal Trees. Loosely speaking, the Assertion Tree holds propositions whose validity ANDS has established, that is, propositions that directly follow from the premises. The Subgoal Tree, on the other hand, contains propositions that are capable of proving the conclusion, but that may or may not themselves be valid. Put slightly differently, the Assertion Tree handles propositions that arise in working forward from the premises of the to-be-proved argument, whereas the Subgoal Tree is in charge of propositions (subgoals) that come from working backward from the conclusion. In the best situation, the forward and backward processes will intersect when a proposition is found that is contained in both trees. Because such a proposition is guaranteed by the premises (since it's part of the Assertion Tree) and itself guarantees the conclusion (since it's a subgoal), it completes the proof of the argument. This type of bidirectional strategy has been adopted in many (nonresolution) theorem provers in AI and has recently been incorporated in a psychological model of geometry proofs by Anderson, Greeno, Kline, and Neves (1981).

Figure 3.1 shows ANDS' two working memory trees at the conclusion of its proof of Argument (3). The premises of (3) appear at the top of the Assertion Tree and the conclusion at the top of the Subgoal Tree. (The premises are labeled "1" and "2" in the figure and the conclusion "3." In general, the numbers in the figure indicate the order in which the corresponding propositions are entered in memory.) As we will see, ANDS' proof of (3) is in most ways the same as the one we have just gone through. A glance at Figure 3.1 shows that all of the critical propositions that we considered are contained somewhere in the trees.

126

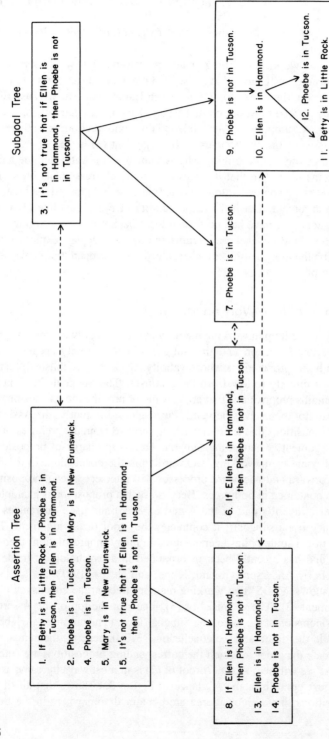

FIG. 3.1. ANDS' memory structure at the conclusion of the proof of the argument: *If Betty is in Little Rock or Phoebe is in Tucson, then Ellen is in Hammond; Phoebe is in Tucson and Mary is in New Brunswick; therefore, it's not true that if Ellen is in Hammond, then Phoebe is not in Tucson.*

We examine this parallel more closely below, looking first at the subgoals and then at the assertions.

The Subgoal Tree.   The main goal of a proof is to establish the argument's conclusion, and so it is usually helpful in finding a proof to take cognizance of the conclusion from the start. Attending to the conclusion keeps us from wasting time in deducing propositions that have no bearing on the current task. Furthermore, the conclusion can often tell us something about the route that a successful proof must take. We may learn that in order to get the conclusion, we will first have to prove some other proposition that stands as a lemma or subgoal. Often this subgoal will have subgoals of its own, and this process of finding subgoals can be continued until an achievable subgoal is found. This is the way that ANDS works backwards, and the purpose of the Subgoal Tree is to keep track of the relations among these steps.

In the proof at hand, ANDS first discovers that the conclusion of the argument will be valid if the negation of this conclusion leads to a contradiction, the same reductio strategy followed above. This is indicated in the Subgoal Tree by pointers leading from the conclusion to the two contradictory propositions, 7 and 9, that it intends to prove. The arc on the pointers leading to these propositions indicates that both of them must be proved before the conclusion can be considered valid.

One of these propositions, *Phoebe is in Tucson,* is established immediately, but the second requires more work. As in our informal proof above, ANDS notices that it can derive *Phoebe is not in Tucson* if it can show that *Ellen is in Hammond,* and this is represented by the link between Subgoals 9 and 10. In turn, *Ellen is in Hammond* will be true if *Betty is in Little Rock* because of the argument's first premise. *Betty is in Little Rock* is proposed as Subgoal 11; but because ANDS knows no way to prove it, this subgoal fails. When this happens, ANDS goes back to the last choice point and tries again. In this case, it goes back to Subgoal 10 and looks for another way to deduce this proposition. Concentrating again on the first premise, ANDS proposes the alternative Subgoal 12, *Phoebe is in Tucson.* This time the subgoal succeeds on the basis of the second premise, and this success completes the proof: Subgoal 12 ensures that Subgoal 10 is true; Subgoal 10 guarantees Subgoal 9; and Subgoals 7 and 9 entail the conclusion itself.

In short, ANDS does a depth-first search of the subgoals of the conclusion. The general form of the subgoals is a tree structure that could conceivably have many branches. However, when ANDS is working at its best, only a small number of subgoals will be necessary to complete the proof. The links in the tree indicate which propositions are deducible from others, given the premises of the argument. The aim of the Subgoal Tree, like that of any working-backward strategy, is to keep the solution process headed as directly as possible toward the conclusion.

The Assertion Tree. What's missing so far in our examination of ANDS' proof is an account of the "givens" of the problem: The premises and other suppositions that are used in deriving subgoals. It's the Assertion Tree that holds these givens, along with propositions that are derived from them.

In Figure 3.1 the Assertion Tree is composed of three blocks of propositions, outlined by rectangles and connected to similar blocks in the Subgoal Tree. As already mentioned, the topmost block contains the premises as Assertions 1 and 2, as well as three other propositions that follow from them. Assertions 4 and 5 are just the two halves of the second premise (*Phoebe is in Tucson and Mary is in New Brunswick*), which are separated at the beginning of the problem in order to simplify later steps. Simplifications of this sort constitute the forward motion of the proof and contrast with the backward motion of the Subgoal Tree. Assertion 15 is the conclusion of the argument itself, and it is placed there as the very last step of the proof, the step that finally allows us to see that the conclusion follows from the premises.

The other two blocks of propositions in the Assertion Tree are concerned with the proposition *If Ellen is in Hammond, then Phoebe is not in Tucson,* which is the hypothesis we made to get the reductio inference going. This proposition is obviously not one that follows from the premises, but is merely one we wish to consider temporarily for the sake of the effect it will ultimately have on the proof. Its status as an assumption or supposition is indicated by placing it in a new block in the Assertion Tree. In fact, we do this twice: The supposition is recorded as Assertion 6, when we derive the first half of the contradiction, and as Assertion 8, when we derive the second half.[6] To represent the fact that this supposition is in effect during this particular phase of the proof, the blocks containing it are attached to the relevant subgoals (by dotted lines in the figure). In other words, the connection between the blocks containing Assertion 6 and Subgoal 7 indicates that 7 is to be deduced under the assumption that 6 is true. Similarly, Subgoals 9–12 are attached to the block containing Assertion 8 to show that these subgoals can be deduced with the help of that assumption. Any deductions that are made on the basis of the assumption are stored in the same block. Thus, Assertions 13 and 14 are stored with Assertion 8.

In sum, although the Assertion Tree contains many of the same propositions as the Subgoal Tree, it provides a different, "premise-side" perspective on the proof. As we have seen, the Assertion Tree establishes the scope of the premises and of the other "givens" of the problem. That is, it shows which propositions are true on the basis of the premises alone and which are true on the basis of the premises plus ancillary suppositions. This idea will be familiar to readers who have had experience with natural deduction proofs, and indeed, the Assertion

---

[6]We could have used just a single Assertion block for both parts of the contradiction. This would, in fact, be somewhat closer to the way ANDS actually operates. However, the use of two blocks gives a better picture of the branching that can occur in the Assertion Tree.

Tree is such a proof, with the tree supplanting the numbering or bracketing devices that are more often used in logic textbooks.

Inference Rules

Both the Assertion and Subgoal Trees are constructed by the inference procedures; examining these procedures will give us a deeper insight into the nature of ANDS' proofs. The rules themselves are listed in abbreviated form in Table 3.1, and they roughly divide into two species. The rules whose numbers are primed in the Table (i.e., R1', R2', R3', and R5') are called "forward" rules; the remaining unprimed items are "backward" rules. As their names suggest, forward rules are responsible for deducing propositions in the premise-to-conclu-

TABLE 3.1
ANDS' Inference Rules

R1.   Backward Modus Ponens:
     Subgoal (q)
     Assert (IF p, q)
     ————————
     Subgoal (p)

R1'. Forward Modus Ponens:
     Assert (IF p, q)
     Assert (p)
     ————————
     Assert (q)

R2'. Forward De Morgan:
     Assert [...NOT (p AND q) ...]
     ————————————
     Assert (...NOT p OR NOT q...)

R3.   Backward Disjunctive Syllogism:
     Subgoal (q)
     Assert (p OR q)
     ————————
     Subgoal (NOT p)

R3'. Forward Disjunctive Syllogism:
     Assert (p OR q)
     Assert (NOT p)
     ————————
     Assert (q)

R4.   Backward Disjunctive Modus Ponens
     Subgoal (q)
     Assert (IF p OR r, q)
     ————————————
     Subgoal (p) or Subgoal (r)

R5.   Backward And Elimination:
     Subgoal (q)
     Assert (...p AND q...)
     ————————————
     Subgoal (p AND q)

R5'. Forward And Elimination:
     Assert (p AND q)
     ————————
     Assert (p) and Assert (q)

R6.   Backward And Introduction:
     Subgoal (p AND q)
     ————————
     Subgoal (p) and Subgoal (q)

R7.   Backward Or Introduction:
     Subgoal (p OR q)
     ————————
     Subgoal (p) or Subgoal (q)

R8.   Backward Restricted Law of Excluded Middle:
     Subgoal (p OR q)
     Assert (NOT p)
     ————————
     Assert (p OR NOT p)

R9.   Backward If Introduction:
     Subgoal (IF p, q)
     ————————
     Assume (p) and Subgoal (q)

R10. Backward Not Introduction:
     Subgoal (NOT p)
     ————————
     Assume (p) and Subgoal (q);
     Assume (p) and Subgoal (NOT q)

R11. Backward Or Introduction:
     Subgoal (r)
     Assert (p OR q)
     ————————
     Assume (p) and Subgoal (r);
     Assume (q) and Subgoal (r)

sion direction, whereas backward rules operate from the conclusion to the premises. Because forward rules are somewhat simpler, we consider them first.

The forward rules bear a close resemblance to rules in logic texts, and inspection of Table 3.1 shows that all of them have a form similar to:

(5) Assert (P1)
     Assert (P2)

     _____

     Assert (P3)

The meaning of this is that if *P1* and *P2* are both propositions in the Assertion Tree (roughly speaking, propositions that ANDS already knows to be true), then *P3* can also be added to the Assertion Tree. An example is forward modus ponens, Rule R1'. This rule stipulates that if the Assertion Tree contains the propositions *IF, p, q* and *p*, then the new proposition *q* can also be added to the tree. Forward rules are the simpler members of ANDS' repertoire precisely because they refer only to assertions, never to subgoals.

The form of the backward rules varies a bit more widely than that of the forward rules, but the usual components are the following ones:

(6) Subgoal (P1)
     Assert (P2)

     _____

     Subgoal (P3)

This is intended to indicate that if the current subgoal is *P1* and if *P2* appears in the Assertion Tree, then *P3* is added as the new subgoal. Because the main function of backward rules is to propose subgoals on the basis of old ones, these are the rules responsible for the subgoal chains that we noticed in Figure 3.1. Whether it is worth ANDS' while to try to prove a subgoal will generally depend on what else ANDS happens to know. ANDS may therefore check one or more assertions (*P2* above) before going ahead. As an example, take the backward modus ponens rule, R1 in Table 3.1. If the current subgoal is *q* and one of the assertions is *IF p, q*, ANDS will propose as the new subgoal *p* on the grounds that if *p* can be established then the conditional will guarantee that *q* is true. In terms of Schema (6), *q* plays the role of *P1*, *IF p, q* that of *P2*, and *p* that of *P3*.

A Second Look at ANDS' Proof of Argument (3).   With this background, it should be easy to see how the rules produce the proof in Figure 3.1. At the very beginning of the proof, the Assertion Tree contains only the two premises (Assertions 1 and 2) and the Subgoal Tree contains only the conclusion (Subgoal 3). ANDS looks over its set of rules to see if any of them apply to this configuration, and the first one it notices is Rule R5', a forward rule that takes an assertion of the form *p AND q* and adds the separate propositions *p* and *q* to the Assertion Tree. In this case, the second premise (*Phoebe is in Tucson and Mary is in New Brunswick*) has the required form, and as a result the corresponding Assertions 4 and 5 are added to working memory.

As a second step, ANDS again looks around for applicable rules and, this time, sees that the conclusion of the argument (*It's not true that if Ellen is in Hammond . . .*) has a negative form. This triggers its reductio rule, R10, which tells it to assume the part of the conclusion inside the negation and see if this leads to a contradiction. A heuristic incorporated in this rule (but not shown in Table 3.1) advises that if the conclusion or premises contain within them propositions of opposite sign, then these contradictory propositions are reasonable candidates to try to deduce. For instance, if one of the premises is of the form . . . *p* . . . and if the conclusion is of the form . . . *NOT p* . . . , then ANDS should try to use *p* and *NOT p* as the contradiction in the reductio proof. Because ANDS realizes that *Phoebe is in Tucson* appears in the second premise and *Phoebe is not in Tucson* appears in the conclusion, it tries to prove both of these. Rule 10 sets up these two subgoals and the assumption from which they are to be derived.

The first subgoal, *Phoebe is in Tucson,* succeeds right away because it has already been deduced as Assertion 4. Heartened by this success, ANDS turns to the tougher part, *Phoebe is not in Tucson,* Subgoal 9. The remainder of the proof conforms quite closely to the steps of our informal reasoning at the beginning of this section: Using the backward modus ponens rule just discussed, ANDS notes that Subgoal 9 follows if it can show that *Ellen is in Hammond,* and *Ellen is in Hammond* thus becomes Subgoal 10. In the same way, Rule R4 recognizes that Subgoal 10 can be fulfilled if it can prove that *Betty is in Little Rock* and sets up this proposition as Subgoal 11. As we've already seen, this subgoal fails because there are no rules that can help prove it, and Rule R4 next tries Subgoal 12, *Phoebe is in Tucson,* the second part of the antecedent in Premise 1. This time the subgoal succeeds (Assertion 4 to the rescue again!), and this means that Subgoals 10, 9, and 3 succeed as well, since each of them is dependent on the propositions below it in the Subgoal Tree. But Subgoal 3 is just the main conclusion of the argument. ANDS therefore places this conclusion in the Assertion Tree (as Assertion 15) and prints out the fact that the argument is valid.

Summary.   What I hope this example brings out is that reasoning in ANDS amounts to specific ways of manipulating propositions in memory. ANDS' operations are generally consistent with production systems that have been successfully used to model many cognitive phenomena (Anderson, 1976; Newell & Simon, 1972). However, the productions in ANDS are specialized to handle propositional connectives, and take the form of Schemas (5) and (6) above, the basic formats for forward and backward inferences. Moreover, the memory structures they produce have the characteristic form of partitioned hierarchies. It is obvious that the rules presently included in ANDS do not exhaust all of the principles that people use in deductive inference; the model is therefore not a final theory of deduction (much less a general theory of reasoning). However, the basic aspects of the current rules—including the use of assumptions and the forward/backward distinction—should carry over to other possible inference rules as well. Of course, one can ask why these particular principles in a computer simulation ought to be taken as reasonable constraints on a theory of human inference. To answer this question we need to evaluate the accuracy of the model in predicting subjects' reasoning performance.

ADEQUACY ISSUES

To the developer of a system like the one just described, it often seems impossible that evolution could have designed the mind in any other way. To a reader, however, claims on behalf of such a system are likely to seem Panglossian at best, given the theory's complexity and its arbitrariness over points of detail. Witness the exasperation with Osherson's monographs on the part of reviewers, many of whom regarded the project as a kind of cabalistic logico-mathematical exercise (Gellatly, 1977; Pufall, 1978; Wason, 1975). I hope to have prepared the ground for a theory of deduction by showing that its cognitive mission is a central one and is unlikely to be fulfilled by other theories otherwise needed (problem solving or fact retrieval). Nevertheless, readers are likely to ask whether ANDS in particular can provide a reasonable empirical and conceptual return on their investments, and I've therefore tried to answer this question below in the context of some relevant experimental findings.

ANDS' Empirical Dividends

ANDS has proved successful in accounting for a number of different sorts of reasoning tasks, described in what follows. I'll be brief for those cases in which a full account of the experiments appears elsewhere.

Memory for Proofs.   Because ANDS makes specific assumptions about the representation of proofs in working memory, it should be able to predict which portions of these proofs will be best remembered. Previous research on text memory suggests that propositions are more memorable if they occupy a top-level position in a hierarchical reconstruction of a passage (e.g., Kintsch, Kozminsky, Streby, McKoon, & Keenan, 1975; Meyer, 1975). Given a proof like that of Figure 3.1, we would therefore expect that propositions at the top of the trees would be better recalled than propositions at lower levels. For instance, subjects who read or listen to a prose version of the Figure 3.1 proof should be more apt to remember the proposition *Mary is in New Brunswick,* which appears in the top block of the Assertion Tree, than *Ellen is in Hammond,* which appears only in the lower blocks.

This prediction has been tested by Marcus (1982) with results that support the ANDS theory. Marcus constructed two sets of proofs: Embedded proofs like Figure 3.1 that contain propositions in lower blocks of the Assertion Tree, and unembedded proofs, whose Assertions Trees contain only one block. Each embedded proof was paired with an unembedded proof so that propositions in the lower blocks of the embedded proof matched propositions in the single block of the unembedded proof. Both proof types were translated into English passages, tape-recorded, and played to subjects, who were told that they would be tested on the passages' content. Subsequent free recall of these passages revealed a memory advantage for the unembedded propositions. Whereas embedded propositions were recalled on 25.4% of trials, the matching unembedded propositions were recalled on 44.6% of trials. This is clearly consistent with ANDS' working memory structure, but cannot be explained by the alternative deduction theories without further assumptions.

Reasoning Aloud.   As another test of ANDS, we can ask whether it can account for the strategies apparent in subjects' protocols when they are asked to decide, while thinking aloud, whether arguments are valid or invalid. In one experiment of this type (Rips, 1983), subjects were presented a series of arguments, half of them valid and the other half invalid. The subjects (none of whom had taken courses in logic) were strongly encouraged to say whatever occurred to them during their initial solution and then to re-explain their answer in the simplest possible terms, as if they were talking to a child. Both the original solution and subsequent explanation were recorded and transcribed. Two judges familiar with formal logic compared ANDS' proof of the valid arguments to the transcripts. The judges also compared to the same transcripts proofs based on Osherson's (1975) theory.

Overall, ANDS' proofs were rated fairly similar to the subjects' informal reasoning, with Osherson's proofs rated significantly less similar. Mean similarity between ANDS and the transcripts was 3.64 on a 0–to–5 scale, where larger numbers indicated more similarity. In many cases, ANDS' predictions were quite close to subjects' explanation (see Rips, 1983, for examples). With one or two exceptions, the low ratings that ANDS received were due to lack of explicitness on the part of subjects; vague responses impose an upper limit on how well any system can do under these circumstances. The mean rating for the Osherson model was 3.21 on the same scale, reliably less than ANDS'. Other psychological deduction systems (Braine, 1978; Johnson-Laird, 1975) are too underspecified to make any predictions at all for these problems.

An important qualitative finding in this experiment is that subjects were able to change their approach to a problem in midstream if they observed new relations among the features of the argument. This process can be modeled in a system like ANDS, because the Subgoal Tree allows the exploration of new solution paths when old ones have failed. However, strategy shifts are a problem for systems like Osherson's that predict a single linear route from the premises to the conclusion.

Argument Evaluation and Probabilistic Proofs.   Besides giving an account of correct responses, ANDS can also be used to generate predictions about erroneous ones in a situation where subjects decide about an argument's validity. We assume as before that such a decision reflects the subjects' skill in coming up with a mental proof. This in turn depends on whether the subjects have the necessary rules available to them; for if one of the rules crucially needed for the proof of a valid argument is unavailable, no proof will be forthcoming and the argument will be incorrectly labeled invalid. The phrase "crucially needed" is important here, because ANDS can sometimes find more than one way to prove an argument. In these cases, loss of a rule can lead to a new proof rather than a failure. Nevertheless, if enough rules are missing, no proof can be constructed. Although there are likely to be other sources of error besides unavailability of rules, let's assume for simplicity that their effect is comparatively small and unsystematic. Then apart from this "noise," we can think of ANDS' derivations as "probabilistic proofs," where the probabilities depend solely on the likelihood that the proper rules are employed. Because ANDS tells us which rules are needed for any argument, we can predict error rate quantitatively by estimating these likelihoods.

This approach has received support in a study described in an earlier paper (Rips, 1983), and the results have since been replicated with a new group of subjects (Rips & Conrad, 1983). In the replication, subjects were given the 32 valid arguments listed in Table 3.2. For each item, they were asked whether the conclusion followed from the premises. The arguments were presented as English sentences about the location of people in cities, as in Argument (3). Subjects saw a given argument twice, once in each of two sessions separated by six weeks. At each presentation, the argument was instantiated with different sentences to keep subjects from recognizing the problem on the basis of superficial features. The Table 3.2 arguments were mixed with an approximately equal number of invalid arguments, and the entire set was randomized in a new order for each subject and session. Subjects saw the arguments in a booklet and worked at their own pace until they had finished all of the items. The subjects were introductory psychology students who had no previous training in logic.

Table 3.2 contains the new data for each argument, collapsed over sessions, as the percentage of correct "valid" responses. The overall rate of correct responding was 62.2%, with a range from 17.6% to 97.0% on individual prob-

TABLE 3.2
Observed and Predicted Percentage of "Valid"
Responses to Stimulus Arguments

Argument	Observed	Predicted	Argument	Observed	Predicted
A. (p v q) & ¬ p	55.9	50.8	O. ¬(p & q)	85.3	77.1
———————			(¬p v ¬q) → r		
q v r			———————		
B. s	73.5	74.6	¬(p & q) & r		
p v q			P. (q v r) & s	70.6	72.0
———————			———————		
¬p → (q & s)			¬q → r		
C. p → ¬(q & r)	29.4	44.6			
(¬q v ¬r) → ¬p			Q. p	58.8	56.1
———————			(p v q) → ¬r		
¬p			———————		
D. ¬¬p	50.0	43.8	p & ¬(r & s)		
¬(p & q)			R. p → r	73.5	81.4
———————			(p & q) → r		
¬q v r			S. s	82.4	84.5
E. (p v r) → q	76.5	71.8	p → r		
———————			———————		
(p v q) → q			p → (r & s)		
F. ¬p & q	67.6	56.1			
———————			T. p v q	55.9	49.7
q & ¬(p & r)			———————		
G. (p v q) → ¬r	73.5	74.6	¬p → (q v r)		
r v s					
———————			U. p	58.8	58.3
p → s			(p v q) → r		
H. (p → q) & (p & r)	91.2	87.0	r → s		
———————			———————		
q & r			s v t		
			V. p & q	61.8	61.5
I. (p v q) → ¬s	70.6	58.0	———————		
s			q & (p v r)		
———————					
¬p & s			W. ¬(p & q)	32.4	46.5
J. q	47.0	60.0	(¬p v ¬q) → ¬r		
———————			———————		
p → ((p & q) v r)			¬(r & s)		
			X. (p v s) → r	61.8	53.4
K. (p v ¬q) → ¬p	17.6	46.7	s		
p v ¬q			———————		
———————			¬(r → ¬s)		
¬(q & r)			Y. p → ¬q	67.6	49.1
L. (p v q) → ¬(r & s)	79.4	60.0	———————		
———————			p → ¬(q & r)		
p → (¬r v ¬s)			Z. ¬(p & q) & r	58.8	74.3
M. ¬p	47.0	39.5	(¬p v ¬q) → s		
q			———————		
———————			s		
¬(p & r) & (q v s)					
N. (p v r) → ¬s	70.6	53.1			
———————					
p → ¬(s & t)					

(continued)

TABLE 3.2 (*Continued*)

1. (p v q) → (r & s)	97.0	89.8	4. (p v q) & ((r vs)→¬p)	73.5	76.7
p → r			r		
			q		
2. r	26.5	54.8	5. p v s	44.1	50.7
q v r			(p v r) → s		
r → ¬¬q			s v t		
3. ¬(p & q)	79.4	64.0	6. t	52.9	52.2
¬¬q			¬(r & s)		
¬p & ¬(p & q)			((¬r v ¬s) & t) v u		

Note: Arguments are given in logical form, where & = "and", v = "or", → = "if . . . then", and ¬ = "not". The original arguments appeared as English sentences.

lems in the table. Subjects false alarmed to only 19.2% of the invalid filler arguments, so subjects were fairly successful in discriminating valid from invalid problems. Performance was, in fact, better than in the original study (Rips, 1983), where the percentage of "valid" responses was 50.6% for the valid problems and 16.7% for the invalid ones. The correlation between the observed values in Table 3.2 and the corresponding figures from the earlier study is .86, which provides an index of the reliability of the data. The standard error of the individual values in Table 3.2 is 7.8.

Table 3.2 also shows ANDS' predicted scores for the same problems. These were derived by running ANDS on the arguments and observing which rules were used in the proof of each. Subsequent runs were done with these rules omitted to determine whether ANDS could construct secondary proofs using new rule combinations. This simulation process was repeated until no new proofs were forthcoming. Given this information, we can find for each argument an equation predicting the probability of finding a proof (and so correctly determining the argument's validity) as a function of the availability of the individual rules. The entire set of equations was fit to the Table 3.2 data using STEPIT (Chandler, 1969) to minimize squared deviations between predicted and observed values (see Rips, 1983, for more on model fitting). Besides the predicted values, the procedure yields availability estimates for each of the main inference rules.

Overall the correlation between predicted and observed scores was .78, and the root mean square deviation was 11.5. These figures can be compared to the reliability and standard error mentioned above. This fit is reasonable, but not as good as in the earlier study. In combination with the higher level of performance, it suggests that subjects may have been using rules or rule combinations that are not in ANDS' current repertoire. Some further evidence for this possibility is discussed below.

TABLE 3.3
Availability Parameters for Rules in ANDS

Rule		Parameter Estimate
R1	(Modus ponens)	.88
R2	(DeMorgan)	.74
R3	(Disjunctive syllogism)	.75
R4	(Disjunctive modus ponens)	1.00
R5	(And elimination)	.95
R6	(And introduction)	1.00
R7	(Or introduction)	.55
R8	(Restricted excluded middle)	——[a]
R9	(If introduction)	.92
R10	(Not introduction)	.48
R11	(Or elimination)	.71

[a]Rule R8 was not used in the proofs of the experimental problems.

The estimated availability of the rules (i.e., the probability that they are correctly employed) is shown in Table 3.3, and for the most part, these values match our intuitions about the rules' obviousness. Among the most available rules are those for handling conjunctions (inferring p from $p\ AND\ q$ or inferring p $AND\ q$ from p and q). Among the least available is the rule for Disjunction Introduction that allows one to derive $p\ OR\ q$ on the basis of p alone. In Grice's (1967) terms, the assertion of $p\ OR\ q$ is conversationally misleading when the stronger statement p is already known to be true, and this pragmatic fact may account for subjects' hesitancy in applying the rule. (Note that the forward and backward rules from Table 3.1 that perform similar operations—e.g., the modus ponens rules R1 and R1'—have been fit by a single value in order to reduce the total number of free parameters in Table 3.3.)

Generality and Individual Differences

Of the criteria for a theory of reasoning that were discussed in the first part of this chapter, the centrality of ANDS seems assured by the inherent centrality of the sentence connectives—*and, or, if . . . then,* and *not*—whose logic it governs. Generativity, the second criterion, is also secured by the generativity of ANDS' inference rules. The difficult problem is the generality criterion. We have very little indication that ANDS applies to different subject groups or to tasks other than the evaluation and memory studies outlined in the last few paragraphs. This issue will not be resolved here. However, we can at least illustrate some of the obstacles to generality, using some additional data from the above replication experiment (see also Rips & Conrad, 1983).

In a pleasantly simple state of affairs, subjects' deduction skills would be uniform and isomorphic to the processes in a deduction model like ANDS. Of course, it is too much to expect that subjects will reason uniformly in the sense of giving exactly the same answers to the same problems; factors irrelevant to reasoning can drastically alter individual subjects' performance. But there may yet be uniformity at the level of the representations and rules posited by the theory of deduction. This question about the universality of deduction is important, not only because of the light it sheds on reasoning models, but also because of its implications for human rationality more generally. In a recent paper, Cohen (1981) has argued that every normal adult is necessarily rational because these same adults are the arbiters of what counts as rational behavior. What's more, according to Cohen, the deductive competence of each of these individuals is isomorphic to the contents of the best normative logic theory. In his words, "where you accept that a normative theory has to be based ultimately on the data of human intuition, you are committed to the acceptance of human rationality as a fact of the matter in that area, in the sense that it must be correct to ascribe to human beings a cognitive competence—however faulted in performance—that corresponds point by point with normative theory [p. 321]." Because deductive competence and normative theory are supposed to be isomorphic, Cohen's position entails the view that—barring some form of extreme relativism—deductive competence is uniform (as Stich, 1981b, has pointed out). That is, there can be no individual differences in those aspects of deduction that the theory describes.

Do individual differences in deductive competence exist? If Cohen is right, it's useless to hunt for them, since they are ruled out a priori. Moreover, even if Cohen is wrong, there are empirical problems to be met because it is almost always possible to come up with a performance factor to explain any observed discrepancies. Nevertheless, it may be possible to eliminate experimentally some of the more obvious sources of performance error; if the differences persist, then we will at least have put some pressure on the universal competence view. Let's take another look, then, at the replication experiment with an eye toward such differences.

A first indication of differences in subjects' reasoning is that the absolute level of performance varied widely: Average scores for the subjects ranged from 26% to 89% correct for the Table 3.2 problems. Of course, although this spread reflects subject differences, it does not necessarily represent the true range in specifically deductive ability. If some subjects are simply more cautious than others about making a "valid" response, then this bias will be reflected in their overall score. Furthermore, the differences could be due to temporary problems in motivation, concentration, and the like. What we really want to know is whether subjects consistently differ in the arguments they regard as valid. This is essentially a question about the interaction between subjects and arguments, and our experiment provides one way of assessing it. Because subjects evaluated the same arguments in each of two sessions (separated by six weeks), we can test whether differences in their choices held up over that interval. In fact, an F-test for the subject-by-argument interaction is significant when tested over the triple interaction of subjects, arguments, and sessions [$F(496, 496) = 1.42, p < .001$].

This evidence would carry more weight if we could relate the obtained subject-argument variance to peculiarly deductive factors. Simply displaying the (17 by 32) matrix of subjects' responses will not be very revealing, so we need to look to techniques that will help us recover some of the underlying structure in this matrix. One way to proceed is to compute correlations between each pair of arguments across subjects and submit the resulting correlations to factor analysis. Figure 3.2 shows part of the output from such an analysis (actually principal components, rather than factor analysis) after varimax rotation. Nine factors in the original solution have eigenvalues greater than one and together account for 91% of the variance. However, two of these factors (after rotation) alone account for 41% and are relatively easy to interpret; the rest are less obviously interpretable and individually pick out only one or two arguments from the rest of the pack. The arguments are plotted in Figure 3.2 with respect to the first pair of factors and are tagged to correspond to Table 3.2.

Inspection of this figure reveals a tight connection between the recovered dimensions and some of ANDS' inference rules. The arguments that receive high loadings on the first factor are exactly those that depend for their solution on Disjunction Introduction (Rule R7 of Table 3.1). This is highlighted in the figure by the circles, representing all of the arguments that ANDS proves by means of this rule. The natural interpretation is that subjects vary in whether or not they possess Rule R7 or in the extent to which they are willing to apply it, perhaps for the Gricean reasons mentioned above.

The second dimension is slightly less straightforward in its import. However, four of the five arguments with high loadings on the factor (loadings greater than .5) are ones that ANDS proves using both If Introduction (Rule R9) and the Disjunctive Syllogism (Rule R3). Conversely, of the five arguments from Table 3.2 whose proofs utilize these two rules (indicated by squares in Figure 3.2), four are among the high-loading items. Some further information can be gleaned by comparing the arguments with high positive loadings to the single argument that received a high negative loading on this factor. Apart from details, the two highest positive arguments are of the form:

(7) p OR q
_____

IF NOT p, q

Here the trick is to assume that *NOT p* is true (from the antecedent of the conclusion) and show that under this assumption *q* must also be true because of the first premise. Rule R3 gives us this result. It follows that if *NOT p* is true, then so is *q;* that is, *IF NOT p, q,* by Rule R9. But notice that this sequence of moves, although tempting, is powerless with the high negative argument:

140

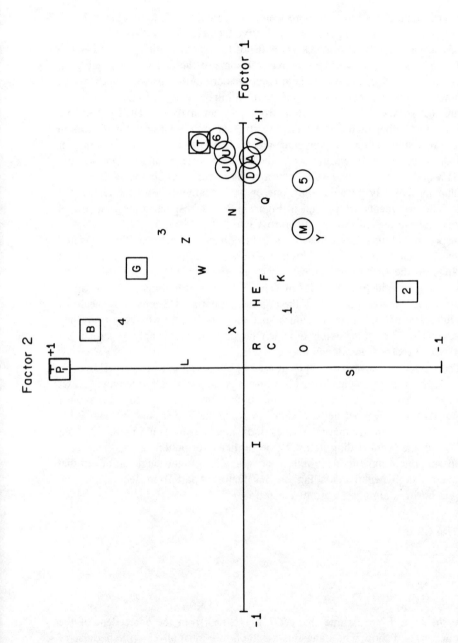

FIG. 3.2. The first two rotated factors for 32 propositional reasoning problems. The problems in the figure are labeled to correspond to those listed in Table 3.2. Problems outlined with circles require Rule 7 for their solution; problems outlined with squares require both Rules 3 and 9.

(8) NOT r
     q OR r
     _____

     IF r, NOT NOT q

Although this argument can also be proven valid by the same two rules, they have to be applied in a different way. In particular, assuming r to be true doesn't help with the disjunction in the way it did above, because q (or *NOT NOT q*) doesn't follow from r and q *OR r*. What seems to be happening is that subjects who are successful with arguments like (7) see the failure of the same operations on (8) as a sign that the latter argument is invalid. This would explain the negative weight for this problem. It is worth noting that this argument provides the next-to-largest deviation between predicted and observed scores in Table 3.2 and so accounts for some of the lack of fit between the model and the data.[7]

These results suggest that changes in ANDS may be warranted. The availability parameters in Table 3.3 can no longer be taken to reflect mere retrieval failures that are equally likely from one subject to the next. Rather, the probabilities are due in part to stable differences between subjects in their possession or handling of the rules. Other individual differences are also possible—for example, differences in the order in which the rules are applied, the amount of working memory capacity allotted to the trees, or willingness to try again once a dead end subgoal is reached. These sources are suggested by the ANDS framework. However a systematic look at them is likely to require adding more parameters to an already large set, and this will have to await a bigger experiment than the one reported here. Because individual differences in this experiment were consistent over six weeks and because they are apparently bound up with the inference schemas, it is hard to write them off as simple performance slips. Recall, too, that subjects had as much time as they wished to study the problems, a condition that should also have reduced simple processing mistakes. Still, it is possible for advocates of universal competence to defend their theory against these findings. For example, they could treat the evidence surrounding Rule R7 as indicating merely a longstanding bias against this rule on the part of certain recalcitrant subjects. Indeed, this same argument would work even if some subjects never use R7 in any concrete instance: The rule could still be a potential, but never manifest, part of these subjects' deductive competence. If one main-

_____

[7]The other big deviation in Table 3.2 occurs in Argument K and appears to be the result of a similar process. This argument invites the use of modus ponens because its premises match the modus ponens schema. However, the result of applying this rule yields a result that may appear to subjects to be unrelated to the conclusion. [Modus ponens produces *NOT p*, but the conclusion is *NOT (q AND r)*.] If subjects take this as evidence for the invalidity of the argument, it would explain why ANDS overpredicts the subjects' accuracy.

tains with Cohen (1981) that competence is necessarily uniform, then these experimental facts are ultimately irrelevant—such is the force of the phrase "however faulted in performance" in the quotation above. Perhaps the best one can do against this sort of argument is to try to construct working theories of reasoning and let the question of individual differences be settled by the usual canons of theory evaluation. ANDS and its predecessors are first starts on this theory-construction program, but the application to subject differences in reasoning has barely begun.

PRINCIPLE THEMES

From the most general perspective, cognitive psychology claims to explain mental life by positing a set of possible representations that are causally interrelated by internal processes. Among these representation-transforming processes, reasoning stands as an important type. I've tried to demonstrate that cognitive psychology is already wedded to the idea that reasoning is a central mental component, and although my arguments were based on cognitive warhorses like perception and comprehension, many other mental activities work equally well. Because reasoning is one of the main ways of modifying beliefs, we are usually forced to take reasoning into account when we invoke beliefs in our explanations.

As we might expect from a skill that is as broadly applicable as reasoning, it is not always clear where other processes stop and reasoning begins. For example, it's possible to explain simple arithmetic without invoking reasoning since a problem like adding 7 and 1 can probably be answered by a kind of table look up (though even for single digit arithmetic, other processes may be involved). But if 7 plus 1 is handled by fact retrieval, what about 7 plus 10 or 735 plus 1018? Borderline cases make it unlikely that any theory of reasoning will have a sharply defined domain among the set of tasks that are of interest to psychologists. On the other hand, I don't think it follows from this that reasoning is nothing but fact retrieval (or some other process). Nor does it follow that reasoning can't be more precisely articulated than it is at present. Such structuring is, in fact, badly needed to avoid the experimentation on arbitrary problems that is one of the more troublesome aspects of this field.

My guess is that an understanding of this area is most likely to result from attempts to come up with explicit models of reasoning for arguments within some theoretically motivated domain. The ANDS model is one attempt of this kind. ANDS reasons by examining the sentences of an argument, using inference routines that are sensitive to propositional connectives. These routines attempt to construct a proof in memory by filling in intermediate steps that aren't stated in the argument but that are easier to grasp. ANDS identifies the cognitive requirements for propositional inference, thus helping to pinpoint those aspects that are unique to reasoning and those that are more likely to be general-purpose mechanisms. Chief among the former are the inference rules themselves and the proof structures they create. Among the latter are the memory demands of the rules and the executive routines that apply the rules in a given order. In any particular piece of reasoning, these factors interact in complex ways—certain rules, for example, need more memory than others—but these factors are nevertheless analytically separable within the model's framework.

The same specificity is an advantage in locating the sources of individual differences in reasoning. As mentioned above, these sources could include both general-purpose factors like working memory capacity and reasoning-specific factors like the availability of certain rules. Results from the experiment reported here suggest that rule availability does indeed vary from subject to subject. Other kinds of differences have not yet been tested but might be studied by incorporating subject parameters for these factors in a mathematical model similar to the one described. Such an investigation is appropriate. For if reasoning is a central ability, then any differences in its constituent factors are likely to show up in the many tasks that rely upon it.

ACKNOWLEDGMENT

I would like to thank Adele Abrahamsen, Ned Block, Norman Brown, Christopher Cherniak, Jennifer Church, Fred Conrad, Donald Fiske, David Malament, Steve Schact, and Robert Sternberg for their help with this chapter. The research reported here was supported by U.S. Public Health Service Grant K02 MH00236 and National Science Foundation Grant BNS 80–14131.

REFERENCES

Adams, M. J. Inductive deductions and deductive inductions. In R. S. Nickerson (Ed.), *Attention and performance VIII*. Hillsdale, N.J.: Lawrence Erlbaum Associates, 1980.

Adkins, D. C. & Lyerly, S. B. *Factor analysis of reasoning tests*. Chapel Hill: University of North Carolina Press, 1952.

Anderson, J. R. *Language, memory, and thought*. Hillsdale, N.J.: Lawrence Erlbaum Associates, 1976.

Anderson, J. R., Greeno, J. G., Kline, P. J., & Neves, D. M. Acquisition of problem-solving skills. In J. R. Anderson (Ed.), *Cognitive skills and their acquisition*. Hillsdale, N.J.: Lawrence Erlbaum Associates, 1981.

Braine, M. D. S. On the relation between the natural logic of reasoning and standard logic. *Psychological Review*, 1978, *85*, 1–21.

Brown, J. S. & Burton, R. R. Multiple representations of knowledge for tutorial reasoning. In D. G. Bobrow & A. Collins (Eds.), *Representation and understanding: Studies in cognitive science*. New York: Academic Press, 1975.

Chandler, J. P. STEPIT: Finds local minima of a smooth function of several parameters. *Behavioral Sciences*, 1969, *14*, 81–82.

Chomsky, N. *Syntactic structures*. The Hague: Mouton, 1957.

Chomsky, N. *Aspects of a theory of syntax*. Cambridge, Mass.: MIT Press, 1965.

Church, J. Personal communication, June 1982.

Clark, H. H. Linguistic processes in propositional reasoning. *Psychological Review*, 1969, *76*, 387–404.

Clark, H. H. Bridging. In R. Schank & B. L. Nash-Webber (Eds.), *Proceedings of the Conference on Theoretical Issues in Natural Language Processing*. Cambridge, Mass.: 1975.

Cohen, L. J. Can human irrationality be experimentally demonstrated? *Behavioral and Brain Sciences*, 1981, *4*, 317–370.

Collins, A. Fragments of a theory of human plausible reasoning. In D. L. Waltz (Ed.), *Theoretical issues in natural language processing—2*. New York: Association for Computing Machinery, 1978.

Davidson, D. Mental events. In L. Foster & J. W. Swanson (Eds.), *Experience and theory*. Amherst: University of Massachusetts Press, 1970.

de Kleer, J. & Brown, J. S. Mental models of physical mechanisms and their acquisition. In J. R. Anderson (Ed.), *Cognitive skills and their acquisition*. Hillsdale, N.J.: Lawrence Erlbaum Associates, 1981.

Dennett, D. C. Intentional systems. *Journal of Philosophy*, 1971, *68*, 87–106.

Dennett, D. C. True believers: The intentional strategy and why it works. In A. F. Heath (Ed.), *Scientific explanation*. Oxford: Clarendon, 1981.

Erickson, J. R. A set analysis theory of behavior in formal syllogistic reasoning. In R. L. Solso (Ed.), *Theories in cognitive psychology: The Loyola symposium*. Potomac, Md.: Lawrence Erlbaum Associates, 1974.

Evans, J. St. B. T. Selective processes in reasoning. In J. St. B. T. Evans (Ed.), *Thinking and reasoning: Psychological approaches*. London: Routledge & Kegan Paul, 1982. (a)

Evans, J. St. B. T. *The psychology of deductive reasoning*. London: Routledge & Kegan Paul, 1982. (b)

Feather, N. T. Acceptance and rejection of arguments in relation to attitude strength, critical ability, and intolerance of inconsistency. *Journal of Abnormal and Social Psychology*, 1964, *69*, 127–136.

Fillenbaum, S. How to do some things with *if*. In J. W. Cotton & R. L. Klatzky (Eds.), *Semantic factors in cognition*. Hillsdale, N.J.: Lawrence Erlbaum Associates, 1978.

Fodor, J. A. & Pylyshyn, Z. W. How direct is visual perception? Some reflections on Gibson's "ecological approach." *Cognition*, 1981, *9*, 139–196.

Galambos, J. A. & Rips, L. J. Memory for routines. *Journal of Verbal Learning and Verbal Behavior*, 1982, *21*, 260–281.

Gellatly, A. Review of *Logical abilities in children* (Vol. 1–3) by D. N. Osherson. *Quarterly Journal of Experimental Psychology*, 1977, *29*, 171–172.

Gentzen, G. Investigations into logical deduction. In M. E. Szabo (Ed. & trans.), *The collected papers of Gerhard Gentzen*. Amsterdam: North-Holland, 1969. (Originally published 1935.)

Goldman, A. I. *A theory of human action*. Princeton: Princeton University Press, 1970.

Gorden, R. L. The effect of attitude toward Russia on logical reasoning. *Journal of Social Psychology*, 1953, *37*, 103–111.

Green, R. F., Guilford, J. P., Christensen, P. R., & Comrey, A. L. A factor-analytic study of reasoning abilities. *Psychometrika*, 1953, *18*, 135–160.

Greeno, J. G. Process of understanding in problem solving. In N. J. Castellan, Jr., D. B. Pisoni, & G. R. Potts (Eds.), *Cognitive theory* (Vol. 2). Hillsdale, N.J.: Lawrence Erlbaum Associates, 1977.

Greeno, J. G. Natures of problem-solving abilities. In W. K. Estes (Ed.), *Handbook of learning and cognitive processes* (Vol. 5). Hillsdale, N.J.: Lawrence Erlbaum Associates, 1978.

Grice, H. P. *Logic and conversation*. Unpublished William James Lectures, Harvard University, 1967.

Griggs, R. A. & Cox, J. R. The elusive thematic materials effect in Wason's selection task. *British Journal of Psychology,* 1982, *73,* in press.

Guyote, M. J. & Sternberg, R. J. A transitive-chain theory of syllogistic reasoning. *Cognitive Psychology,* 1981, *13,* 461–525.

Harris, R. J. Inferences in information processing. In G. H. Bower (Ed.), *Psychology of learning and motivation* (Vol. 15). New York: Academic Press, 1981.

Henkin, L. A. The completeness of the first-order functional calculus. *Journal of Symbolic Logic,* 1949, *14,* 159–166.

Henle, M. & Michael, M. The influence of attitudes on syllogistic reasoning. *Journal of Social Psychology,* 1956, *44,* 115–127.

Huttenlocher, J. Constructing spatial images: A strategy in reasoning. *Psychological Review,* 1968, *75,* 550–560.

James, W. *The principles of psychology* (Vol. 2). New York: Holt, 1890.

Janis, I. L. & Frick, F. The relationship between attitudes toward conclusions and errors in judging logical validity of syllogisms. *Journal of Experimental Psychology,* 1943, *33,* 73–77.

Jaskowski, S. On the role of supposition in formal logic. *Studia Logica,* 1934, *1,* 5–32.

Jepson, C., Krantz, D. H., & Nisbett, R. E. *Normative implications of individual differences in inductive reasoning.* Unpublished manuscript, University of Michigan, 1981.

Johnson-Laird, P. N. Models of deduction. In R. J. Falmagne (Ed.), *Reasoning: Representation and process in children and adults.* Hillsdale, N.J.: Lawrence Erlbaum Associates, 1975.

Johnson-Laird, P. N. Thinking as a skill. *Quarterly Journal of Experimental Psychology,* 1982, *34A,* 1–29.

Johnson-Laird, P. N. & Steedman, M. The psychology of syllogisms. *Cognitive Psychology,* 1978, *10,* 64–99.

Johnson-Laird, P. N. & Wason, P. C. A theoretical analysis of insight into a reasoning task. *Cognitive Psychology,* 1970, *1,* 134–148.

Kahneman, D. & Tversky, A. The simulation heuristic. In D. Kahneman, P. Slovic, & A. Tversky (Eds.), *Judgment under uncertainty: Heuristics and biases.* New York: Cambridge University Press, 1982.

Kintsch, W., Kozminsky, E., Streby, W. J., McKoon, G., & Keenan, J. M. Comprehension and recall of text as a function of content variables. *Journal of Verbal Learning and Verbal Behavior,* 1975, *14,* 196–214.

Lakoff, G. The role of deduction in grammar. In C. J. Fillmore & D. T. Langendoen (Eds.), *Studies in linguistic semantics.* New York: Holt, Rinehart, & Winston, 1971.

Lefford, A. The influence of emotional subject matter on logical reasoning. *Journal of General Psychology,* 1946, *34,* 127–151.

Legrenzi, P. Relations between language and reasoning about deductive rules. In G. B. Flores D'Arcais & W. J. M. Levelt (Eds.), *Advances in psycholinguistics.* Amsterdam: North-Holland, 1970.

Marcus, S. L. Recall of logical argument lines. *Journal of Verbal Learning and Verbal Behavior,* 1982, *21,* 549–562.

Marcus, S. L. & Rips, L. J. Conditional reasoning. *Journal of Verbal Learning and Verbal Behavior,* 1979, *18,* 199–223.

Meyer, B. J. F. *The organization of prose and its effects on memory.* Amsterdam: North-Holland, 1975.

Moore, R. C. The role of logic in knowledge representation and commonsense reasoning. *Proceedings of the National Conference on Artificial Intelligence.* Pittsburgh, 1982.

Morgan, J. J. B. & Morton, J. T. The distortion of syllogistic reasoning produced by personal convictions. *Journal of Social Psychology,* 1944, *20,* 39–59.

Newell, A. Production systems: Models of control structures. In W. G. Chase (Ed.), *Visual information processing.* New York: Academic Press, 1973.

Newell, A. Reasoning, problem solving, and decision processes: The problem space as a fundamental category. In R. S. Nickerson (Ed.), *Attention and performance VIII.* Hillsdale, N.J.: Lawrence Erlbaum Associates, 1980.

Newell, A. & Simon, H. A. *Human problem solving.* Englewood Cliffs, N.J.: Prentice-Hall, 1972.

Newell, A. & Simon, H. A. Computer science as an empirical inquiry: Symbols and search. *Communications of the Association for Computing Machinery,* 1976, *19,* 113–126.

Nisbett, R. & Ross, L. *Human inference: Strategies and shortcomings of social judgment.* Englewood Cliffs, N.J.: Prentice-Hall, 1980.

Osherson, D. N. *Logical abilities in children* (Vol. 2). Potomac, Md.: Lawrence Erlbaum Associates, 1974.

Osherson, D. N. *Logical abilities in children* (Vol. 3). Hillsdale, N.J.: Lawrence Erlbaum Associates, 1975.

Osherson, D. N. *Logical abilities in children* (Vol. 4). Hillsdale, N.J.: Lawrence Erlbaum Associates, 1976.

Pellegrino, J. W. & Glaser, R. Components of inductive reasoning. In R. E. Snow, D.-A. Federico, & W. Montague (Eds.), *Aptitude, learning, and instruction: Cognitive process analysis.* Hillsdale, N.J.: Lawrence Erlbaum Associates, 1980.

Pollard, P. Human reasoning: Some possible effects of availability. *Cognition,* 1982, *12,* 65–96.

Pylyshyn, Z. W. Computation and cognition: Issues in the foundations of cognitive science. *Behavioral and Brain Sciences,* 1980, *3,* 111–169.

Pufall, P. B. Deductions that do not compute. *Contemporary Psychology,* 1978, *23,* 420–421.

Revlin, R. & Leirer, V. O. The effect of personal biases on syllogistic reasoning: Rational decisions from personalized representations. In R. Revlin & R. E. Mayer (Eds.), *Human reasoning.* Washington, D.C.: Winston, 1978.

Revlis, R. Two models of syllogistic reasoning: Feature selection and conversion. *Journal of Verbal Learning and Verbal Behavior,* 1975, *14,* 180–195.

Rips, L. J. Cognitive processes in propositional reasoning. *Psychological Review,* 1983, *90,* 38–71.

Rips, L. J. & Conrad, F. G. Individual differences in deduction. *Cognition and Brain Theory,* 1983, in press.

Rips, L. J. & Marcus, S. L. Suppositions and the analysis of conditional sentences. In M. A. Just & P. A. Carpenter (Eds.), *Cognitive processes in comprehension.* Hillsdale, N.J.: Lawrence Erlbaum Associates, 1977.

Rips, L. J. & Stubbs, M. E. Genealogy and memory. *Journal of Verbal Learning and Verbal Behavior,* 1980, *19,* 705–721.

Schank, R. & Abelson, R. *Scripts, plans, goals, and understanding.* Hillsdale, N.J.: Lawrence Erlbaum Associates, 1977.

Simon, H. A. Information-processing theory of human problem solving. In W. K. Estes (Ed.), *Handbook of learning and cognitive processes* (Vol. 5). Hillsdale, N.J.: Lawrence Erlbaum Associates, 1978.

Staudenmayer, H. Understanding conditional reasoning with meaningful propositions. In R. J. Falmagne (Ed.), *Reasoning: Representation and process in children and adults.* Hillsdale, N.J.: Lawrence Erlbaum Associates, 1975.

Sternberg, R. J. Representation and process in linear syllogistic reasoning. *Journal of Experimental Psychology: General,* 1980, *109,* 119–159.

Sternberg, R. J. Toward a unified componential theory of human intelligence: I. Fluid ability. In M. Friedman, J. Das, & N. O'Connor (Eds.), *Intelligence and learning.* New York: Plenum, 1981.

Sternberg, R. J., Conway, B. E., Ketron, J. L., & Bernstein, M. People's conceptions of intelligence. *Journal of Personality and Social Psychology,* 1981, *41,* 37–55.

Stich, S. P. Dennett on intentional systems. *Philosophical Topics,* 1981, *12,* 39–62. (a)

Stich, S. P. Inferential competence: Right you are, if you think you are. *Behavioral and Brain Sciences*, 1981, *4*, 353–354. (b)

Taplin, J. E. & Staudenmayer, H. Interpretation of abstract conditional sentences in deductive reasoning. *Journal of Verbal Learning and Verbal Behavior*, 1973, *12*, 530–542.

Thistlethwaite, D. Attitude and structure as factors in the distortion of reasoning. *Journal of Abnormal and Social Psychology*, 1950, *45*, 442–458.

Thomason, R. H. *Symbolic logic*. Toronto: Macmillan, 1970.

Thouless, R. H. Effect of prejudice on reasoning. *British Journal of Psychology*, 1959, *50*, 289–293.

Thurstone, L. L. Primary mental abilities. *Psychometric Monographs*, 1938 (No. 1).

Ullman, S. Against direct perception. *Behavioral and Brain Sciences*, 1980, *3*, 373–415.

Warren, W. H., Nicholas, D. W., & Trabasso, T. Event chains and inferences in understanding narratives. In R. O. Freedle (Ed.), *New directions in discourse processing: Advances in discourse processing* (Vol. 2). Norwood, N.J.: Ablex, 1979.

Wason, P. C. Reasoning: Uncertain steps. *Contemporary Psychology*, 1975, *20*, 642–643.

Wason, P. C. & Johnson-Laird, P. N. *Psychology of reasoning*. Cambridge, Mass.: Harvard University Press, 1972.

Deductions About Induction: Analyses of Developmental and Individual Differences

Susan R. Goldman
James W. Pellegrino
University of California,
Santa Barbara

INTRODUCTION AND OVERVIEW

In recent years, attention has shifted away from global measurement of aptitude and intelligence toward an analysis of the cognitive skills underlying performance on aptitude and intelligence test tasks. The most extensive application of this ''cognitive components'' approach to aptitude analysis has been to inductive reasoning tasks (Pellegrino & Glaser, 1979). There are several reasons why inductive reasoning tasks have been targeted for such an in-depth analysis. Perhaps the most important reason is that induction problems have been a part of aptitude tests and psychometric theory almost from the inception of the testing movement. Spearman (1923) and Raven (1938) both argued that inductive reasoning was central to the concept and measurement of intelligence. Figure 4.1 illustrates major types of induction problems and typical content. One or more of these problem types can be found on virtually any standardized aptitude or intelligence test at any developmental level. The most frequently occurring is the analogy problem. The extensive use of analogy items in intelligence and aptitude tests was documented by Dawis and Siojo (1972), and more recently, Sternberg (1977a) has provided a detailed review and discussion of the importance of analogical reasoning within the field of differential psychology.

Another major reason for the emphasis on inductive reasoning tasks is that they are not simply a psychometric curiosity but are relevant in the broader domain of cognitive theory and research. Greeno (1978), for example, has characterized rule induction problems as instances of a major type of problem-solving task within a general problem typology. Egan and Greeno (1974) have considered rule induction in the framework of semantic memory research and have

CLASSIFICATION PROBLEMS

Verbal

mouse	wolf	bear		A. rose	B. lion	C. run	D. hungry	E. brown
Bob	Jack	Fred	Bill	A. Mary	B. boy	C. name	D. Ed	E. Jones

Figural

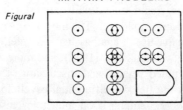

SERIES COMPLETION PROBLEMS

Letter Series

c d c d c d – – – –
j k q r k l r s l m s – – – –

Number Series

32 11 33 15 34 19 35 – – – –
72 43 90 71 47 85 70 51 80 – – – –

ANALOGY PROBLEMS

Verbal (A:B :: C:D′)

Sugar:Sweet :: Lemon: _____
  Yellow   Sour   Fruit   Squeeze   Tea
Abate:Decline :: Wax: _____
  Increade Improve Blemish Polish Wane

Numerical (A:B :: C:D :: E:F′)

7:21 :: 5:15 :: 4: __
15:19 :: 8:12 :: 5: __
10:40 :: 6:36 :: 5: __
28:21 :: 24:18 :: 20: __

Geometric

MATRIX PROBLEMS

Figural

FIG. 4.1. Examples of typical inductive reasoning problems. From "Analyzing Aptitudes for Learning: Inductive Reasoning," by J. W. Pellegrino and R. Glaser, in R. Glaser (Ed.), *Advances in Instructional Psychology*, Vol. 2, Hillsdale, N.J.: Lawrence Erlbaum Associates, 1982. Copyright 1982 by Lawrence Erlbaum Associates, reprinted by permission.

pointed out that analogical reasoning, series completion, problem solving, and concept formation all require a search for relations among elements resulting in new interconnections between the nodes of a network structure. The importance of inductive thought processes and reasoning by analogy has been emphasized in science (e.g., Oppenheimer, 1956), mathematics (Polya, 1965), and in the acquisition of information in the classroom (Bruner, 1957; Norman, Gentner, & Stevens, 1976).

Research on inductive reasoning fits within the general scheme for cognitive components research outlined by Pellegrino and Glaser (1980, 1982). This includes: (a) the construction and validation of theories and models of aptitude task performance; (b) the application of such models to developmental and individual differences analysis; and (c) the multitask analysis of individual differences in aptitude. These sequential stages of research are necessary for understanding any general or specific cognitive aptitude. During the past eight years, process models have been developed for performance on a number of induction tasks, including analogy, classification, matrix completion, and series extrapolation. The lion's share of attention has been to analogical reasoning because it is the most frequently occurring of all induction tasks. The present chapter is an attempt to examine the theoretical and empirical state-of-the-art regarding performance on analogy and classification tasks. We emphasize these two tasks because research on analogy and classification solution has progressed to the point where information is currently available about all three of the above issues.

The structure of this chapter reflects the above progression of research issues. The next section reviews theories and models of the processes involved in solving analogy problems. Included in this section is a discussion of how chronometric techniques have been used to test specific models and isolate component process latencies as well as empirically based conclusions about component processes and process execution. This section also considers the issue of modeling component process accuracy. The third section briefly reviews similar analyses of classification solution. The fourth and fifth sections focus on applications of latency and accuracy models to the analysis of developmental and individual differences, respectively. The sixth section considers some recent research examining concurrent performance in two or more inductive reasoning tasks. The final section is a summarization of what is currently known and a discussion of its significance.

COGNITIVE COMPONENTS OF ANALOGY SOLUTION

Basic Performance Components

A general theory of analogy solution can be derived from the work of several individuals (e.g., Pellegrino & Glaser, 1982; Spearman, 1923; Sternberg, 1977a; Whitely, 1977). They have described analogy solution in terms of several basic or elementary information processes. The list of processes constitutes a theory of performance; the details of process sequencing and execution constitute various specific models of solution. The process list can be divided into three general classes. The first class represents what Sternberg (1977a) has termed attribute discovery or encoding processes: The important attributes of each individual term in the analogy problem must be activated and internally represented. For verbal items, encoding involves activating a set of semantic features associated with a concept. Given the term dog, encoding would involve activation of semantic features representing superordinate, subordinate, property and other-labeled relationships. For geometric items, encoding constitutes a description of the constituent elements, their specific properties and relationships. An example term might be a rectangle containing two adjacent circles, one shaded and the other unshaded.

Attribute discovery or encoding is essential for execution of other component processes. The second set of processes involves attribute comparison for specific pairs of terms. The first such process has been labeled inference and it involves determining the attribute relationship between the first two terms of the analogy (A and B). For verbal stimuli this constitutes determining semantic features that directly or indirectly link the two concepts. For an A–B pair like ''Dog–Wolf'' this might include common features such as *animal* and *canine* as well as differentiating features such as *size, ferocity,* and *domesticity.* When geometric stimuli are involved, the inference process involves defining a set of feature changes or transformations applied to the A term to produce the B term. If the A term is the one described earlier and the B term consists of only two adjacent circles, then the inference process yields a transformation involving deletion of one of the elements indicating that it is the external shape. Mapping is a similar type of attribute comparison process. It refers to finding possible correspondences between the first and third terms (A and C) of an analogy. The third attribute comparison process is referred to as application. This process involves applying the specific rule inferred for the A–B pair to the attributes of the C term to produce a candidate or ''ideal'' D term for item solution. Inference, mapping, and application are component processes associated with the stem terms of an analogy, i.e., the A, B, and C terms.

The other major set of processes necessary for analogy solution are evaluation components. These determine the adequacy of any completion or D term. In simple analogies where the ideal D term can be generated easily, evaluation is a confirmation process wherein features of a given completion term are matched against the ideal answer. This process leads to rejection of inappropriate completions and selection of the correct response. However, many analogies involve ambiguity with respect to the exact rule and/or they may have several possible answers. Evaluation of the alternatives may yield two or more completion terms that partially match the features of an acceptable answer. In this case, rule comparison and discrimination processes are required and this general aspect of performance has been labeled justification. The final component process involves executing an overt response.

Models of Process Execution Latency

Given the set of component processes, several different models can be specified for the solution of forced-choice analogy items, or for items presented in a true-false verification format. The latter involves a completed analogy A--→B::C--→D whose overall truth value must be evaluated. Models vary with respect to process sequence and the way each process is executed. The major question about process execution is whether it is exhaustive or self-terminating, i.e., it ceases once disconfirming evidence is obtained. Sternberg (1977a,b) has delineated a number of possible models that involve the same sequence of processes but that differ with respect to assumptions about the exhaustive execution of each process. Two general sequences for process execution are shown in Figure 4.2. The generic model shown on the left in Figure 4.2 assumes that the A and B terms are encoded and this is followed by execution of the A–B inference process. Following this, the C term is encoded and the A–C mapping process is executed. Then, a D term is encoded and a combined application-confirmation process is executed, leading to acceptance or rejection of the given D term. If the term is in a verification format then a true or false response is emitted. If the item is in a forced-choice format then another completion term is encoded with execution of a combined application-confirmation process. This cycle continues until all the options have been evaluated and the correct response identified. For both verification and forced-choice items it is possible that a unique response cannot be determined, thus necessitating use of a justification process prior to final response. A slightly different generic model is shown on the right in Figure 4.2. The process sequence remains essentially the same except that application occurs prior to encoding the D term and this is followed by a confirmation process.

Differences among models reflect differences in assumptions about the processes that are executed in a self-terminating vs. exhaustive manner. At one extreme is a model in which each process in the sequence is exhaustively executed prior to execution of the next process. At the other extreme is a model in which each attribute comparison and evaluation process is executed in a self-terminating manner. Models falling along this continuum differ in terms of the exhaustive nature of inference and/or mapping. A concrete example of the sequence of process execution within a given model is provided by Figure 4.3. The analogy shown at the top of the figure is a schematic-figures item representing the true-false verification format of the analogy task. For purposes of discussion it can be assumed that the different figures vary in four attribute dimensions, each of which has only binary values. Thus the total population of unique figures is 16 and many individual analogies can be constructed from this stimulus population.

In attempting to solve the item shown in Figure 4.3, the first term (A) must be encoded, i.e., the figure (words in verbal or shapes in geometric analogies) must be represented in some abstract propositional form in memory. This representation is assumed to be an exhaustive attribute-value list that adequately serves to

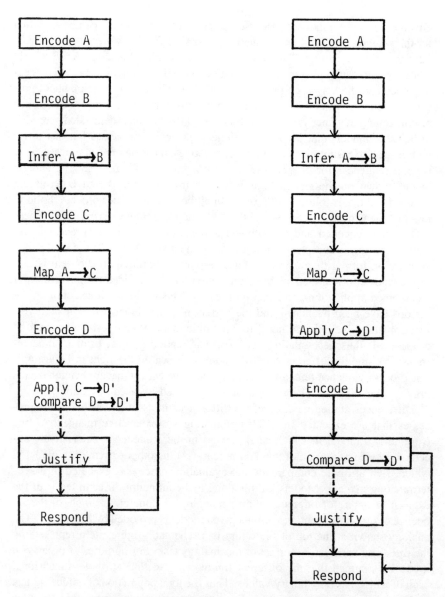

FIG. 4.2.   Simplified process models for analogy solution.

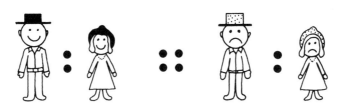

OPERATION	RESULT				TIME
1. encode A	male	tall	happy	solid hat	a
2. encode B	female	short	happy	solid hat	a
3a. infer transformation on attribute 1 (t_1)	male to female				x
b. infer transformation on attribute 2 (t_2)		tall to short			x
c. infer transformation on attribute 3 (t_3)			ϕ		
d. infer transformation on attribute 4 (t_4)				ϕ	
4. encode C	male	tall	sad	dotted hat	a
5. map transformation on attribute 1 (m_1)	ϕ				
6. encode D	female	short	sad	dotted hat	a
7a. apply t_1 to C yielding D'	female				z
b. compare D to D'	(match)				
8. map transformation on attribute 2 (m_2)		ϕ			
9a. apply t_2 to C yielding D'		short			z
b. compare D to D'		(match)			
10. map transformation on attribute 3 (m_3)			happy to sad		y
11a. apply t_3 to C yielding D			sad		
b. compare D to D'			(match)		
12. map transformation on attribute 4 (m_4)				solid to dotted	y
13a. apply t_4 to C yielding D'				dotted	
b. compare D to D'				(match)	
14. respond TRUE					c

FIG. 4.3. Procedure for solving a typical figural analogy according to Sternberg's model with self-terminating mapping and application. From ''Components of a Componential Analysis,'' by J. W. Pellegrino and D. R. Lyon, *Intelligence*, 1979, *3*, 169–186. Copyright 1979 by Ablex, reprinted by permission.

describe the figure (word or shape) presented. The second term (B) must also be exhaustively encoded and represented in memory. The time to execute each separate encoding process is measured by parameter a. After the initial two terms have been encoded, there is an inference process that exhaustively proceeds through the attribute list for A and B, comparing the values and determining entries in a transformation vector. This inference process takes time x for each attribute on which the values for A and B do not match, that is, for attributes on which a transformation is required. Thus the inference time for the analogy in Figure 4.3 is 2x. The next phase of processing involves exhaustive attribute encoding of the C term (again with time a). This is followed by a mapping process that selects the first attribute of A and determines its value in C to compute entries in a new transformation vector relating A and C. Because mapping in this specific model is self-terminating, no other attributes are mapped yet. Instead, the next step is to exhaustively encode the D term (again with time a). The model now specifies an application process in which the initial transformation in the A–B transformation vector is applied to the corresponding attribute value of C to yield an attribute value for an ideal answer D'. This is followed by a comparison of D and D' on the values of the designated attribute (e.g., sex). If these do not match, a "false" response is given and the problem is solved. If a match *is* obtained, then control returns to the mapping process, which determines the value change (if any) for the next A to C attribute comparison. There follows an application of the appropriate A–B transformation to yield the value of D' to be compared to D. If the analogy is true, then the mapping and application processes will work through all of the attributes, with the time for each process being a function of the number of non-null transformations that must be processed. In the case of the item in Figure 4.3, the mapping process has value 2y whereas application has a value 2z. The final process is response selection and execution, which takes time c and is a constant across items.

Chronometric Methods for Model Testing. Evaluating the adequacy of a given model or set of models has been based upon the application of chronometric methods, specifically subtractive and additive factors logic (S. Sternberg, 1969). The basic assumption is that the total time to verify the truth of a given analogy item is the sum of the times associated with each of the independent component processes. Thus, for the item illustrated in Figure 4.3, the total time is a composite of four separate encoding latencies plus inference, mapping, application, and response component latencies. The overall reaction-time equation for the item shown in Figure 4.2 would be as follows:

$$4a + 2x + 2y + 2z + c$$

To test such a model and the resultant equations for specific conditions and items, it is necessary to obtain estimates of the duration of each of the component processes and evidence of additivity. This can be done in several ways.

One way to decompose total solution time is by the precuing method (Stern-berg, 1977a). This method employs subtractive logic and can be illustrated very simply. For any given analogy item that represents a true-false verification format, the basic equation for total reaction time is:

$$4a + x + y + z + c$$

This represents a 0 cues condition, i.e., no cues or parts of the item are presented prior to measuring final solution time. This can be contrasted with a 1 cue condition: The A term is presented alone for as much time as an individual needs to encode it. The remaining B, C, and D terms are then presented. The time to solve the item upon presentation of the remaining terms is presumed to reflect the following components:

$$3a + x + y + z + c$$

The difference between the 0 and 1 cue conditions provides an estimate of *a* or encoding time. In a 2 cue condition, A and B are presented for initial processing with subsequent presentation of C and D. The time to solve the item upon presentation of C and D represents fewer components.

$$2a + y + z + c$$

Similarly, in a 3 cue condition, A, B, and C are presented prior to the D term. The time to solve the item once D is presented represents the smallest number of processing components:

$$a + z + c$$

By solving this set of simultaneous equations, estimates can be derived for encoding, inference, mapping, and a combined application + response compo-nent. When this method is applied across a set of items that vary with respect to the predicted times for one or more component processes, it is possible to test the adequacy of a given model on a large data set.

Another method that can be used to obtain estimates of individual component latencies is to vary the number of times a given process needs to be executed. This can be done by varying item format in a forced-choice paradigm (Stern-berg, 1977a; Sternberg & Nigro, 1980). In a standard two-alternative forced-choice task the individual sees A$\rightarrow$B::C$\rightarrow$_____ with two alternatives: D_1 and D_2. The reaction-time equation for item solution is:

$$5a + x + y + 2z + c$$

If the task is now modified such that the individual is presented A$\rightarrow$B::_____ $\rightarrow$_____ with alternatives $C_1\rightarrow D_1$ and $C_2\rightarrow D_2$ then the reaction time equation is now:

$$6a + x + 2y + 2z + c$$

A third possible task variant is A--→_____::_____→_____ with alternatives $B_1::C_1 \rightarrow D_1$, $B_2::C_2 \rightarrow D_2$ in which case the reaction time equation is now:

$$7a + 2x + 2y + 2z + c$$

A combination of this method with the method of precuing and item manipulations can lead to a large number of "experimental" conditions for estimating latency parameters and testing specific models. As in all applications of simple subtractive logic, there is a potential concern about violations of the assumption of additivity when tasks are simplified (see for example Pachella, 1974).

These general methods for reaction time decomposition do not take into account the difficulty of process execution. Items often differ along this dimension. A process like encoding may be relatively easy to execute for highly familiar as compared with less common concepts, e.g., dog vs. unicorn. Therefore, in order to test specific models, it is necessary to develop reaction time equations that consider factors relevant to the duration of each stage of processing. The encoding process for geometric types of stimuli should be a function of stimulus complexity because more individual elements or geometric figures need to be represented. Differences among individual items can be included in the reaction-time equations by a direct manipulation of the number of stimulus elements (e.g., Mulholland, Pellegrino & Glaser, 1980) or by a weighting function based upon ratings of stimulus complexity (e.g., Sternberg, 1977a). As a concrete example, consider the contrast between a geometric analogy that involves a single stimulus element for each term versus one that involves three separate stimulus elements for each term. If a now represents the time to encode a single element then the reaction time equations for these items in a forced-choice format would be:

$$4a + x + y + z + c$$

$$12a + x + y + z + c$$

The difference in total time is attributed entirely to the encoding component.

The difficulty of attribute comparison processes such as inference, mapping, and application are also presumed to differ across items. These processes should be a function of the number of feature changes that define the relationships between pairs of terms (A–B, A–C, C–D). This was illustrated earlier in Figure 4.2 for the schematic-figures item. Differences between items in the time for inference, mapping, and application can be incorporated into reaction time equations by either direct manipulations of item features or by utilizing rating data. Direct manipulations are possible for schematic-figure and geometric items. For a geometric analogy that contains three separate stimulus elements in each term, it is possible to construct items that involve 0, 1, 2, or more separate transformations defining the relationships between terms. These differences can be incorporated directly into the reaction time equations for sets of items. Rating data can be used for verbal analogies to create differential weighting of components for sets of items.

An additional factor that serves to differentiate among items involves response evaluation and the need to include a possible justification component. For difficult verbal and geometric analogies, there are completion terms that constitute potentially acceptable answers that cannot be immediately accepted or rejected. This can affect processing in one of two ways. In a verification task, the D term requires additional feature analysis before its appropriateness can be verified. In a forced-choice task, two or more D terms are similar to each other and also related to the C term. This requires additional feature analysis and rule comparison before the best choice can be selected. Items can be scaled with respect to the probability of such additional processing and this can be incorporated into reaction time equations to obtain estimates of justification latency.

One of the most important aspects of model testing has involved the differentiation between exhaustive and self-terminating modes of process execution. By definition, verification of true items always requires exhaustive processing. In order to differentiate between exhaustive and self-terminating processing assumptions, it is necessary to contrast performance on true and false items and/or to examine differences among false items that vary in the amount of incorrect or disconfirming evidence. This requires the generation of different sets of equations for false items under different process models. A completely exhaustive process model yields the same reaction time equations for true and false items of the same type. Thus, the general prediction is that true and false items should not differ in overall reaction-time or the difference should be constant over all items. In contrast, models with self-terminating process assumptions predict systematic variations between true and false items, as well as within false items, given other variations in item complexity.

In summary, specific models of analogy solution are evaluated by applying the assumptions of a given model to individual items or sets of items under different formats of presentation. The predictions of a model are represented by a set of specific reaction time equations that differentially weight the individual component processes. The equations are then evaluated by determining their fit to actual latency data from a large set of individual items, often several hundred. The outcomes of such model fitting are estimates of the goodness-of-fit of a model to the data as well as estimates of the times associated with each of the component processes. The selection of the ''best'' model is based upon multiple criteria that include actual variance in the data that are accounted for, the magnitude of the average deviation between observed and predicted values, and the plausibility of the estimated latencies for each component process.

Empirical Results. Several studies have been conducted with adult, college-age individuals examining actual performance on verbal, geometric, and schematic-figure or people-piece items (e.g., Mulholland et al., 1980; Pellegrino &

Glaser, 1982; Sternberg, 1977a,b; Sternberg & Gardner, 1982). A major goal of these studies was to evaluate different models of analogy solution and to obtain estimates of individual component latencies. In all these studies, the items were selected or constructed so that accuracy would be high. This permits the collection of a large amount of latency data that can be reliably modeled.

All of the studies of adult performance have yielded support for models that assume self-terminating process execution for item falsification. When a completion term is found to violate a criterial feature of the A–B relation, processing of that term ceases and it is rejected. In a verification task, this means that item processing terminates and a false response is emitted. In a forced-choice task, processing shifts to consideration of the remaining alternatives. Although there is strong support for a model that assumes self-terminating process execution, it has proven difficult to discriminate among alternative models within this class. Sternberg (1977a,b) has contrasted three different models on verbal, geometric, and schematic-figure analogies. The general model that Sternberg preferred was one in which only mapping and application are self-terminating. Alternative models that were less preferred assumed that inference, mapping, and application were all self-terminating or that only application was self-terminating. The data, however, did not show a very substantial difference in the quality of fit of the preferred model and the one in which all three attribute comparison processes were assumed to be self-terminating.

Two additional results are of interest. The first involves overall differences among item types in the time for solution. Schematic-figure items are solved more rapidly than verbal or geometric analogies with an average latency of approximately 1.5 sec. Verbal analogy items also tend to be solved more rapidly than geometric items. In Sternberg's (1977a) study of verbal analogy solution, the average latency was approximately 2.5 sec. This is consistent with data obtained in studies conducted by Pellegrino and Ingram (1977). Geometric analogies require considerably longer average latencies, on the order of 4 sec for verification tasks (Mulholland et al., 1980) and 7 sec for forced-choice tasks (Sternberg, 1977a). A second possible difference among these three types of items is the need to postulate the existence of a mapping component. Evidence for mapping was considerably greater for the schematic-figure analogies than for either the verbal or geometric items. The similarities and differences suggested by the preceding global description of performance on these three types of items are elaborated by examining results specific to each.

Schematic-figure or people-piece analogies have been studied by Sternberg (1977a) and used in developmental research (e.g., Sternberg & Rifkin, 1979). There are certain interesting aspects of these materials that should be noted. Because these items are relatively simple with a well-defined set of dimensions and attributes, most of the time spent in item processing is distributed over the encoding and response components (70%). Attribute comparison processes require only 30% of the total solution time and none of these processes seems to be associated with external measures of inductive reasoning skill. As noted above, mapping appears to be a significant component of performance and accounts for 13% of the variance in item solution latency. The existence of a mapping component may be a function of the systematic nature of the item set where the A–C relationship is easily identifiable and may be useful for item verification.

Geometric analogy solution has been examined in forced-choice (Sternberg, 1977a) and verification formats (Mulholland et al., 1980). Both studies provided support for self-terminating processing in item solution. Sternberg found evidence for an option processing strategy that involved alternation between options with respect to attribute comparison. His data also indicated that a justification process was needed to account for performance. This process made a highly significant contribution to the overall model fitting. Of particular interest is the partition of solution time relative to the different sets of processes. Encoding required 36% of total solution time whereas response only required 7%. Attribute comparison processes (including justification) required 57% of the total time. In contrast to schematic-figure items, a greater amount of absolute and relative time was spent on attribute comparison. These processes were associated with performance on standardized reasoning tests. The Mulholland et al. study also found that the greatest single proportion of processing time (44%) was associated with attribute comparison processes. Encoding required 36% of total solution time; response accounted for 20%.

The Mulholland et al. (1980) study was designed to permit an analysis of the time spent on processing stimulus attributes (elements), and attribute changes (transformations), and the additivity of these aspects of processing. They found that transformations took longer to process than individual elements. For complex items involving multiple elements and transformations, the latencies were longer than those predicted by a simple additive model. This was explained in terms of time associated with control or executive processing components necessary to monitor or keep track of the total information stored in working memory. The false item data collected by Mulholland et al. also permitted a test of different models for the sequence of processing stimulus elements and transformations. Their data supported a process sequence in which elements and their transformations are processed in a pairwise sequential manner. The suggestion was also made that processing conforms to a different model than the one proposed by Sternberg. The sequence of processing events in their model can be characterized as Encode A, Encode B, Infer A–B, Encode C, Encode D, Infer C–D relational features, Compare to A–B, and Respond. This model is similar to one proposed by Evans (1968). It substitutes a second inference process for application with a subsequent mapping or comparison process. Sternberg's data on geometric analogy solution provided the weakest evidence for a mapping component; its existence may be attributable to the presence of transposition items. Items of this type are solved more readily by considering A–C as the primary relationship; more will be said about this factor in the following discussion of verbal analogy solution.

Verbal analogies have been studied more extensively than any other type of analogy. In addition to Sternberg's original 1977 study, latency studies have been conducted by Pellegrino and Ingram (1977) (see Pellegrino & Glaser, 1982), Barnes and Whitely (1981), and Grudin (1980). The basic findings in Sternberg's (1977a) research are similar to those discussed earlier in this chapter. His data on component process latencies indicated that the largest proportion of processing time was distributed between encoding (54%) and attribute comparison (29%) processes. A different set of results was obtained by Pellegrino and Ingram (1977). They found that encoding required 23% of the total solution time whereas 61% of the total time was associated with attribute comparison processes, including an extended feature analysis or justification component. One possible explanation for the differences between these two studies is the nature of the items. Sternberg employed verbal items where there was a high degree of preexperimental consensus about the D term that completed a given item. Thus, there was little ambiguity or uncertainty with respect to the semantic features defining the rule for the item. In contrast, Pellegrino and Ingram (1977) used items that varied considerably in the degree of consensus about the semantic features of the item and the best completion term. This characteristic may have made attribute comparison processes more difficult and time consuming. Thus, item differences may have produced the difference in the relative times for encoding vs. attribute comparison processes in the two experiments.

Mapping as a required component of verbal analogy solution has been questioned. Grudin (1980) argued that evidence for mapping may be due to modeling a large item set that contains both standard items and transposition items. An example transposition item is Sugar : Grapefruit : : Sweet : Sour. Items of this type are solved more readily by treating A–C as the primary relation and then applying this relation to the B term to verify the appropriateness of the D term. An implication of Grudin's argument is that mapping may not be a required process but may be part of a strategy for dealing with analogies where inference of the A–B relation is difficult or the relationship is unclear. Two experiments were conducted by Grudin to examine how transposition affected analogy solution. In the first study, performance on standard and transposed items was examined under different precuing conditions. The results showed asymmetries in solution time that were attributed to the differential utility of inference processes executed during precuing conditions. His second experiment examined possible set or bias effects in solving verbal analogies. The four conditions that he used represented the crossing of an initial set favoring an A–B vs. A–C solution strategy with a subsequent test on items that favored either the A–B or A–C solution mode. His data indicated that an A–B set impedes solution of A–C transposition items. An A–C set had no effect on solution of standard items. He thus proposes a refinement of the model of analogy solution such that A–C mapping may be optional and individuals first consider A–B. If this does not appear useful, then they use mapping and focus on the A–C relationship to guide solution.

Related work has been reported by Barnes and Whitely (1981) in the context of problem restructuring processes for ill-structured verbal analogies. They delineated three types of ill-structured items. One type is the transposition item studied by Grudin. This type requires semantic restructuring. Two additional types both require perceptual restructuring. Perceptual restructuring is required if the item is presented in reverse order :_____:C::B:A. Both perceptual and semantic restructuring are required for an item that is in reversed order and transposed :_____:B::C:A. Two studies were conducted with these types of items and evidence was obtained for both types of restructuring processes. The effects of both restructuring processes were additive and appeared to be relatively automatic in execution. Perceptual restructuring occurs early in the solution process. Semantic restructuring occurs later, presumably after a subject experiences difficulty in executing the initial inference process.

Models of verbal analogy solution have been extended to include other aspects of processing that govern solution latency. One such extension has been the consideration of executive or control functions associated with global and local strategy planning for solving analogies that are not in the canonical form A:B::C:_____. Sternberg (1981) has reported the results of a study where latency on different types of analogies was compared under blocked and mixed presentation conditions. The different types of items varied the number of missing terms and their location. Both global and local planning components were found to contribute to solution latency, indicating that these are additional aspects of analogy solution that need to be incorporated into specific models and the general theory.

Other extensions of the theory of analogy solution (Heller, 1979; Whitely & Barnes, 1979) based upon protocol data are designed to handle two related issues. The first of these involves recursive processing events that may often occur in the solution of ambiguous or difficult items. The second involves within and between individual differences in the sequence of process execution for a given item or set of items. Difficult items often demand a refinement or redefinition of individual terms and relationships in order to achieve solution. This involves various amounts of recursive processing. The possibility of such events is generally handled by the concept of a justification component. However, this general component can subsume a number of possible recursive processing sequences. Solution of items representing the difficulty levels found on actual standardized tests may involve significant amounts of such recursive processing. How such a complex process is monitored and its interaction with individual subject characteristics remain largely unexplored areas. Sophisticated eye-movement protocols together with verbal report data can provide important information about these additional problem-solving aspects of analogy solution. The limited eye-movement data that are available (Bethell-Fox, Lohman, & Snow, 1982) suggest that it is inappropriate to conclude that all analogy solution conforms to the simple linear process sequences that have been verified chronometrically for proficient adult reasoners.

Process Outcome Models

The use of chronometric methods for theory and model development requires high levels of solution accuracy. However, a cognitive components approach can also be applied to differences in performance accuracy. Such a focus is important for several reasons related to both developmental and individual differences analysis. This can be illustrated by considering a prototypical standardized test of analogical reasoning. The Cognitive Abilities Test (CAT) developed by Thorndike and Hagen (1971) contains a set of 60 verbal and 60 geometric analogies. The structure of this group test involves overlapping item sets for successive age groups starting at grade 3 and continuing through grade 12. Each age group solves a set of 25 items. The third graders solve problems 1–25, fourth graders solve problems 6–30 and so on. Thus, children of several different ages solve similar subsets of items. Normative data on item solutions reveal two important things. First, children typically complete all 25 items within the time allotted. Second, the probability of correct solution of a given item increases with age. Developmental changes in analogical reasoning performance are therefore more a function of accuracy than speed. To maintain the same average accuracy over age groups, each age group is required to solve successively harder sets of items. Given that children within a given age group attempt to solve all 25 items, the major factor associated with individual differences is accuracy. If we are to understand developmental and individual differences in analogical reasoning it will be necessary to consider accuracy of executing component processes as well as speed.

There are three possible relationships between accuracy and latency at the individual subject level. The first of these is a speed-accuracy tradeoff across individuals such that individuals who show lower mean solution times have higher mean error rates, producing a negative correlation between mean latency and errors. The second is a complete independence of latency and accuracy, yielding a zero correlation of the two measures over individuals. The third possibility is a positive relationship such that individuals who make more errors are also slower in average solution latency. Data tend to support the last relationship. As an example, Holzman (1979) examined the performance of adults on three types of inductive reasoning items: geometric analogies, numerical analogies, and number series problems. For all three tasks, an individual's mean solution time over a set of items was positively correlated with mean errors. The implication of these results is that skill is often associated with faster *and* more accurate process execution.

The data obtained in a number of studies of analogy solution support a similar relationship between latency and accuracy at the level of individual items. An item that is predicted to have a longer solution latency due to increased time for execution of encoding, attribute comparison, or response evaluation processes also has a lower mean accuracy (e.g., Sternberg, 1977a). When equations designed for chronometric modeling are fit to accuracy data, there is a moderate level of fit to the data. As an example, Sternberg (1977a,b) was able to account for 60% of the variance in error rates on schematic-figure items, 50% for geometric items but only 14% for verbal items. Similarly, Mulholland et al. (1980) obtained data on geometric analogies showing a partial relationship between the item features yielding longer average solution latencies and lower mean accuracy. However, there was a major difference between latency and accuracy. Whereas the number of stimulus elements significantly affected solution time via encoding processes, this number contributed little to solution accuracy. The major factor predicting accuracy differences was the complexity of the item rule, i.e., the number of transformations relating the A–B and C–D pairs of terms. The error function that best fit the accuracy data was different from the best fitting function for the latency data.

There are several reasons why prediction equations derived for chronometric modeling are not adequate for the modeling of accuracy data. Such equations reflect assumptions about independence and additivity of processing stages. The independence assumption means that the time and outcome of a prior stage of processing has no effect on the time or outcome of a subsequent stage of processing. However, if a term is incorrectly encoded, then the outcomes of all subsequent mental operations are affected and solution will probably be incorrect. This misencoding may have little effect on the time to execute subsequent processing operations. Second, although latencies are additive over stages, accuracies are not. There is no upper limit on solution time and it is not a dichotomous variable. Accuracy has an upper limit and is dichotomous for a given item.

One way to approach the problem of modeling accuracy in a task like analogy solution is to assume accuracy is a function of the appropriate representation of each unit of information necessary for solution. In the case of geometric analogies, the units of information include the individual stimulus elements and the transformations defining relationships between elements. It is assumed that over an entire set of items there is some average probability $\propto$ of misrepresenting individual transformations and a similar probability β of misrepresenting individual elements. Thus, the general equation for predicting the average error rate on a given class of items would be:

$$\text{Probability (error)} = 1 - (1-\propto)^T (1-\beta)^E$$

where T equals the total number of transformations to be represented and E equals the total number of stimulus elements to be represented. This equation further assumes independence of element and transformational processing. The adequacy of such an expression is determined by its ability to fit actual data and the estimates derived for $\propto$ and β.

An equation having this form was used by Mulholland et al. (1980) to model accuracy on a set of geometric analogies. The error function that best fit their accuracy data takes two factors into account: attribute comparison and memory load. Number of transformations to be inferred and evaluated, but not number of elements to be encoded, constitute the attribute comparison component. The specific form of the error function that best fit their accuracy data was:

$$\text{Probability (error)} = 1 - (1-\propto)^T(1-\lambda^{M-\lambda})$$

The $\propto$ parameter represents the probability of incorrectly representing or applying a specific transformation, T represents the total number of transformations that must be processed, λ is a parameter reflecting the maximum amount of information that can be held in working memory, and M represents the number of working memory placekeepers required during the solution of a given problem. When this function was fit to the data, the value of $\propto$ was equal to .044, indicating that the probability of misrepresenting or misapplying a simple transformation is very low. The value of λ was equal to 5.8, which is quite close to the magical number 7 that is often cited as the capacity limit of short-term or working memory. This particular model of accuracy implies that complex items involving many attributes or feature changes will be very difficult to solve and the likelihood of correct solution will be close to zero. It predicts performance on an item or class of items with certain specifiable characteristics.

Several problems exist, however, if one wishes to extend this type of model. For some types of items, e.g., verbal analogies, the precise specification of item characteristics is not possible. Second, attribute comparison involves a number of component processes. The model used by Mulholland et al. (1980) does not allow the examination of accuracy of each of these components. Third, and most important, the model ignores the sequential dependency of processing stages such that the outcome of each process affects the outcome of subsequent processes and the likelihood that the final outcome will be a correct solution.

A more complete approach to modeling accuracy builds on the general theory of analogy solution and examines differences among individuals in overall accuracy in terms of the successive outcomes of individual component process execution. By determining how accurately individuals execute each component process, explicit process accuracy comparisons between individuals and age groups can be performed. These comparisons emphasize the explanation of accuracy differences of the sort found on standardized tests. Such data are complementary to latency data obtained at the group and individual subject level.

The development of a process outcome model is based on a consideration of possible relationships between processes that operate on the stem and processes operating on the alternative set. Consider the typical forced-choice format for analogy problems. A three term stem is presented, i.e., A is to B as C is to ?, with four or five alternatives. In a slightly different form of the task, a generation task, no alternatives are presented and choice of a completion term is not restricted to the alternative set. This form of the task allows the examination of a joint inference x application process: The individual may infer any possible A–B relationship and then attempt to apply that relation to the C term to produce an ideal D′ term. For the generated completion term to be correct, both inference and application must be executed correctly. The accuracy of *each* of these can be examined by presenting A is to B prior to the full stem and requiring the statement of a relationship.

The forced-choice task requires the same inference and application processes as the generation task plus discrimination-choice components that may affect performance. There are three possible ways in which stem and alternative set processing may be related. These possibilities are shown in Table 4.1. In the simplest case, encoding, inference, and application have been successfully executed. Each of the alternatives is evaluated for consistency with the semantics of the item stem, and the correct choice is selected. The second possibility also involves accurate stem processing. However, certain kinds of distractors, e.g., salient free associates to the C term, may cause the rejection of a previously generated analogically appropriate response. Additionally, the distractor set may contain multiple alternatives that match the ideal D′ term equally well. The individual may be unable to select the C–D pairing that yields the most precise matching relation.

TABLE 4.1
Relationship Between Stem and Option Processing in Analogy

	Stem Processing Outcome	*Option Processing Outcome*	*Overall Accuracy*
I.	Accurate execution of *Encoding, Inference* and *Application*	Accurate execution of response selection	Correct
II.	Accurate execution of *Encoding, Inference* and *Application*	*Distraction* during response selection	Incorrect
III.	Inaccurate execution of *Encoding, Inference* and/or *Application*	*Recognition* of appropriate rule during response selection (or successful guessing)	Correct

Prediction Equation

$$P_{FC} = \overbrace{\left[P_{Inf}P_{App} \right]}^{\substack{\text{Stem} \\ \text{Processing}}} + \overbrace{\left[\underbrace{R_{Rec}(1\text{-}P_I P_A)}_{\substack{\text{Response} \\ \text{Recognition}}} + \underbrace{1/K \left\{ 1\text{-}[P_I P_A + P_R(1\text{-}P_I P_A)] \right\}}_{\text{Guessing}} - \underbrace{P_{Dist}P_I P_A}_{\substack{\text{Distractor} \\ \text{Interference}}} \right]}^{\text{Option Processing}}$$

The third possibility involves inaccurate stem processing. However, the alternatives may permit the individual to recognize the correct relation and completion term. A final component of alternative processing is guessing. Here inference, application, and/or response recognition processes have failed and only random guessing leads to a correct response.

The different outcomes for stem and option processing apply to each analogy item solved. By considering performance over an entire set of items, the general prediction equation shown at the bottom of Table 4.1 can be derived from overall forced-choice performance. The equation represents the separate contributions of inference, application, recognition, distraction, and guessing. If the probabilities of recognition and distraction are zero, then fored-choice accuracy is predicted by stem processing accuracy plus guessing. The equation is appropriate for group and individual subject data. Its application requires independent estimates of each probability. The latter can be obtained through an incremental presentation methodology in conjunction with the more typical forced-choice format. The essence of this approach is to present the first pair of stem terms in the analogy so that initially only the relational inference process is required. Subsequently, all of the stem terms are presented and the task is to generate a correct completion term. Finally, the stem is represented along with an alternative set and the task is the typical forced-choice format (see Goldman, Pellegrino, Parseghian, & Sallis, 1982). This methodology is similar to precuing but emphasis is on the outcome of process execution rather than latency.

Whitely (1980a,b,c) has described in detail a very powerful extension of this type of approach to process outcome modeling that she refers to as multicomponent latent trait modeling. The essence of this approach is to treat performance on a task such as analogy or classification as the result of two factors. The first involves the probability of success in executing each of the separate component processes necessary for item solution. This results in a prediction function similar to the one presented earlier in Table 4.1, where the likelihood of success is a joint function of the individual's ability on each of the separate component processes. The second factor involves the difficulty of executing each separate process in solving a given item. Items are assumed to differ in the ease or likelihood of inferring the appropriate rule and/or in selecting the best alternative completion term. A model of item difficulty can be derived that is then combined with a model of individual ability to provide a composite model in which the performance of an individual on a specific item is described in terms of both subject and item variables. Process outcome models can be tested and the result is a characterization of the components of performance that contribute to item difficulty and individual differences. Factors that affect item difficulty may not necessarily be important individual difference components and her procedures allow for such an evaluation.

To conduct a multicomponent latent trait analysis, it is necessary to obtain independent estimates of an individual's performance on each process on each item of a total item set. A procedure that Whitely (1980c) has used is similar to the incremental procedure in which different amounts of information are presented and the individual is asked to provide some explicit response. In modeling performance on analogy tasks, she has used three separate tasks that are designed to evaluate three major aspects of analogy solution. The first type of task is to present the A:B::C stem of the item and ask for specification of the item rule. Performance on this task defines the measure of *image construction* and represents a composite of several processes such as encoding, inference, and possibly application. The second type of task involves presenting the stem and the set of possible completion terms. The individual is not asked to select the best answer but is asked to specify any new rule that might be needed to discriminate effectively among the alternatives. Performance on this task defines the measure of *event recovery* and this measure is similar to the recognition measure described earlier where a new or refined rule is specified because stem processing was incorrect or insufficient for the item. The third task involves presenting the stem and the alternatives together with an explicit statement of the correct rule for the item. The individual is then required to select the correct answer. Performance on this task defines the measure of *response evaluation*. Applications of this multicomponent measurement approach to individual differences analysis for analogy and classification tasks will be discussed subsequently.

COGNITIVE COMPONENTS OF CLASSIFICATION SOLUTION

The type of componential analysis done for analogy has been extended to performance in verbal classification tasks. Sternberg and Gardner (1982) have developed and tested latency models of verbal classification and Pellegrino and his associates (e.g., Alderton, Goldman, & Pellegrino, 1982; Parseghian & Pellegrino, 1980; Pellegrino & Goldman, 1983) have extended process outcome models to this task. The typical psychometric verbal classification item involves a three term stem and a set of four or five alternatives. The task is to choose the answer that is consistent with the features shared by all three terms in the stem. The most common features defining the rule for the stem involve a similar function, property or superordinate category.

Latency Models

Sternberg and Gardner (1982) have outlined five processes in solving verbal classification problems. The individual must encode each of the terms and infer a relation or rule that describes what the stem terms have in common. Application, an important process in analogy, does not operate in classification because all the stem terms are members of the same set. The individual must compare each alternative to an ideal fourth term or rule. If a perfect match is not present, justification is used to choose the option closest to the ideal. The final process is response. Sternberg and Gardner (1982) indicate that in some presentation formats mapping may be required. However, this would not be typical of the standard form of this task.

It is also important to note that the exact process by which the ideal fourth term is determined and the execution of the comparison process would be expected to vary across semantic domains. For some rules, individuals may generate an ideal term and look for a match in the alternatives. In other cases, the rule may not be precise enough to have a specific ideal until the alternatives are examined. This issue is considered in the process outcome model described next.

Process Outcome Models

The development of a process outcome model for classification items follows a logic similar to that which was applied to analogy items (see for example Pellegrino & Goldman, 1983). Given a three term stem the individual must infer a relation that holds across all three terms; an examplar of this same relation may then be generated. As noted above, the application process of analogy is not characteristic of classification. When the alternatives are presented, as in the forced-choice format, distractor inference and response recognition must be considered. In the former case, stem processing is correct, but the alternative set leads the individual astray. In the latter case, the presence of the alternatives may enable the individual to recognize the most appropriate or "more correct" relation and select the correct alternative. In fact, for many classification items, it is not possible to determine the exact rule until the alternatives are examined. As in analogy, there is also a random guessing component, and the prediction equation over a set of classification items is:

$$P_{fc}(\text{Corr}) = P_{Inf} + P_{Rec}(1-P_I) + 1/K \ 1-[P_I + P_R(1-P_I)]-P_{Dist}P_I.$$

This equation is similar in structure to the one discussed earlier for analogy performance and illustrated in Table 4.1. Estimates for each of the separate process outcome probabilities can be obtained by a sequential presentation of stem and alternative set terms with responses elicited from the individual at each stage of processing.

The multicomponent latent trait approach developed by Whitely (1980a,b,c) has also been applied to performance on classification items. A task presentation format similar to the one described earlier for analogy problems has been used to obtain process outcome measures of stem processing (image construction) and alternative processing (response evaluation and event recovery). Empirical results dealing with both latency and process outcome models are discussed in subsequent sections of this chapter.

Before discussing applications of chronometric and process outcome modeling procedures to the analysis of developmental and individual differences, a brief summarization of possible results is needed. A major goal of developing and validating process theories and performance models for tasks such as analogy and classification is to apply them to the analysis of performance differences as manifest on standard psychometric tasks. In this way, understanding can be gained of the specific sources of age and skill differences in this cognitive aptitude. The types of analyses outlined in this and the preceding section provide the basis for examining two types of differences among individuals. Qualitative differences would be manifest by evidence of differences in the model or solution strategy that an individual employed for task performance. Older and/or more skilled reasoners may utilize a solution strategy that includes all of the necessary component processes, and their sequence and mode of execution may show optimal efficiency. Younger and/or less skilled reasoners may employ solution strategies that lack one or more component processes, or they may utilize a less efficient sequence and mode of process execution. Quantitative differences would be manifest by evidence of differences in the speed and/or power of executing the same component processes. Both types of differences have been investigated and supported in the developmental and individual differences literature.

DEVELOPMENTAL CHANGES IN INDUCTIVE REASONING

A variety of studies have addressed issues associated with sources of developmental change in inductive reasoning. These studies indicate that both qualitative and quantitative changes occur in elementary school-aged children. Qualitative changes refer to changes in strategies used in solution and to changes in understanding task constraints. Such changes are demonstrated by data that (1) indicate differential importance of processing components in accounting for children's as compared to adults' performance; and/or (2) assess children's thinking about the rules and relations that constrain their solutions. Sternberg (1979) has recently referred to the latter as metacomponents. Quantitative generally refers to changes in the efficiency with which a process is executed. Efficiency may be indexed by speed of process execution or by the degree of accuracy with which a process is executed. From studies of analogy and classification tasks using verbal, figural, and geometric stimuli, it can be concluded that the development of inductive reasoning involves all of the aforementioned loci of change. The remainder of this section examines the data supporting this conclusion in the various task and stimulus-type situations that have been investigated.

Nonverbal Analogies

In an early effort to extend component process analysis to children, Sternberg and Rifkin (1979) presented two types of figural analogies to 8-, 10-, 12-, and 19-year olds. The task was to choose the better of two completion terms. Both types of analogies varied on four attribute dimensions. However, for the schematic-picture analogies these attributes are separable, that is the presence or absence of one attribute does not affect the presence or absence of any other. In contrast, the second type are described as integral stimuli. These were humanlike figures (people-piece analogies) and in order to depict any one attribute, the other three must be assigned some value.

The analogies were presented in a series of booklets. Component process time was determined by dividing total time by number of problems solved correctly. Bisanz (1979) has noted that this method of obtaining latency data is appropriate only if error rates are the same across the different age groups. Because error rates decreased significantly with age, it is difficult to compare absolute times per process across ages. The data do, however, illustrate some important developmental differences in the processes used at different ages and self-terminating vs. exhaustive execution of these processes.

Encoding, inference, and application were used at each age level for both types of analogies. Mapping was used only for integral analogies and only by the 10-, 12-, and 19-year-old groups. Thus, although mapping is required when attributes are integrated, according to Sternberg and Rifkin (1979), the 8-year olds did not use this process. Sternberg and Rifkin (1979) concluded from these data that mapping is unavailable or inaccessible to 8-year olds and they appeared to solve analogies in ways that bypassed mapping. Parallel developmental trends were observed when Sternberg and Rifkin (1979) examined how each process was executed. For the schematic stimuli, all component processing was self-terminating. Eight-year olds solved the integral stimuli in the same way. However, the older groups employed both self-terminating and exhaustive processing. For the 10-year olds, encoding was exhaustive, but inference, application, and mapping were self-terminating. For the 12- and 19-year olds, encoding and inference were exhaustive, but the other operations were self-terminating. Sternberg and Rifkin (1979) speculated that two factors could account for this change: (1) exhaustive processing is associated with lower error rates than self-terminating processing; and (2) older children may be better able to handle the increased memory load of exhaustive inference and mapping. Sternberg (1979) has also suggested that younger children seem more willing to trade accuracy for speed. In contrast, older individuals choose the type of processing that will minimize error rate but still permit them to maintain a reasonable solution rate.

The Sternberg and Rifkin (1979) study suggests that older individuals alter their solution process in response to differences in the type of item; younger individuals do not. Common across ages was the presence of encoding, inference, and application. Conclusions from these data regarding speed of processing changes are somewhat problematic due to the method employed. Bisanz (1979) pursued the issue of developmental changes in speed and the types of processing in geometric analogy solution. True–false decisions were made by 10-, 12-, and 14-year olds. Latency and accuracy were recorded for each item. The items consisted of four terms in which number of elements (1 or 3) and type of transformation were manipulated independently. Transformations were of three types: changes in orientation, size, or number of figures per element. False analogies differed in the number of C-->D mismatches.

Bisanz (1979) found that on one element analogies, speed of processing was equivalent across age groups. For three element analogies, 10-year olds were slower than the two older groups. Bisanz (1979) discusses two complementary interpretations of these data. First, three element analogies involve the execution of three times as many component processes as one element analogies. Consistent with the conclusions of Sternberg and Rifkin (1979), the decrease in latency between 10- and 12-year olds could reflect increased speed on one or more component processes. However, this interpretation would predict differences on one element analogies as well. Alternatively, Bisanz suggests that three element analogies may involve factors that do not apply to one element analogies. With the greater amount of information in the former, time to initiate any one process might increase and/or additional time might be needed to monitor processing. One possible source of developmental change that has both quantitative and qualitative aspects might thus be the ability to maintain efficient execution of a set of processes in the face of a complex stimulus.

The false analogy latency data revealed that 10-year olds were slower than the two older groups. However, time to detect a mismatch was similar across ages regardless of the number of C-->D mismatches. Bisanz's investigation of the type of processing indicated that C-->D processing was self-terminating for false analogies. Thus, the number of mismatches did not have a differential developmental effect because all groups responded when a mismatch was detected. Further, the rate of discovering a single C-->D mismatch did not change with age.

Bisanz (1979) also evaluated the goodness-of-fit of a number of processing models to the group mean data. Models with exhaustive C-->D relationship testing were unacceptable. However, two models yielded similar fits to the data for each age group, each accounting for over 95% of the variance among latencies. The first model involves exhaustive A-->B inference and self-terminating testing of the C-->D relationship. The second model assumes selective A-->B inference, nonexhaustive C-->D testing and a degree of processing inefficiency on three element problems. Although the two models could not be distinguished statistically from one another, Bisanz favored the second model. He argued that this model has implications for determining if changes with age in processing speed are due to increases in the speed(s) of specific components or to how these components are initiated, monitored, and executed.

Subsequent work by Stone and Day (1981) suggests that both factors are significant sources of developmental changes in solution time. Eleven- and 14-year olds and adults solved geometric matrix problems. The design was similar to Mulholland, et al. (1980) in that number of elements (1–3) and number of transformations (0–3) were varied. Latency to decide whether a matrix was correct or incorrect was measured. Replicating Mulholland et al. (1980), processing time per element and transformation was nonadditive: Multiple element and transformation items were not predicted by an additive model for any age group. Consistent with Sternberg and Rifkin (1979), overall solution time decreased with age and this was due to decreases in latency of executing each component process. In addition, differences in latency between ages increased as the number of elements and transformations increased.

These three studies of various types of nonverbal analogies indicate that the basic component processes of encoding, inference, and application are executed by children as young as eight. The efficiency with which these are executed appears to increase with age. Furthermore, as age increases, there is an increased tendency to adjust information-processing activities to stimuli that differ in complexity, either in terms of separability of attributes, number of attributes, or transformations. Such adjustments tend to be focused on processes associated with encoding and understanding the relationship represented in the stem of the item.

Verbal Analogies

Research has indicated that developmental changes in verbal analogical reasoning stem from qualitative differences in how such items are solved. During midchildhood, children have a tendency to choose alternatives that are highly associated with the C term (Achenbach, 1970; Gentile, Tedesco-Stratton, Davis, Lund, & Agunanne, 1977). It also appears that inferring the relationship between the A–B terms is a potential source of difficulty especially for certain types of relationships (e.g., Levinson & Carpenter, 1974; Lunzer, 1968). Other data indicate that the A–B terms play a very minor and nonsignificant role in the first stage of analogy solution (Gallagher & Wright, 1979; Piaget, Montangero, & Billeter, 1977). Using these findings as a starting point, Sternberg and Nigro (1980) and Goldman, Pellegrino, Parseghian, and Sallis (1982) examined developmental changes in verbal analogical reasoning within the current component process framework. The former study concentrated on model testing based primarily on latency data and comparisons of best fitting models for different age groups. Goldman et al. compared the accuracy of component processes for different age groups and examined the processes that contributed most to individual differences in overall performance.

Sternberg and Nigro (1980) had 20 children at each of four age levels (9, 12, 15, and 18 years) solve forced-choice verbal analogies. In order to collect latency data appropriate to Sternberg's (1977a) component process modeling techniques, the number of alternatives was varied (from two to four) and three different presentation formats were used. These formats varied in terms of the number of stem terms that were presented prior to the response options and, concurrently, in terms of the number of terms in each of the alternatives. For example, in the standard presentation format, and one of those used by Sternberg and Nigro (1980), the A, B, and C terms appear in the stem. Then possible D terms appear as alternatives. In the second presentation format used by Sternberg and Nigro (1980), A and B appeared in the stem, and each alternative consisted of a C–D pair. In the third type, only A appeared as a stem term and each alternative consisted of B, C, and D terms. These presentation techniques allowed the identification and estimation of component process latencies and the determination of whether a particular process was self-terminating or exhaustive.

Of particular importance from a developmental perspective is that Sternberg and Nigro (1980) found a significant item form x age interaction for both latency and errors: The performance of the 9- and 12-year olds was comparable and differed from that of the 15- and 18-year olds, which was also comparable. Simple correlations indicated that three components were predictive of latency at each age level: encoding, application, and mapping. In addition, the degree of association between the stem and alternatives was predictive of the 9- and 12-year olds' performance but not of the older groups. Multiple regression analyses indicated that the best fitting models were also different across age groups. The data of the 9- and 12-year-old groups were best fit by a model that assumes an exhaustive scan of all the options if working memory is not exceeded but a self-terminating scan of the options if working memory capacity is exceeded. In contrast, the data of the 15- and 18-year-old groups were best fit by a model that assumes exhaustive scanning of the options. Thus, there was a developmental difference in how the processes were executed. The multiple regression analyses further indicated that the component processes that were the two best model predictors were encoding and justification. This was the case at each grade level. In essence, latency was predicted best by the number of terms that had to be encoded (β's = .94 to .85) and second best by the degree of fit or relatedness between the two pairs of terms in the analogy (β's = .26 to .17).

Sternberg and Nigro (1980) interpret these data as indicating two levels of performance. At the first level, solution is partly governed by associative relations among the terms. Processing partially reflects analogical reasoning but when working memory is exceeded, processing is affected by associative relatedness and is self-terminating. At the second level, there is complete encoding of relations such that the two halves of the analogy are fully related to one another. In essence, verbal reasoning overrides verbal association. Thus, processing becomes more exhaustive with increasing age and the effect of verbal association decreases. As Sternberg and Nigro (1980) note, precisely how association affects the solution process is unclear. Speculatively, an alternative with high associative relatedness may contribute to only global processing of other alternatives. This may produce the premature termination such that the analogically-but-not-associatively-correct option is not sufficiently processed.

Goldman et al. (1982) also found evidence for the presence of associative solution strategies among younger, as well as less skilled, reasoners. Their conclusions were based on process outcome measures and children's verbal justifications of their responses. As described in a previous section, process

TABLE 4.2
Mean Accuracy on Process Outcome
Measures in Analogy Problems

	Age	
	8	10
Overall Forced-Choice Performance	.40	.52
Process Measures		
Inference x Application	.30	.40
Response recognition	.10	.19
Distractor interference	.36	.27

outcome modeling involves obtaining probability estimates of the success of two processes operating on the item stem, inference and application, and two processes related to processing of the alternatives, response recognition and distractor interference. Goldman et al. (1982) conducted two experiments with 8- and 10-year olds. In the first experiment, a sequential presentation procedure was used to obtain four probabilities: overall forced-choice performance, inference x application, response recognition, and distractor interference. Significant age group differences were obtained on each measure. The means are shown in Table 4.2. Older children were more accurate in inferring and applying the A–B relation to the second pair. They were also more likely to recognize the correct response from among a set of alternatives in cases where inference x application had been incorrect. Finally, they were less likely to have previously accurate processing disrupted by distractors in the alternative set.

There was also substantial variability in forced-choice accuracy within each age group, and the ranges of the two groups were overlapping. Correlation-regression analyses, in which age was entered as a predictor along with the three process outcome measures, indicated that this variability was not significantly predicted by age, although the simple correlation was significant. Rather, performance on each of the process measures significantly predicted overall performance. These data are shown in Table 4.3. Thus, older children tend to do better

TABLE 4.3
Simple and Multiple Regression Results
Predicting Forced-Choice Performance in Analogy

Predictor	Simple r	β	F (1,42)
Age	.41*	.02	1.0
Inference x application	.77**	.28	137.1**
Response recognition	.91**	.58	559.3**
Distractor interference	-.69***	-.35	305.5**

*p < .01
**p < .001

than younger children but the degree to which an individual between 8 and 10 years successfully executes each process is more predictive of performance. These results were replicated in a second experiment, using 8- and 10-year olds, in which inference and application measures were independently estimated. Inference was a significant predictor of overall performance ($\beta = .19$, $F[1,18] = 10.1$, $p < .01$), but it was less important than the other three processes. This is demonstrated by the beta values associated with application ($\beta = .34$), response recognition ($\beta = .36$), and distractor interference ($\beta = .40$), significant at the p $< .001$, level.

A plausible interpretation of these developmental differences is that a child's understanding of the constraints on analogical solutions and the characteristics of the best answer is initially very weak and easily subject to disruption. Verbal justifications of the alternatives chosen support this notion. Children in both studies were asked to state why they picked the answer they did. Three major categories were used to classify the responses: parallel relations, nonparallel relations, and no relation. Those statements that indicated an understanding that the A-->B and C-->D relations must match were classified in the first category. The nonparallel category comprises statements that violate this matching-relations constraint. In the no relation category were statements about the chosen response that did not relate it to any of the stem terms. When justifications for all responses were considered, 10-year olds had significantly more statements in the parallel relations category (.50) than 8-year olds (.34), $t(45) = 2.81$, $p < .01$. However, when only justifications for analogically correct responses were considered, the only developmental difference was in the greater tendency of younger children to have more statements in the no relation category (.20) than the older children (.08), $t(45) = 2.26$, $p = .03$. These results were replicated in the second experiment.

Goldman et al. (1982) interpreted these results as indicating that younger children are aware of the constraints that are supposed to hold in analogical reasoning, but that their understanding is weak. When they do choose the correct alternative, they are as likely as older children to verbalize appropriate relational constraints. However, they choose an inappropriate option more frequently than older children and their post hoc rationalizations reflect little awareness of the relational constraints on the four terms. Weaker understanding in conjunction with the process component differences provide further support for the notion that different models of analogy solution are necessary to characterize the development of analogical reasoning (e.g., Piaget et al., 1977; Sternberg & Nigro, 1980). Consistent with Sternberg and Nigro (1980), the data of Goldman et al. (1982) support the proposal that mature analogical reasoning involves an understanding of the parallelism and directional constraints on solution as well as the efficient and appropriate management of inference, application, and discrimination-choice processes. Developmentally earlier models of analogical reasoning involve some type of associative processing component, although the precise understanding of its characteristics is presently lacking. A factor contributing to the presence of such a strategy may be whether or not demands imposed by content and process execution exceed the child's capacity to manage a solution requiring the coordination and comparison of multiple relations. Such coordination and comparison involve the ability to deal with a higher order relation-of-relations. It was this ability that Piaget (1977) cited as a critical feature in the acquisition of analogical reasoning, and one typically acquired by adolescence.

To pursue the development of analogical reasoning during adolescence, Sternberg and Downing (1982) had adolescents solve higher order analogies: subjects evaluated analogies between analogies, e.g., $(A1:B1::C1:D1)::(A2:B2::C2:D2)$. Such a task essentially involves comparing the relation-of-relations of the first analogy with the relation-of-relations of the second analogy. Sternberg and Downing (1982) predicted that development on this task among adolescents would parallel the qualitative stages observed during midchildhood for standard analogies. This parallel was obtained. Latency data were obtained from students in eighth (13.5 years) and eleventh (16.5 years) grades and from college freshmen (18.5 years). The results of the modeling indicated that associative relatedness was a significant predictor for the 13-year olds but not for the two older groups. The relatedness of the inference and application between the two analogies was a significant predictor at each age level. The relatedness of mapping between the two analogies was a significant predictor only for the oldest group. These data thus replicate the developmental pattern across midchildhood on standard analogy items.

The hallmark of mature analogical reasoning thus appears to be the ability to coordinate and compare multiple relationships, which may differ in terms of their distance from the presented terms. As mentioned previously in our process model discussion, inductive reasoning tasks such as classification do not involve relational coordination and comparison to the same extent as analogy. Thus, it might be expected that developmental differences during midchildhood would be less evident.

Verbal Classification

Classification behavior has been the object of a number of developmental studies (e.g., Anglin, 1977; Nelson, 1979; Inhelder & Piaget, 1964). The focus of these studies has largely been on the dimensions children use when putting two objects in the same group and on the emergence of higher order classes. Superordinate category labels emerge during preschool years in at least one or two familiar domains (e.g., Nelson, 1979). However, consistently successful performance on the typical Piagetian class-inclusion task is a characteristic of midchildhood. This task requires the coordination and comparison of superordinate and subordinate classes. These operations often do not appear until age 8 or 9.

Psychometric instruments feature verbal classification tasks at the third-grade level. These items require the induction of a class to which each term in the item belongs. The correct alternative is an additional member of the class. Thus, in terms of complexity of processing, the psychometric form of a classification problem lies somewhere between requiring the ability to give exemplars of a class (e.g., Nelson, 1979) and requiring the ability to perform the Piagetian class-inclusion task.

In contrast to analogy, there appears to be only one developmental study of performance on classification items of the type found on psychometric instruments, and the developmental focus in this study was of secondary interest (Parseghian & Pellegrino, 1980). The authors employed a process outcome approach to examine sources of individual differences. In the course of that study, third-grade (9-year-old) and fifth-grade (11-year-old) children were tested on 150 classification items, all of which used vocabulary within the third-grade level. Items were presented in a three alternative forced-choice format and were group administered. Overall correct forced-choice performance was significantly higher in 11-year olds (.61) than in 9-year olds (.47). However, the primary focus was on individual differences and a subsequent phase of this study suggested that this mean difference between age groups was far less important than within-age group differences. The latter are discussed in the subsequent section on individual differences. It may be tentatively concluded that performance on classification items that use vocabulary within the child's level does not show major developmental differences.

INDIVIDUAL DIFFERENCES IN INDUCTIVE REASONING

Adults

Analyses of adult individual differences have considered both the latency and accuracy of executing components of analogical reasoning. In each case, estimates of process speed or accuracy are determined by modeling the data of individual subjects over an entire set of items. The resultant parameter estimates are then used in either correlational analyses, where external reference test performance is the criterion variable, or in a contrastive analysis comparing high vs. low reasoning groups as defined by an external reference measure. The purpose is to determine those measures of task performance related to reasoning skill and their absolute and relative importance.

Studies where process latency has been the critical individual difference measure are considered first. These include Sternberg's (1977a,b) analysis of people-piece, verbal, and geometric analogies, Mulholland et al.'s (1980) analysis of geometric analogies, and Pellegrino and Ingram's (1977) and Sternberg's (1981) analyses of verbal analogies. The obtained results show both consistency and inconsistency, which may be attributed to several factors including differences in the range of item difficulty and the range of subject ability. Another factor that needs to be considered is the size of the subject sample, which is often relatively small (20–30).

Across studies, one of the most consistently observed sources of individual differences is associated with the response component. Skilled reasoners have shorter latencies for this component of processing when solving people-piece and verbal analogies (Sternberg, 1977a,b; 1981) and geometric analogies (Mulholland et al., 1980). Although the response component may not appear to be a terribly significant aspect of inductive reasoning, in chronometric modeling of analogy solution this process is estimated as a constant across items. The resultant estimated value may be a conglomerate of several cognitive functions. It has been argued (Sternberg, 1977a; Mulholland et al., 1980) that certain executive or metacognitive functions associated with executing and monitoring the analogy solution strategy are "dumped" into this parameter, thereby yielding the pattern of reasoning skill differences that has been observed consistently.

Ability differences in encoding speed have also been observed, but the direction of the differences shows that skilled reasoners are slower at encoding than less skilled reasoners. In Sternberg's study of verbal analogy solution, there was a significant 96 msec difference favoring less skilled reasoners. Mulholland et al. (1980) observed a nonsignificant positive correlation between encoding (element processing) latency and reference ability scores. Sternberg (1977a,b) suggested that such counterintuitive results might reflect a strategy difference between ability groups. High ability individuals spend more relative time on encoding because more precise encodings facilitate or speed up subsequent processing operations. When time spent on encoding is considered as a proportion of the total time required for item solution, then substantial differences between skill groups emerge on verbal (Sternberg, 1977a,b; Pellegrino & Ingram, 1977), geometric (Mulholland et al., 1980), and people-piece items (Sternberg, 1977a,b). Accurate encodings seem to greatly enhance subsequent processing speed as indexed by attribute comparison and response components.

Attribute comparison components such as inference, mapping, application, and justification have all yielded significant latency differences favoring skilled over less skilled reasoners. In verbal analogy solution, Sternberg (1977a,b) obtained data indicating that skilled reasoners were 243 msec faster than less skilled reasoners for a combined estimate of inference, mapping, and application. Pellegrino and Ingram (1977) obtained a 181 msec difference for inference, mapping, and application as well as a 120 msec difference for justification. Related results have been obtained by Sternberg (1981), where a combined estimate of processing component latencies was correlated −.42 with reference test performance. Geometric analogies have also yielded similar reasoning skill differences for application and justification components (Sternberg, 1977a,b). The one discrepancy is data obtained by Mulholland et al. (1980), showing a nonsignificant positive correlation between attribute comparison (transformation) latencies and reference test scores. However, the latter result may be a function of a general speed-accuracy tradeoff that was observed for their subjects.

Two other latency contrasts are of interest. In both verbal analogy (Sternberg, 1977a) and geometric analogy solution (Mulholland et al., 1980), a positive correlation of .44 has been obtained between the estimate of goodness-of-fit of the process model and reference test performance. A possible interpretation of such results is that reasoning ability may also be associated with the consistent application of the same basic processing strategy over a wide range of problems. Systematic performance in the experimental task would result from a well-developed performance routine that leads to stable reaction-time data as well as high levels of accuracy in the standard psychometric testing format. The second result involves metacomponents associated with global and local planning of solution for analogies varying in format (Sternberg, 1981). When latencies for such components are estimated from blocked and mixed analogy conditions, there is a .43 correlation between global planning and reference test performance but a $-.33$ correlation for local planning. It appears that skilled reasoners spend relatively more time in global planning of a strategy for problem solution when diverse item forms occur together but relatively less time on local planning and actual execution of the global strategy. Superior local planning speed may explain the previously mentioned latency differences obtained for the response component.

The individual difference data summarized above are based upon different subject samples performing a single analogy task. Recently, Sternberg and Gardner (1982) have reported the results of an extensive individual differences study (Exp. 3) examining performance of 18 adults over a series of nine inductive reasoning tasks. More will be said about the significance of this study in a subsequent section of this chapter. Of present concern are the individual difference data relating component process latency measures to reasoning factor scores. The 18 individuals solved 2880 individual induction problems representing the crossing of three task forms—analogy, classification, and series completion, with three types of content—verbal, geometric, and schematic. When performance on all nine tasks was considered collectively, reasoning factor scores from a reference battery were negatively correlated with three aspects of processing. A component score representing inference, mapping, and application yielded a correlation of $-.79$, whereas one representing confirmation yielded a correlation of $-.75$. The component score for justification yielded a correlation of $-.48$. All of these represent attribute comparison and evaluation processes and the results are generally consistent with those obtained in earlier studies. Encoding also yielded a negative but nonsignificant correlation with the external reference score. Of particular interest was the lack of any correlation involving the response component. This is contrary to previous findings. The collective results were representative of correlational analyses based upon collapsing task form or item content. It would thus appear that adult individual differences in inductive reasoning ability are partly attributable to more efficient execution of component processes involving the attribute relationships between and among individual pairs of terms.

Results obtained in adult individual differences studies focusing on component process accuracy support the conclusions obtained from latency analyses. Two such studies have been reported and both examined the performance of several adult subjects on verbal analogy and classification tasks (Alderton, Goldman & Pellegrino, 1982; Whitely, 1980c). In the Alderton et al. (1982) study, 80 undergraduates were tested on a set of 40 analogy and 40 classification items. The method of item presentation permitted the measurement of accuracy components associated with stem (A,B,C) and option processing.

Table 4.4 contains a summary of the major results for the analogy task. Results are shown for the entire sample of subjects as well as the upper and lower quartiles defined by overall forced-choice accuracy. Accuracy of stem processing was 50% with a 33% difference between quartiles. Of particular interest are data for the two measures of option processing. The overall probability of recognizing a correct solution when stem processing was incorrect was .33 and there was a three-fold difference in recognition between the upper and lower quartiles. In contrast, the probability of distraction was extremely low and this was true for all subjects. In fact, 59 of the 80 adults showed a zero likelihood of being

TABLE 4.4
Analogy Performance Measures

	Group Mean (N = 80)	Upper Quartile (N = 20)	Lower Quartile (N = 20)	Correlation with FC Accuracy
Forced-Choice Accuracy	.74	.90	.55	—
Stem Processing Inference x Application	.50	.67	.34	.80
Option Processing				
Recognition	.33	.52	.14	.83
Distraction	.04	.01	.09	-.44

Multiple Regression (N = 80)			Multiple Regression (N = 40)		
R^2 = .88			R^2 = .87		
Predictor	β	F	Predictor	β	F
Inf x Appl	.44	106.72	Inference	.27	16.81
Recognition	.48	156.03	Application	.14	7.09
			Recognition	.56	101.64

distracted by the option set when prior stem processing was correct. The last column of Table 4.4 shows the simple correlations between each performance measure and overall forced-choice accuracy. These data verify that inference, application, and recognition are all important contributors to individual differences in analogy solution. This conclusion is confirmed by the results of a multiple regression analysis, which are also shown in Table 4.4. The combined inference and application measure and the recognition measure were both significant predictors of overall forced-choice accuracy and had approximately equivalent beta weights.

It was possible to conduct a more detailed analysis of performance for 40 of the subjects. They solved the items under a presentation format that yielded separate estimates of inference and application. The multiple regression results for this subgroup are also shown in Table 4.4. Both inference and application were significant contributors in the prediction of forced-choice accuracy and their combined contribution approximates the value obtained for the entire sample of subjects.

Table 4.5 shows a similar breakdown of the data for adult performance on the classification task. Overall forced-choice accuracy was 72% and the upper and lower quartiles showed a 37% difference in accuracy. All of the measures of stem and option processing showed substantial differences between the upper

TABLE 4.5
Classification Performance Measures

	Group Mean (N = 80)	Upper Quartile (N = 20)	Lower Quartile (N = 20)	Correlation with FC Accuracy
Forced-Choice Accuracy	.72	.87	.50	—
Stem Processing				
Inference x Application	.61	.71	.43	.68
Option Processing				
Recognition	.44	.56	.22	.72
Distraction	.22	.08	.43	-.80

Multiple Regression (N = 80) $R^2 = .91$			Multiple Regression (N = 40) $R^2 = .91$		
Predictor	β	F	Predictor	β	F
Inf x Appl	.09	3.50	Inference	.10	3.97
Recognition	.37	162.25	Application	.00	.00
Distraction	-.56	224.53	Recognition	.39	101.13
			Distraction	-.58	82.98

and lower quartiles. Of particular interest is the fact that the upper quartile subjects continue to show a relatively low probability of distraction. However, distraction is now substantial in the performance of the lower quartile subjects. The correlational results shown in Table 4.5 confirm the fact that each performance component is significantly related to individual differences in forced-choice accuracy. However, the most important components of processing are those associated with evaluating the options. This is indicated by the results of the multiple regression analysis. In fact, distraction is the most highly weighted predictor of performance differences.

The reduced importance of the stem processing measure in the multiple regression analysis may be a function of including the application component. Theoretical analyses (e.g., Pellegrino & Goldman, 1983; Sternberg & Gardner, 1982) have claimed that application is not essential in solving classification items. Its inclusion in the stem processing measure may suppress a significant individual contribution of inference. It was possible to test these assumptions for a subgroup of 40 subjects. They provided separate data for the inference and application components. The results of the multiple regression for this subgroup are also shown in Table 4.5. The data clearly show that application makes no contribution to predicting individual differences in forced-choice accuracy. Inference is a significant predictor but its contribution is considerably less than recognition and distraction. The beta weights for the latter two measures are virtually identical to those obtained for the entire sample of 80 subjects.

The Alderton et al. (1982) results for analogy and classification performance lead to a general conclusion that both stem and option processing accuracy contribute to individual differences in overall task performance. High ability individuals are more accurate in initial encoding and attribute comparison processes and are also more accurate in subsequent response evaluation components. What differs across analogy and classification tasks is the relative importance of accuracy on initial vs. subsequent component process execution. These conclusions are supported by Whitely's (1980c) data for these two induction tasks. She examined the performance of 104 adults on similar types of problems and obtained estimates of both stem and option processing accuracy. Her performance measures showed individual differences in both aspects of processing in both induction tasks. Like Alderton et al. (1982), stem and option processing accuracy were of equal importance in analogy solution, whereas option processing accuracy was a more important factor in classification solution.

Both latency and accuracy data support the general conclusion that adult individual differences in inductive reasoning are associated with the efficiency of processing. Efficiency can be viewed as a composite of both speed and accuracy of component process execution. Even though speed differences may be relatively small among college-age individuals they are nonetheless significant and co-occur with substantial accuracy differences. A composite efficiency score such as Mean Latency/Mean Accuracy may ultimately prove useful in examining efficiency differences among individuals for specific components of inductive reasoning.

Adolescents and Children

The work conducted with adults suggests that individual differences largely reside in the efficient and accurate execution of the same set of processes. This implies a common understanding of the task constraints relevant to different types of inductive reasoning tasks. Studies of high school students (Heller, 1979) as well as within-age group comparisons of elementary school children (Goldman et al., 1982; Parseghian & Pellegrino, 1980) indicate that there are also individual differences in task understanding per se. Thus, when one examines a range of skill levels wider than that typically found among college students, individual differences in what people are doing, as well as in how well they are doing it, are observed. This parallels the findings of age-based comparisons (e.g., Goldman et al., 1982; Sternberg & Nigro, 1980; Sternberg & Rifkin, 1979).

Heller (1979) examined the verbal analogical reasoning performance of vocational high school and college students. Protocols of solution episodes were analyzed to determine the degree to which analogical task constraints were reflected in the behaviors. Three types of solutions were identified. Analogical solutions showed no behaviors that violated any of the task constraints: Consistent attention to the relations contained in two allowable word pairs and to the match between these pairs of relations was present. Nonanalogical solutions violated one or more task constraints in three primary ways: (1) relations between "illegal" pairs of elements were the only ones to which attention was given; (2) the match between inappropriately selected pairs of relations in two word-pairs was attended to consistently; (3) the match between relations contained in two word-pairs was disregarded consistently. Borrowing a term from the computer programming notion of procedural bugs with missing or faulty subroutines, "Buggy" analogical solutions were also identified. Behaviors indicative of both analogical and nonanalogical solution were present but the match requirement was "forced," not considered, or considered between inappropriate pairs of words.

These three solution types were observed differentially in the three groups comprising the sample. High ability solvers (20 college students) used analogical solutions 99% of the time and "Buggy" solutions 1%. Intermediate ability solvers (6 tenth-grade students in the upper quartile of verbal ability) used analogical solutions 71% of the time, "Buggy" 13% of the time and nonanalogical in 16% of the cases. The percentages for the low ability solvers (9 tenth-grade students in the lower quartile of verbal ability) were 34% analogical, 15% "Buggy" and 50% nonanalogical. These group data suggest overall strategy differences. Heller (1979) further examined the performance of individuals within each group to look at consistency in an individual's performance as well as within-group variability. She described the behavior of each individual in terms of the types of solutions used over the set of items. The profile data indicated that 85% of the high ability solvers consistently used analogical solutions; none of the intermediate or low ability solvers did. Individuals in both of these groups used analogical solution sometimes but did not do so consistently. Further, three of the individuals in the low group never used analogical solution. These data indicate the existence of global solution strategy differences, which reflect partial or weak understanding of task constraints on analogy.

Heller (1979) also examined those cases in which analogical solutions were used. These analyses indicated that high as opposed to intermediate and low ability solvers were more likely to engage in interactive processing, i.e., mapping and justification processes. Thus, even when analogical solutions were used, an important individual difference was the tendency to capitalize on information and relations present among multiple stem terms and response options. This finding may reflect a problem in comparing and coordinating multiple sets and multiple levels of relationships.

Heller's (1979) examination of nonanalogical solutions supported this notion. She identified three types of nonanalogical solutions: Only C–D relations were attended to; interrelationships among three or four terms were attended to but pair relationship comparison was ignored; A–B and C–D relations were identified but there was no attempt to compare the relation of relations. These ability differences parallel the developmental differences reported above.

Examination of ability differences among same-age children have also been found to parallel developmental differences between age groups. In their work with 8- and 10-year olds, Goldman et al. (1982) found significant developmental differences in overall forced-choice performance. However, they also found substantial variability within each age group. The range on this measure was .18 to .70 for the 8-year olds and .22 to .78 for the 10-year olds in the first experiment. Correlation-regression analyses indicated that all three process outcome measures (inference × application, recognition, and distractor interference) were significant predictors of overall forced-choice performance. However, the recognition and distractor interference processes were relatively more important than the combined inference × application processes. The former are associated with the coordination and comparison of multiple relations; the latter is basically a stem process involving fewer relationships. To illustrate the magnitude of individual differences on these measures, the means for the top and bottom thirds within each grade are shown for each process measure in Table 4.6. Of particular interest is the greater similarity between scorer groups across grades as compared with scorer groups within grades. This pattern was replicated in the second experiment as well. Additionally, inference and application were independently assessed in that experiment. The correlation-regression analyses showed that although all four process components predicted individual differences, inference

TABLE 4.6
Process Outcome Measures on Analogy

	8 year olds		10 year olds	
Process Measure	Top Third	Bottom Third	Top Third	Bottom Third
Inference x Application	.37	.22	.52	.29
Response Recognition	.21	.01	.34	.03
Distractor Interference	.26	.52	.18	.41

was the least important. It is the only process that deals with one relation. The recognition and distractor components were found to make the largest total contribution to predicting forced-choice performance. In addition, analyses of the verbal justification data from both experiments indicated individual differences in understanding the task constraints. The probability of justifying correct responses in terms of parallel relations was significantly correlated with overall forced-choice performance, $r(45) = .73$, $p < .001$ in the first experiment and $r(18) = .74$, $p < .001$ in the second. Furthermore, the bottom-third scorers in each grade justified only about half of their correct responses in terms of relational parallelism.

Heller's (1979) individual difference work with adolescents and Goldman et al.'s (1982) with 8–10 year olds indicate that solution strategies reflect different conceptions of the constraints that govern analogical reasoning. In addition to a weaker understanding of the task, individuals differ in the accuracy of process execution. Those factors that seem to characterize developmental differences based on age-group comparisons are similar to those characterizing individual differences among children and adolescents solving verbal analogy problems. Individual differences in college-age populations are associated largely with differences in the efficiency of process execution. The relatively minor role of distractor interference and consistent use of an analogical solution strategy indicate that weak understanding of the task and task constraints is not a particular problem for college populations. The weaker understanding manifests itself in inconsistent use of analogical solutions. In particular, the coordination and comparison of multiple relations among stem terms as well as stem terms and response options appears problematic. Mature analogical reasoning involves the ability to manipulate second and sometimes third order relationships. Less mature forms of analogical reasoning are characterized by failure to deal successfully and/or efficiently with this manipulation. These "failures" appear to be related to a weak understanding of task constraints such that more global and less specific evaluations and solutions are conducted.

Tentative solution strategies are also a major source of individual differences in the verbal classification performance of 9–11-year-old children. The major focus of the Parseghian and Pellegrino (1980) study, described above, was the identification of process component and solution strategy factors contributing to performance on verbal classification tasks. The study was conducted in two phases. In the first phase, approximately 30 9-year olds and 30 11-year olds took a group-administered test consisting of verbal classification items. Performance on this test was used to identify six high and six low scorers at each age level. These children were then seen individually and solved a subset of the items from the group test. The individual sessions were highly structured, incremental presentations so that three process outcome measures could be obtained: relational inference, response evaluation, and response recognition. Detailed verbal protocols of the solution attempts were also collected: Children justified the answer they had chosen as well as providing justifications for why nonchosen alternatives were incorrect.

One aspect of the data strongly supports the notion of tentative or weak solution strategies. A comparison of performance on the same items in the group and individual testing formats indicated a 40% increase in accuracy for the low scorers in both grades. There was a lack of a change in performance in the high skill groups, 80% in each, indicating that the effect in the low skill group was more than a retesting effect. The incremental presentation procedure essentially constituted the child's executive control over a set of processing stages. The high skill children tended to internalize the testing procedure; the low skill children required many more prompts from the experimenter. For example, high skill children's justifications for chosen and nonchosen alternatives were often spontaneous whereas the low skill children often had to be prompted for a response and reminded of the next step in the task. The simple correlation between the number of experimenter interventions and performance on the 16 problems in the individual test was significant, $r = -.60$, $p < .004$. Thus, the structured format improved performance over the group test for the low scorers by reminding them of what to do next.

However, even when prompted for relational inferences, the low scorers were not as accurate as the high scorers, .18 as compared to .47. Correlation-regression analyses indicated that this process was the best predictor of group test performance ($\beta = .79$) and accounted for 62% of the variance in performance. Although response evaluation and recognition also differentiated between skill groups, they were far less important than the initial inference process. In contrast to the adult data discussed above (Alderton et al., 1982), the alternative set does not seem to provide a helpful clue for solution in less skilled children when earlier inferences have failed.

Further analyses of the inference behavior of the high and low groups were conducted. Statements that were not correct inferences for the stem terms were examined. The high skill children tended to state relationships; the low skill children tended to make statements that failed to specify information about the semantic features of the individual terms. This was the dominant type of response among the low skill children. Such differences in inference behavior were also evident in the statements about the alternatives. Each child's approach to the set of alternatives was analyzed in terms of the use of a relevant consistent rule. Four types of rule-governed behavior were typical: (1) use of a previously inferred relationship; (2) elaboration of a previously inferred relationship; (3) use of a new, different rule; and (4) identification and use of the correct rule. High skill individuals worked through the set of alternatives with a rule for evaluating each word 55% of the time, but low skill individuals operated with rules only 29% of the time.

The Parseghian and Pellegrino (1980) study indicates that for 9–11-year olds, two primary factors contribute to individual differences. One is a general management-of-solution factor. Low skill individuals have a difficult time consistently executing an appropriately ordered set of steps. In addition, inferring and evaluating relationships among sets of terms is a source of difficulty. For all children, when the initial inference was the one needed for correct solution, subsequent processing tended to be successful. The low skill children were, however, less likely to get started on the right foot. They were more likely to be attempting to evaluate and recognize appropriate alternatives with no relation among the stem terms to guide them.

MULTITASK PERFORMANCE ANALYSIS-UNITIES IN INDUCTIVE REASONING

Both psychometric theory and measurement of intelligence and aptitude emphasize the importance of a general intelligence or g factor. This factor is extracted from the patterns of intercorrelations among a host of individual tasks. Those loading the highest on such a general factor are inductive reasoning items such as analogy, classification, series extrapolation, and matrix completion. Performance on these tasks tends to be highly correlated even when differences in content (e.g., verbal vs. geometric stimuli) are reflected in the test battery. Correlations for common content tend to be higher than those for common tasks differing in content (see Pellegrino & Glaser, 1982). To adequately understand individual differences in a general cognitive aptitude such as inductive reasoning, it is not sufficient to analyze only a single task form such as analogy. Efforts must be made to develop models and conduct performance analyses for related tasks that define the same aptitude construct.

Recently, research has been reported attempting to examine performance in two or more induction tasks. The studies have two important characteristics. First, they attempt to show that component processes postulated in the theory and models of analogy solution are also present to varying degrees in other tasks such as classification and series completion. This is done by specifying process models for these tasks and validating them in the same way that models of analogy solution were validated. Second, and most important, data collection and model testing is done in a multitask design where the same individuals are tested on all the tasks.

Most process models for cognitive tasks describe performance in terms of the same basic or elementary information processes such as encoding, response, inference, comparison, etc. Psychologists currently use the same limited set of process labels to describe performance on a wide range of simple and complex tasks and this partially reflects an assumption that there are a core set of elementary information processes that serve as the building blocks for all cognitive activity (e.g. Chase, 1978; Simon, 1976). Unfortunately, little has been done to support or document their existence and generality. Data on the existence and duration of specific mental processes comes from independent studies, using different stimuli, with different groups of individuals. All that appears to be common is the labels and the assumption that the processes are the same across tasks, subjects, etc. Multitask component process analyses with the same individuals make two important contributions. First, they permit a general test of the comparability of common component process measures across tasks. Second, they permit a more specific test of comparability through individual differences analysis. If a process such as inference is present in two separate tasks then individuals who are efficient in executing this process in analogy solution should also show high efficiency for process execution in classification. The extent to which two measures of performance reflect the same basic cognitive process can only be determined by correlational analyses across tasks based on individual differences data. Thus, individual differences become a critical aspect of theory testing when multiple tasks are hypothesized to share the same basic processes. Perfect correlations are not necessarily expected because the execution of a process such as inference may well depend on the nature of the information being manipulated. However, correlations for corresponding measures should exceed correlations for noncorresponding measures. An example of such a pattern of correlations has been reported by Mumaw, Pellegrino, Kail, and Carter (1982) for performance in spatial processing tasks.

Sternberg and Gardner (1982) described two experiments that support common aspects of processing in analogy, classification, and series completion tasks. Their experiments employed a restricted set of stimuli representing animal names. Previous multidimensional scaling of similarly judgment data for this stimulus set (Henley, 1969) was used by Rumelhart and Abrahamson (1973) to construct analogy items. The analogies used animal pairs that reflected different dimensional features within the multidimensional semantic space. An A:B::C: D_1, D_2, D_3, D_4, analogy format was used and the D terms systematically deviated from the ideal answer. Sternberg and Gardner used these same concepts to construct similar classification and series completion items. The two experiments tested similarities across tasks for response choice (Exp. 1) and process latency (Exp. 2). In the first experiment, individuals were required to rank order the four

D terms with respect to their suitability as a completion term for a specific item. Rumelhart and Abrahamson (1973) previously showed that rank ordering of alternatives in this analogy task is a systematic function of semantic distance from the ideal answer and conforms to Luce's (1959) choice rule. A single parameter from the choice rule is estimated from the rank ordering data over a set of items. The value of this parameter was compared across the three tasks. The choice model based upon semantic distance fit performance in all three tasks and the value of the single estimated parameter was comparable across tasks.

These same items and tasks were then used in the second experiment, which assessed latency of solution. Process models for each task were specified and reflected common processes such as inference, encoding, application, confirmation (comparison), and justification. Model testing was done for each task and models were fit to individual subject data for each task. A comparison of estimated values for encoding, comparison, and response processes showed equivalent values across tasks. Only justification showed a significant difference in estimated latency across tasks. Model fitting for group mean data also showed equivalent model fits in all three tasks. Unreliability of individual subject component process estimates prevented a more specific test of process commonality over tasks. Nevertheless, these two experiments provide support for the existence of common processes in induction tasks with a general equivalence of process latencies when content is common across tasks.

Individual difference data have been used to test process commonality across tasks in three studies (Alderton et al., 1982; Whitely, 1980c; Sternberg & Gardner, Exp. 3, 1982). As discussed earlier, Alderton et al. and Whitely examined performance on both verbal analogy and classification tasks. Accuracy scores were determined for individual subjects for both stem and option processing components. In the Alderton et al. study, inference accuracy was positively correlated across tasks (r = .47, p < .005), as was the measure of recognition (r = .42, p < .001). Data were also available for application accuracy in both tasks and a nonsignificant correlation was obtained. This was predicted on the basis of prior models of task performance. Application is a necessary component of analogy solution and significantly contributes to individual differences in overall task performance. In analogy, application involves applying a specific relationship to a term from a new semantic domain. In classification, application is not necessary for item solution and does not contribute to individual differences in overall performance. When application is requested in a classification task it also involves a different psychological process representing the generation of a new instance consistent with the general rule inferred across all stem terms.

Whitely (1980c) failed to find evidence supporting common components across analogy and classification tasks and this was attributed to measuring components at too global a level. For example, she used a measure of overall stem processing accuracy in both tasks and the correlation across tasks was lower than the correlation between stem processing in classification and option processing in verbal analogies. However, as noted above, stem processing in analogy and classification does not represent completely overlapping sets of processes. The common components are encoding and inference and inference accuracy does seem to be correlated across tasks.

The most extensive multitask analysis of common processing components is the third study conducted by Sternberg and Gardner (1982), described in the earlier section on individual differences. Component process latencies were derived for individual subjects by collapsing over tasks (analogy, classification, series) or contents (verbal, geometric, schematic-figures). Correlations were then computed for corresponding and noncorresponding measures. The results for corresponding component processes are shown in Table 4.7. The mean correlation for corresponding process components was .32 when collapsed over contents and .40 when collapsed over tasks. The mean correlation for noncorresponding process components was .24 for both collapsings. Thus, evidence was obtained for convergent and discriminant validity with regard to corresponding and noncorresponding process components. Of significance is the fact that greater commonality is shown for common content than common task forms. This is

TABLE 4.7
Intercorrelations of Corresponding Components
Scores Over Tasks and Contents

Collapsed Over tasks		Collapsed Over Contents	
Schematic-picture − Verbal		Analogies − Series Completions	
Encoding	-.04	Encoding	-.08
Reasoning	.40*	Reasoning	.69**
Comparison	.40*	Comparison	.54**
Justification	−	Justification	.19
Schematic-picture − Geometric		Analogies − Classifications	
Encoding	.16	Encoding	-.02
Reasoning	.40*	Reasoning	.48*
Comparison	.71**	Comparison	.43*
Justification	−	Justification	−
Verbal − Geometric		Series Completions − Classifications	
Encoding	.36	Encoding	.43*
Reasoning	.55**	Reasoning	.10
Comparison	.74***	Comparison	.80***
Justification	.43*	Justification	−

Note: Significance Tests are one-tailed. Raw parameter estimates were used in these computations.
  *$p < .05$
  **$p < .01$
  ***$p < .001$

consistent with an assumption that the instantiation of a process is dependent upon the nature of the information to be processed. An individual who is efficient in processing verbal information may not show the same absolute or relative efficiency in processing geometric information.

Multitask studies of performance in inductive reasoning tasks provide support for unities in inductive reasoning. Similar processes are required in analogy, classification, and series tasks. Individual differences in process execution are consistent across tasks producing the high average intertask correlations typically found in psychometric measurement. Although there is consistency in process execution across tasks, the correlations obtained for corresponding processes indicate that there are unique aspects of process execution associated with individual tasks and task demands as well as specific content.

CONCLUSIONS AND FUTURE DIRECTIONS

The various theoretical approaches and empirical data discussed in this chapter have significantly contributed to an understanding of one aspect of aptitude, inductive reasoning. Both process latency and process outcome modeling support the existence of similar cognitive components in typical psychometric inductive reasoning tasks. All involve inferential and attribute comparison processes associated with the stem of an item and discrimination-choice processes associated with processing the alternatives. The research also suggests that the visual or semantic complexity of a particular item affects the degree to which general system characteristics such as working memory and executive monitoring strategies become important cognitive components of performance.

Within these frameworks, developmental and individual differences analyses of analogy and classification solution lead to several important general conclusions and future areas of research. First, there are impressive parallels in the sources of variability between and within age groups. These parallels imply that inductive reasoning may not be an ability that gradually develops over time and on its own. This statement is not meant to suggest that reasoning does not improve over time. Rather, the processes that are problematic for younger children appear to be the primary problem areas for older individuals as well. Identifying these in children requires accuracy and verbal protocol analysis, whereas latency measures reveal such problem areas among adult populations. These parallels suggest the need for two types of longitudinal studies of inductive reasoning. The first is the standard longitudinal study in which the same individual is tested over a period of years. The second, typically called learning or instructional studies, are conducted over shorter periods of time during which the individual might do many induction problems. Both types of work are needed in order to begin to understand how the interaction between general executive, memory, and knowledge characteristics of the individual and specific experiences with inductive reasoning tasks contribute to performance.

A second important conclusion from the research is that processes that deal with multiple relationship comparison and evaluation are consistent sources of differences between high and low ability reasoners. This problem manifests itself somewhat differently in adults than in children. Differences among adults in processes involving comparison and evaluation are largely efficiency differences. Among children, qualitative differences emerge when comparison and evaluation become extremely difficult. Appropriate inductive reasoning seems to be replaced by a more global associate reasoning process. This change has led to the conclusion that an important individual difference factor among children is their understanding of task constraints, of the procedures necessary to meet those contraints, and of how to evaluate the success of those procedures. Future research exploring the nature of such metacognitive activities is clearly needed.

A third area is implicated by the work done on unities in inductive reasoning. This work indicates that there are indeed cross-task as well as cross-content area commonalities, at least at the level of process labels, i.e., inference in analogy is correlated with inference in classification. A set of labeled inductive reasoning processes has emerged but subsequent work devoted to understanding what these labels refer to and the nature of the factors that affect them is needed. These efforts will undoubtedly need to consider a person's knowledge base in a particular content area as well as prior experience analyzing the particular type of stimulus. These appear to be critical issues when one goes beyond grade school vocabulary and relatively simple geometric figures.

Finally, one future direction for research on inductive reasoning needs to be considered. It is commonly noted that aptitude tests predict school success (e.g., Pellegrino & Glaser, 1982). One potential reason for this is the large degree of inductive reasoning required for accurate performance on many school tasks. It may be profitable to begin to explore the ways and situations in which children are expected to infer task structure. Poor performance on tasks where the constraint must be inferred from sometimes obtuse instructions may not be related to ability to execute the task. Rather, it may be related to the same types of general inference, application, and evaluation skills required by psychometric estimates of inductive reasoning.

ACKNOWLEDGMENTS

The authors' research reported in this chapter was supported by funds provided by the Learning Research and Development Center, University of Pittsburgh, which is supported in part by the National Institute of Education, U.S. Department of Education. The authors also wish to acknowledge the research and editorial assistance of David Alderton and Connie Varnhagen.

REFERENCES

Achenbach, T. The children's associative responding test: A possible alternative to group IQ tests. *Journal of Educational Psychology,* 1970, *61,* 340–348.

Alderton, D. L., Goldman, S. R., & Pellegrino, J. W. *Multitask assessment of inductive reasoning skill.* Paper presented at the annual meeting of American Educational Research Association, New York, March 1982.

Anglin, J. M. *Word, object and conceptual development.* New York: Norton, 1977.

Barnes, G. M. & Whitely, S. E. Problem restructuring processes for ill structured verbal analogies. *Memory & Cognition,* 1981, *9,* 411–421.

Bethell-Fox, C. E., Lohman, D. F., & Snow, R. E. *Adaptive reasoning: Componential and eye movement analysis of geometric analogy performance.* Unpublished manuscript, Stanford University, 1982.

Bisanz, J. *Processes and strategies in children's solutions of geometric analogies.* Unpublished doctoral dissertation, University of Pittsburgh, 1979.

Bruner, J. S. Going beyond the information given. In H. Gruber (Ed.), *Contemporary approaches to cognition.* Cambridge, Mass.: Harvard University Press, 1957.

Chase, W. G. Elementary information processes. In W. K. Estes (Ed.), *Handbook of learning and cognitive processes* (Vol. 5). Hillsdale, N.J.: Lawrence Erlbaum Associates, 1978.

Dawis, R. V. & Siojo, L. T. *Analogical reasoning: A review of the literature. Effects of social class differences on analogical reasoning* (Tech. Rep. No. 1). Minneapolis: University of Minnesota, 1972.

Egan, D. E. & Greeno, J. G. Theory of rule induction: Knowledge acquired in concept learning, serial pattern learning, and problem solving. In L. W. Gregg (Ed.), *Knowledge and cognition.* Hillsdale, N.J.: Lawrence Erlbaum Associates, 1974.

Evans, T. G. Program for the solution of a class of geometric-analogy intelligence-test questions. In M. Minsky (Ed.), *Semantic information processing.* Cambridge, Mass.: MIT Press, 1968.

Gallagher, J. M. & Wright, R. J. Piaget and the study of analogy: Structural analysis of items. In J. Magary (Ed.), *Piaget and the helping professions* (Vol. 8). Los Angeles: University of Southern California, 1979.

Gentile, J. R., Tedesco-Stratton, L., Davis, E., Lund, N. J., & Agunanne, B. A. Associative responding versus analogical reasoning by children. *Intelligence,* 1977, *1,* 369–380.

Goldman, S. R., Pellegrino, J. W., Parseghian, P. E., & Sallis, R. Developmental and individual differences in verbal analogical reasoning. *Child Development,* 1982, *53,* 550–559.

Greeno, J. G. Natures of problem-solving abilities. In W. K. Estes (Ed.), *Handbook of learning and cognitive processes* (Vol. 5). Hillsdale, N.J.: Lawrence Erlbaum Associates, 1978.

Grudin, J. Processes in verbal analogy solution. *Journal of Experimental Psychology: Human Perception and Performance,* 1980, *6,* 67–74.

Heller, J. I. *Cognitive processing in verbal analogy solution.* Unpublished doctoral dissertation. University of Pittsburgh, 1979.

Henley, N. M. A psychological study of the semantics of animal terms. *Journal of Verbal Learning and Verbal Behavior,* 1969, *8,* 176–184.

Holzman, T. G. *A cognitive-developmental analysis of performance on rule induction tests.* Unpublished doctoral dissertation. University of Pittsburgh, 1979.

Inhelder, B. & Piaget, J. The early growth of logic in the child. New York: Norton, 1964.

Levinson, P. J. & Carpenter, R. L. An analysis of analogical reasoning in children. *Child Development,* 1974, *45,* 857–861.

Luce, R. D. *Individual choice behavior.* New York: Wiley, 1959.

Lunzer, E. A. Formal reasoning. In E. A. Lunzer & J. R. Morris (Eds.), *Development in human learning.* New York: American Elsevier Publishing Co., 1968.

Mulholland, T. M., Pellegrino, J. W., & Glaser, R. Components of geometric analogy solution. *Cognitive Psychology*, 1980, *12*, 252–284.

Mumaw, R. J., Pellegrino, J. W., Kail, R. V., & Carter, P. *Different slopes for different folks: Process analyses of spatial aptitude*. Unpublished manuscript, University of California at Santa Barbara, 1982.

Nelson, K. Explorations in the development of a functional semantic system. In W. A. Collins (Ed.), *Children's language and communication. The Minnesota Symposia on Child Psychology* (Vol. 12). Hillsdale, N.J.: Lawrence Erlbaum Associates, 1979.

Norman, D. A., Gentner, D. R., & Stevens, A. L. Comments on learning schemata and memory. In D. Klahr (Ed.), *Cognition and instruction*. Hillsdale, N.J.: Lawrence Erlbaum Associates, 1976.

Oppenheimer, J. R. Analogy in science. *American Psychologist*, 1956, *11*, 127–135.

Pachella, R. G. The interpretation of reaction time in information-processing research. In B. H. Kantowitz (Ed.), *Human information processing: Tutorials in performance and cognition*. Hillsdale, N.J.: Lawrence Erlbaum Associates, 1974.

Parseghian, P. E. & Pellegrino, J. W. *Components of individual differences in verbal classification performance*. Paper presented at the annual meeting of the American Educational Research Association, Boston, April 1980.

Pellegrino, J. W. & Glaser, R. Cognitive correlates and components in the analysis of individual differences. *Intelligence*, 1979, *3*, 187–214.

Pellegrino, J. W. & Glaser, R. Components of inductive reasoning. In R. E. Snow, P-A Federico, & W. E. Montague (Eds.), *Aptitude, learning and instruction: Cognitive process analyses of aptitude* (Vol. 1). Hillsdale, N.J.: Lawrence Erlbaum Associates, 1980.

Pellegrino, J. W. & Glaser, R. Analyzing aptitudes for learning: Inductive reasoning. In R. Glaser (Ed.), *Advances in instructional psychology* (Vol. 2). Hillsdale, N.J.: Lawrence Erlbaum Associates, 1982.

Pellegrino, J. W. & Goldman, S. R. Developmental and individual differences in verbal and spatial reasoning. In R. F. Dillon & R. R. Schmeck (Eds.), *Individual differences in cognition* (Vol. 1). New York: Academic Press, 1983.

Pellegrino, J. W. & Ingram, A. L. *Components of verbal analogy solution*. Paper presented at the annual meeting of the Midwestern Psychological Association, Chicago, May 1977.

Pellegrino, J. W. & Lyon, D. R. The components of a componential analysis. *Intelligence*, 1979, *3*, 169–186.

Piaget, J. (with Montangero, J., & Billeter, J.). Les correlats. *L'Abstraction reflechissante*. Paris: Presses Universitaires de France, 1977.

Polya, G. *Mathematics and plausible reasoning: Induction and analogy in mathematics* (Vol. 1). Princeton, N.J.: Princeton University Press, 1965.

Raven, J. C. *Progressive matrices: A perceptual test of intelligence*. London: Lewis, 1938.

Rumelhart, D. E. & Abrahamson, A. A. Toward a theory of analogical reasoning. *Cognitive Psychology*, 1973, *5*, 1–28.

Simon, H. A. Identifying basic abilities underlying intelligent performance of complex tasks. In L. B. Resnick (Ed.), *The nature of intelligence*. Hillsdale, N.J.: Lawrence Erlbaum Associates, 1976.

Spearman, C. *The nature of intelligence and the principles of cognition*. London: MacMillan, 1923.

Sternberg, R. J. *Intelligence, information processing and analogical reasoning: The componential analysis of human abilities*. Hillsdale, N.J.: Lawrence Erlbaum Associates, 1977. (a)

Sternberg, R. J. Component processes in analogical reasoning. *Psychological Review*, 1977, *84*, 353–378. (b)

Sternberg, R. J. *The development of human intelligence*. Cognitive Development Series, Technical Report No. 4, Yale University, April 1979.

Sternberg, R. J. Intelligence and nonentrenchment. *Journal of Educational Psychology*, 1981, *73*, 1–16.

Sternberg, R. J. & Downing, C. J. The development of higher-order reasoning in adolescence. *Child Development*, 1982, *53*, 209–221.

Sternberg, R. J. & Gardner. *Unities in inductive reasoning*. Unpublished manuscript, 1982.

Sternberg, R. J. & Nigro, G. Developmental patterns in the solution of verbal analogies. *Child Development*, 1980, *51*, 27–38.

Sternberg, R. J. & Rifkin, B. The development of analogical reasoning processes. *Journal of Experimental Child Psychology*, 1979, *27*, 195–232.

Sternberg, S. The discovery of processing stages: Extensions of Donder's method. *Acta Psychologica*, 1969, *30*, 276–315.

Stone, B. & Day, M. C. A developmental study of the processes underlying solution of figural matrices. *Child Development*, 1981, *52*, 359–362.

Thorndike, R. L. & Hagen, E. *Cognitive abilities test*. Boston: Houghton Mifflin, 1971.

Whitely, S. E. Information processing on intelligence test items: Some response components. *Applied Psychological Measurement*, 1977, *1*, 465–476.

Whitely, S. E. Multicomponent latent trait models for ability tests. *Psychometrika*, 1980, *45*, 479–494. (a)

Whitely, S. E. Latent trait models in the study of intelligence. *Intelligence*, 1980, *4*, 97–132. (b)

Whitely, S. E. Modeling aptitude test validity from cognitive components. *Journal of Educational Psychology*, 1980, *72*, 750–569. (c)

Whitely, S. E. & Barnes, G. M. The implications of processing event sequences for theories of analogical reasoning. *Memory & Cognition*, 1979, *7*, 323–331.

5 Analogical Thinking and Human Intelligence

Keith J. Holyoak
University of Michigan

INTRODUCTION

Lori's Magic Carpet: An Illustration of Analogy in Use

Broad abstractions are best clarified by concrete examples. It therefore seems appropriate to begin a discussion of analogy and human intelligence—broad abstractions indeed—with an example of the intelligent use of analogy. The example that follows is a small one, and is due to a small person—a little girl named Lori, who was four years old when she served as a subject in one of our studies (Holyoak, Junn & Billman, 1982). As in most of our earlier work with adults (Gick & Holyoak, 1980, 1983), described below, our experimental procedure involved two steps: (1) the subject was first presented with a story describing a problem and its solution; (2) then the subject attempted to solve a superficially dissimilar but analogous problem. In this case the experimenter first read Lori a fairy tale, accompanied by pictures. The story described a genie who wished to move his home from one bottle to another, and who faced the problem of safely transferring a number of precious jewels to the new bottle. The genie's solution was to command his magic carpet to roll itself into a tube, place it so as to form a "hollow bridge" between the two bottles, and then roll his jewels through it.

After ensuring that Lori understood the story (that she knew what a "genie" is, for example), the experimenter posed a problem for her to solve. Two bowls were set about three feet apart on a table. One bowl contained a number of small round balls and the other was empty. Lori was seated beside the filled bowl. She was asked to remain seated, and hence could not reach the empty bowl. A variety of other objects were available on the table, including a rectangular sheet of heavy paper. Lori's task was to devise as many ways as possible, using the materials provided, of transferring the balls from the filled to the empty bowl. No mention was made of any relationship between this problem and the fairy tale she had just heard.

At this point one of Lori's first reactions was to say, ''Let's pretend they're real jewels'' (the balls, that is). After considering a couple of the objects on the table, she looked at the sheet of paper and said, ''That will be a magic carpet.'' She then laughed as she picked it up, rolled it, and asked the experimenter to help to tape it. ''That's the way the genie did it,'' she exclaimed as she rolled the ball through her newly constructed tube; ''I did it just like the genie!''

The use of analogy is manifest in Lori's derivation of this solution to the ball problem. The tale of the genie constituted a known problem situation, which was used to construct a parallel solution to a novel problem drawn from a different semantic domain. I will refer to the known problem as the *base* and to the transfer problem as the *target* (adopting the terms used by Gentner, in press). Analogical problem solving involves four steps (not necessarily serial), which Lori's protocol illustrates:

(1) Mental representations of the base and target problems must be constructed.
(2) The potential analogy must be noticed; i.e., some aspect of the target must serve as a retrieval cue that reminds the person of the base. Lori immediately noticed the relevance of the base problem to the target.
(3) An initial partial *mapping*, or set of correspondences, must be found between the elements (objects and their attributes and relations) of the two situations. Lori noted the mapping between the balls and the genie's jewels, and also that between the paper and the magic carpet.
(4) Finally, the mapping must be *extended* by retrieving or constructing new knowledge about the target problem. Thus Lori constructed a paper tube analogous to the rolled carpet, explicitly mapping herself with the genie.

As in most realistic uses of analogy, the mapping between the two situations in the above example is in fact imperfect. Lori didn't really construct a tube ''just like the genie;'' the genie rolled his carpet by using his magical power, whereas Lori had to roll the paper by hand and ask for help to tape it. Part of skilled analogical problem solving is the ability to identify analogous elements embedded in representations that also include elements that are nonanalogous. In addition, knowledge derived by analogy often must be augmented by additional information in order to achieve a complete solution to the target problem.

Centrality of Analogical Thinking

Analogical thinking is a pervasive component of human intelligence and manifests itself in many forms throughout most of the lifespan. Lori's skill in using analogy was probably more sophisticated than that of the typical 4-year old; nonetheless, even preschool children can reliably solve the ball problem by analogy to a fairy tale when the solution mapping is relatively simple (Holyoak et al., 1982). Such early use of analogy in a goal-directed task may draw upon the mapping skills exhibited in social modeling (Holyoak & Gordon, in press) and "make-believe" play, which are clearly present in the behavioral repertoires of 3-year old children. From its orgins in early childhood, analogical thinking may develop into a major basis for the construction of scientific models (Oppenheimer, 1956). Analogical thought is used not only to derive solutions to problems but to make predictions, strengthen arguments, and generate literary metaphors. The observations of Lakoff and Johnson (1980) suggest that many metaphorical sentences are not isolated verbal flourishes, but rather systematic products of a broad analogical system. They point out, for example, that a logical "argument" can be mapped with the relations associated with the concept of a "building." The result is a diverse set of metaphorical expressions, such as "That is the foundation of the entire argument;" "His argument collapsed under its own weight;" and "The argument badly needs buttressing." Although the present discussion will focus on the role of analogy in problem solving, I will occasionally touch on other functions of analogy. (Miller, 1979, provides a careful analysis of the analogical basis of metaphor; and Gentner, in press, and Holyoak, 1982, discuss the similarities and differences between scientific analogies and literary metaphors.)

Given the central role of analogy in cognition, it is natural to view the development of a theory of analogical thinking as a major focus of cognitive science. The function of analogy is to allow transfer of knowledge from a known situation to a novel one, even if the two situations are superficially dissimilar. Such transfer is central to learning and reasoning. Indeed, various theorists have raised the possibility that *all* problem solving is fundamentally analogical (Moore and Newell, 1973; Sternberg, in press). However, this idea has not been developed in detail, and current models of problem solving have stressed the importance of abstract "problem schemas" as mediators of transfer (Chi, Feltovich & Glaser, 1981; Larkin, McDermott, Simon, & Simon, 1980). Here I will argue an intermediate position, shared with Winston (1980), according to which reasoning by analogy and from schemas are distinct but intimately related mechanisms of transfer. Reasoning by analogy implies a comparison of two concepts ("analogs") at the same level of abstraction. This level is typically relatively concrete, as is the case when two actual problem situations are mapped; however, an analogy can also be drawn between a pair of abstract concepts, such as two scientific theories (e.g., wave models of sound and of light). In contrast, reasoning from a schema implies a comparison of the representation of a concrete situation to a more abstract mental representation (the schema). Thus one can speak of a particular situation being an instance of a "category" defined by a problem schema; but one concrete situation is not an instance of another, although they may be analogous. Nonetheless, reasoning from a schema appears to involve mapping processes, and, as I will elaborate below, analogical thinking may actually underlie the acquisition of schemas.

Finally, it is also natural to suppose that a theory of analogical thinking will be central to a theory of human intelligence. In one sense this has long been recognized; "analogy problems," typically presented in a "proportional" format (i.e., A:B::C:?), have long served as a major component of intelligence tests. Furthermore, performance on such analogy items is highly correlated with measures of "general intelligence" (see Sternberg, in press, for a review). I will argue, however, that analogical thinking of the sort illustrated by Lori's problem-solving protocol involves mental processes that go beyond those tapped by typical analogy test items. A general process model of analogical thinking is therefore likely to have significant implications for current conceptions of intelligence.

Overview

The remainder of this chapter consists of three major sections. In the first section I will present in more detail a theoretical framework for understanding analogical thinking and its relationship to the acquisition of schemas, developed in collaboration with Mary Gick (Gick & Holyoak, 1980, 1983). This framework is by no means wholly original; some aspects of it can be traced back to Aristotle (Hesse, 1966), and it has been especially influenced by Hesse's (1966) analysis of the role of analogy in science, the concept of analogical mapping as it has been used by Sternberg (1977) and others, and the various schema-based models of cognitive processes that have flourished in recent years (see Rumelhart, 1980). The conception of analogy presented here has many commonalities with recent work in artificial intelligence by Winston (1980) and in psychology by Gentner (in press).

The second section provides a review of our recent experimental work on the process of analogical problem solving and the induction of problem schemas. Recent relevant work by other investigators will also be touched upon. Finally, in the third section I will discuss the import of current work on analogical thinking for a variety of issues related to human intelligence.

A THEORETICAL FRAMEWORK FOR ANALOGICAL THINKING

Psychological Causality and Analogical Mapping

As our earlier description of the mapping process suggests, each analog can be conceptually divided into two parts: That which provides the basis for an initial partial mapping; and that which constitutes the extension of the mapping (i.e., the derived solution, hypothesis, or prediction). To use the terms introduced by Hesse (1966), analogy involves two distinct types of relationships: the "horizontal'' mapping between elements of the two analogs, and the ''vertical'' relationship between the two parts of a single analog. Vertical relationships hold between relevant antecedent conditions and their correlated consequences; more specifically, at least in the case of analogies between problems, vertical relationships correspond to causal relations within the person's mental model of each situation (Winston, 1980). For example, certain aspects of the base problem will be viewed as ''enabling conditions'' for the attained solution. The critical point to note is that the vertical and horizontal relationships within an analogy are intimately related. Although it will seldom be possible to map *all* elements of the base and target, those base elements causally related to the solution must be mappable. If causal elements cannot be mapped, the putative analogy can be rejected as misleading. I will discuss types of mapping failures in more detail below.

Gentner (in press) argues that analogy requires mappings between object *relations* (multiplace predicates), but not between object *attributes* (one-place predicates). For example, in the analogy between atomic structure and the solar system, objects in each domain share the relation of *revolving around* each other (mapping of a multiplace predicate), but they differ across domains in the attribute of size (mapping failure of a one-place predicate). Although I agree that as a general rule mapping of relations is more critical to successful analogy than is mapping of attributes, I would claim that this is a consequence of the fact that relations typically have greater causal importance than do attributes (a point also made by Winston, 1981). It is easy to find exceptions in which an attribute mapping is more critical than is a relational one. In Lori's use of analogy, for example, the successful mapping between the magic carpet and the piece of paper on shape was important because in each case the shape attribute was an enabling condition for construction of a tube. In contrast, the relation of location failed to map (the paper was initially located on the table, whereas the initial location of the magic carpet was unspecified); however, this mapping failure was irrelevant because initial location was not causally related to the solution achieved in the base problem.

The role of causal relationships also helps to elucidate the distinction between analogy and the broader concept of similarity. For example, cats are clearly quite similar to dogs, yet it seems curious to claim that cats are ''analogous'' to dogs. This is so despite the fact that one could derive a rich mapping between elements associated with the two concepts. Neither does the difficulty simply stem from cats and dogs being *too* similar to each other to constitute an analogy (i.e., they share many attributes, and hence would be termed ''literally similar'' by Gentner, in press). To clarify the latter point, note that it is possible to construct a scenario in which an analogy is in fact apparent. Suppose you are trying to convince someone that cats can swim. Assume the person knows a good deal about both cats and dogs, including the fact that dogs can swim. You might then bolster your case by reminding the doubter that cats are analogous to dogs. This remark should trigger a mapping between elements of the two concepts, concentrating on aspects of dogs that seem causally relevant to their swimming (e.g., the structure of their legs). If it seems that cats are comparable to dogs with respect to such factors, the person may agree that cats probably also swim.

Often the functional basis of a putative analogy will be readily apparent, even without an explicit context. For example, in 1982 the statement that "El Salvador is analogous to Vietnam" was easily interpreted, serving as shorthand for the view that the increasing American involvement in El Salvador's civil war was analogous to the early stages of intervention by the United States in Vietnam. The initial partial mapping, as argued by critics of American policy, included American collusion with an unpopular government, an opposing guerrilla movement based in the countryside, and attempts to justify intervention on the basis of a theory of Communist conspiracy. The mapping was extended to derive predictions about the consequences to be expected if American policy did not change— bitter divisions at home, pointless bloodshed abroad.[1] In general, a comparison statement can be interpreted as an analogy whenever it is possible to divide each concept into causal antecedents and relevant consequences. Analogy involves similarity, but it is structured similarity with functional import. Let us now examine that structure in more detail.

Representation of Mapping Relations

Analogical mapping raises a variety of thorny issues that lie at the heart of cognitive science. Mapping relationships hold between elements of mental representations of situations, and depend on some form of propositional representation. Because mapped elements (corresponding to objects and their attributes and relations) are typically similar but not identical, they must be decomposable into more primitive components. Mappings often involve situational elements that were never explicitly stated. Consequently, the various inference processes required for everyday understanding must play a role in analogical thinking. In addition, mappings can be defined at multiple levels of abstraction, perhaps corresponding to "macrostructures" in the sense of Kintsch and van Dijk (1978; van Dijk, 1980). For example, the degree of analogy between the Soviet Union's invasion of Czechoslovakia in 1968 and the imposition of martial law in Poland

---

[1]Debate about American policy in Central America has afforded an interesting case study in extended analogical argumentation. For example, proponents of military intervention countered the Vietnam analogy by pointing out mapping failures (e.g., because El Salvador was smaller and closer than Vietnam, military success would be easier to achieve). They also raised rival analogies, portraying El Salvador and Nicaragua as potential "new Cubas." Critics, meanwhile, compared American intervention in Central America to Soviet intervention in Poland, in order to emphasize the hypocrisy of the Reagan administration's posturing. A normative analysis of analogical reasoning could make a valuable contribution to critiques of foreign policy discussions, a domain in which argument by analogy is commonplace.

in 1981 varies with the specificity of description. At a specific level of description numerous mapping failures can be identified, most notably that the Czech situation involved an external invasion whereas the Polish case did not. However, if the two events are described more abstractly, as the reimposition of Soviet dominance in the face of a perceived threat from an internal popular movement, then the apparent degree of analogy is increased.

In order to make our discussion more concrete, it will be useful to introduce the main target problem used in the experiments of Gick and Holyoak (1980, 1983), as well as a story used as a base analog. The target was Duncker's (1945) radiation problem:

Suppose you are a doctor faced with a patient who has a malignant tumor in his stomach. It is impossible to operate on the patient, but unless the tumor is destroyed the patient will die. There is a kind of ray that can be used to destroy the tumor. If the rays reach the tumor all at once at a sufficiently high intensity, the tumor will be destroyed. Unfortunately, at this intensity the healthy tissue that the rays pass through on the way to the tumor will also be destroyed. At lower intensities the rays are harmless to healthy tissue, but they will not affect the tumor either. What type of procedure might be used to destroy the tumor with the rays, and at the same time avoid destroying the healthy tissue?

Prior to their attempt to solve the radiation problem, our subjects often read a story about an analogous military problem and its solution, in which a general wishes to capture a fortress located in the center of a country. There are many roads radiating outward from the fortress. All have been mined so that although small groups of men can pass over the roads safely, any large force will detonate the mines. A full-scale direct attack is therefore impossible. The general's solution is to divide his army into small groups, send each group to the head of a different road, and have the groups converge simultaneously on the fortress. Note that there is an analogous "convergence" solution to the radiation problem. The doctor could direct multiple low-intensity rays toward the tumor simultaneously from different directions, so that the healthy tissue will be left unharmed, but the effects of the low-intensity rays will summate and destroy the tumor.[2]

Figure 5.1 provides a propositional representation of the military and medical problems, with propositions numbered to indicate mapping relations. The propositions corresponding to the convergence solution to the radiation problem (which subjects had to generate) are italicized. The propositional-function notation is augmented by labeled arcs that represent the major causal relations within

---

[2]In our initial paper (Gick & Holyoak, 1980) we referred to this as the "dispersion" solution, emphasizing the initial division of the single large force into several small ones and their dispersal to multiple locations. However, in some forms of the problem a single large force may not initially exist, making our original name for the solution quite misleading. Calling it the convergence solution emphasizes its central property, the convergence of multiple forces on the target.

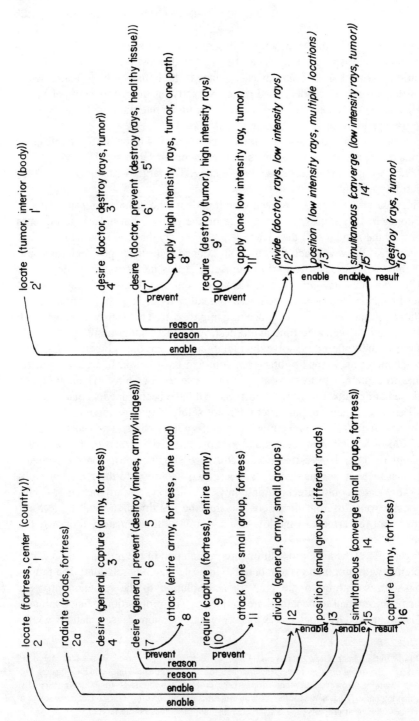

FIG. 5.1. Analogical correspondences between a military story and the radiation problem (from Gick & Holyoak, 1980).

the two analogs. The causal types are based on those proposed by Schank and Abelson (1977). As Figure 5.1 suggests, at this level of macrostructure there is a high degree of correspondence between the two analogs. However, they are not perfectly isomorphic. Proposition 2a in the military story, which states that many roads radiate outward from the fortress, has no parallel in the statement of the radiation problem. Presumably people must infer that there may be multiple potential "routes" to the tumor (an important enabling condition) in the course of generating the convergence solution. A more direct mapping failure is also apparent. In a complete analogy there is a consistent mapping between pairs of elements; i.e., wherever element A occurs in one relational system, A' occurs in the other. In the two analogs in Figure 5.1, the role of the army usually corresponds to that of the rays. However, this mapping is violated in propositions 5 and 5'. In the military story, sending the entire army down one road will result in destruction of the *army* (as well as neighboring villages) by *mines*; whereas in the radiation problem applying high-intensity rays will result in destruction of the *healthy tissue* by the *rays*.

TABLE 5.1
Correspondences among Two Convergence Problems and Their Schema
(From Gick & Holyoak, 1983)

Military Problem

   Initial State
      Goal: Use army to capture fortress
      Resources: Sufficiently large army
      Constraint: Unable to send entire army along one road

   Solution Plan: Send small groups along multiple roads simultaneously

   Outcome: Fortress captured by army

Radiation Problem

   Initial State
      Goal: Use rays to destroy tumor
      Resources: Sufficiently powerful rays
      Constraint: Unable to administer high-intensity rays from one direction

   Solution Plan: Administer low-intensity rays from multiple directions simultaneously
   Outcome: Tumor destroyed by rays

Convergence Schema

   Initial State
      Goal: Use force to overcome a central target
      Resources: Sufficiently great force
      Constraint: Unable to apply full force along one path

   Solution Plan: Apply weak forces along multiple paths simultaneously

   Outcome: Central target overcome by force

This mapping failure is removed when the two analogs are represented slightly more abstractly, as in Table 5.1. The informal notation used in Table 5.1 emphasizes the hierarchical structure of the analogs, each of which is represented as an instance of a very general "problem schema," composed of an initial state (goals, available resources, and constraints), a solution plan, and an actual or anticipated outcome of realizing the plan. The problem schema reflects the vertical causal organization of the analogs, and can be readily related to the causal-network notation of Figure 5.1. The components of the initial state are all causally related to the solution plan: the goal is a *reason* for it; the resources *enable* it; and the constraints *prevent* alternative plans. The outcome is then a *result* of executing the solution plan.[3] The task of the analogist is to construct a partial mapping between the two initial states, which in turn can be used to construct the analogous solution plan and expected outcome for the radiation problem.

Schema Induction

Table 5.1 also includes a statement of a "convergence schema"—a representation of the *type* of problem for which convergence solutions are possible. This schema contains the "core ideas" shared by the two analogs, and it can be abstracted from the analogs by "eliminative induction" (Mackie, 1974; see Winston, 1980, for a computational implementation). The schema can be viewed as an abstract category of which the specific analogs are instances.

In essence, the process of abstracting a schema by eliminative induction involves deleting differences between the analogs while preserving their commonalities. To clarify the relationship between analogs and their schema, let us consider in detail the mapping between two propositions, the analogous expected outcomes of our two convergence problems: roughly, "army captures fortress" and "rays destroy tumor." It is apparent that the two propositions have the same abstract semantic structure, namely, a relation between an instrument and an object. However, this level of mapping is so general that it makes the two propositions no more analogous than either one would be to, say, "key locks door."

To find a more specific mapping, it is necessary to analyze the concepts in the two propositions in order to show how the mapped pairs are similar. I assume that a similarity relation can be decomposed into a set of differences and a set of identities (Hesse, 1966; Tversky, 1977), and that a decomposition can be achieved by means of an abstraction operator, as illustrated in Table 5.2 for our

---

[3]The present conception of the causal elements within a problem schema seems to correspond closely to the top three levels in Carbonell's (1981) "invariance hierarchy" for analogical interpretation: goals, plans, and causal structures. He has found that these types of elements are the most likely to be shared by two domains linked by a metaphor.

example. The function of the abstraction operator is to separate each concept into a "core meaning" that is identical across the mapped elements (a kind of "greatest common denominator"), and a "residual meaning" specific to the particular analog, which is represented as a predicate operating on the core meaning. For example, the core meaning common to both "capture" and "destroy" may be glossed as "overcome." The abstraction operator must therefore transform "capture" into "capture' (overcome)," where the prime indicates that "capture'" is to be understood as the residual meaning of the concept "capture" that remains after the core meaning has been factored out. That is, the meaning of "capture'" is that of "capture" minus that of "overcome." The transformed equivalent of "army captures fortress" might be stated as, "a kind of overcoming (namely, capturing) has as its instrument a kind of force (namely, an army) and as its object a kind of target (namely, a fortress);" the transformed version of "rays destroy tumor" can be interpreted analogously. As Table 5.2 indicates, the meaning components common to the two analogs can be directly translated into a representation of a more abstract shema. (The "schema" in Table 5.2 is a fragment of the convergence schema presented in Table 5.1.) In a sense, then, each analog has the schema embedded in it. However, I will argue below that there are psychological advantages in inducing a schema and storing it as a concept separate from any individual analog.

The above description of the abstraction operator is much too sketchy to constitute a computational model, and many difficult problems need to be solved in order to formulate such a model. One constraint worth emphasizing is that the decomposition process cannot simply operate in a word-by-word fashion using information stored in the mental lexicon for each concept. Rather, the abstraction operator must take account of the broader relational context. To take an obvious example, the lexical entry for the word *fortress* is unlikely to contain the infor-

TABLE 5.2
The Abstraction Operation in Analogical Mapping

An example:	
Analog 1	capture (army, fortress) → capture' (overcome) (army' (force), fortress' (target))
Analog 2	destroy (rays, tumor) → destroy' (overcome) (rays' (force), tumor' (target))
Schema	overcome (force, target)
More generally:	
Analog 1	$R_1 (A_1, B_1) \rightarrow R_1' (R) (A_1' (A), B_1' (B))$
Analog 2	$R_2 (A_2, B_2) \rightarrow R_2' (R) (A_2' (A), B_2' (B))$
Schema	$R (A, B)$

mation that a fortress is a kind of target. In the proposition "army destroys fortress," the fortress is a target solely by virtue of its semantic role with respect to the relation, "destroys." Indeed, the analogy between the two propositions in our example is entirely relational. Thus the residual meaning glossed as "fortress'" is in fact the entire meaning of "fortress" other than its contextual meaning of "target." As this example suggests, the process of mapping dissimilar analogs is likely to be governed by analyses of corresponding relations (Gentner, in press; Gick & Holyoak, 1980).[4]

Taxonomy of Mapping Relations

Postulating an abstraction operator, as discussed above, affords a basis for constructing a taxonomy of mapping relations. Mapping relations are of two basic types: successful mappings, and potentially problematic mapping failures. Successful mappings can be divided into two subtypes. First, there are *mapped identities,* the core meaning components that are shared by the two analogs and that correspond to the schema (e.g., "overcome" in Table 5.2). Second, there are *structure-preserving differences,* the corresponding differences associated with the mapped identities (e.g., "capture'" and "destroy'"). These differences are structure-preserving in that they reflect a general transformation relating the schema to a set of concepts appropriate to the domain of the specific analog. In our example, the military analog can be viewed as a transformation of the convergence schema into concepts appropriate to a military domain, and the medical analog can be viewed as a transformation of the same schema into concepts appropriate to a medical domain. Because the schema is implicitly embedded in each analog (in the form of identities), and assuming the mapped identities are causally sufficient to yield the outcome associated with the schema, it follows that structure-preserving differences do not alter the causal relations in the schema. Accordingly, such differences are not problematic. Other types of relations represent mapping failures. At best these fail to support the analogy, and at worst they destroy it. Mapping failures can be divided into two subtypes: *structure-violating differences* and *indeterminant correspondences.* A structure-violating difference is one that is inconsistent with the general transformation relating the schema to its analog. The lack of role parallelism between the army and rays in propositions 5 and 5', mentioned above (Figure 5.1), is an example of a structure-violating difference. Structure-violating differences, although they may take many forms, all make it impossible to find a single consistent schema that "fits" both analogs. Normatively, a structure-violating difference should lead to rejection of the analogy *if* such a difference alters a causally necessary element of the base analog. The above example is not fatal to the analogy

---

[4]The remarks in the above paragraph result from suggestions made by Dedre Gentner (personal communication).

because proposition 5 is not causally necessary to the convergence solution to the military problem.

Indeterminate correspondences arise when the analogist fails to map conclusively some elements of the base and target. Two subclasses of indeterminate correspondences can be illustrated with a single example from the convergence analogy. An implicit aspect of the military analog, causally related to its solution, is that the effects of the small attacking groups will summate, yielding a strength equivalent to that of the undivided army. A parallel assumption is required for the radiation problem—the effects of multiple low-intensity rays applied simultaneously must summate. The problem statement, however, provides no information about the validity of this assumption (although actual medical practice in fact supports it). An indeterminate correspondence will arise if the analogist has yet to determine whether rays summate or not. If the person has noticed the importance of summation in the military problem, but remains in doubt about ray summation, then the correspondence is *undetermined*. Although such a mapping failure does not justify confident rejection of the analogy, it does leave its appropriateness in doubt (again assuming the difficulty involves a causally necessary aspect of the base).

Alternatively, the person may have yet to notice that the military solution depended on a summation principle; indeed, unless the person makes the prerequisite inferences, the question may never be considered. In this case the indeterminate correspondence remains *latent*. In complex analogies there may be an indefinite number of indeterminate correspondences latent in the analogs. Because some of these might yield to structure-violating differences, an analogy can at best yield plausible conjectures, not irrefutable certitudes. But the open-endedness of analogy is a strength as well as a limitation. As Hesse (1966) has argued, explorations of indeterminate correspondences (which she terms the "neutral analogy") drive the generative use of scientific models: They represent hypotheses yet to be tested, or perhaps even to be derived.

Dimensions of Analogy: Similarity and Completeness

The distinction between mapped identities and structure-preserving differences helps to elucidate the intuitive notion that analogs differ in their similarity to one another. The similarity of any pair of mapped concepts will increase with the extent of the meaning captured by a mapped indentity (Tversky, 1977). In general, if the mapped concepts are either identical or instances of a close superordinate concept, the analogs will be very similar (yielding, one might say, a "literal" rather than a "metaphorical" analogy). Thus a story about a doctor treating a brain tumor with multiple lasers would obviously be more similar to the radiation problem than is our military story. A "deep" analogy, the sort that captures our admiration, is an analogy between disparate situations in which only the essential causal relations are maintained. In what Hesse terms "formal analogies,'' which are common in science, two systems may be analogous by virtue of being alternative interpretations of a logicomathematical model, without any residual similarities between corresponding elements.

Another major dimension of analogy, completeness, is based on the distinction between successful mappings and mapping failures, A complete analogy is an isomorphism in which all mappings are between either identities or structure-preserving differences; an analogy is incomplete to the extent that it includes mapping failures. The completeness of an analogy will usually depend on the level of macrostructure at which the mapping is attempted. For example, although our convergence analogy is complete at the level at which the two analogs are represented in Table 5.1, it is incomplete at the more specific level represented in Figure 5.1. In general, increasing the level of representational abstraction will increase the completeness of an analogy, by deleting mismatching details. However, greater completeness need not be entirely a virtue. For example, one might claim that any two problems are completely analogous at the level of the abstract problem schema corresponding to the headings used in Table 5.1. But such abstract analogies will seldom trigger development of a realizable solution procedure (just as one is unlikely to solve a calculus problem by analogy to repairing a typewriter). In general, increasing the level of abstraction will at some point delete correspondences as well as mismatches, and consequently diminish the value of the analogy. A tendency to maximize the completeness of an analogy by moving to a more abstract level of macrostructure may therefore often compete with a tendency to maximize the extensiveness of the mapping between causal relations by moving to a more detailed representational level. As a result, the ''optimal'' level of representation for successful analogical thinking may typically lie at an intermediate level of abstraction, and it may yield an analogy that is less than complete. (For a somewhat different analysis of dimensions of analogy, see Gentner, in press).

Mechanisms of Analogical Transfer

The above analysis of analogical thinking and schema induction suggests how analogical transfer can take place. Transfer has two basic components: (1) accessing the base from the target problem to make the analogy available; and (2) applying the analogy by mapping elements of the base and the target. In some cases a base analog may be constructed by transforming the representation of the target (Clement, 1981). In other cases it will be necessary to retrieve the base analog from memory when the target is presented, so as to notice the potential analogy between them. Because human memory research is guided by semantic retrieval cues, any semantic aspect of the target could potentially provide access to a relevant analog. In general, many cues are available to remind the person of similar problems from the same domain; for example, the radiation problem will likely call to mind prior knowledge about related medical procedures. However, a dissimilar analog from a remote domain will lack such transparent resemblances. Consequently, the potential semantic links between two dissimilar analogs will simply correspond to the basis of the analogy: the identities that comprise the implicit schema embedded within each analog.

The advantages of having an independent schema stored in memory, alluded to earlier, can now be made explicit. If an appropriate schema has not been at least partially abstracted, it will be relatively difficult to retrieve a base analog when given the target problem because it is the schema that affords potential retrieval cues. Tversky's (1977) analysis of similarity implies that an analog will be more similar to its schema than to another analog, because the schema contains all the aspects common to the two analogs (mapped identities), and none of the differences between them. An independent schema will therefore facilitate the retrieval and noticing of an analogy.

In addition, it should be easier to apply a schema than an analog. An explicit problem schema will make salient those causal aspects of a situation that should trigger a particular plan of action. When two analogs are drawn from disparate domains, the inference processes underlying the abstraction operator will be difficult to execute; if the optimal mapping is therefore not found, the analogist may fail to generate the corresponding solution to the target problem. In general, mapping an analog to a schema will be simpler than mapping one analog with another; in the former case it will only be necessary to map identities, rather than both identities and differences.

It is thus possible to distinguish three important mental activities that involve mapping. First, reasoning from one analog to another involves abstracting the identities within each analog, and mapping both identities and structure-preserving differences. Second, schema induction requires the same abstraction and mapping processes, plus a process of eliminative induction to establish the mapped identities as an independent schema. A schema may be incidentally induced in the course of reasoning between two analogs. Third, reasoning from a schema to an analog involves mapping the components of the schema with the identities implicit in the analog. The residual differences contained in the analog need not be mapped.

EXPERIMENTAL STUDIES OF ANALOGICAL PROBLEM SOLVING

Basic Methodological Issues

The theoretical framework for analogical thinking described above has in part guided and in part emerged from our experimental studies of analogical problem solving. (Gick & Holyoak, 1980, 1983). Our development of an experimental paradigm was influenced by several basic considerations. First, a relevant base analog must be made available to subjects. This was accompanied by presenting subjects with a story analog, such as the military story discussed earlier, prior to an analogous transfer problem. Second, the target problem must be such that its solution can be attained at least as efficiently by using an analogy as by other problem-solving heuristics. Subjects are unlikely to bother to apply an analogy if a solution procedure for the target problem is readily apparent, or if the mapping between the two analogs is complex. For example, Reed, Ernst, and Banerji (1974) observed little transfer between two semantically dissimilar, homomorphic versions of the "missionaries and cannibals" problem. But this multimove problem seems quite ill-suited for the study of analogy. On the one hand, the space of legal moves is so constricted that there is virtually no branching at each step, so that the problem can be efficiently approached by a variant of means-ends analysis. And on the other hand, its sequential, multimove nature makes the number of mapping relations required to develop a solution by analogy extremely high. Consequently, such a problem has little a priori likelihood of revealing subjects' analogical problem-solving skills.

Our own investigations to date have used as targets three problems from the Gestalt tradition. The "ball problem" (adapted from a similar problem described by Raaheim, 1974), was used with preschool and elementary school children (Holyoak et al., 1982); this problem yielded the protocol of 4–year old Lori, discussed earlier. The "cord problem" (Maier, 1930, 1931) was used with high school students (Gick & Holyoak, 1983). And, last in mention but foremost in its contribution to our work, Duncker's (1945) radiation problem has been administered to hundreds of University of Michigan undergraduates (Gick & Holyoak, 1980, 1983). All of these problems are "ill-defined," particularly in that the permissible operations that might be used to achieve the goal are left very open-ended. As a result, it is not immediately obvious how to apply a means-ends strategy, making it more likely that an available base analog will be perceived as useful.

Our convergence with Gestalt psychology is theoretical as well as methodological. Gestalt theory stressed the importance of "restructuring" the problem representation in order to effect a solution; doubtless for that reason, Gestalt psychologists tended to study problems that seem to require such restructuring. The process of analogical mapping, as described earlier, can readily be viewed as a mechanism for restructuring one problem in terms of another. It is probably more than an historical accident that, as we only recently discovered, Duncker himself (1926) performed a preliminary study of analogical problem solving using the radiation problem as target, thus anticipating our own work by over half a century. (See Sternberg, in press, for an analogical interpretation of the process of solving ill-defined problems.)

In addition to providing a base analog and an appropriate transfer problem, other considerations arise if one wishes to assess subjects' ability to *notice* an analogy separately from their ability to subsequently *apply* it. Subjects must be led to process the initial base analog in such a way that the subsequent target problem will potentially serve to remind them of it. Task demands should neither make it obvious to subjects that they should use the base analog, nor preclude the possibility of their noticing its relevance. As we will see below, such methodological issues are an integral part of the study of analogical problem solving.

I will now provide an overview of our empirical results, interpreted in the context of our theoretical framework. This review is organized around four major issues that our studies have addressed. First, it was necessary to establish that people can in fact use analogies to generate problem solutions. The fact that two situations are analogous by no means guarantees that the analogy will have functional significance, especially when the analogs are drawn from disparate domains; each problem might be solved independently, and the analogy recognized post hoc or not at all. Second, we went on to experimentally separate the processes of noticing and applying analogies. Third, we investigated factors that influence the degree of transfer from a single base analog to a target problem. And fourth, we explored transfer from multiple analogs, with emphasis on the role of schema induction as a mediator of analogical transfer.

Problem Solving by Analogy: Basic Evidence

The radiation problem, because it is ill-defined, allows a variety of potential solution plans. We were able to exploit this feature of the problem to demonstrate the use of analogy. Our basic procedure was first to present a military story, and then to ask subjects to give as many solutions as possible to the radiation problem, using the prior story to help them. In GH1:1[5] different subjects received one of three different versions of the story, differing only in the general's solution to his problem. In the version discussed earlier, the general had small groups of men converge on the fortress; in a second version he took advantage of an unguarded road to send his army to the fortress; and in a third version he dug an underground tunnel to the fortress and sent his army through it. Each of these solutions corresponds to a type of solution to the radiation problem that Duncker's (1945) subjects sometimes produced without a prior analog. The three types are the convergence solution that was discussed earlier; sending rays down an existing open passage, such as the stomach; and operating to create an open passage to the tumor. We also tested a control group that did not receive a prior story.

The results were clear-cut: Each solution type was produced most frequently

---

[5]To concisely identify specific experiments in our two papers (Gick & Holyoak, 1980, 1983), I will refer to the former as GH1 and the latter GH2. Numbers after the colon refer to experiment numbers in the specified paper. Thus GH1:1 refers to Experiment I of Gick and Holyoak (1980).

by the group that received the corresponding story analog. Subsequent experiments focused on the convergence solution, which a stable figure of approximately 75 percent of our college subjects generated after receiving the corresponding military story and a hint to apply it. This high solution frequency was obtained even when the critical story analog was presented between two disanalogous "distractor" stories (GH1:4). In contrast, the convergence solution was produced by less than 10 percent of our control subjects (whether they received no prior story at all, or disanalogous stories). We have also used story analogs from semantically distant domains to influence the frequencies with which high school students generate an analogous solution to the cord problem (GH2:1), and the frequencies with which children as young as five years old generate solutions to the ball problem (Holyoak et al., 1982). Such findings constitute strong evidence that many of our subjects in fact used the presented story as a base analog to derive an analogous solution to the target problem. Using similar logic, Gentner and Gentner (1983) have demonstrated that different base analogs lead to systematically varying patterns of difficulty among types of electricity problems.

In most of our experiments, the initial story described both a problem and its solution. In GH1:3, however, we first gave subjects a description of the general's problem and asked them to suggest solutions to it; afterwards they received the radiation problem. About half the subjects gave the convergence solution to the military problem; of these, 41 percent went on to generate the parallel solution to the radiation problem. The latter figure was significantly higher than that for control subjects, indicating that self-generated solutions can also be successfully mapped with a subsequent transfer problem. However, at least in this particular experiment, self-generated solutions to the base analog produced less transfer than did solutions provided by the experimenter.

Our experiments have provided other types of evidence that story analogs can play a causal role in problem solving. For example, not only did the appropriate military story increase the frequency of the convergence solution to the radiation problem (relative to the frequency observed with control subjects), but it also *decreased* the frequency of certain disanalogous solutions, such as desensitizing the healthy tissue (GH1:2). Our analysis of analogical thinking predicts such inhibitory effects of analogy because an attempt to map a target problem with a base analog will necessarily compete with alternative problem-solving strategies that might yield solutions other than those suggested by the analog.

Other evidence regarding the use of analogy was provided by oral problem-solving protocols obtained from subjects solving a target problem by analogy. Such protocols have seemed to us to be limited in their informativeness, because subjects often first stated the analogous solution and only later alluded to the prior story. However, some adult subjects (like 4-year old Lori, whose protocol we discussed earlier) did mention spontaneously correspondences between the problems. For example, one subject in GH1:1 (Gick & Holyoak, 1980), who received the convergence version of the military story, read the radiation problem and then immediately said:

"Like in the first problem, the impenetrable fortress, the guy had put bombs all around, and the bombs could be compared to the healthy tissue. And so they had to, they couldn't go in in mass [sic] through one road, they had to split up so as not to damage the healthy tissue. Because if there's only a little bit of ray it doesn't damage the tissue, but it's all focused on the same spot [p. 327]."

Our paradigms have always involved experimental manipulation of the prior analog; therefore, our subjects have never been encouraged to respond spontaneously with analogies based on their preexperimental knowledge. However, the radiation problem reminded one subject in GH1:1 of another analog, a situation in which the filament of a light bulb was repaired by directing lasers from multiple directions so as not to damage the intervening glass. Instances of the use of subject-generated analogs were also observed in the protocols of children solving the ball problem (Holyoak et al., 1982). In addition, the work of other researchers has produced more extensive evidence suggesting that the spontaneous use of analogies to solve problems is not uncommon, at least in scientific problem solving (Gentner & Gentner, in press; Clement, 1981).

To summarize, the evidence regarding our first and most basic issue is overwhelming: People, including young children, are often able to apply analogies to generate problem solutions.

Noticing Vs. Application of Analogy

Once we had established that analogies can indeed be used to solve problems, we attempted to separate the process of initially noticing the analogy from the subsequent application process. In our earliest experiments, subjects were always given an explicit hint to use the prior story to help solve the radiation problem. The experimenter thus played a role similar to that of a teacher who draws a student's attention to a potential analogy. The hint was entirely nonspecific, as subjects were not told *how* the story might help; however, it obviated any need for subjects to spontaneously notice the analogy.

To investigate the noticing process we had subjects memorize the military story analog in the guise of a study of story recall, and then immediately go on to work on the radiation problem, without any hint to use the prior story (GH1:4, 5). Under these conditions only about 30 percent of our subjects produced the convergence solution, as opposed to about 75 percent who produced it when a hint was given. Assuming that about 10 percent of subjects would produce the solution in the absence of any analogy, these results indicate that that only a third of less of the subjects who could potentially apply the analogy spontaneously noticed it.

In a further experimental variation, we had subjects read and recall the story analog between two attempts to solve the radiation problem, in the guise of a study of the effects of "incubation" on problem solving (GH1:5). These subjects thus encoded and recalled the story *after* being confronted with the rradiation problem, and knowing they would soon return to it. Nonetheless, the frequency with which subjects spontaneously noticed and applied the analogy was no greater in this condition than when the story preceded the target problem. Most subjects in both conditions failed to notice spontaneously an analogy they could successfully apply. (See also Schustack & Anderson, 1979, for evidence that potentially useful analogies are often not noticed in a memory paradigm.)

Such striking gaps between noticing an analogy and applying it seemed surprising for several reasons. Our procedure did not involve any deception; subjects were told at the outset that the experiment would have two parts, story recall and then problem solving. The delay between the two tasks was minimal. One might well have supposed that the demand characteristics of being in a psychology experiment would have led virtually all subjects to consider how the first part might be related to the second.

What might account for the apparent difficulty of noticing an analogy between semantically dissimilar problems? According to our earlier analysis of analogical retrieval, elements of the implicit schema afford potential retrieval cues by means of which the target problem may call to mind a relevant base analog. It follows that if the problem solver fails to encode elements of the schema, in either the base or the target, the potential analogy may be missed. In our paradigm, it seems especially likely that subjects may often fail to encode schema elements in the base analog. It is presented as a "story" rather than as a "problem," and subjects are not encouraged to represent it in alternative ways. In general, the analogist is free to transform the representation of a current target situation, but the memory representations of potential base analogs will have been "fixed" at the times of their encodings and cannot be processed further until they have been retrieved. The accessibility of a base analog will therefore be especially dependent on the nature of its initial encoding. But once a "teacher" calls the analogist's attention to the potential analogy, the representations of both analogs can be transformed in an attempt to find a satisfactory mapping. As a result, the analogist may be able to apply an analogy even though it was not noticed spontaneously.

This semantic retrieval-cue explanation of failures to notice analogies is supported by the results of a condition tested in GH2:3, in which the base analog was not a story but rather the pair of diagrams depicted in Figure 5.2. Subjects in this condition were told that the first part of the experiment involved pattern recognition, and that they were to study the diagrams so they could later reproduce them. All the subjects were able to reproduce the diagrams from memory. They were then presented with the radiation problem, at first without any hint to use the diagrams to help solve it. Later, after subjects had given as many solutions as they could initially think of, they were told to try to use the diagrams to generate

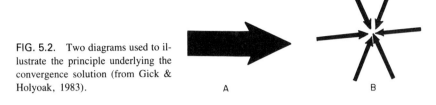

FIG. 5.2.   Two diagrams used to illustrate the principle underlying the convergence solution (from Gick & Holyoak, 1983).

A   B

further solutions. (This "two-pass," within-subjects procedure was used in most of our studies of noticing.)

The diagrams in Figure 5.2 were intended to serve as an abstract visual representation of key elements of the convergence schema. Diagram A, a single large arrow, represents the desirable but blocked plan of sending a large force from a single direction. Diagram B, several smaller converging arrows, represents the alternative plan of sending small forces from multiple directions. This diagram condition yielded the most striking discrepancy between initial noticing and eventual application we have ever observed in our studies. Of 15 subjects who were tested, only one gave the convergence solution prior to the hint, and he apparently solved the radiation problem without reference to the diagrams. But once the hint was given, another nine subjects were able to use their memory of the diagrams to generate the convergence solution.

This result is in accord with our retrieval-cue analysis. When the diagrams were presented in the context of a "pattern recognition" task, it is unlikely that subjects assigned any semantic interpretation to them and undoubtedly no interpretations even approximating the convergence schema. As a result, no semantic retrieval cues were subsequently available to link the radiation problem with the diagrams. But once subjects had been explicitly told to consider the prior diagrams, they were often able to interpret them by means of a mapping process. Once the initial arrow has been interpreted as a representation of the intensity and direction of rays, the relationship between the two diagrams can be construed as a transformation of one large unidirectional ray into several small converging ones, thus illustrating the convergence solution. Such a chain of reasoning, which might be termed "analogical bootstrapping," seems similar to the use of formal models in science to derive predictions. Once the elements of a formal model have been interpreted by a mapping with elements of the relevant domain, the model can be manipulated, using permissible inference rules, to derive predictions about the target domain.

We will see shortly that our analysis of noticing an analogy and applying it derives further support from experiments designed to investigate conditions that facilitate analogical transfer.

Determinants of Transfer from a Single Analog

The theoretical framework presented earlier suggests several factors that should facilitate transfer from a base analog to a target problem. One such factor is the overall similarity of the elements of the two analogs: The greater their similarity, the more potential retrieval cues will link the two analogs, and the easier the mapping process will be. Our experiments have not tested this hypothesis directly, but a comparison across target problems provides suggestive evidence. In GH2:1, we had subjects solve Maier's (1930) cord problem after reading a story in which a "pendulum" solution was used to solve an analogous problem involving the need to tie together two widely separated ribbons. Seventy-one percent of the subjects given the story analog generated the parallel pendulum solution to the cord problem prior to receiving a hint, as opposed to only 20 percent of control subjects who did not read the story analog. Once the hint to consider the story was given, 98 percent of the subjects in the analogy conditions eventually generated the critical solution. Subjects were thus more successful in solving the cord problem by analogy, in terms of both initial noticing and eventual application, than were subjects in comparable experiments that used the radiation problem and its military analog. Because these two analog pairs differ in many ways, strong conclusions are unwarranted. Nonetheless, it is intuitively clear that the two analogs were more similar in the case of the cord problem than in that of the radiation problem (e.g., ribbons are more similar to cords than armies are to rays). The above results are thus consistent with the predicted positive effect of similarity on the use of analogy in problem solving.

The completeness of an analogy should also be positively related to transfer. This prediction was tested directly in GH1:2. One group of subjects received the usual military story with the convergence solution. A second group received an alternative version of the story that included the identical solution but a very different initial problem state. In the latter version, the general's goal was not to attack the fortress but to stage an elaborate military parade that would be seen throughout the country. Because this initial state was substantially disanalogous to that of the radiation problem, substituting the Parade for the Attack story reduced the completeness of the analogy between the base and target. As predicted, the percentage of subjects who were able to generate the convergence solution to the radiation problem (with a hint to use the story) declined significantly across these two story conditions (76 percent in the Attack condition vs. 49 percent in the Parade condition).

As I argued earlier, analogical transfer should be facilitated to the extent that the problem solver in fact encodes the schema elements implicit in the base analog. When the base and target are relatively dissimilar, and when the base is encoded incidentally in the context of a task other than problem solving (as in all our experiments), the problem solver may often fail to encode the critical elements of the base. In several experiments (GH2:Part I) we attempted to facilitate analogical transfer by manipulations intended to foster a more abstract encoding of the base while still presenting it in an incidental context. None of our attempts were successful. In GH2:1 we compared the performance of subjects instructed to summarize the story analog to that of subjects instructed to recall it. No differences were observed in degree of transfer to the target problem. However, we also found no evidence that summarization instructions led to more extensive encoding of the schema elements than did recall instructions, so the failure to find transfer differences was not surprising. In two other experiments, we took a more direct approach, augmenting the story with references to either a verbal or a diagrammatic statement of the implicit convergence schema. The verbal statement (GH2:2) was, "The general attributed his success to an important principle: If you need a large force to accomplish some purpose, but are prevented from applying such a force directly, many smaller forces applied simultaneously from different directions may work just as well." The diagrammatic representation (GH2:3) consisted of the arrow diagrams depicted in Figure 5.2. Neither of these devices facilitated analogical transfer from the story analog to the radiation problem (although both were effective solution prompts when presented alone). But as in the case of our summarization manipulation, we found no evidence that either the verbal or visual statements of the principle actually yielded more abstract representations of the story. For example, some subjects given the story and the diagrams seemed to interpret the arrows simply as roads rather than as abstract directions of access.

It should be kept in mind that the above encoding manipulations were always made in an incidental context; subjects were never directly told, when first given the story, to try to use it to learn about a type of problem. It is quite possible that with more explicit guidance, presentation of abstract principles along with a single example may facilitate transfer (Krantz, Fong, & Nisbett, 1982). But from the present perspective, the critical point is that all manipulations involving a single example share a common limitation: They do not allow induction of a schema by mapping. Because the schema is defined by the correspondences between two analogs, at least two examples are required. Let us now consider the results of some experiments in which this prerequisite for schema induction was met.

Schema Induction and Analogical Transfer

In order to investigate the effects of providing multiple base analogs, we wrote several new stories illustrating convergence solutions. Each described either a military situation (as in the original version) or a fire-fighting situation (e.g., "Red Adair," in which the hero extinguished an oil well fire by using multiple small hoses). In GH2:4, subjects first read either two of these story analogs, or else one convergence story and one disanalogous story. They were asked to write brief summaries of each story, and (in the procedural aspect most critical to our subsequent analyses) to describe as clearly as possible ways in which the stories were similar. The latter task was intended to elicit a mapping between the two stories, and hence potentially to lead to abstraction of a convergence schema. These written descriptions were later scored for presence and quality of the schema. All subjects then attempted to solve the radiation problem, both before and after a hint to consider the stories.

As our analysis of schema induction predicts, two story analogs produced significantly greater transfer than did one. More importantly, in all the experiments in GH2:Part II, we observed striking relationships between the quality of the schemas induced from the two story analogs, as revealed by subjects' descriptions of similarities between the stories, and success in generating the convergence solution to the radiation problem. Descriptions were categorized into three levels of schema quality: good (e.g., "Both stories used the same concept to solve a problem, which was to use many small forces applied together to add up to one large force necessary to destroy the object"); intermediate (e.g., "In both cases many small forces were used"); and poor (e.g., "In both stories a hero was rewarded for his efforts"). Poor schemas contained none of the essential elements of the convergence schema. In GH2:4, 91 percent of the subjects generated the convergence solution to the radiation problem *prior* to the hint for those who wrote good schemas; 40 percent of those who wrote intermediate schemas generated it; as did 30 percent of those who wrote poor schemas. Similar dramatic differences were observed in subsequent experiments.

In addition, the same verbal statements and diagrams that had failed to facilitate transfer from a single analog (as discussed above) proved highly beneficial when paired with two. For example, in GH2:6 some subjects received two story analogs that both referred to the diagrams shown in Figure 5.2. Over half of these subjects wrote good schemas, and 92 percent of the group eventually produced the convergence solution. This frequency, nine times higher than the base rate for generation of the solution without any analog, is clearly close to the maximum any manipulation could achieve.

These central results support our analyses of analogical mapping, schema formation, and semantically driven retrieval. A mapping process cannot operate on only a single prior analog to derive a schema; hence the most direct mechanism for schema induction is inapplicable. Two analogs, on the other hand, can be mapped together to derive a more general schema; furthermore, any device that highlights the causally relevant correspondences will facilitate abstraction of a more optimal schema. To the extent that the schema implicit in the prior analogs has been made explicit, analysis of a disparate transfer problem may yield semantic retrieval cues that prompt recall of the prior information. Schema induction will thus increase the probability that an analog will subsequently be noticed; in addition, a problem schema will simplify the process of mapping the prior information with the new problem in order to generate an analogous solution.

ANALOGICAL ASPECTS OF INTELLIGENCE

Overview

I will now consider the implications of our theoretical framework and empirical evidence for the goal of understanding human intelligence. Here I am using the term "intelligence" in a broad sense that includes the mental processes used to reason and solve problems (Sternberg, in press), rather than as the equivalent of mental ability as measured by conventional tests. An obvious gap in our research to date has been the lack of any assessment of individual differences in analogical problem-solving skill, a central issue in any theory of intelligence. Nonetheless, it is possible to speculate regarding potential sources of individual differences in the use of analogy. I will first consider some central distinctions between the present theoretical framework and models that deal with "analogy problems" of the sort typically used in intelligence tests. We will see that analogical problem solving invokes mental processes that go beyond those postulated by models of solving analogy items. I will then discuss the relationship between the use of analogy and other problem-solving heuristics, particularly in relation to the development of expertise. The nature of analogical memory retrieval will then be considered. Finally, I will sketch some avenues of approach to the problem of improving analogical thinking by instruction.

Alternative Conceptions of Analogy

The conception of analogy that has emerged from work on problem solving is substantially different from that reflected in models based on studies of "proportional" analogy problems (such as those models reviewed and proposed by Sternberg, 1977). It is possible to describe an analogy between a base and a target problem in the proportional format; i.e., $Problem_B:Solution_B:: Problem_T:Solution_T$, where the analogist must generate the solution to the target problem, $Solution_T$. However, the resemblance between such problem analogies and conventional analogy items such as tree:trunk::person:legs is quite superficial. Several of the most basic distinctions were first noted by Hesse (1966). Perhaps the most critical of these is functional: Analogy items are simply to be solved for their own sake, whereas in problem solving the base analog must be selected and evaluated with respect to its usefulness in generating an effective solution to the target problem. This functional distinction entails several structural ones. In standard analogy items the kinds of relationships that can hold between the A and B terms and between the C and D terms are relatively arbitrary (e.g., "has as supporting part" in the above example). But in problem analogies the corresponding links between each problem and its solution are causal relations, as discussed earlier. Similarly, the terms in standard analogy items can often be rearranged in the manner of mathematical proportions (e.g., our example might be transformed into legs:trunk::person:tree). In contrast, problem analogies lose their functional significance if the canonical format given above is violated. It makes little sense, for example, to consider using the relationship between a target solution and a base solution to generate the base problem from the target problem.

The functional and structural differences between problem analogies and analogy problems have led to differing models. For example, the theoretical framework presented here can be compared with the models of solving analogy problems proposed by Sternberg (1977). These models divide the solution process into stages of *encoding* the presented terms, *inference* (to discover a rule relating A to B), *mapping* (to discover a higher order rule relating A and C), *application* (to construct a rule to generate an "ideal" fourth term, D), and *response* execution. Such models are certainly similar in some respects to a model of analogical problem solving (particularly with respect to mapping and application processes), but the latter is necessarily more complex. In the case of problem solving, the stages of encoding and inference merge into a process of analyzing the causal structure of the base analog and of the target problem. Mapping is used to relate not just two concepts, but two *sets* of interrelated concepts. Mapping can involve not only the problem statements (equivalent to the A and C terms), but also the solution to the base problem (B) and an hypothesized solution to the target (D). Models of solving analogy problems typically employ simple attribute-value or spatial representations, whereas a model of analogical problem solving must necessarily be based on elaborated propositional representations that can represent causal relations.

From the perspective of the research issues I reviewed earlier, an especially important distinction is that noted by Weitzengfeld and Klein (1979): The question of how analogies are retrieved or generated is entirely evaded in the context of analogy items, since both domains are explicitly given in the statement of the question. As was argued earlier, the process of retrieving a base analog depends on finding some minimal initial mapping with schema elements implicit in the statement of the target problem. Whereas models such as those proposed by Sternberg (1977) include mapping as an intermediate stage in the solution process, mapping seems to initiate the process of analogical problem solving. More generally, analogical problem solving seems less serial than models of solving analogy problems would imply. The use of analogy in problem solving appears to be a complex and interactive process involving the retrieval of plausible base analogs, assessment of the causal relations in the base, reformulation of the target problem, tentative attempts at partial mapping, integration with other problem-solving heuristics, and evaluation of potential solutions. The selection, order, and duration of such processes are likely to be highly flexible and under the strategic control of the analogist. Such control processes correspond closely to what Sternberg (in press) has termed "metacomponents" of the process of solving analogy items. In reaction-time analyses such as those of Sternberg (1977), time to perform such operations is included in the parameters representing encoding and response time (both of which are significantly related to measured intelligence). In contrast to their subsidiary role in models of solving analogy items, analogical control processes are of central importance within the present theoretical framework.

I have emphasized the differences between analogical problem solving and solving analogy items, but I do not mean to imply that the two types of tasks are entirely unrelated. On the contrary, I would expect to find a substantial positive relationship between the ability to solve problems by analogy and standard measures of analogical reasoning (a worthwhile direction for future research). The entire range of analogy tasks most likely taps some very general cognitive processes related to skill in flexibly transforming information. However, analogical problem solving seems especially relevant to the broader range of cognitive skills basic to human intelligence.

Analogical Thinking and Problem-Solving Expertise

Given our focus on analogical problem solving, and the centrality of problem-solving skill as a manifestation of intelligence, it is important to consider the place of analogy in a broader theory of problem solving. Over the past two decades the information-processing approach to problem solving has passed through two major phases. The first phase emphasized the specification of general, domain-independent heuristics (now often called "weak methods"), such as means-ends analysis and hierarchical planning (Newell & Simon, 1972). It soon became apparent that the general heuristics alone could not account for the levels of problem-solving expertise achieved by humans. Consequently, the second phase of research has emphasized domain-specific heuristics and knowledge representations (Feigenbaum, Buchanan, & Lederberg, 1971; Davis, Buchanan, & Shortliffe, 1977; Larkin et al., 1980). In many respects the second phase has clearly built on the first, especially because domain-specific heuristics can often be viewed as specializations of more general methods. Nonetheless, the more recent emphasis on domain-specific expertise has perhaps not encouraged the investigation of analogical reasoning between deomains. Indeed, a certain amount of stress has been placed on the apparent *absence* of transfer between various expert skills, such as chess playing and mass spectrum analysis.

It is important to realize, however, that the concept of a domain is intrinsically hierarchical. When we look within the various subareas of a single discipline, analogical transfer is commonplace. To draw an example from close at hand, our own research was influenced by an apparent analogy between the formation of problem schemas and perceptual category learning. Such cases are mini-analogies between microdomains; however, examples of analogies between more general domains are also easily found. Within cognitive psychology, influential ideas have been based on parallels between organizational decision making and human problem solving; between machine computations and human intelligence; between biological evolution and human learning. Furthermore, important scientific analogies often transfer knowledge that is more procedural than substantive: what goals to set for theory, how to design informative experiments, how to evaluate an explanation. In all such examples, both small and large, the fruitfulness of the analogy is ultimately limited by the degree of correspondence between the two domains of knowledge. If mastery of chess provides few insights into mass spectral analysis, it may simply reflect the lack of deep correspondences between these particular domains.

Work on analogical problem solving has several links to other current problem-solving research. For example, evidence that analogical transfer is facilitated by explicit encoding of the schema implicit in each analog suggests that expert knowledge of each domain is a prerequisite for optimal transfer. The abstract problem schemas apparently available to experts (Larkin et al., 1980) may arise as the result of mappings between specific problems. Novices will encode relatively superficial features of individual problems, whereas experts will encode more abstract causal relations (Chi et al., 1981). Consequently, experienced problem solvers will be better able to recognize analogical relationships between superficially dissimilar problems. As a problem-solving method, the use of analogy can be viewed as a general heuristic that can be specialized to operate between particular domains of expertise. Skill in analogical thinking will likely exhibit some degree of domain specificity, rather than solely reflecting "general intelligence."

Analogical Memory Retrieval

In much of the research reviewed earlier we distinguished between the initial noticing of a potential analogy and its eventual use. The processes by which analogies are noticed very likely play a major role in memory retrieval, even when no explicit problem needs to be solved. A new situation very often spontaneously reminds us of related ones that were encountered in the past. Sometimes the two situations are superficially dissimilar, in which case it seems that analogical mappings between corresponding relations must trigger the retrieval process. Let me use an example from my own experience to illustrate what I mean by analogical retrieval. I recently read a brief biographical sketch of Karl Marx in a book on economics, and the following day I was discussing the book with a friend. I mentioned the author's contention that Marx was personally dogmatic, which may have contributed to the dogmatism of his followers. My friend pointed out that disciples often tend to be more dogmatic than their masters, and we mentioned psychoanalysis and major religions as examples. She asked me if Marx had ever expressed doubts about his tenents. I answered yes, and repeated an enigmatic remark that Marx purportedly made shortly before his death: "I am not a Marxist." At that point I suddenly thought of a parallel: Christ's cry from the cross, "My God, my God, why have you forsaken me?"

What triggered this association? This question leads me from description into speculation. As far as I know I had never previously thought of these two remarks together. Yet they are clearly related analogically. Both situations involve expressions of loss of faith by the founders of ideologies. In each case the doubt arose shortly before death, it is uncertain whether the doubt was later resolved, and the ideology was nevertheless destined to flourish and grow. There is thus an implicit schematic structure shared by the cue situation and the analog retrieved from memory. The analysis of analogical retrieval presented earlier suggests that elements of such a schematic structure provide potential retrieval cues. In this example it is clear that some of these elements had been activated by the preceding conversation; e.g., ideologies (with Marxism and Christianity as eamples), and differences in rigidity of beliefs between founders and their disciples. I had thus encoded the cue situation in a manner conducive to retrieval of its analog. In addition, Marx's remark yielded a sense of ironic paradox, engendered by the contrast between a doubt-ridden founder and his many later believers. Being reminded of the remark in the conversational context may thus have invoked an implicit reasoning heuristic of the form, "If you've stumbled upon one interesting example, look for others." Accordingly, I may have searched the small set of ideologies that had been primed, actively seeking a parallel to Marx's remark. (Freud, to the best of my knowledge at the time, died a faithful Freudian.)

Analogical memory retrieval may well serve as the interface between passive memory storage and the creative generation of new ideas. Two important properties of such retrieval support this contention. First, it can relate ideas that were not directly associated in prior experience. Second, the relationship between the two ideas is not simply haphazard; rather, the ideas share certain elements of an abstract relational structure. The resulting association is thus not only novel but potentially useful, as it may trigger the induction of a new, more abstract concept (such as "doubt-ridden founder of an ideology," perhaps).

Analogical retrieval is surely important in literary creativity. This may be particularly true of writing poetry, given the highly metaphorical nature of the product. A good poet may be one who encodes experiences in a way that facilitates subsequent analogical transfer. Such trasfer very likely depends on shared affective and esthetic structure, as well as abstract semantic overlap. These suggestions seem to be in accord with an observation made by the poet Stephen Spender (1952): "A memory once clearly stated ceases to be a memory, it becomes perpetually present, because each time we experience something which recalls it, the clear and lucid original experience imposes its formal beauty on the new experiences [p. 121]."

Can Analogical Thinking Be Trained?

I have argued that analogical thinking develops in early childhood, and that it is a pervasive aspect of human intelligence. Nonetheless, it is clearly a skill (or more accurately, set of skills) in which a wide range of individual differences can be observed. An important question, then, is whether analogical thinking can be improved by appropriate training.

This question seems to have received little serious research. Nonetheless, I would venture a positive answer, and I believe the framework we have been examining at least suggests some important points to consider in attempting to develop an effective training program. As noted earlier, analogical thinking is probably to some degree a domain-specific skill; certainly the poet and the scientist must process analogies in significantly different ways. If we consider the use of analogy in problem solving, several suggestions can be made. As has been emphasized repeatedly, analogical transfer depends critically on the way in which the potential base analog was initially encoded. Perhaps people could be taught to explicitly note the abstract goals, plans, and causal relations embodied in problem situations that they encounter, thus establishing the bases for potential analogies (Carbonell, 1981). Appropriate encoding might be facilitated if useful taxonomies of such problem elements were developed and taught. In addition, optimal encoding of causal relations will inevitably depend on the acquisition of expertise in the subject area.

Once an anlogy has been spontaneously noticed or provided by someone else, it still must be evaluated and applied. Success will depend on a variety of skills that may prove open to training (Clement, 1981). For example, Weitzenfeld and Klein (1979) emphasize the importance of "refining the causal description [p. 8];" i.e., consciously analysing the causal basis of the outcome observed in the base analog. It might prove valuable to teach explicitly a taxonomy of mapping relations such as that described earlier. Examples could be introduced to illustrate different types of mapping failures, with discussion of implications for the usefulness of the analogies. Consider, for example, the reasoning task confronted by a judge who must relate a current case to a putative precedent. It will be necessary to identify the causal elements underlying the original decision (the points of law that were applied), and to separate these from irrelevant aspects of the precedent. A mapping must then be performed between the causal elements of the precedent and elements of the current case. The current case may have to be redescribed in order to effect a mapping, and the implications of apparent mapping failures will need to be evaluated. Explicit training in the nature of this type of analogical reasoning might well prove beneficial.

Analogical thinking is one of the most powerful tools of the human mind. It is a complex tool, and we still have only a sketchy understanding of its internal workings. As we learn more about how the tool is designed, we may also learn how it can be most effectively used.

ACKNOWLEDGMENTS

Preparation of this paper was supported by an NIMH Research Scientist Development Award, 1–K02–MH00342–02. The research I review was sponsored by NIMH Grant 5–R01-MH332878. The ideas presented here were developed jointly with my collaborator Mary Gick, who provided valuable comments on an earlier draft. Richard Nisbett and Robert Sternberg also contributed helpful suggestions.

REFERENCES

Carbonell, J. G. Invariance hierarchies in metaphor interpretation. *Proceedings of the Third Annual Conference of the Cognitive Science Society,* Berkeley, 1981.

Chi, M. T. H., Feltovich, P. J., & Glaser, R. Categorization and representation of physics problems by experts and novices. *Cognitive Science,* 1981, *5,* 121–152.

Clement, J. Analogy generation in scientific problem solving. *Proceedings of the Third Annual Conference of the Cognitive Science Society,* Berkeley, 1981.

Davis, R., Buchanan, B., & Shortliffe, E. Production rules as a representation for a knowledge-based consultation program. *Artificial Intelligence,* 1977, *8,* 15–45.

Duncker, K. A qualitative (experimental and theoretical) study of productive thinking (solving of comprehensible problems). *Journal of Genetic Psychology, 33,* 1926, 642–708.

Duncker, K. On problem solving. *Psychological Monographs,* 1945, *58* (Whole No. 270).

Feigenbaum, E. A., Buchanan, B. G., & Lederberg, J. On generality and problem solving: A case study using the DENDRAL program. In B. Meltzer & D. Michie (Eds.), *Machine intelligence 6.* Edinburgh: Edinburgh University Press, 1971.

Gentner, D. Are scientific analogies metaphors? In D. S. Miall (Ed.), *Metaphor: Problems and perspectives.* Brighton, Sussex: Harvester Press, in press.

Gentner, D., & Gentner, D. R. Flowing waters or teeming crowds: Mental models of electricity. In D. Gentner & A. Stevens (Eds.), *Mental models.* Hillsdale, N.J.: Lawrence Erlbaum Associates, 1983.

Gick, M. L. & Holyoak, K. J. Analogical problem solving. *Cognitive Psychology,* 1980, *12,* 306–355.

Gick, M. L. & Holyoak, K. J. Schema induction and analogical transfer. *Cognitive Psychology,* 1983, *15,* 1–38.

Hesse, M. B. *Models and Analogies in Science.* Notre Dame: University of Notre Dame Press, 1966.

Holyoak, K. J. An analogical framework for literary interpretation. *Poetics,* 1982, *11,* 105–126.

Holyoak, K. J., & Gordon, P. C. Information processing and social cognition. In R. S. Wyer, Jr., T. K. Srull, & J. Hartwick (Eds.), *Handbook of social cognition.* Hillsdale, N.J.: Lawrence Erlbaum Associates, in press.

Holyoak, K. J., Junn, E. N., & Billman, D. O. *Development of analogical problem-solving skill.* Manuscript in preparation, 1982.

Kintsch, W. & van Dijk, T. A. Toward a model of text comprehension and production. *Psychological Review,* 1978, *85,* 363–394.

Krantz, D. H., Fong, G. T., & Nisbett, R. E. Manuscript in preparation, 1982.

Lakoff, G. & Johnson, M. *Metaphors We Live By.* Chicago: University of Chicago Press, 1980.

Larkin, J. H., McDermott, J., Simon, D., & Simon, H. A. Expert and novice performance in solving physics problems. *Science,* 1980, *208,* 1335–1342.

Mackie, J. L. *The cement of the universe.* Oxford: Oxford University Press, 1974.

Maier, N. Reasoning in humans. I. On direction. *Journal of Comparative Psychology,* 1930, *10,* 15–43.

Maier, N. Reasoning in humans. II. The solution of a problem and its appearance in consciousness. *Journal of Comparative Psychology,* 1931, *12,* 181–194.

Miller, G. A. Images and models, similes and metaphors. In A. Ortony (Ed.), *Metaphor and thought.* Cambridge: Cambridge University Press, 1979.

Moore, J. & Newell, A. How can MERLIN understand? In L. W. Gregg (Ed.), *Knowledge and cognition.* Hillsdale, N.J.: Lawrence Erlbaum Associates, 1973.

Newell, A. & Simon, H. A. *Human problem solving.* Englewood Cliffs: N.J.: Prentice-Hall, 1972.

Oppenheimer, J. R. Analogy in science. *American Psychologist,* 1956, *11,* 127–135.

Raaheim, K. *Problem solving and intelligence.* Oslo: Universitetsforlaget, 1974.

Reed, S. K., Ernst, G. W., & Banerji, R. The role of analogy in transfer between similar problem states. *Cognitive Psychology,* 1974, *6,* 436–450.

Rumelhart, D. E. Schemata: The building blocks of cognition. In R. Spiro, B. Bruce, & W. Brewer (Eds.), *Theoretical issues in reading comprehension.* Hillsdale, N.J.: Lawrence Erlbaum Associates, 1980.

Schank, R. C. & Abelson, R. P. *Scripts, plans, goals, and understanding.* Hillsdale, N.J.: Lawrence Erlbaum Associates, 1977.

Schustack, M. & Anderson, J. R. Effects of analogy to prior knowledge on memory for new information. *Journal of Verbal Learning and Verbal Behavior,* 1979, *18,* 565–583.

Spender, S. The making of a poem. In B. Ghiselin (Ed.), *The creative process: A symposium.* University of California Press, 1952 (Mentor Books, 1955). Originally published in *Partisan Review,* Summer 1946.

Sternberg, R. J. *Intelligence, information processing, and analogical reasoning: The componential analysis of human abilities.* Hillsdale, N.J.: Lawrence Erlbaum Associates, 1977.

Sternberg, R. J. Reasoning, problem solving, and intelligence. In R. J. Sternberg (Ed.), *Handbook of human intelligence.* New York: Cambridge University Press, in press.

Tversky, A. Features of similarity. *Psychological Review,* 1977, *84,* 327–352.

van Dijk, T. A. *Macrostructures.* Hillsdale, N.J.: Lawrence Erlbaum Associates, 1980.

Weitzengfeld, J., & Klein, G. A. *Analogical reasoning as a discovery logic.* Technical Report TR–SCR–79–5, Klein Associates, Yellow Springs, Ohio, 1979.

Winston, P. H. Learning and reasoning by analogy. *Communications of the ACM,* 1980, *23,* 689–703.

Winston, P. H. *Learning new principles from precedents and exercises.* Technical Report AIM 632, Massachusetts Institute of Technology, 1981.

6

A Cognitive Analysis of Mathematical Problem-Solving Ability

Richard E. Mayer
University of California, Santa Barbara

Jill H. Larkin
Joseph B. Kadane
Carnegie-Mellon University

INTRODUCTION

Mathematical Ability

Issue. Why is it that some people, when faced with a mathematics problem, are able to generate clever solutions, whereas other people cannot? What makes people differ in their performance on mathematics problems? What is it that good mathematics problem solvers possess that poor mathematics problem solvers do not possess? In other words, what is the nature of mathematical ability? The goal of the present chapter is to describe recent research that attempts to provide a better understanding of the nature of mathematical ability.

General vs. specific ability. A psychological study of mathematical ability is similar to a study of general ability, except that the focus is on performance within the domain of mathematical problems. Resnick & Ford (1981) have argued the merits of such an approach.

> As psychologists concerned specifically with mathematics, our goal is to ask the same questions that experimental and developmental psychologists ask about learning, thinking, and intelligence but to focus these questions with respect to a particular subject matter. What this means is that instead of asking ourselves the general question, "How is it that people think?" we ask ourselves, "How is it that people think about mathematics?". . . . We want to know what mixture of experience and intellect makes that thing called *mathematical ability* happen. As psychologists of a subject matter, we want to know not simply how overall human performance becomes skillful but how human performance of mathematically significant skills

becomes fluent, and how those skills are integrated in the context of mathematical problem solving [p. 3].

One reason for focusing on a specific domain such as mathematical ability is that important questions are posed for psychology that might not have been posed if we focused solely on general ability.

Example. In particular, this chapter focuses on algebra story problems—what Hinsley, Hayes, and Simon (1977) have called "those 20th century fables." Algebra story problems are important because they form the core of the mathematics curriculum in secondary schools, and because they are typically used in tests of mathematical ability, mathematical achievement, general intelligence, and special aptitude. Thus, algebra story problems are a typical or representative mathematical problem solving task.

As an example of a problem found in tests of mathematical ability, consider the astronaut problem, given in Table 6.1. This problem was taken from the California Assessment Program (1980), a test of achievement given to all 12th graders in California public schools each year. It should be noted that approximately one-third of the 12th graders in California schools were unable to give the correct answer. Furthermore, performance was even worse on many other story problems, despite years of training in mathematics.

Why do so many people have trouble with story problems such as the astronaut problem? This question is important on both theoretical and practical grounds. For theory, an answer to this question would provide a better understanding of the nature of mathematical ability, i.e., an attack on the mathematical ability problem. For practice, an answer would have implications for how to improve students' learning in mathematics, a skill that is essential in a technological society.

There are two basic approaches to answering the mathematical ability question: the psychometric approach and the cognitive approach.

Psychometric Approach. The psychometric approach to the mathematical ability problem offers a seemingly straightforward solution: people's performances differ because people possess different amounts of mathematical ability. Mathematical ability refers to the ability to efficiently solve mathematics prob-

TABLE 6.1
The Astronaut Problem

An astronaut requires 2.2 pounds of oxygen per day while in space. How many pounds of oxygen are needed for a team of 3 astronauts for 5 days in space?

_____13.2   _____15.2   _____33   _____330

lems. Thus, mathematical ability is viewed as a trait or factor that can be measured.

Measurement of mathematical ability is a key component in tests of general intelligence, achievement, and aptitude. For example, most intelligence tests such as the Otis contain arithmetic story problems. Most achievement tests like the Scholastic Aptitude Test (SAT) or the previously cited California Assessment Program (CAP) devote one entire subscale to "quantitative" ability as measured by mathematical problem solving. Even aptitude tests such as the Programmer Aptitude Test (PAT) devote an entire subscale to "arithmetic reasoning," a test consisting of arithmetic story problems. Hence, the psychometric approach has clearly designated mathematical ability as a key trait or factor.

How well does the psychometric approach answer our questions? On the positive side, the psychometric approach tells us how to measure mathematical ability, and provides evidence concerning the reliability and validity of the measurements. In a recent review, Sternberg (1977) listed six major contributions of the psychometric approach: (1) it provided the Zeitgeist for two generations of ability researchers; (2) it permitted the investigation of complex psychological constructs; (3) it generated theories at a macrotheoretical level; (4) it provided a systematic means for studying individual differences; (5) it fostered a symbiotic relationship between theories of measurement and intelligence that led to greater sophistication in each; and (6) it proved itself relevant to the needs of applied settings. On the negative side, the psychometric approach seems to have begged the question, for its definition of mathematical ability is circular. As Sternberg (1977) points out, "There has never been much consensus among factor analysts as to just what a factor is [p. 34]."

Cognitive Approach. The cognitive approach also offers a solution to the mathematical ability problem: People's performances differ because people possess information processing systems that differ and because people possess differing amounts and kinds of knowledge. Mathematical ability can be expressed in terms of: (1) structural and operating characteristics of the information processing system (such as size of working memory, access time for a target in long memory); and (2) knowledge contained in long term memory (such as knowledge of appropriate algorithms, strategies, schemas, concepts, etc.).

The analysis of ability in terms of the structure of the information processing system is exemplified by recent work of Hunt and his colleagues (Hunt, 1978; Hunt, Lunneborg, & Lewis, 1975) on locating some cognitive correlates of verbal ability. The information processing system analysis focuses on components that may be fairly permanent features of a person's mathematical ability. The analysis of ability in terms of specific knowledge is exemplified by recent work of Greeno and his colleagues (Anderson, Greeno, Klinc, & Neves, 1981; Greeno, 1978; 1980a; 1980b) on building formal models of geometry problem-solving ability. The knowledge analysis focuses on components that may be changeable through learning and practice.

Role of Knowledge in Mathematical Problem-Solving

Issue. The present chapter focuses on the cognitive approach to the mathematical ability problem and in particular focuses on the nature of knowledge that is required for mathematical problem solving. Thus, the approach of this chapter is to ask, "What does a person have to know in order to be a good mathematical problem solver?" In short, this paper assumes that mathematical ability—at least to some extent—depends on what a person *knows*. Admittedly, the operating characteristics and capacities of the person's information processing system are another important aspect of mathematical ability, but these will not be directly investigated in this chapter.

Recent work comparing expert and novice problem-solving performance has suggested that knowledge is at the heart of problem-solving performance. In distinguishing what experts in physics problem solving know that novices do not know, Larkin, McDermott, Simon, & Simon (1980) concluded that experts possess domain specific knowledge, organized in efficient ways, and experts possess solution strategies that can be applied to that knowledge.

Similarly, most modern theories of problem solving are based on the idea that solving a particular problem requires both domain-specific knowledge and general strategies (Greeno, 1980a; Simon, 1980). For example, in a recent review, Greeno concludes: "All problem solving is based on knowledge. A person may not have learned exactly what to do in a specific problem situation, but whatever the person is able to do requires some knowledge, even if that knowledge is in the form of general strategies for analyzing situations and attempting solutions [p. 10]." Simon (1980) provides a similar thesis: "There is no such thing as expertness without knowledge—extensive and accessible knowledge.[p. 82]."

Framework. Let's return to the astronaut problem shown in Table 6.1. What steps are involved in solving this problem? Table 6.2 suggests four major activities that may be involved in solving algebra story problems such as the astronaut problem. First, the problem must be translated from words into an internal representation. A literal, phrase-by-phrase translation will yield a fragmented representation such as the following four facts: (1) (OXYGEN PER ASTRONAUT PER DAY) = 2.2; (2) (NUMBER OF ASTRONAUTS) = 3; (3) (NUMBER OF DAYS) = 5; and (4) (TOTAL OXYGEN) = UNKNOWN. Second, the problem must be understood by organizing the internal representation into coherent structure. The astronaut problem can be fit into the general schema (TOTAL OXYGEN) = (OXYGEN PER ASTRONAUT PER DAY) × (NUMBER OF ASTRONAUTS) × (NUMBER OF DAYS). This is a more unified representation of the problem. Third, a plan must be developed for how

TABLE 6.2
Four Phases in Solving An Algebra Story Problem

Phases	Input and Output	Example from Astronaut Problem
1. Translate	Words to fragmented internal representation.	(OXYGEN PER ASTRONAUT PER DAY) = 2.2 (TOTAL OXYGEN) = UNKNOWN (NUMBER OF ASTRONAUTS) = 3 (NUMBER OF DAYS) = 5
2. Understand	Fragmented internal representation to integrated internal representation.	(TOTAL OXYGEN) = (OXYGEN PER ASTRONAUT PER DAY) x (NUMBER OF ASTRONAUTS) × (NUMBER OF DAYS) (TOTAL) = (RATE PER UNIT) × (NUMBER OF UNITS)
3. Plan	Internal representation to plan for solution.	MULTIPLY 3 BY 5 MULTIPLY RESULT BY 2.2
4. Execute	Solution plan answer.	3 x 5 = 15 15 x 2.2 = 33

to generate an answer. The strategy in the astronaut problem might be summarized as: $(2.2 \times 3) \times 5 =$ _____. Fourth, the computations must be carried out, using appropriate arithmetic algorithms. This yields an answer of 33. Table 6.2 refers to these four basic phases in problem solving respectively as, translation, understanding, planning, and execution.

Knowledge. Each phase in the solution of a story problem requires different knowledge in the problem solver. Table 6.3 suggests what a problem solver

TABLE 6.3
Four Types of Knowledge Required in Solving
An Algebra Story Problem

Phase	Type of Knowledge	Example from Algebra Problem
1. Translate	linguistic and factual knowledge	Variables are (TOTAL OXYGEN), (OXYGEN PER ASTRONAUT PER DAY), (NO. OF DAYS), (NO. OF ASTRONAUTS).
2. Understand	schematic knowledge	"Time-Rate" problem schema is TOTAL = RATE × TIME. TOTAL is (TOTAL OXYGEN) RATE is (OXYGEN PER ASTRONAUT PER DAY)
3. Plan	strategic knowledge	First figure out TIME, (TIME) = (NO. OF DAYS) × (NO. OF ASTRONAUTS). Then figure out TOTAL, (OXYGEN) = (OXYGEN PER ASTRONAUT PER DAY) × (TIME)
4. Execute	algorithmic knowledge	Carry out procedure for 3×5, such as adding $5 + 5 + 5$.

might have to know in order to accomplish each of the four problem-solving phases for the astronaut problem. For the translation phase, a person needs linguistic knowledge such as distinguishing among variables, operators, and numbers; and a person needs factual knowledge, such as knowing there are seven days in a week. For the understanding phase, a person needs schematic knowledge, such as knowledge of problem forms involving "total = rate × time." For planning, a person needs strategic knowledge, such as how to solve for X. For execution, a person needs algorithmic knowledge, such as the procedure for finding "3 × 5 = _____."

Individual differences in solving algebra story problems may be due to differences in the quantity and quality of each of these four kinds of knowledge. The following four sections respectively explore the role of these four types of knowledge in algebraic problem solving.

LINGUISTIC AND FACTUAL KNOWLEDGE ARE NEEDED FOR TRANSLATION

Example

According to most theories of mathematical problem solving, the first phase is to translate the words of the problem into an internal representation. For example, the words of the astronaut problem may be translated into a list of propositions, as shown in the upper right portion of Table 6.2. During the translation phase, a problem solver needs access to linguistic knowledge—such as knowing that "astronaut" is a noun or knowing that "an astronaut" and "a team of astronauts" refer to the same variable; and factual knowledge—such as knowing that "days" is a measure of time consisting of 24 hours or that "oxygen" is required to stay alive in space.

Review

Computer simulations of algebra problem solving suggest the important role of linguistic and factual knowledge. For example, Bobrow (1968) developed a computer program called STUDENT that solves simple story problems such as the following:

> If the number of customers Tom gets is twice the square of 20 percent of the number of advertisements he runs, and the number of advertisements he runs is 45, what is the number of customers Tom gets?

The translation phase of the program involves steps such as: (1) Copy the problem word for word. (2) Substitute words like "two times" for twice. (3) Locate each word or phrase that describes a variable, such as "the number of customers Tom gets" and note if two or more phrases refer to the same variable. (4) Break the problem into simple sentences. (5) Convert each simple sentence into variables, numbers, and operators, such as, (NUMBER OF CUSTOMERS TOM GETS) = 2 (.20(NUMBER OF ADVERTISEMENTS))^2, (NUMBER OF ADVERTISEMENTS) = 45, (NUMBER OF CUSTOMERS TOM GETS) = (X).

As you can see, STUDENT performs a very literal translation of words into equations. To do even this, however, requires that STUDENT have: (1) knowledge of the English language, such as the ability to distinguish between operators and variables; and (2) knowledge of the world, such as knowing that there are 10 dimes in a dollar or seven days in a week. In fact, a great portion of the STUDENT program is devoted to domain-specific information concerning linguistic and factual knowledge. Without this knowledge, the program would not be able to solve story problems. More recently, Hayes and Simon (1974) have developed a program called UNDERSTAND that translates problems into an internal representation; it also requires a great deal of specific linguistic and factual knowledge.

Recent empirical research tends to confirm the important role played by linguistic and factual knowledge in algebra problem solving. For example, Greeno and his colleagues (Greeno, 1980b; Heller & Greeno, 1978; Riley & Greeno, 1978) asked children to listen to problems and then repeat them. The children were quite proficient at repeating problems in which each sentence dealt with one variable, such as "Joe has 3 marbles. Then Tom gave him 5 more marbles. How many does Joe have now?" However, younger children made many errors when a sentence involved a relation between two variables such as, "Joe had 3 marbles. Tom has 5 more marbles than Joe. How many marbles does Tom have?" Typically, students would repeat this problem as: "Joe has 3 marbles. Tom has 5 marbles. How many marbles does Tom have?" Apparently, young children had more difficulty in translating sentences that involve relation information.

This finding is consistent with earlier studies by Loftus & Suppes (1972) in which sixth graders were asked to solve a variety of story problems. For example, the hardest problem for children to solve was one that contained a relational proposition: "Mary is twice as old as Betty was 2 years ago. Mary is 40 years old. How old is Betty?"

Clement, Lochhead, & Soloway (1979, 1980) have shown that difficulties in translating relational propositions are not limited to primary school children. College students were asked to write equations to represent propositions such as: "There are 6 times as many students as professors at this university." One-third of the students produced incorrect equations, with the most typical wrong answer being, "6S = P." However, when students were asked to translate relational statements like this one into a computer program, the error rate fell dramatically. Such results suggest that people have difficulty in interpreting what a relational proposition means, especially when they must use a static format such as equations or simple sentences.

Research on Language: Memory Study

Introduction. The foregoing review suggests that the translation process requires extensive linguistic and factual knowledge. In particular, humans may often lack the linguistic knowledge required for representing relational information. In order to investigate this idea in more detail, we recently conducted a series of experiments in our lab at Santa Barbara (Mayer, 1982a).

Method. First, we asked college students to read (but not solve) a series of eight story problems, devoting 2 minutes to each. For example, one of the problems was: "A river steamer travels 36 miles downstream in the same time that it travels 24 miles upstream. The steamer's engine drives in still water at a rate of 12 miles per hour more than the rate of the current. Find the rate of the current." Then, we asked each subject to recall each of the eight problems, and we supplied a "cue" for each. For example, the cue for the above problem was, "river." The experiment was also repeated with different sets of story problems. A list of some of the 16 problems, and cues for each, is given in Table 6.4.

In order to score the recall protocols, each problem was analyzed into propositions. For example, the river problem contained five propositions, as shown below:

(DISTANCE DOWNSTREAM) = 36 miles

(DISTANCE UPSTREAM) = 24 miles

(TIME DOWNSTREAM) = (TIME UPSTREAM)

TABLE 6.4
Some of the Sixteen Story Problems Used in the Memory Study

Title	Problem
River	A river steamer travels 36 miles downstream in the same time that it travels 24 miles upstream. The steamer's engine drives in still water at a rate of 12 miles per hour more than the rate of the current. Find the rate of the current.
Freeway	A truck leaves Los Angeles en route to San Francisco at 1 p.m. A second truck leaves San Francisco at 2 p.m. en route to Los Angeles going along the same route. Assume the two cities are 465 miles apart and that the trucks meet at 6 p.m. If the second truck travels at 15 mph faster than the first truck, how fast does each truck go?
Frame	The area occupied by an unframed rectangular picture is 64 square inches less than the area occupied by the picture mounted in a frame 2 inches wide. What are the dimensions of the picture if it is 4 inches longer than it is wide?
Race	In a sports car race, a Panther starts the course at 9:00 a.m. and averages 75 miles per hour. A Mallotti starts 4 minutes later and averages 85 miles per hour. How many miles will the first car have driven when it is passed?

(RATE IN STILL WATER) = 12 mph + (RATE OF CURRENT)

(RATE OF CURRENT) = UNKNOWN

Protocols were also parsed into propositions and then compared against the propositions in the original problem. A match was recorded if a proposition contained the same variables and relations as an original proposition, even if the specific numerical values did not match.

Three kinds of propositions were identified among the set of story problems:

1. *Assignment proposition.* This proposition gives a single numerical value for some variable. Examples include, "The cost of the candy is $1.70," "The time to fill one pipe is 6 hours," or "Total amount invested was $4000."

2. *Relation proposition.* This proposition gives a single numerical relationship between two variables. Examples include, "The length is 2½ times the width," "The area of one rectangle is 64 square inches less than the area of the second rectangle," or "The rate in still water is 12 mph more than the rate in the current."

3. *Question proposition.* This proposition involves a question concerning a single numerical value for some variable. Examples include, "How much time will it take to empty the tank?" or "How many miles will the first car have gone before it is passed?"

In addition, some problems contain "fact propositions" such as "The same route was used" on a round trip. In the river problem, given above, the first two propositions are assignments, the next two are relations, and the last one is a question.

Results.   If relation propositions are more difficult to represent internally than other types of propositions, we can expect relatively higher error rates for recall of relational propositions. Figure 6.1 shows the proportion of errors by type of proposition across the two experiments. As can be seen, error rates were three times as high for relation propositions as compared to assignment propositions.

In addition, a regression analysis was conducted based on each problem, with number of assignments and number of relations as the independent variables and number of subjects (out of 24) correctly recalling the problem as the dependent variable.[1] The resulting function was: (PROPORTION OF SUBJECTS WHO CORRECTLY RECALL A PROBLEM) = 1.17 − .14 (NUMBER OF AS-SIGNMENT PROPOSITIONS) − .30 (NUMBER OF RELATION PROPOSI-

---

[1]We are aware of a theoretical difficulty in this regression, as the dependent variable is limited to the interval between zero and one. A logistic regression would be one method that would properly accept such a dependent variable. The regressions reported here should be taken in the spirit of curve-fitting over a part of the apparent range of the dependent variable.

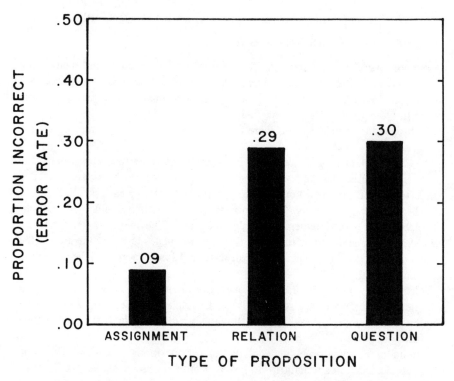

FIG. 6.1.   Error Rates for Recall of Three Types of Propositions from Story Problems

TIONS). The correlation between obtained and predicted probability of recall is .942, indicating that number of assignment and number of relation propositions account for 89% of the variance in recall performance. These analyses indicate that humans have particular difficulty in remembering relational propositions.

If people lack sufficient linguistic knowledge to correctly represent relational propositions, we can predict that relational propositions will generate qualitatively different kinds of errors in recall than assignment propositions. In particular, if relations are linguistically more difficult to represent than assignments, we can predict that subjects might convert relations into assignments in their recall protocols but that assignments will not be converted into relations.

In order to test this idea, each error committed in the experiments was classified as one of the following:

1. *Omission error.* A proposition from the original problem was not produced in the recall protocol for that problem.

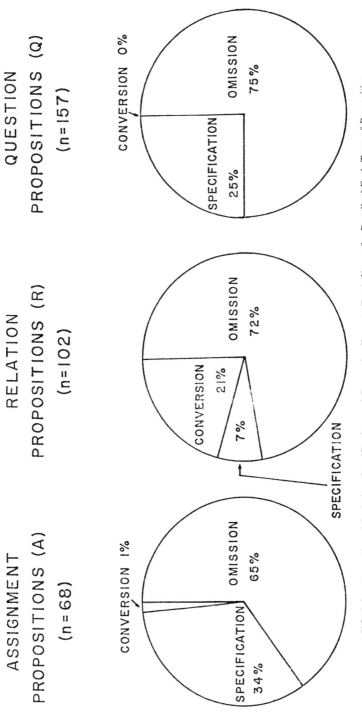

ASSIGNMENT PROPOSITIONS (A) (n=68)

RELATION PROPOSITIONS (R) (n=102)

QUESTION PROPOSITIONS (Q) (n=157)

FIG. 6.2. Proportion of Omission, Specification, and Conversion Errors to Total Errors for Recall of Each Type of Proposition

241

2. *Specification error.* A variable in the proposition was changed to a different variable in the recall protocol. For example, the proposition, "A river steamer travels 36 miles downstream," may be recalled as, "A river steamer travels 36 mph downstream."

3. *Conversion error.* The form of the proposition was changed from a relation to an assignment or from an assignment (or question) into a relation. For example, the proposition, "The steamer's engines drive in still water at 12 mph more than the rate of the current," may be recalled as, "The steamer's engines drive in still water at 12 mph."

Figure 6.2 gives the percentage of omission, conversion, and specification errors for assignment propositions, for relation propositions, and for question propositions. As can be seen, almost none of the assignments (or questions) are converted into relations, whereas 21% of the relations are converted into assignments. In all, there were 20 instances of relation propositions being recalled as assignments, and only one case of an assignment being converted to a relation. For example, in 10 cases, the relational proposition, "The steamer's engine drives in still water at a rate of 12 mph more than the rate of the current" was recalled as an assignment, such as, "Assume it goes 12 mph by motor alone (with no current)," or "In smooth water the engine causes it to move 12 mph," or "Its engines push the boat 12 mph in still water." As another example, in four cases the relational proposition "The area occupied by an unframed rectangular picture is 64 square inches less than the area occupied by the picture mounted in a frame" was converted into an assignment such as, "A picture has an area of 64 inches" or "If an unframed picture is 64 sq. in. . . . ."

Conclusion. These results provide consistent evidence concerning how humans represent propositions from algebra story problems in memory. In particular, these results suggest that many subjects may simply not be prepared for the necessary parsing of relational propositions. One hypothesis consistent with these findings is that subjects tend to expect a story can be parsed into a list of assignments; thus, propositions that are not assignments may be converted to fit slots that are expected.

SCHEMATIC KNOWLEDGE IS NEEDED FOR UNDERSTANDING

Example

Let's return to the astronaut problem. The previous section explored how linguistic and factual knowledge are used to translate a problem into a set of simple equations or propositions. Is there anything else one needs to know in order to understand the problem?

The next step in working on the astronaut problem might be to see how the bits of information fit together into a coherent whole. In short, one needs a schema—a structure that clarifies the internal relations among variables in the problem. Thus, the understanding process takes a list of equations or pieces of information as input and gives a coherent integrated representation of the problem as output. For example, the integrated relations in the astronaut problem may be represented as a single equation, TOTAL OXYGEN = (AMOUNT PER DAY PER ASTRONAUT) × (NUMBER OF DAYS) × (NUMBER OF ASTRONAUTS). We can refer to this structure as a schema because it provides a unified representation of the relations among variables.

Schematic knowledge refers to knowledge of problem types. For example, one might decide that the astronaut problem fits into a family of problems that rely on the general form (TOTAL AMOUNT) = (RATE PER UNIT) × (NUMBER OF UNITS). In this case, the relationships you would look for in the astronaut problem would be (TOTAL AMOUNT OF OXYGEN) = (RATE PER ASTRONAUT PER DAY) × (NUMBER OF ASTRONAUTS × NUMBER OF DAYS). Thus, a schema allows one to fit the variables of the problem into a structure that is already familiar.

Review

As can be seen in the previous discussion of Bobrow's (1968) STUDENT, it is possible to translate each phrase of a problem, using appropriate linguistic and factual knowledge. However, there is a sense in which literal translation of each phrase is not the only process involved in representing a problem. For example, Paige and Simon (1966) developed ''impossible'' problems such as the following:

> The number of quarters a man has is seven times the number of dimes he has. The value of the dimes exceeds the value of quarters by $2.50. How many has he of each coin?

When asked to solve this problem, some students behaved like STUDENT by generating literal translations of each sentence into an equation. Other students misread the problem in a way that made it coherent, such as changing the second sentence to, ''The value of quarters exceeds the value of dimes by $2.50.'' Finally, some students were able to recognize that the problem is impossible, i.e., the first two sentences contradict one another. Thus, although some students may use literal translations of each sentence, others may try to understand the problem by building a coherent representation.

In order to recognize the inconsistency, a problem solver needs to represent the problem as a coherent whole. The problem solver must see how variables relate to one another. In other words, the problem solver must build a structure that clarifies the internal relations among variables. When students produce a series of sentence-by-sentence translations, they can be led astray. Thus, in addition to linguistic and factual knowledge, a student needs knowledge about how to put variables together into a coherent problem type—knowledge of problem type.

More recently, there has been increasing evidence that humans possess and use schematic knowledge—i.e., knowledge of problem types—for understanding algebra story problems. Hinsley et al. (1977) gave subjects a series of algebra problems from standard textbooks and asked the subjects to sort the problems into categories. Subjects were quite proficient and showed high levels of agreement on the task. In all, the subjects produced 18 different categories such as river current, distance-rate-time, work, triangle, interest, etc. Apparently, subjects possessed schemas for each category, i.e., knowledge of the structure of at least 18 distinct problem types.

Hinsley et al. (1977) also found that subjects tended to categorize a problem almost as soon as the problem was presented. After hearing the first phase or two, subjects determined which type of problem was being presented. In other studies, Hayes, Waterman, and Robinson (1977) and Robinson and Hayes (1978) presented problems and asked subjects to judge which information was important. Subjects were able to quickly categorize a problem, and then accurately distinguish between information that was and was not important. These results suggest that schemas can be rapidly accessed and used to guide the problem solver's attention.

Errors in problem solving may occur when a subject miscategorizes a problem, i.e., uses an inappropriate schema. In a supplemental study reported by Hinsley et al., (1977), subjects were given an ambiguous problem that could be interpreted as either a triangle problem or a distance-rate-time problem. Half of the subjects interpreted it as a triangle problem and half as a distance-rate-time problem. The two groups focused on entirely different information and even misread facts in a way that was consistent with their schemas. For example, a "triangle subject" misread "four minutes" as "four miles," assumed this was the leg of a triangle, and applied the Pythagorean theorem. These results are consistent with Loftus and Suppes' (1972) finding that a word problem was much more difficult to solve if it was a different type from ones preceding it.

Greeno and his colleagues (Greeno, 1980b; Heller & Grenno, 1978; Riley & Greeno, 1978) have located schemas for children's word problems, such as, "cause/cause" (for example, "Joe has 3 marbles. Tom gives him 5 more marbles. How many does Joe have now?"), "combine" (for example, "Joe had 3 marbles. Tom has 5 marbles. How many do they have together?), and "compare" (for example, "Joe has 3 marbles. Tom has 5 more marbles than Joe. How many marbles does Tom have?"). There is some evidence that children may develop these schemas in the above order. For example, second graders perform poorly on compare problems but well on cause/change problems.

Research on Schemas: Textbook Study

Introduction. The foregoing review suggests that schematic knowledge may play an important role in how students represent story problems. In particular, knowledge of problem types is used to select and connect information from the problem. In order to gain a broader perspective on the nature of schemas for story problems, we recently conducted a study in our lab in Santa Barbara.

Method. We compiled a list of all story problems from exercise sections of 10 major algebra textbooks used in California secondary schools. The books yielded approximately 1100 story problems, not including simple "arithmetic word" problems such as used by Greeno. Word problems were not included because they are generally part of elementary school curriculum and represented only a "review" in secondary school mathematics books.

Analysis. The 1100 problems were sorted into eight major "families," with each family based on a different source formula (or set of source formulas). A source formula is a simple three-variable equation that can be used to solve the problem, such as: output = rate × time. Table 6.5 lists typical source formulas and example problems for each of the eight families. As can be seen, the "number story" family does not involve any specific source formula, and the "geometry," "physics," and "statistics" families each involve formulas that are specific to their respective domains. The example problems in the table show that "simple" problems use the source formula directly, whereas "complex" problems require extensions to the source formula.

Although the problems within each family all are based on the same set of source formulas, there are many different categories of problem within each family. Thus, the problems in each family were further sorted into categories, as summarized in Table 6.6.

One major question concerns the reliability of the 18 categories that were reported by Hinsley et al., (1977). Each of these 18 problem categories is represented in the larger set of categories shown in Table 6.10. Thus, Hinsley et al. seem to have identified a substantial subset of textbook problems, but did not identify *all* types.

In order to provide a more detailed structural analysis of algebra story problems, each of the 1100 algebra story problems was parsed into a list of propositions. The list of propositions consisted of assignments, relations, and questions, as described previously, and summarized in Tables 6.5 and 6.6. Each problem was then represented as a "template," i.e., a list of propositions (without specific numbers or names) that followed a certain story line. Problems within each category were sorted into template groups with all members sharing the same set of assignment, relation and/or question propositions (regardless of specific wordings and numbers).

TABLE 6.5
Examples of Source Formulas and Simple Problems for Eight Families of Story Problems

Family	Example Simple Category	Example Source Formula	Example of Simple Problem
Amount-per-Time Rate	Simple DRT	distance = rate x time	If a car travels 10 hours at 30 miles per hour, how far will it go?
	Simple work	output = rate x time	If a machine can produce 10 units per hour, how many units can be produced in an 8 hour day?
Cost-per-Unit Rate	Simple unit cost	total cost = unit cost x number of units	If pencils cost 5¢ each, how much will a dozen pencils cost?
Proportion-to-Total Cost Rate	Simple interest	interest = interest rate x principal	How much will be earned if $1000 is invested at 8% interest for 1 year?
	Simple profit	profit = markup rate x cost	If a TV set costs the seller $300 and the markup is 20%, how much profit will be made?
	Simple discount	discount = discount rate x cost	A TV set regularly sells for $400. A certain store is offering 25% off the regular price. How much can you save?

Amount-to-Amount Rate	Simple percent	amount 1 = rate x amount 2	Of 300 votes cast in an election, Tom received 30% of the votes. How many votes did he get?
Number-Story	NONE		John cuts a 6 foot board into two pieces, with one piece twice as long as the other. How long is each piece?
Geometry	Simple area	area = length x width	John's living room is 9 feet long and 12 feet wide. How many square feet of carpet is required to cover the floor?
Physics	Ohm's Law	current = voltage/resistance	If the voltage of a dry cell is 1.5 volts, find the current that cell will produce in a single cell flashlight bulb having a resistance of 10 ohms.
Statistics	Combinations	number of permutation = number of trials factorial ÷ number of successes factorial	How many different ways can you arrange 3 people at a dinner table that has 4 places?

TABLE 6.6

Families, Simple Categories, and Complex Categories for Story Problems

Family	Amount-per-time rate (time rate)	Cost-per-unit rate (unit cost rate)	Portion-to-total cost rate (percent cost rate)	Amount-to-amount rate (straight rate)	Number-story	Geometry	Physics	Statistics
Simple category (source formula)	Simple DRT Simple work	Simple unit cost	Simple interest Simple profit Simple discount	Simple rate* Simple percent* Simple-fraction* Simple proportion* Simple index* Simple ratio*		Simple area* Simple perimeter* Simple circumference* Simple pythagorean* Simple trapezoid*	Falling body* Ohm's Law* Other*	Permutations/ combinations* Probability*
Complex categories	Motion Current Work	Fixed cost Coin Dry mixture	Interest/ investment Profit Discount	Direct variation Inversion variation Wet mixture	Part* Age* Consecutive integer* Digit** Angle** Number**	Area* Frame Perimeter	Fulcrum*	Progression* Exponential* Maximization

*Indicates some problems are not story problems.
**Indicates all problems are not story problems.

248

TABLE 6.7
Examples of Four Templates for Motion Problems

Name & Frequency	Description	Propositional Structure	Example Problem
Overtake (N = 23)	One vehicle starts and is followed later by a second vehicle that travels over the same route at a faster rate.	(RATE FOR A) = _____ (RATE FOR B) = _____ (TIME FOR A AND B) = _____ (TIME FOR B TO OVERTAKE A) = UNK	A train leaves a station and travels east at 72 km/h. Three hours later a second train leaves on a parallel track and travels east at 120 km/h. How long will it take to over-take the first train?
Opposite Direction (N = 23)	Two vehicles leave the same point traveling in opposite directions.	(RATE FOR A) = _____ (RATE FOR B) = _____ (DISTANCE BETWEEN A & B) = _____ (TIME) = UNK	Two trains leave the same station at the same time. They travel in opposite directions. One train travels 64 km/h and the other 104 km/h. In how many hours will they be 1008 km apart?
Round Trip (N = 13)	A traveler (or vehicle) travels from point A to point B and returns.	(RATE FROM A TO B) = _____ (RATE FROM B TO A) = _____ (TIME FOR ENTIRE TRIP) = _____ (DISTANCE FOR ENTIRE TRIP) = UNK	George rode out of town on the bus at an average speed of 20 miles per hour and walked back at an average speed of 3 miles per hour. How far did he go if the entire trip took 6 hours?
Closure 1 (N = 12)	Two vehicles start at different points traveling towards one another.	(RATE FOR A) = _____ (RATE FOR B) = _____ (DISTANCE BETWEEN A AND B) = _____ (TIME) = UNK	Two cyclists start at the same time from towns 36 miles apart. The cyclists move toward each other; one travels at 4 mph and the other at 8 mph. How long will it take for them to meet?

249

Table 6.7 shows four templates within the motion category (selected from the 12 templates observed). In all, approximately 100 templates were identified within the 1100 problems, with approximately 50 templates occuring in five or more problems. A tally was made of the frequency of occurrence (within 1100 problems) for each problem template. The numbers in parentheses in Table 6.7 indicates the frequencies. Thus, the 1100 problems in our sample contained 23 different "overtake" problems but only 12 "closure" problems.

Conclusion.   This analysis extends earlier work by providing a broader range of problem types, based on all story problems from 10 textbooks, and a more detailed structural analysis, at the level of template. A detailed listing of each template is available elsewhere (Mayer, 1981).

Research on Schemas: Memory Study

Introduction.   The foregoing analysis generated a list of approximately 100 templates, with observed frequency values for each. The textbook analysis motivates a hypothesis that typical problems (i.e., problems corresponding to high frequency templates) should be easier to represent in memory than atypical problems (i.e., problems corresponding to low frequency templates). In order to provide data on this question, several studies were conducted in our lab concerning students' recall for story problems.

Method.   Two studies were conducted, as described in a previous section on the "memory study." In those studies, subjects read a list of eight problems (each for two minutes) and then took a cued recall test for each problem. As described earlier, the recall protocol or each problem was parsed into a list of propositions.

Results.   Earlier work by Hayes and his colleagues (Hinsley et al., 1977; Hayes et al., 1977; Robinson & Hayes, 1978) suggested that subjects use schemas to separate "important" from "unimportant" information. With respect to the present studies, Figure 6.3 shows the proportion of error in recall for propositions that are essential to the problem (i.e., part of the template) and for information that is irrelevant (i.e., unnecessary details). As can be seen in the figure, there is a clear "levels effect" in which recall is better for relevant as compared to irrelevant information. These results are consistent with the idea that subjects use schemas to make judgments about importance of information.

Another way to investigate the role of schematic knowledge on subjects' memory is to examine the relationship between frequency with which a problem is cited in textbooks and the probability that the problem is correctly recalled in the memory study. If schemas aid memory, then recall should be better for more typical problem types. In order to test this idea, frequency values were obtained

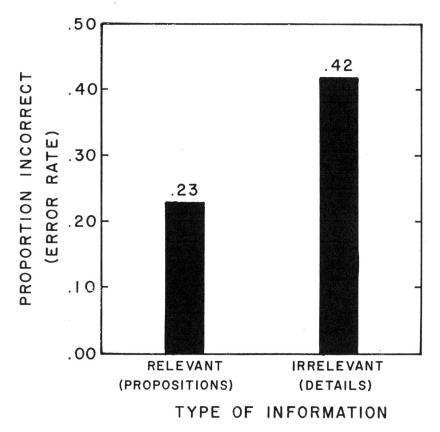

FIG. 6.3.   Error Rates for Recall of Relevant and Irrelevant Information

for each of the problems used in memory study, using frequency data collected in the textbook analysis (describe above). The 16 problems were rank ordered, based on frequency values, with 1 being least typical and 16 being most typical. In addition, for each problem, the proportion of subjects who correctly remembered the problem was determined, and these were rank ordered.

The relationship between frequency rank and recall rank for the 16 problems suggests a trend in which recall performance increases as the typicality of problem increases. This pattern produced a rank order correlation of $r = .66$, indicating that frequency rank was able to account for approximately 44% of the variance in recall rank.

As a follow-up, an analysis was conducted using only the seven problems from the amount-per-time family, i.e., motion, current, and work problems. There is a strong relationship between typicality and recall performance, yielding a correlation of $r = .85$ between frequency rank and recall rank.

TABLE 6.8

Examples of Conversions from Low Frequency to High Frequency Problems

Problem (Number of Cases)	Converted From (Name, Frequency, Example)	Converted To (Name, Frequency, Example)
River (N = 10)	Current: Equal-Time-2 Frequency = 0 A river steamer travels 36 miles downstream in the same time that it travels 24 miles upstream. The steamer's engine drives in still water at a rate of 12 miles per hour more than the rate of the current. Find the rate of the current.	Current: Equal-Time-1 Frequency = 9 A river steamer travels 36 miles downstream in the same time that it travels 24 miles upstream. The steamer's engine drives in still water at a rate of 12 miles per hour. Find the rate of the current.
Freeway (N = 2)	Motion: Closure-2 Frequency = 4 A truck leaves Los Angeles enroute to San Francisco at 1 p.m. A second truck leaves San Francisco at 2 p.m. en route to Los Angeles going along the same route. Assume the cities are 465 miles apart and that the trucks meet at 6 p.m. If the second truck travels 15 mph faster than the first truck, how fast does each truck go?	Motion: Closure-1 Frequency = 12 A truck leaves Los Angeles en route to San Francisco at 1 p.m. A second truck leaves San Francisco at 2 p.m. en route to Los Angeles going along the same route. Assume the cities are 465 miles apart and that the trucks meet at 6 p.m. If the second truck travels 15 mph, how fast does the other truck go?
Frame (N = 5)	Rectangle: Frame-Relative-3 Frequency = 0 The area occupied by an unframed rectangular picture is 64 square inches less than the area occupied by a picture mounted in a frame 2 inches wide. What are the dimensions of the picture if it is 4 inches longer than it is wide?	Rectangle: Frame-Absolute-1 Frequency = 11 The area of an unframed rectangular picture is 64 square inches. The width of the frame is 2 inches. If one side of the frame is 4 inches, how long is the other side?

Another way to investigate the role of schematic knowledge on recall involves an analysis of errors. If subjects are more likely to possess schemas for typical problem types than atypical types, this should be reflected in the pattern of recall errors. In the recall experiments, there were several instances in which a problem belonging to one template was recalled as another template. For example, during the course of the two experiments, there were 21 instances of conversion—i.e., a problem of one type was remembered as a problem of another type. Of these 21 conversions, 17 involved a change from a low frequency version of the problem to a higher frequency version of the problem, and 4 could not be scored. Examples are given in Table 6.8. Thus, when subjects make conversion errors, they tend to change the problem from a low frequency template into a more typical template of the same category.

Conclusion. These results are consistent with the idea that high frequency problem structures are easier to represent in memory than low frequency problem structures. It must be noted, however, that high frequency problems tend to contain fewer relational propositions than low frequency problems. Apparently, problems that do not match a well-learned problem "template" are harder to represent than problems that do match well-learned templates. The present results do not help determine whether the advantage for high frequency templates is due to their being fundamentally more obvious or due to the fact they are more heavily drilled in textbooks.

STRATEGIC KNOWLEDGE IS NEEDED FOR PLANNING

Example

Let's return to the astronaut problem. The previous two sections have shown that linguistic, factual, and schematic knowledge are needed in order to build a coherent representation of the problem. Once you have built an internal representation, the next step is to devise a plan for solving the problem. For example, in the astronaut problem, once you have a representation such as (TOTAL OXYGEN) = (AMOUNT PER DAY PER ASTRONAUT) × (NUMBER OF DAYS) × (NUMBER OF ASTRONAUTS), the next step is to devise a plan for finding the value of an unknown. Your plan might be: multiply (NUMBER OF DAYS) times the (NUMBER OF ASTRONAUTS); then multiply the result times (RATE PER ASTRONAUT PER DAY); and give this result as the answer.

As you can see, a strategy is a general plan for how to go about solving the problem. Strategic knowledge refers to the problem solver's knowledge concerning how to establish and monitor plans for goals. In a recent study of students' learning of geometry, Greeno (1978) noted that "some students' difficulty in the subject may be due to their not having acquired the strategic knowledge they need to solve some of the problems they are given" [pp. 60–61].

Review

Strategic knowledge for solving algebra equations involves knowledge of how to set goals and knowledge of which procedures are productive in carrying out these goals. Bundy (1975) has provided a formal analysis of the strategies involved in solving algebra equations. Three basic strategies are: (1) *attraction*—moving two instances of the unknown closer to one another, such as moving from $(X)/2 + (2X)/2 = 1$ to $(X + 2X)/2 = 1$; (2) *collection*—carrying out a computation that reduces the number of instances of the unknown, such as moving from $(X + 2X)/2 = 1$ to $(3X)/2 = 1$; and (3) *isolation*—getting the unknown alone on one side and getting a numerical value on the other side of the equality, such as moving from $(3X)^{1/2} = 1$ to $X = 1/3$. According to Bundy's model, planning a problem solution involves employing one or more of these strategies in a given order.

Lewis (1981) has analyzed the strategic errors committed by mathematics experts in solving equations. Following Bundy's model, Lewis distinguished between two kinds of knowledge needed for solving problems—knowing procedures such as how to add a quantity to both sides of an equality, and knowing how to select appropriate procedures during solution. The latter type of knowledge involves strategy. Lewis (1981) points out: "It is always legal to add any quantity to both sides of an equation, but it is rarely advisable. The knowledge needed to make this selection can be called strategic knowledge [p. 87]." Lewis found that although experts were able to combine many procedures into single steps, experts also displayed a surprisingly large number of strategic errors. These errors can be described as selecting a procedure that is not appropriate for the problem.

In a recent study of equation solving, Matz (1980) identified over 30 common errors. Further, Matz was able to distinguish between planning errors—deciding what procedures to perform—and execution errors—carrying out the procedures. Planning errors were the main focus of Matz's analysis. In particular, she proposed that problem solvers may know rules or procedures from previous experience, but problem solvers tend to extrapolate incorrectly to new problems. For example, a problem solver may incorrectly decide that a problem is similar to a previous problem, and then use a technique that was effective for the previous problem.

Larkin (1981) and Larkin et al. (1980) identified qualitative differences between the strategies used by experts and novices in solving physics story problems. For example, novices tended to possess a list of fragmented principles and to work backwards from the givens to the goal; in contrast, experts tended to possess knowledge that was integrated into larger units and tended to work forward from the goal to the givens. Further, Larkin and her colleagues were able to develop formal models of the strategies used by experts and novices.

The foregoing work summarized some attempts to represent problem solvers' strategies for solving algebra problems. One important implication of research on strategies is that different problem solvers may use qualitatively different solution strategies. For example, the "means-ends analysis" procedure, once thought to characterize general problem solving (Newell & Simon, 1972), appears to be consistent with "novice" performance but not "expert" performance in physics problem solving.

The strategy that a problem solver uses for a particular problem may be influenced by the format of the problem, i.e., different problem representations may lead to qualitatively different solution strategies. In a lengthy series of studies involving several deductive reasoning tasks, subjects given premises in a meaningful or organized format used qualitatively different procedures to solve problems as compared to subjects given premises in fragmented or nonsense format. This finding was replicated using linear ordering premises (Mayer, 1978a, 1979), conditional reasoning premises (Mayer, 1976a), network structure premises (Mayer, 1976b), and simultaneous algebra equations (Mayer & Greeno, 1975; Mayer, 1978b).

Research on Strategies: Single-Variable Equations Study

Introduction.   The foregoing review revealed that several theorists have developed models of equation solving. The main question dealt with in this section concerns whether different models are required to describe performance on algebra word vs. algebra equation problems. In particular, we focus on how humans solve single equations (or word problems) that involve just one variable. Further, we seek to determine whether subjects use qualitatively different strategies to solve algebra problems expressed in equation format as compared to problems expressed in word format.

Method.   A group of 21 subjects solved 98 algebra equations, and a group of 21 subjects solved an isomorphic set of 98 algebra word problems. The equation problems were of the form

$$(8 + 3X)/2 = 3X - 11$$

The word problems were identical except that the equation was expressed in words such as

Find a number such that if 8 more than 3 times the number is divided by 2 the result is the same as 11 less than 3 times the number.

There were seven basic formulas, each similar in form to the example given. In addition, there were 14 problem states used for each equation (or isomorphic word problem), corresponding to locations in partial problem space, as shown in Figure 6.4. The code number for each problem state corresponds to the minimum

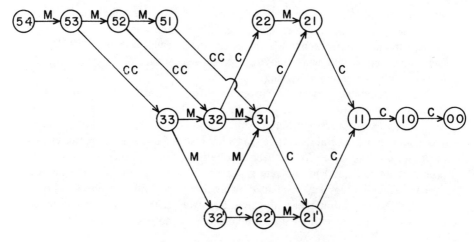

FIG. 6.4.   Partial Problem Space for $(8 + 3X)/2 = 3X - 11$

number of moves (M) and computations (C) that must be carried out to solve the problem. A prime mark (') indicates this state has the same number of moves and computations as another state. Thus, the initial state, 54, corresponds to the equation, $(8 + 3X)/2 = 3X - 11$; the goal state 00, corresponds to the answer, $X = 10$. State 53, corresponds to the equation $8 + 3X = (3X - 11) \times 2$, and thus involves one less move than state 54. Similarly, state 33, corresponding to the equation $8 + 3X = 6X - 22$, involves two fewer computations than state 53. Thus, the 98 problems in each set consisted of 14 problem states from each of 7 basic equations (or corresponding word problems).

The problems were individually presented on a CRT screen, and subjects responded by pressing a button corresponding to the answer. A microcomputer recorded the response times and controlled the order of presentation.

Results.   Preliminary studies suggested two distinct strategies for solving problems like the ones used in this study: (1) The *reduce strategy* involves trying to carry out any indicated operations or clearing of parentheses as soon as possible. This strategy may be preferred by subjects solving word problems. Table 6.9 provides a partial list of condition-action pairs for solving problems in this study, using a reduce strategy. The left side of each statement gives a general description of a situation that may be encountered in solving a problem and the right side gives a general description of the action to be taken. When a subject is given a problem, the subject searches for the conditions that are met. If more than one condition is met, the reduce strategy calls for choosing one based on the priority ordering, R–1, R–2, R–3, R–4, I–1, I–2. Another way of stating this priority ordering is to say that a subject first looks for a reduce condition and carries out actions associated with it if possible.

TABLE 6.9
Some Condition-Action Pairs for Solving Problem 54

Reduce Expression

(R-1)   2 Xs on one side of the equation →
         Combine them
(R-2)   2 Ns on one side of the equation →
         Combine them
(R-3)   Parenthesis on one side of the equation attached to division →
         Move divided term to other side of equation
(R-4)   Parenthesis on one side of equation attached to multiplication →
         Carry out the multiplications

Isolate Variable

(1-1)   Xs are on both sides of the equation →
         Move X to left side and combine with other X
(1-2)   Ns are on both sides of the equation →
         Move N to right side and combine with other N

For example, the solution process for problem 54 is shown in Table 6.10. First, for problem 54, three conditions are met: There are Xs on both sides (I–1), there are numbers of both sides (I–2), and there are parentheses (R–3). According to the reduce strategy, the selected statement will be R–3. The action involves a MOVE—multiplying both sides by 2—and yields a new problem state 53. Second, for problem 53, three conditions are met: There are Xs on both sides (I–1), there are numbers on both sides (I–2), and there are parentheses (R–4). According to the reduce strategy, the selected statement will be R–4. The action involves two COMPUTEs—distributing the 2 across the parentheses—and yields a new problem state 33. As shown in Table 6.10, the next actions selected by the reduce strategy are, respectively, to subtract 3X from both sides, to add 22 to both sides, and to divide both sides by 10. For problem 54, the reduce strategy calls for 5 COMPUTEs and 4 MOVEs. As can be seen, the reduce strategy predicts that solution time for any problem will be a function of two factors: number of MOVEs and number of COMPUTEs.

(2) The *isolate strategy* involves trying to move all the Xs to one side and all the numbers to the other side of the equality. This strategy may be preferred by subjects solving equation problems. For example, the isolate strategy would reorder the condition-action pairs in Table 6.14 to I–1, I–2, R–1, R–2, R–3, R–4. Another way to state this priority ordering is to say that subjects first look for isolate conditions and try to carry out the associated actions. However, unlike the reduce strategy, there are instances when a selected action cannot be directly carried out. In these cases, the to-be-performed action must be held in a goal stack (this is called a STACK operation) and some other action is performed.

Table 6.11 gives an example of how the isolate strategy would be applied to problem state 54. First, problem state 54 meets conditions I–1, I–2, and R–3.

TABLE 6.10
Solution of Problem 54 Using Reduce Strategy

Problem State	Event	Calculation	Move	Stack
(54)	$3X - 11 = (8 + 3X)/2$			
	Conditions: 1-1, 1-2, R-3			
	Goal: R-3			
	Succeed		1	
(53)	$2(3X - 11) = 8 + 3X$			
	Conditions: 1-1, 1-2, R-4			
	Goal: R-4			
	Succeed	2		
(33)	$6X - 22 = 8 + 3X$			
	Conditions: 1-1, 1-2			
	Goal: 1-1			
	Succeed	1	1	
(22)	$3X - 22 = 8$			
	Conditions: 1-2			
	Goal: 1-2			
	Succeed	1	1	
(11)	$3X = 30$			
	Conditions: 1-2			
	Goal: 1-2			
	Succeed	1	1	
(00)	$X = 10$	1	1	

According to the isolate strategy, the selected condition will be I–1. The action—to move and combine 3X terms—cannot be directly carried out because of the parentheses. Thus, the move and combine action for I–1 must be stacked onto a goal stack and a new condition is attended to, namely removing the parentheses (R–3). The action—to multiply both sides by 2—can be carried out so one MOVE operation is executed and a new state (53) is created. For problem 53, the conditions met include I–1, I–2, and R–4. According to the isolate strategy, the condition that is selected will be I–1; however, the action—to move and combine X terms—again cannot be directly carried out. Thus, this action is stacked while another (R–4) can be carried out to yield problem 33. Thus, the isolate strategy predicts that solution time for any problem will depend on three factors: number of MOVEs, number of COMPUTEs, and number of STACKings. A more formal description of the isolate and reduce strategies is provided in Larkin, Mayer, & Kadane (1981), and Mayer (1982b.)

The reduce and isolate strategies suggest two different patterns of solution time by problem state. If the equation group uses an isolate strategy and the story group uses a reduce strategy, then there should be differences in the pattern of solution times. An inspection of the solution times by problem state suggests a pattern for the story group in which RT increases with the number of moves and computes required in a problem. In contrast, the equation group displays a more complex pattern, involving sharp drops in RT from state 54 to 53 (i.e., moving from 2 stackings to 1 stacking), and from 54, 53, and 51 to 33, 32, or 31 (i.e.,

TABLE 6.11
Solution of Problem 54 Using Isolate Strategy

Problem State	Event	Calculation	Move	Stack
(54)	$3X - 11 \ (8 = 3X)/2$			
	Conditions: 1-1, 1-2, R-3			
	Goal: 1-1			
	Fail due to PARENS (R-3)			1
	Goal: R-3			
	Succeed		1	
(53)	$2(3X - 11) = (8 + 3X)$			
	Conditions: 1-1, 1-2, R-4			
	Goal: 1-1			
	Fail due to PARENS (R-4)			1
	Goal: R-4			
	Succeed	2		
(33)	$6X - 22 = 8 + 3X$			
	Conditions: 1-1, 1-2			
	Goal: 1-1			
	Succeed	1	1	
(22)	$3X - 22 = 8$			
	Conditions: 1-2			
	Goal: 1-2			
	Succeed	1	1	
(11)	$3X = 30$			
	Conditions: 1-2			
	Goal: 1-2			
	Succeed	1		
(00)	$X = 10$	—	—	—
	From Problem State 54	5	4	2
	From Problem State 53	5	3	1
	From Problem State 33	3	3	0
	From Problem State 22	2	2	0
	From Problem State 11	1	1	0

TABLE 6.12
Values of R^2 and Variable Weighings for Three Multiple Regressions
Fit to Two Treatment Groups

Treatment	One Variable	Two Variables	Three Variables
	(Reduce Model)	(Reduce Model)	(Isolate Model)
Equation Group	R^2 = .83	R^2 = .84	R^2 = .99
	Step = 2.63 sec	Computation = 3.02 sec	Computation = .69 sec
	Intercept = -4.40 sec	Move = 2.04 sec	Move = 1.42 sec
		Intercept = -4.59 sec	Stack = 7.25 sec
			Intercept = .90 sec
Story Group	R^2 = .95	R^2 = .98	R^2 = .98
	Step = 4.37 sec	Computation = 5.63 sec	Computation = 5.42 sec
	Intercept = 3.58 sec	Move = 2.47 sec	Move = 2.43 sec
		Intercept = 3.94 sec	Stack = .61 sec
			Intercept = -3.39 sec

moving from 1 stacking to 0 stackings). An ANOVA carried out on the RT data revealed a significant group × problem type interaction, which is consistent with the above description.[2]

In order to provide a more detailed and formal analysis of these observations, several multiple regression functions were fit to the mean RTs for the 14 problem states for each group. Table 6.12 summarizes these analyses. First, a simple linear regression was used with the independent variable being the number of steps (i.e., sum of the number of MOVEs and COMPUTEs). As shown in the table, the model fit the word group reasonably well (R^2 = .95) but did not fit the equation group as well (R^2 = .83). Second, a multiple regression was conducted with the independent variables being number of MOVEs and number of COM-PUTEs. As shown in the table, this model produced similar results to the step model. Finally, a multiple regression was used that included three independent variables: number of MOVEs, number of COMPUTEs, and number of STACK-ings. This model resulted in no improvement for the word group, but produced a large improvment of fit for the equation group (R^2 = .99). Thus, the word group was well fit by models involving only number of moves and computes, whereas the equation group required a model involving stacking operations. This same pattern was found for data from the first trial and the last trial, suggesting that subjects did not change strategies during the experiment. It should also be noted that negative intercepts were obtained only for the rejected models.

The foregoing analysis was based on group means. In order to provide additional data concerning individual subjects, each of three regression models was

---

[2]A more sophisticated method of analyzing these results is discussed in Kadane, Larkin, & Mayer (1981), and is employed in subsequent sections of this chapter.

fit by the RT data for each of the 42 subjects. For purposes of analysis, "best fit" was defined as a model producing an R^2 that was at least .03 higher than the next simplest model. Twenty of the 21 equation subjects were best fit by a stacking model; 17 of 21 word subjects were best fit by simpler models involving only moves and computes.

Conclusion.   These results indicate that presentation format of problems influenced the solution procedure used by subjects. Even though subjects apparently possessed adequate knowledge of arithmetic and algebra procedures (e.g., the error rates were low), subjects differed in their solution strategies. When problems were presented in story form, the subjects seem to have relied on a reduce strategy; when problems were presented in word form, the subjects seem to have been able to use a strategy that involved more planning (i.e., goal stacking).

Research on Strategies: Simultaneous Equations Study

Introduction.   The foregoing study indicated that presenting a problem in word vs. equation format can affect the solution strategy used by subjects. The present section further explores this hypothesis, but involves problems with simultaneous equations.

Method.   Subjects read four sets of premises and answered 12 questions after each. Half the subjects received problems in equation format; the other subjects

TABLE 6.13
Example Problems in Story and Equation Formats

Equation Format	Story Format
Premises	Premises
F = 10 x R H = 20 x B F = 40 x B	In a certain forest the animals are voting for their leader. The frog gets 10 times as many votes as the rabbit. The hawk gets 20 times as many votes as the bear. The frog gets 40 times as many votes as the bear.
Size 1 Question	Size 1 Question
F > R?	Does the frog get more votes than the rabbit?
Size 2 Question	Size 2 Question
R > B?	Does the rabbit get more votes than the bear?
Size 3 Question	Size 3 Question
H>R?	Does the hawk get more votes than the rabbit?

received isomorphic problems in story format, such as shown in the top of Table 6.13. After each set of premises, subjects received 12 "comparative questions," with each question involving one premise (size 1 question), 2 premises (size 2 question) or all 3 premises (size 3 question), as shown in the bottom of Table 6.13. The format of the questions corresponded to the format of the premises for each subject. All stimuli were presented on a CRT screen, and all responses consisted of pressing buttons labeled "yes" and "no." A microcomputer controlled the presentation of stimuli and recorded the subjects' responses.

Results.   Figure 6.5 shows the proportion correct on problems involving 1, 2 and 3 premises for the equation and story groups averaged over the four problems. As can be seen, the story group shows decreasing performance with number of equations required, but the equation group does not.

The performance of the word group is consistent with an "inference strategy" as summarized in Table 6.14. According to the inference strategy, a problem

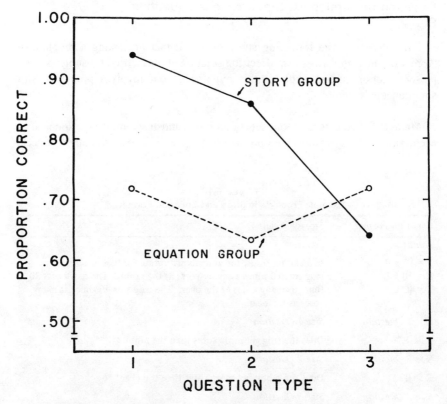

FIG. 6.5.   Proportion Correct Response by Question Type for Equation and Story Problems

TABLE 6.14
Memory Structure and Solution Algorithm
for an Inference Strategy

Memory structure for inference model:
Referenced, tagged list of pairs
    1. $A(3) - C \rightarrow + 4$
    2. $B - D(3) \rightarrow + 2$
    3. $A(1) - D(2) \rightarrow + 5$

A, B, C, D are terms; numbers in parentheses are references to other locations; and numbers to right of the arrows indicate tags such as +4 for "add 4."

Algorithm for inference model	
Size 1 question	$A > C$?
Retrieve A–C proposition	$A = C + 4$
Transform proposition	$A > C$
Match question	Yes
Size 2 question	$A > B$?
Retrieve proposition	$A = D + 5$
Retrieve proposition	$B = D + 2$
Rearrange proposition	$D = B - 2$
Substitute propositions	$A = B - 2 + 5$
Rearrange proposition	$A = B + 3$
Transform proposition	$A > B$
Match question	Yes
Size 3 question	$B > C$?
Retrieve proposition	$A = C + 4$
Retrieve proposition	$B = D + 2$
Retrieve proposition	$A = D + 5$
Rearrange proposition	$D = A - 5$
Substitute proposition	$B = A - 5 + 2$
Substitute proposition	$B = C + 4 - 5 + 2$
Rearrange proposition	$B = C + 1$
Transform proposition	$B > C$
Match question	Yes

Note: Size 1 has 1 retrieval and 0 substitutions; Size 2 has 2 retrievals and 1 substitution; Size 3 has 3 retrievals and 2 substitutions.

solver generates a numerical answer for each question by substituting equations into each other. Thus, size 1 questions involve 0 substitutions, size 2 involves 1 substitution and size 3 involves 2 substitutions; thus, performance should be a direct function of step size.

The performance of the equation group is consistent with a "feature strategy," as summarized in Table 6.15. According to the feature strategy, a problem solver remembers that frog has been "greater than" 2 times, hawk has been greater than once, rabbit has been less than once and bear has been less than twice. Whenever a question is asked, the problem solver compares the two

TABLE 6.15
Memory Structure and Solution Algorithm
for a Feature Strategy

Memory structure for feature model:
Unordered feature lists
Terms = A++, C-, B+, D–
Quantities = +4, +2, +5

+ indicates that the term occurred on the left of an equation and - indicates
it occurred on the right, for the terms list; and the quantities come from
the numbers in the equations or stories.

Algorithm for feature model	
Size 1 question	A > C?
Match A	yes, yes
Match C	yes
Add	yes, yes, yes (3)
Respond	yes
Size 2 question	A > B?
Match A	yes, yes
Match B	no
Add	yes (1)
Respond	yes (maybe)
Size 3 question	B > C?
Match B	yes
Match C	yes
Add	yes, yes (2)
Respond	yes

Note: Size 1 has 2 consistent matches and 3 (or 4) consistent tags; Size 3
has 2 consistent matches and 2 consistent tags; Size 2 has 1 match,
1 mismatch, and 1 consistent tag.

terms: If one term was "greater than" and the other "less than" (as in size 1 and
3) the answer is easy, but if both were "greater than" or both were "less than,"
then it is harder (as in step size 2). Thus, the feature strategy predicts the most
errors for size 2, with least for 1 and 3.

In order to provide a more detailed test of the foregoing observations, several
regression analyses were performed. Table 6.16 gives the obtained scores and
the scores predicted by the inference strategy and the feature strategy on each of
the three types of questions for each of the two groups. As can be seen, the
inference strategy best fits the performance of the story group ($r = .90$), but the
feature strategy best fits the performance of the equation group ($r = .99$). These
results were replicated in several other studies, and have been described in more
detail elsewhere (Mayer, 1978b).

Conclusion.   These results indicate that subjects tended to use qualitatively
different solution strategies to solve problems presented in equation form as

TABLE 6.16
Predicted and Obtained Guess Rates for Story and Equation Groups

	Equation Group				Story Group			
	Question Size			R^2	Question Size			R^2
	1	2	3		1	2	3	
Obtained	.60	.76	.58		.16	.28	.72	
Predicted – Inference Strategy	.63	.64	.65	.02	.10	.38	.66	.90*
Predicted – Feature Strategy	.59	.76	.59	.99*	.44	.44	.44	.02

compared to problems presented in story form. Apparently, a meaningful story tended to elicit a classic "deductive reasoning" strategy, based on substituting equations into one another; in contrast, the equation format tended to elicit a more superficial strategy. The results of this research suggest that problem solvers have several possible strategies available to them. Formal models should be developed with an eye to how individual differences among subjects' strategies may be described.

ALGORITHMIC KNOWLEDGE IS NEEDED FOR PROBLEM EXECUTION

Example

The previous section suggested that strategic knowledge is required for determining which actions will be carried out. The present section focuses on the actual process of carrying out the actions. For example, in the astronaut problem, a problem solver needs to know how to perform arithmetic operations such as $3 \times 5 = \underline{\hspace{1cm}}$ or $3.3 \times 15 = \underline{\hspace{1cm}}$. Even if a problem solver can translate, understand, and plan a problem, the problem solver must also be able to carry out the plan.

Algorithmic knowledge refers to knowledge about how to do something, i.e., how to carry out some procedure. Examples of algorithmic knowledge relevant for story problems include: (1) arithmetic procedures such as knowing how to perform long division or three column substraction; and (2) algebraic procedures such as knowing how to divide both sides of an equality by the same number.

Review

In order to solve problems like the astronaut problem, one has to be able to perform computations. In order to perform computations, a learner needs to know the algorithm for generating the correct answer. An algorithm is an exact procedure for carrying out some task, such as adding two numbers. Thus, one component of a person's algorithmic knowledge involves arithmetic algorithms—procedures for carrying out arithmetic computations.

Groen & Parkman (1972) suggested five different process models to represent children's addition algorithms for single column problems of the form, m + n = _____. For example, the min model states that a child begins with the larger number and increments it by the size of the smaller number. This model predicts that RT performance will be a linear function of the value of the smaller number. In a study involving school children, RT performance involving single digit addition was best described by the min model for older children, but some younger children may have been using less sophisticated models.

Similar models have been developed by Resnick and her colleagues (Resnick, 1976; Woods, Resnick, & Groen, 1975) to describe five "counting models" of subtraction. This work also suggests that there is a developmental trend in which inefficient models are used by younger children but more complex and efficient ones are used by older children.

More recently, Brown and Burton (1978) investigated "bugs" in students' knowledge of how to carry out three column subtraction. In an analysis of errors committed by 1325 primary school students, Brown and Burton identified procedural bugs such as, "borrowing from zero" ($103-45 = 158$ or $803-508 = 395$), "subtracting smaller from larger" ($253-118 = 145$), as well as dozens of others. According to Brown and Burton's analysis, even incorrect answers could be explained by assuming that students used algorithms that contained one or more bugs. Thus, students may have a subtraction algorithm that they consistently apply, but bugs in that algorithm can systematically generate incorrect answers on certain problems.

In a recent article, Simon (1980) has argued that although algorithmic knowledge is emphasized in mathematics instruction (e.g., drill in arithmetic and algebra operations), other forms of knowledge are generally not taught. Furthermore, algorithmic knowledge alone will not sustain creative problem-solving performance. Simon argues that students must also know "when" to apply operators as well as "how" to apply them.

Research on Algorithms: Single Variable Equation Study

Introduction. Part of algebra problem solving involves carrying out actions such as MOVEs, COMPUTEs, and STACKs as discussed in the previous section on strategies. A MOVE procedure involves bringing a variable or number from one side of the equation to another, adding or multiplying or subtracting or dividing both sides of the equation by the same value. A COMPUTE procedure involves carrying out an arithmetic operation on one side of the equality, such as adding two numbers together. A STACK procedure involves placing a goal into a goal stack. Table 6.17 provides examples of each of these algorithms.

TABLE 6.17
Examples of MOVE, COMPUTE, and STACK Procedures

Type of Procedure Required	Input State	Output State
MOVE	$(5X + 8)/3 - 2X = X$	$(5X + 8)/3 = 2X + X$
COMPUTE	$(5X + 8)/3 = 2X + X$	$(5X + 8)/3 = 3X$
STACK, MOVE, COMPUTE	$(5X + 8)/3 = 3X$	$5X + 8 = 9X$
MOVE	$5X + 8 = 9X$	$8 = 9X - 5X$
COMPUTE	$8 = 9X - 5X$	$8 = 4X$
MOVE	$8 = 4X$	$8/4 = X$
COMPUTE	$8/4 = X$	$2 = X$

In order to provide more information concerning the nature of algorithmic knowledge in problem solving, a study was conducted. (For more detail see Larkin et al., 1981.) One goal of this study was to determine the role of each type of algorithm—MOVE, COMPUTE, and STACK—in determining subjects' performance in equation solving.

Method. Four subjects participated in the experiment. Subject A was a faculty member in psychology. Subject B was a psychology graduate student who studied mathematics abroad. Subject C was an undergraduate student majoring in music. Subject D was a graduate student in psychology. All subjects were mathematically sophisticated and readily able to solve equations at error rates under 3%. All subjects received the same treatment and solved the same problems.

Subjects solved 270 linear equations during each of four sessions, for a total of 1080 equations. There were three basic problem forms, such as the one shown in Table 6.18. Each problem form was broken down into problem states, such as the 8 problem states shown in Table 6.18. The table also shows the number of

TABLE 6.18
Eight Problem States for $(5X + 8)/3 - 2X = X$

Problem State	Operations Required to Transform Current Problem State Into Next Problem State		
	COMPUTES	MOVES	STACKS
8. $(5X + 8)/3 - 2X = X$	0	1	0
7. $(5X + 8)/3 = 2X + X$	1	0	0
6. $(5X + 8)/3 = 3X$	1	1	1
5. $5X + 8 = 9X$	0	1	0
4. $8 = 9X - 5X$	1	0	0
3. $8 = 4X$	0	1	0
2. $8/4 = X$	1	0	0
1. $2 = X$	0	0	0

MOVEs, COMPUTEs, and STACKs required for moving from each problem state to the next. Nine alternatives were included for each problem state, such that the same number of MOVEs, COMPUTEs, and STACKs were involved but different specific numbers were used. The equations were presented, in a semi-randomized order, on a CRT screen, and subjects responded by pushing a button corresponding to the correct answer. The experiment was controlled by a microcomputer.

Results.   The results were transformed to "change scores": for each pair of problem states that were adjacent in the problem space for a problem, we recorded the change in RT from the longer to the shorter problem state, as well as the differences in the number of MOVEs, COMPUTEs, or STACKs between the two adjacent states. For example, in Table 6.18, problem state $5X + 8 = 9X$ involves one more MOVE than problem state $8 = 9X - 5X$, so the difference in RTs between the two states corresponds to the time for one MOVE.

The rationale for using change scores and the statistical model used to analyze the results has been described in detail elsewhere (Kadane, Larkin, & Mayer, 1981). The model takes difference scores as input and is able to distinguish between two types of error in RT: (1) *random error* is due to an absolute RT being higher or lower than predicted; (2) *systematic error* is due to deviation of difference score data from the model. Thus, random error reflects fluctuation in the subject's performance, assuming the model correctly describes performance; systematic error reflects misfit of the model to the subject's performance.

The three variable models for the isolate strategy (as discussed in the previous section on strategic knowledge) was fit to the performance of each subject. Table 6.19 gives the average systematic and random error for each subject on each of

TABLE 6.19
Estimates of Systematic Error and Random Error for
Four Subjects on Each Session

Systematic Error (Sec.)				
	Session 1	*Session 2*	*Session 3*	*Session 4*
Subject A	2.8	2.1	1.2	.7
Subject B	2.2	1.9	1.0	1.1
Subject C	5.2	2.3	1.9	1.9
Subject D	3.1	3.1	1.7	1.3
Random Error (Sec.)				
	Session 1	*Session 2*	*Session 3*	*Session 4*
Subject A	3.8	1.7	1.2	.8
Subject B	2.9	2.1	1.4	1.6
Subject C	4.8	2.1	1.6	1.9
Subject D	3.8	4.8	3.1	3.0

TABLE 6.20
Parameter Estimates (in seconds) for Four Subjects
on Sessions 3 and 4

	Constant	COMPUTE	MOVE	STACK	Systematic Error (s.d.)	Random Error (s.d.)
Subject A	.26	.93	.39	–	.88	1.03
Subject B	.08	.94	.51	.81	1.07	1.42
Subject C	-.45	1.16	1.12	–	1.89	1.73
Subject D	-.02	.68	1.37	1.57	1.17	3.17

the four sessions. As can be seen, both random and systematic error decreases with practice. Two possible explanations are: (1) subject's processing strategy changed across sessions so that the model fit better on later sessions; or (2) subject's performance was quite noisy on the first sessions. It should also be pointed out that Subject D displayed a high level of random error, so that we must interpret his data with caution.

Because error scores were so high during the first two sessions. parameter estimates were obtained using data from sessions 3 and 4. The data from each subject was fit to a three-variable "isolate strategy" model and a two-variable "reduce strategy" model as described in the section on strategic knowledge. Subjects A and C were best fit by the reduce strategy model; subjects B and D were best fit by the isolate strategy model. Table 6.20 gives the parameter values for MOVEs, COMPUTEs, and STACKings based on a three-variable isolate strategy model for subjects B and D and gives the parameter values for MOVEs and COMPUTEs based on a two-variable reduce strategy model for subjects A and C. As can be seen, the time to make a computation averaged between .682 and 1.132 seconds, the time to make a move averaged between .392 and 1.407 seconds, and the time to carry out a goal stacking operation averaged between .811 and 1.573 seconds. Thus, simple procedures seem to require times on the order of about one second.

Conclusion. This study provides for a detailed analysis of the time required for basic algorithms in equation solving performance. In particular, this study suggests that carrying out basic algorithms such as MOVEs and COMPUTEs adds approximately one second to response time. There are, however, large individual differences among subjects in speed and consistency of performance.

IMPLICATIONS

The introduction to this chapter suggested two approaches to the study of human intelligence—the psychometric approach and the cognitive approach. During the first half of this century, when the psychometric approach was dominant, performance on mathematical problems was considered to be a fundamental manifestation of intelligence. For example, solving "number" problems constituted one of Thurstone's (1938) seven primary mental abilities, and "arithmetic reasoning" problems were included on most instruments measuring general intelligence. However, although the psychometric approach stimulated exciting developments in the psychology of human intelligence, it failed to provide a satisfactory description of human intelligence or its component factors such as mathematical ability.

More recently, two varieties of a cognitive approach to human intelligence have emerged. The cognitive correlates approach involves relating individual differences in test performance to individual differences in the structure or operating characteristics of the information processing system (Hunt, 1978). The cognitive components approach involves relating individual differences in test performance to individual differences in the domain-specific knowledge (including information processing algorithms) of the problem solver (Sternberg, 1977).

The present chapter has employed what Sternberg (1977) calls a "componential" approach to intelligence in general, and mathematical ability in particular. Our approach has explored the idea that performance on mathematical problems depends on the problem solver's knowledge, including linguistic, factual, schematic, strategic, and algorithmic knowledge. This chapter has suggested that one source of individual differences in mathematical ability may be differences in people's domain specific knowledge. Other possible sources of individual differences not explored in this chapter include general operating characteristics and structural characteristics of the information processing system.

The central theme of this chapter has been that mathematical ability is related to an individual's knowledge. In summary, let's return to the astronaut problem (Table 6.1) for one final look at sources of individual differences. This chapter has suggested four areas in which people who can solve this problem might differ from people who cannot solve this problem:

(1) Linguistic and Factual Knowledge.   People who are unable to generate the correct answer may lack linguistic or factual knowledge. In particular, this chapter has focused on research evidence that people may have particular difficulty in comprehending sentences that express relations among variables. One implication of this finding is that students need practice in comprehension of sentences in story problems, such as being able to paraphrase each sentence or to represent each sentence using an equation or a picture or concrete objects.

(2) Schematic Knowledge.   People who are unable to generate the correct answer may lack knowledge of problem types. In particular, this chapter has focused on research evidence that people may possess knowledge of only a limited number of problem types. When a presented problem does not fit into one of the student's existing categories, the problem is likely to be misinterpreted. One implication of this finding is that students need practice in representing

problems and in recognizing those problems that go together and those that do not.

(3) Strategic Knowledge.   Failure to solve the problem may be due to lack of knowledge of appropriate strategies. In particular, this chapter has explored alternative techniques for solving equations. One important finding has been that the strategy that a problem solver uses is often tied to the way that the problem is represented. In addition, results demonstrated strong individual differences among students in their preferred strategies for solving equations. An implication of this work is that students need instruction and practice in determining which algorithms to apply and when to apply them.

(4) Algorithmic Knowledge.   Failure to solve the problem may be due to lack of skill at applying arithmetic and algebraic algorithms. In particular, this chapter has indicated great individual differences in the speed and consistency with which students are able to apply algorithms. One implication is that students will always need practice in ''getting the right answer'' when applying basic computational algorithms.

To the extent that differences in mathematical ability are related to differences in students' domain specific knowledge, there is a role for instruction. Future work in this area requires evaluation techniques for analyzing and measuring knowledge, instructional techniques for helping students to acquire knowledge, and research techniques for determining the relationship between specific knowledge and mathematical problem-solving performance. We hope that the preliminary research reported in this chapter will encourage further exploration of the relationship between specific types of knowledge and what has been called mathematical ability.

ACKNOWLEDGMENT

Much of the original research reported in this chapter was supported by Grants NIE–G–78–0162 and NIE–G–0118 from the National Institute of Education, Program in Teaching and Learning. Much of the original research, statistical analyses, and theoretical work in Sections 4 and 5 was conducted in collaboration among the three authors while the first author was on sabbatical leave at the Learning Research and Development Center, University of Pittsburgh. The first author's address is: Richard E. Mayer, Department of Psychology, University of California, Santa Barbara, Calif. 93106.

REFERENCES

Anderson, J. R., Greeno, J. G., Kline, P. J., & Neves, D. M. Acquisition of problem-solving skill. In J. R. Anderson (Ed.), *Cognitive skills and their acquisition.* Hillsdale, N.J.: Lawrence Erlbaum Associates, 1981.

Bobrow, D. G. Natural language input for a computer problem solving system. In M. Minsky (Ed.), *Semantic information processing*. Cambridge, Mass.: MIT Press, 1968.

Brown, J. S. & Burton, R. R. Diagnostic models for procedural bugs in basic mathematical skills. *Cognitive Science*, 1978, *2*, 155–192.

Bundy, A. *Analysing mathematical proofs (or reading between the lines)*. (DAI Report No. 2) Edinburgh, Scotland: University of Edinburgh, Department of Artificial Intelligence, May, 1975.

California Assessment Program. *Student achievement in California schools: 1979–80 annual report*. Sacramento: California State Department of Education, 1980.

Clement, J., Lochhead, J., & Soloway, E. *Translating between symbol systems: Isolating a common difficulty in solving algebra word problems*. (COINS Technical Report 79–19) Amherst, Mass.: University of Massachusetts, Department of Computer and Information Sciences, March, 1979.

Clement, J., Lochhead, J., & Soloway, E. *Positive effects of computer programming on students' understanding of variables and equations*. Paper presented at National Conference of the Association for Computing Machinery, 1980.

Greeno, J. G. A study of problem solving. In R. Glaser (Ed.), *Advances in instructional psychology*. Hillsdale, N.J.: Lawrence Erlbaum Associates, 1978.

Greeno, J. G. Trends in the theory of knowledge for problem-solving. In D. T. Tuma & F. Reif (Eds.), *Problem solving and education: Issues in teaching and research*. Hillsdale, N.J.: Lawrence Erlbaum Associates, 1980. (a)

Greeno, J. G. Some examples of cognitive task analysis with instructional implications. In R. E. Snow, P. Federico, & W. E. Montague (Eds.), *Aptitude, learning, and instruction*. Hillsdale, N.J.: Lawrence Erlbaum Associates, 1980). (b)

Groen, G. J., & Parkman, J. M. A chronometric analysis of simple addition. *Psychological Review*, 1972, *79*, 329–343.

Hayes, J. R. & Simon, H. A. Understanding written instructions. In L. W. Gregg (Ed.), *Knowledge and cognition*. Hillsdale, N.J.: Lawrence Erlbaum Associates, 1974.

Hayes, J. R., Waterman, D. A., & Robinson, C. S. Identifying relevant aspects of a problem text. *Cognitive Science*, 1977, *1*, 297–313.

Heller, J. & Greeno, J. G. *Semantic processing in arithmetic word problem solving*. Paper presented at the annual meeting of the Midwestern Psychological Association, 1978.

Hinsley, D., Hayes, J. R. & Simon, H. A. From words to equations. In P. Carpenter & M. Just (Eds.), *Cognitive processes in comprehension*. Hillsdale, N.J.: Lawrence Erlbaum Associates, 1977.

Hunt, E. B. Mechanics of verbal ability. *Psychological Review*, 1978, *85*, 109–130.

Hunt, E. B., Lunneborg, C. & Lewis, J. What does it mean to be high verbal? *Cognitive Psychology*, 1975, *1*, 194–227.

Kadane, J., Larkin, J. H., & Mayer, R. E. A moving average model for sequenced reaction time data. *Journal of Mathematical Psychology*, 1981, *23*, 115–133.

Larkin, J. Enriching formal knowledge: A model for learning to solve textbook physics problems. In J. R. Anderson (Ed.), *Cognitive skills and their acquisition*. Hillsdale, N.J.: Lawrence Erlbaum Associates, 1981.

Larkin, J. H., Mayer, R. E. & Kadane, J. An information processing model based on reaction times in solving linear equations (Technical Report). Pittsburgh, Penna.: Carnegie-Mellon University, Department of Psychology, April, 1981.

Larkin, J. H., McDermott, J., Simon, D. P., & Simon, H. A. Expert and novice performance in solving physical problems. *Science*, 1980, *208*, 1335–1342.

Lewis, C. Skill in algebra. In J. R. Anderson (Ed.), *Cognitive skills and their acquisition*. Hillsdale, N.J.: Lawrence Erlbaum Associates, 1981.

Loftus, E. F. & Suppes, P. Structural variables that determine problem-solving difficulty in computer assisted instruction. *Journal of Educational Psychology*, 1972, *63*, 531–542.

Matz, M. Towards a computational theory of algebraic competence. *Journal of Mathematical Behavior*, 1980, *3*, 531–542.

Mayer, R. E. Comprehension as affected by the structure of problem representation. *Memory & Cognition*, 1976, *4*, 249–255. (a)

Mayer, R. E. Integration of information during problem solving due to a meaningful context of learning. *Memory & Cognition*, 1976, *4*, 603–608. (b)

Mayer, R. E. Effects of meaningfulness on the representation of knowledge and the process of inference for mathematical problem solving. In R. Revlin & R. E. Mayer (Eds.), *Human reasoning*. Washington: Winston–Wiley, 1978. (a)

Mayer, R. E. Qualitatively different storage and processing strategies used for linear reasoning tasks due to meaningfulness of premises. *Journal of Experimental Psychology: Human Learning and Memory*, 1978, *4*, 5–18. (b)

Mayer, R. E. Qualitatively different encoding strategies for linear reasoning: Evidence for single association and distance theories. *Journal of Experimental Psychology: Human Learning and Memory*, 1979, *5*, 1–10.

Mayer, R. E. Frequency norms and structural analysis of algebra story problems into families, categories, and templates. *Instructional Science*, 1981, *10*, 135–175.

Mayer, R. E. Memory for algebra story problems. *Journal of Educational Psychology*, 1982, *74*, 199–216. (a)

Mayer, R. E. Different problem solving strategies for algebra word and equation problems. *Journal of Experimental Psychology: Learning, Memory and Cognition*, 1982, *8*, 448–462. (b)

Mayer, R. E. & Greeno, J. G. Effects of meaningfulness and organization on problem solving and computability judgments. *Memory or Cognition*, 1975, *3*, 356–362.

Newell, A. & Simon, H. A. *Human problem solving*. Englewood Cliffs, N.J.: Prentice-Hall, 1972.

Paige, J. M. & Simon, H. A. Cognitive processes in solving algebra word problems. In B. Kleinmuntz (Ed.), *Problem solving: Research, method, and theory*. New York: Wiley, 1966.

Resnick, L. B. Task analysis in instructional design: Some cases from mathematics. In D. Klahr (Ed.), *Cognition and instruction*. Hillsdale, N.J.: Lawrence Erlbaum Associates, 1976.

Resnick, L. B. & Ford, W. W. *The psychology of mathematics for instruction*. Hillsdale, N. J.: Lawrence Erlbaum Associates, 1981.

Riley, M. S. & Greeno, J. G. *Importance of semantic structure in the difficulty of arithmetic word problems*. Paper presented at the annual meeting of the Midwestern Psychological Association, Chicago, May, 1978.

Robinson, C. S. & Hayes, J. R. Making inferences about relevance in understanding problems. In R. Revlin & R. E. Mayer (Eds.), *Human reasoning*. Washington: Winston/Wiley, 1978.

Simon, H. A. Problem solving and education. In D. T. Tuma & T. Reif (Eds.), *Problem solving and education: Issues in teaching and research*. Hillsdale, N.J.: Lawrence Erlbaum Associates, 1980.

Sternberg, R. J. *Intelligence, information processing, and analogical reasoning*. Hillsdale, N.J.: Lawrence Erlbaum Associates, 1977.

Thurstone, L. L. *Primary mental abilities*. Chicago: University of Chicago Press, 1938.

Woods, S. S., Resnick, L. B., & Groen, G. J. An experimental test of five process models for subtraction. *Journal of Educational Psychology*, 1975, *67*, 17–21.

7

Factors Affecting Individual Differences in Learning Ability

Lauren B. Resnick
Robert Neches
University of Pittsburgh
Learning Research and Development Center

INTRODUCTION

In this paper we take a step backward to an old definition of intelligence, and several steps forward in a new line of research that we believe is necessary if we are to escape from a continuing tendency to define intelligence in terms of performance on a small number of psychometric instruments. Throughout the history of psychology, two meanings of the term ''intelligence'' have coexisted but rarely interacted. One tradition treats intelligence as something that distinguishes between individuals: Some people are said to be more intelligent than others, presumably because of differences in stable—perhaps innate—mental abilities. The other tradition considers a species-wide capacity for adaptation to the environment: Humans are said to be more intelligent than other species because of their ability to adapt (through learning) to a wider range of specific environmental conditions.

The individual difference, or correlational, branch of research on intelligence has over the decades since Binet sought to refine our knowledge of the nature of the mental abilities that correlate with success in school and other activities. Factor-analytic work was designed to uncover the different *kinds* of mental abilities included in the general rubric of intelligence and to explicate the relations among these abilities. More recently, cognitive analyses of tests of known factorial structure have attempted to press this agenda further (e.g., Carroll, 1976; Glaser, 1981; Sternberg, 1977). As a result of these efforts we are increasingly able to specify the knowledge drawn upon and the processes used in responding to various kinds of test items. We are moving closer to having a well-tested cognitive theory of test taking that can specify in detail how high and low scorers are likely to differ.

Yet despite extensive attention to "test items as cognitive tasks" (cf. Carroll, 1976), most investigators are not fundamentally interested in the tests themselves. Rather, they are interested in the success or failure that the tests *predict*—that is, in whether individuals are likely to be successful in learning something new in the future. The extensive attention given to the cognitive components of test performance is based on an implicit assumption that the processes required for *performance* on the tests are also directly involved in *learning*.

We believe that this is a risky assumption, that it is not at all certain that study of the differences in performance on the tests that predict learning success will actually reveal differences in learning processes. The performance capabilities that people draw upon as they take tests may reveal little about how those capabilities were *acquired*. And it is the processes of acquisition—i.e., of learning—that are what we really mean by the term "intelligence." Tests do not actually engage people in new learning except within very narrow limits (for example, the processes of inferring relations in an analogy item). Tests are primarily indicators of what has already been learned—both knowledge and strategies for using that knowledge. Presumably, people who learned more in the past will be able to learn more in the future. This is why the tests predict future learning reasonably well. However, this does not mean that test items can directly reveal the processes of learning.

We propose to examine intelligence through a more direct look at the learning process itself, rather than at its results. In doing so, we will turn away—temporarily—from a direct focus on *differences* in learning ability. Instead, we will concern ourselves first with the basic mechanisms and structures of learning and only afterward discuss possible individual differences in these structures and processes. By focusing first on what we assume to be the basic "structural" features of performance and learning we will be working more in the spirit of the second major strand of thinking about intelligence, the one that has been primarily interested in the shared mental characteristics of the species that allow it to adapt and survive. By focusing on shared processes of learning, however, we will not be abandoning an interest in individual differences. Rather, we intend to use a small number of well-understood examples of learning as a basis for inferring sources of individual differences. Our work can thus be characterized as an initial step in an effort to bring structuralist approaches to intelligence (Piaget, 1950/1971; Gardner, 1973) into more active communication with individual difference psychology. To the extent that this venture is successful, we will also be constructing links between learning and differential psychology of the kind called for by Cronbach (1957).

In this paper we will examine three specific cases of learning, each drawn from early mathematics and each concerned with the construction, or invention, of new knowledge of children. Following the presentation of the three learning examples, we will explicitly consider the sources of individual differences in learning suggested by the analyses.

In the first case we consider two versions of an artificial intelligence system that invents a new, more efficient procedure for simple addition. It is a procedure that young children (under age 7) are also known to invent. The first version of the system appears to construct the new procedure entirely on the basis of general knowledge about the structure of procedures and a preference for procedural efficiency. But close inspection shows that the new construction also depends *either* upon extensive memory capacity *or* upon assumptions about prior knowledge regarding the equivalence of commutative addition pairs that are not reasonable to assume in children under the age of 7 years (cf. Resnick, in press). For this reason a second version of the system was designed. The second version invents the new procedure without assuming commutativity and with less demand on memory. However, it now explicitly uses certain domain-specific knowledge that is known to be within the competence of preschool children. The second version thus suggests that specific knowledge about the nature of number is almost essential for learning in this domain. The contrast between the two models shows how plausible domain-specific knowledge can allow learning to proceed when more general strategic knowledge alone would surpass the system's memory capacity.

The next example of learning probes more directly the role of domain-specific knowledge in learning. In this case we examine the protocol of an instructional interview during which a child tried to modify one procedure so that it was analogous to another. The instructor's intent was to have the child discover and display the rationale for the source procedure, on the assumption that the process of constructing an analogy would force attention to the meaning of the procedure. Our analysis shows that this assumption is correct: In constructing a procedure that is constrained to "match" another one, schematized domain-specific knowledge must be accessed or constructed. One of the features of this analysis is that it makes evident the nature and extent of interplay between schematic and procedural knowledge in the course of learning.

The final case we consider is one that does not directly involve procedural knowledge. It is a case drawn from experiments (Inhelder, Sinclair, & Bovet, 1974) in which a child learns about liquid conservation through a process of making and verifying predictions and constructing explanations for cases in which his predictions turn out wrong. Our analysis of this episode shows that the learning occurs in ways very similar to those observed in the procedural analogy example. That is, attempts to instantiate simultaneously several schemata force the child to recognize a conflict. The conflict is resolved by a schema modification that clearly depends upon the availability of specific prior knowledge that had not previously been integrated with the child's liquid quantity schemata.

INVENTING AN EFFICIENT PROCEDURE FOR SIMPLE ADDITION

Psychological research using a number of different paradigms has shown that very young children add by a "counting-all" method (Carpenter & Moser, 1982; Fuson, Richards, & Briars, 1982; Ginsburg, 1977a,b; Groen & Resnick, 1977; Steffe & Thompson, 1982). The basic operations of this method consist of counting out separate sets of objects to represent each addend and then counting the total set of objects in order to determine the sum. This has become known as the SUM procedure for addition.

Although there is still room for debate about the nature of adult procedures for solving addition problems (Ashcraft & Battaglia, 1978), there is fairly solid evidence that children at the second-grade level generally solve many addition problems by an efficient "counting-on" procedure (Groen & Parkman, 1972; Ginsburg, 1977a,b; Svenson, 1975; Svenson & Broquist, 1975; Svenson, Hedenborg, & Lingman, 1976). This procedure can be described as starting counting at the larger addend (regardless of presentation order) and counting on from there by the smaller addend (e.g., for 3 + 5, the child would mentally count, "5 . . . 6, 7, 8"). This is called the MIN procedure, because only the minimum of the two addends must actually be counted.

There is reason to believe that MIN is not directly taught, but rather is invented by children (Resnick, 1980). Even if some children are taught or shown MIN, it is clearly inventable by children, even very young ones. For example, Groen and Resnick (1977) taught preschool and kindergarten children to add using a SUM-like procedure. After 12 to 15 weeks of practice (but with no further instruction), half of the children had switched to MIN. Thus, the invention of MIN by children under the age of 7 is a real phenomenon. What we seek here is an explanation of that phenomenon—an account of the specific learning processes involved.

Despite several efforts—most notably Groen and Resnick's (1977), in which children were observed several times per week over several months—it has proved very difficult to actually observe a child in the process of inventing MIN. All we really know is that the earliest observations of young children show them performing SUM and later ones show the same children performing MIN. A possible intermediate procedure, counting on from the first addend (whether it is larger or smaller), has occasionally been observed (cf. Fuson, 1982) but never linked directly to the emergence of MIN.

In the absence of any direct observation of the process of discovering MIN, one way to proceed in attempting to account for it is to build a self-modifying system that begins with SUM and, without any additional external input, changes to the use of MIN. To the extent that such a system accords with what we know about human capacities and knowledge, we can assume that it is a plausible model of human learning performance. In particular, we can inspect its learning processes for clues to human learning processes. We describe here an initial effort along these lines.

An Initial Model of the Invention of MIN

Neches (1981b) has built a program called HPM that starts with a version of the SUM procedure and converts to MIN over a number of "practice trials." The program's initial SUM procedure depends on its ability to form the union of two sets by means of a collection of counting processes that have been shown to be in the repertoire of the typical preschool child (Gelman & Gallistel, 1978; Greeno, Riley, & Gelman, in press). Figure 7.1 is a simplified representation of the goal structure used by this procedure in the process of solving a simple addition problem $(1 + 2 = ?)$.

In this procedure, a goal to ADD is decomposed into subgoals to GENERATE sets and COUNT UP the result. GENERATE is decomposed into goals to MAKE-SET for each of the addends. MAKE-SET in turn is satisfied by meeting goals to CORRESPOND elements until a set has been produced of a size equal to the addend. To meet the CORRESPOND goals, HPM pairs objects (denoted as O_1, O_2, O_3 in the figure) with numerlogs (number names denoted as 1, 2, etc.). The results of the two MAKE-SET goals are pairings of sets (denoted as S_1 and S_2) with numbers representing their size. For the problem shown there are two such sets, one of size 1 (S_1 1) and one of size 2 (S_1 2). Their union is denoted in Figure 7.1 as S_{tc} ("set of things to count"), a set of unknown size. This is marked as the result of the GENERATE goal. Next, S_{tc} is given to the COUNT UP goal as an input. The COUNT UP goal is satisfied by fulfilling CORRESPOND goals until the system has used up all of the objects in S_{tc}. The set of counted objects (denoted as S_c for "set counted") is equivalent in membership to S_{tc} and is of known size (in this case, 3).

Although not shown in the figure, each CORRESPOND goal is achieved by pairing a goal to "GET-NEXT from a supply of objects" with a goal to "GET-NEXT from an ordered string of numerlogs." These are the basic procedures of counting in a program (Greeno, Riley, & Gelman, in press) that formalizes a theory of counting formulated by Gelman and Gallistel (1978) on the basis of extensive observations of preschool children's counting performance. The process of adding by creating a union set and then counting it has been observed for untaught preschool children (e.g., Ginsburg, 1977a), and Groen and Resnick's (1977) subjects performed this procedure after only a few minutes of demonstration. HPM's account of initial knowledge is thus entirely plausible.

HPM's transformation of the SUM procedure to MIN is accomplished by a set of self-modifying processes that operationalize a model of strategy learning and optimization derived from protocol analyses of subjects practicing with several very different tasks (Neches, 1981b, in press). The model posits that a memory trace is left when a procedure is performed. The system has a set of "strategy

280

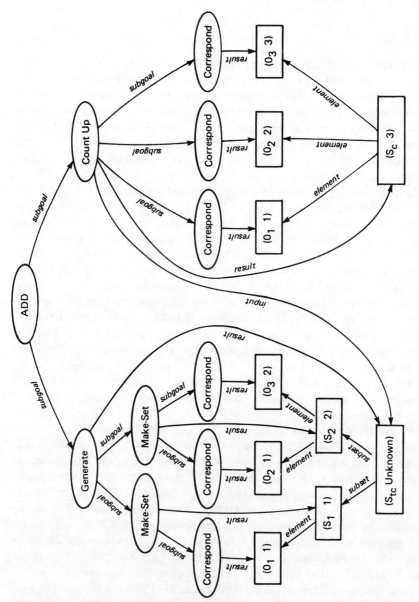

FIG. 7.1. Goal structure of a simple addition problem (1 + 2).

transformation'' heuristics, each of which suggests a change that can be made if certain conditions are detected in the memory trace. The changes compete with the current form of the procedure, and are reinforced or extinguished according to whether they meet expectations about the improvement they will produce. As a modified procedure emerges, it is subject to the same learning processes as the initial procedure. As a result, drastically new strategies are produced through a sequence of small incremental refinements to an initial procedure.

Of the many possible heuristics in this general model, three are used by HPM in the SUM to MIN transition. These are:

1. *Result still available:* If an item of information has previously been computed, try to retrieve it rather than recomputing it.
2. *Untouched result:* If an item of information is computed but not used, try to avoid computing it.
3. *Effort difference:* If the effort required to achieve a goal differs over two occasions, try to use the method involving the lesser effort.

Figure 7.2 illustrates the progression of strategies developed by HPM in the course of its learning (Neches, 1981a,b). The problem pair $2 + 3 = ?$ and $3 + 2 = ?$ are used as an illustration. Consider the left side $(2 + 3 = ?)$ first. To fulfill the MAKE-SET goals of the SUM procedure, HPM pairs two objects with the numerlogs 1 and 2 and then pairs three different objects with the numerlogs 1, 2, 3. Then it begins to COUNT-UP. Partway through the COUNT-UP goal the system, which has been keeping a record of its actions, notes that it has made the same object/numerlog pairing twice. This makes the *result still available* heuristic applicable. That is, the system can use the result of the first pairing rather than repeating the pairing. This is illustrated in the SUM strategy of Figure 7.2 by the objects generated for MAKE-SET 2 having the same number assignments as in the COUNT-UP phase.

When this equivalence is noted, HPM constructs a new rule that will make the system behave according to a procedure that we call SUM/FIRST. The rule, which will fire whenever a COUNT-UP goal is asserted, uses the counts from the first MAKE-SET goal in place of the first part of the COUNT-UP procedure. Because the COUNT-UP goal starts with a counted-objects set already equal to the first addend, the new procedure counts *only* the objects representing the *second* addend. It is worth noting that this procedure is equivalent to treating the set of objects counted by the MAKE-SET goal as a subset (a part) of the COUNT-UP set (the whole). However, the new procedure is generated by HPM without reference to any schema of wholes and parts or of inclusion.

As the new SUM/FIRST procedure is executed, the system notices that the objects representing the first addend (generated under the first MAKE-SET goal) are not really used in determining the final sum. Specifically, the result of

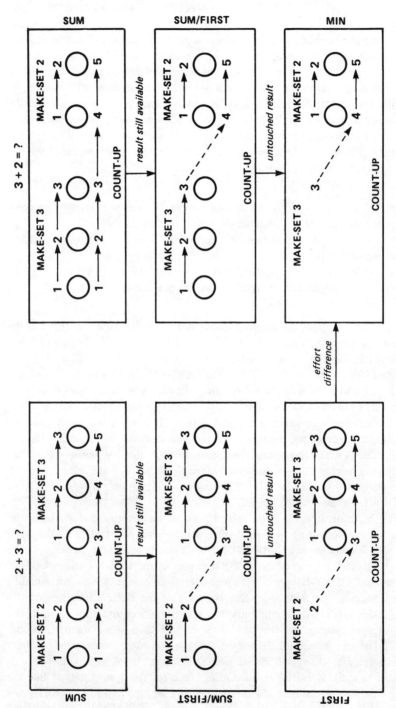

FIG. 7.2. Initial model for inventing MIN.

282

constructing the set is the same numerlog that was given as an addend. This numerlog provides the starting point for the modified COUNTING-UP process, but the *objects* in the first addend set are not operated on during the COUNT-UP phase of the procedure. This is a condition in which the *untouched result* heuristic is applicable. This heuristic causes HPM to respond by constructing a new rule (FIRST), which asserts that the MAKE-SET goal is satisfied as soon as the goal is established and assigns the given addend as the result. Now instead of counting out a two-object set, HPM will simply "assert" 2—in effect stating that the set exists without having actually counted its members. The resulting procedure (FIRST) skips over counting out the first addend, generates objects to represent the second addend, and then counts those objects starting from the numerlog for the first addend. This is the procedure of counting on from the first addend that has been documented in children's behavior (e.g., Fuson, 1982).

The right-hand side of the figure shows exactly the same set of transformations for the 3 + 2 = ? problem. Note, however, that the final result of these transformations is a procedure identical to MIN, because it counts on from the larger addend. A further modification on the left-hand side is needed, however, if the system is to *always* count on from the larger addend, as is demanded by MIN. HPM accomplishes this by application of the *effort difference* heuristic. This heuristic applies when two equivalent problems (i.e., problems that yield the same answer, such as 2 + 3 and 3 + 2) are compared and a difference in number of "steps" (i.e., counts) is found that favors 3 + 2. The heuristic causes HPM to transform the less efficient method (starting to count from 2) into the more efficient method (starting from 3). This is the MIN procedure. We will not elaborate here on this transformation, because several objections to the process have led us to prefer an alternative version of HPM. Before describing this alternative version, however, we want to consider the objections in some detail because they raise important questions about sources of individual differences in learning.

A first question concerns the source of the system's knowledge that pairs such as 2 + 3 and 3 + 2 are equivalent. As it stands here, this knowledge is simply *given* to HPM, thus implicitly endowing the system with knowledge of commutativity relations. This seems questionable in light of data on children's addition performance. Ginsburg (1977a) has shown, for example, that young children given problem sequences in which adjacent problems were commutative pairs (e.g., 4 + 6 followed by 6 + 4) generally solve the second problem by counting, with no mention and no use made of the preceding solution. The HPM model would predict that, if there were prior knowledge of commutativity, children would have copied the problem answer rather than engaging in new computation. HPM would surely be more convincing as a model of children's learning if it *discovered* the equivalence of commutative pairs rather than "knowing" this equivalence from the outset.

For HPM to make this discovery would require the ability to detect that certain pairs of problems yield the same result. We cannot assume that this is done by simply comparing the *answers* to two problems, for if the answers themselves were directly accessible, there would be no need for counting procedures in the first place. Thus the discovery must be based on the system's being able to remember something about the solution processes. However, the semantic structure built by HPM in the course of solving a problem is rather large—typically, over 70 unique nodes and hundreds of relational links. Retention in working memory of that entire structure while solving a second problem seems an unlikely model of human processing. Furthermore, we would like to account for Groen and Resnick's (1977) evidence that children can invent MIN even when there are many unrelated problems between the pairs of problems that this account claims are critical. For the system to meet these constraints, it would have to be able to selectively retrieve execution trace information from long-term memory.

This assumption has some important implications. Current theories of spreading activation in semantic memory (e.g., Anderson & Bower, 1980; Collins & Loftus, 1975) suggest that adding a pair of numbers will re-evoke the memory trace for having added the commuted pair, because the traces would have many common elements. However, the same memory capacity limitations that made it infeasible to retain an entire trace in working memory also make it infeasible for HPM to *retrieve* the entire trace. The system could retrieve only a subset of the trace's propositions. Because HPM would have no systematic way of deciding which propositions were critical, learning would be possible only on the occasional trials where the subset retrieved from the prior trace happened to contain all the key propositions. Thus, the account offered by HPM implies that learning MIN could happen only very slowly.

A Modified System for Inventing MIN

All of these difficulties can be resolved, with learning taking place more quickly and efficiently, in a modified version of HPM now under development. The new version gives HPM initial knowledge of a strong version of one of the principles of counting that Gelman and Gallistel's (1978) research has attributed to preschool children. The principle is referred to as "indifference to order"—the concept that, although the numerlogs must be assigned in a fixed order when counting, it does not matter which object receives which numerlog. In accord with this principle, the new version of HPM tags all objects-to-be-counted as equivalent, while still assigning each numerlog in the string a separate tag. This allows it to recognize certain objects that are not identical as being functionally equivalent. HPM has thus been given an additional piece of "semantic" knowledge about quantification, but it is knowledge that—unlike commutativity—is well established as being in the repertoire of the preschool child. Let us now consider what effect this knowledge has on HPM's account of the transition from SUM to MIN. The sequence of procedure transformations in this revised model is illustrated in Figure 7.3.

The system changes its SUM procedure to SUM/FIRST using the *result still available* heuristic, as in the original version (Figure 7.2). But because the new version is indifferent to the specific objects that are counted, it can also note a *result still available* when it reaches the *third* count in the COUNT-UP goal. Although the set representing the second addend contains different objects than the set of objects counted by the COUNT-UP goal at that point, the tagging of all objects as equivalent allows the system to generalize over the specific objects and to recognize the numerlog produced in both counts as being the same.[1] To avoid this second redundancy, HPM also creates another new rule, SUM/SECOND, which uses the results for the second addend during COUNT-UP and thus is obliged to recount only the objects corresponding to the first addend. HPM has now produced two competing rules, one that counts up from the first addend and one that counts up from the second addend. Because the rules apply under exactly the same conditions, HPM selects one of the two for application on a given trial. Thus, one procedure is used sometimes and the other at other times—by a random choice process.

How does this situation—in which a choice is made on each trial between counting up from the first addend and counting up from the second—become transformed into one in which counting up from the larger, regardless of order, is always chosen? Consider the outcomes of applying the two rules. For any given problem, one of the rules will lead to the system's counting up from the larger addend (SUM/SECOND in this case) and the other rule will lead to counting up from the smaller. We need not be concerned further with developments following from SUM/SECOND; the path from there to a full MIN procedure is a matter of applying the *untouched result* heuristic. However, HPM's handling of the SUM/FIRST procedure bears further examination.

In SUM/FIRST, two MAKE-SET goals produce objects representing each of the addends. The ending point of the smaller addend count is taken as the starting point of the COUNT-UP process, and the set of objects representing the smaller addend is entered as a subset of the COUNT-UP goal's set of "objects already counted." As counting proceeds, HPM notes that the COUNT-UP goal's set of counted objects attains the same size as the set of objects representing the *larger* addend. The system's tagging of all countable objects as equivalent allows it to "ignore" the fact that some of the counted objects compared to the larger-

---

[1]Imagine counting out two pennies ("one, *two*") and then three more ("one, two, *three*"). If you then count up all the pennies together, there will be a point where you have counted two pennies "again" and another where you have counted three "again" ("one, *two, three,* four, five"). You may not have assigned the same number name to the same penny both times, but you have assigned the same number name to *some* penny both times.

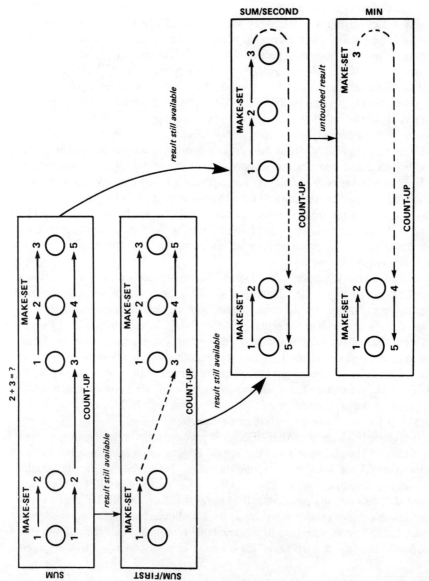

FIG. 7.3. Modified model for inventing MIN.

addend set were from the smaller-addend set. The *result still available* heuristic applies to the SUM/FIRST procedure at that point much as it did to the SUM procedure earlier. A new rule is constructed that uses the count of objects for the larger addend, and thus counts on from the larger addend. When that new rule applies, the COUNT-UP procedure applies only to the objects representing the first addend. This is the same as the SUM/SECOND procedure. The system uses the fact that the same rule has been rediscovered on the basis of different evidence as grounds for preferring that rule over competing rules.[2] As a result, SUM/SECOND comes to be regularly chosen and SUM/FIRST drops out.

The final step in the process is the transition to MIN. Once a preference for starting the COUNT-UP from the larger addend is established, the *untouched result* heuristic can apply much as in the first version of HPM. This leads to elimination of the MAKE-SET count for the larger addend, which results in the MIN procedure.

The new account of the development from SUM to MIN differs in a number of important respects from the initial version of HPM. The transitions depend on two heuristics, *result still available* and *untouched result,* rather than on the three heuristics in the original account. This means that the system is no longer burdened with the need to compare memory traces across different problems; the learning events that take place depend only on observations that the system makes *within* single solution episodes. In addition to allowing the system to function with a smaller active memory, this reduces the system's dependence on "built-in" mathematical knowledge of commutativity and problem equivalence. Finally, it allows the system to give a better account of the empirical observation that children can switch from SUM to MIN under circumstances rendering across-problem comparisons unlikely, if not impossible (Groen & Resnick, 1977).

MIN has been invented, according to this account, through application of a small number of general strategy heuristics by a system that keeps track of and inspects its own procedures. The system can use fewer heuristics and avoid a possible working memory overload because it begins this learning process already in command of certain key information about the *semantics* of counting. Both versions know about one-to-one pairing of count words and countable objects and can be said to know the cardinality principle in Gelman and Gallistel's (1978; cf. Greeno, Riley, & Gelman, in press) sense. The second version also knows the order indifference principle. That is, it is indifferent to *which* objects are counted, thus allowing it to treat as "the same quantity" any count of

---

[2]Although the machinery to actually implement this is not yet in operation, it is easy to see how a system could use the rediscovery of a rule on the basis of different evidence as grounds for increasing the preference for that rule over competing rules. The facilities for simulating this process already exist in the PRISM programming environment in which HPM runs, and have been effectively used in a program that acquires successively more sophisticated grammar rules for language generation (Langley, in press).

objects that arrives at the same ending number regardless of which objects have been counted.

Although MIN performance is well explained, an important limit to HPM's knowledge must be noted. HPM's MIN procedure is based on a set of rules specific to number pairs: When 2 and 3 appear, it will start at 3; when 9 and 7 appear it will start at 9, and so forth. This does not reflect a general principle of commutativity. Although it is easy to imagine that a child might coordinate its existing knowledge of larger and smaller numbers (see Resnick, in press) with its MIN rules to eventually produce a more general commutativity schema based on part-whole understanding, we have not yet taken steps to formulate such a theory explicitly. Such a theory would have to show how schemata can be built from an inspection of procedural rules or procedural traces. In the example that follows, we will consider more explicitly how schematic and procedural knowledge may interact in learning.

CONSTRUCTING PROCEDURES ON THE BASIS OF SCHEMATIC KNOWLEDGE

We have seen that very specific knowledge about counting played a role in HPM's invention of MIN. We turn next to a more explicit examination of the role of schematic declarative knowledge in constructing a new procedure. More broadly, we are interested in constructing a new procedure. More broadly, we are interested in what kinds of understanding may underlie procedural knowledge and how understanding and procedural competence interact.

Over the past several years, we have conducted instructional experiments in which children are taught arithmetic procedures through a form of instruction where they must alternate between steps in a written arithmetic algorithm and steps in a corresponding calculation using Dienes blocks (blocks with different shapes and sizes to represent units, tens, and hundreds). This "mapping instruction" is intended to produce the conditions under which the child will recognize the correspondences between steps in the two procedures and thereby: (a) construct an abstraction that references both domains; and (b) transport into the less well-understood domain (in this case, written arithmetic) declarative knowledge that had already been constructed for the better-understood domain (here, block arithmetic). Although some children make great advances in understanding through such instruction and come to construct elegant explanations of why the written arithmetic procedures work as they do (Resnick, 1982), others make only minimal progress (Omanson, 1982). The differences appear to lie in the kinds of correspondences between the two procedures that they recognize and the kinds of new declarative knowledge about number and arithmetic they thereby construct. This in turn depends at least partly on the kind of declarative knowledge available and accessible at the beginning of a learning segment. It also, of course, depends on certain more general "strategies" of learning.

We can examine the protocols of some of these instructional sessions as a way of gaining a sense of how correspondences are recognized or constructed, and how the recognition of correspondences leads to the construction of both procedural and schematic declarative knowledge. We will focus here on a single child, Molly. Molly was particularly generous with statements and actions that revealed her mental work, and she thus made the task of inducing her cognitive processes less subject to guesswork than might otherwise be the case. Molly is also a good subject for our investigation because, although she is one of the children who eventually offered elegant explanations for her written algorithms, she had a number of ''false starts''—exchanges in which she tried, but failed, to learn how blocks and written algorithms corresponded. We will consider here an initial failure episode in which her learning processes and the role of initial declarative knowledge are particularly evident.

Molly's Prior Knowledge

An introductory interview was used to establish what Molly knew about written arithmetic, Dienes block arithmetic, and the mappings between them prior to our learning episode. Molly's performance and response to questions in this inter-

TABLE 7.1
Production System for Molly's Initial Knowledge
of Adding with Blocks

PS ADDBLOCKS-1

Condition	Action
AB1: Addition problem exists.	Make block displays to represent each addend.
AB2: Addition problem exists. Two block displays are present.	Combine block displays into a single set.
AB3: Addition problem exists. Combined block set is present.	Find largest block shape.
AB4: Addition problem exists. Combined block set is present. Largest block shape is identified but uncounted.	Count largest block shape (using counting string for that shape). Store block count.
AB5: Addition problem exists. Combined block set is present. Largest block shape is counted. Uncounted block shapes are present.	Find next largest block shape.
AB6: Addition problem exists. Combined block set is present. No uncounted block shapes are present. All block counts are stored.	Combine stored block counts into numerlog.

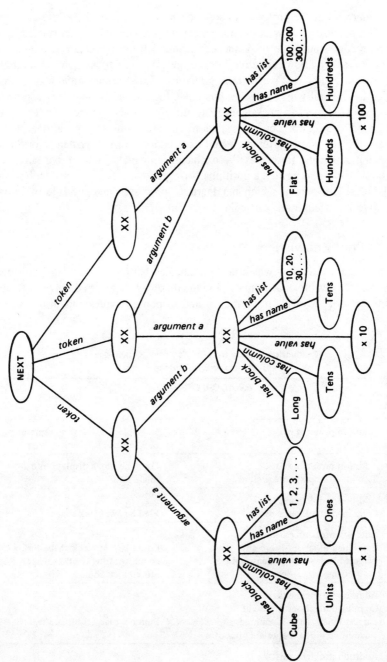

FIG. 7.4. Knowledge structure organizing column information in addition.

view made it clear that she knew how to represent quantities in Dienes blocks and how to use them for performing multidigit addition. Her procedure for adding with blocks can be expressed as the production system shown in Table 7.1. The first step (AB1) is to construct block displays to represent each of the addends in the given addition problem. The action of making block displays could be shown as a small production system that carries out actions such as finding the leftmost column, finding its corresponding block shape, counting the blocks using the appropriate counting string, and then moving to the next column and repeating the process. The actual counting operations of such a system would be identical to those used in HPM's MAKE-SET goal. This is exactly the procedure Molly used in the introductory interview.

Her ability to construct block displays in this way, together with her responses to other questions in the course of the preliminary interview, made it clear that Molly was in command of what we have previously (Resnick, 1982) called a "code map." That is, she knew the correspondences between block shapes, counting strings, and column positions. This knowledge can be represented as a declarative knowledge structure organizing column information (Figure 7.4). We have shown earlier (Resnick, Greeno, & Rowland, 1980) that this structure plays a role in the explanations for borrowing that Molly was able to construct after the mapping instruction.

In AB2, all of the blocks are combined. They are then treated as one large set to be enumerated (AB3, AB4, AB5). The same basic knowledge of the code map plus counting rules is required for this process as for the making of sets in AB1. Enumeration continues until there are no uncounted blocks (AB6), at which point a number name is assigned to the total. The entire PS ADDBLOCKS–1 production system can be thought of as a procedural instantiation of a definition of addition such as is represented by the left (Count method) branch of the ADD schema shown in Figure 7.5. Addition here is a schema whose open slots are the addends and sum and whose action nodes are making, combining, and counting up sets. Note that this is fundamentally the same procedure—now extended to include blocks of different shapes and values—that HPM began with (see Figure 7.1). It is a SUM procedure for addition.

Molly also displayed knowledge of the possibility of exchanges of blocks in the course of the preliminary interview. For example, when she used blocks to find the sums of five two-digit numbers, she accumulated large numbers of tens and ones blocks. When the experimenter suggested doing some "tricks" to make the counting easier, Molly traded 10 tens blocks for one hundreds block. This performance shows us that Molly possessed the Trade Up branch of the TRADE schema shown in Figure 7.6. This schema, which also plays a role in Molly's later explanations of borrowing, specifies that in adjacent trades the pile from which blocks (the From Blocks) are taken will grow smaller by 10 blocks and the pile into which blocks are put (the Into Blocks) will grow larger by one block. Combined with the column-value information specified in the NEXT

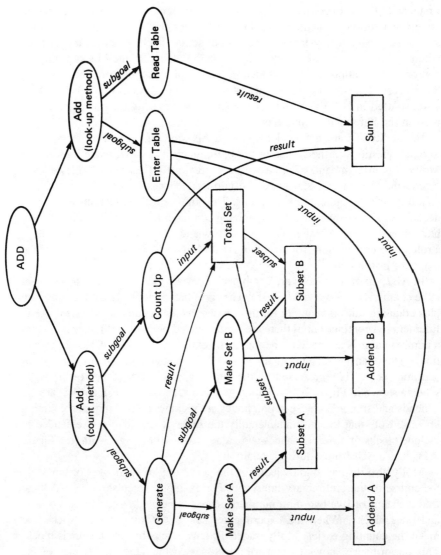

FIG. 7.5. The ADD schema.

292

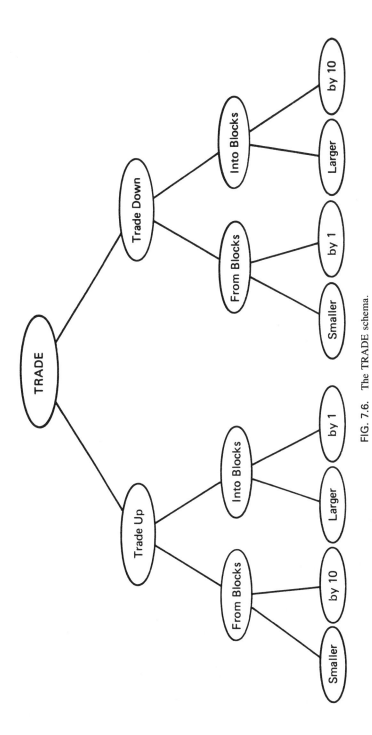

FIG. 7.6. The TRADE schema.

293

structure (Figure 7.4), this permits the conclusion that this transfer or trade has not changed the total value of the blocks.

The protocol, however, makes it clear that although Molly knew that ten-for-one trades were *allowed,* she did not consider more than ten of a shape to be a *necessary* condition for initiating such a trade. In other words, Molly had no *preference* for canonical block representations. Having just done several "making-it-easier" trades from the tens pile, she did not think of trading from the ones pile. Instead, she was content with her ADDBLOCKS procedure (Table 7.1), in which she simply counted across the decade boundary in order to add on as many ones blocks as happened to be accumulated.

TABLE 7.2
Production System for Molly's Knowledge of
Carrying in Addition

PS CARRY	
Condition	*Action*
C1: Addition problem exists.	Find rightmost column. Mark column as active.
C2: Addition problem exists. Active column is present.	Find sum of active column.
C3: Addition problem exists. Active column is present. Sum of active column is present.	Test sum of active column for total number of digits.
C4: Addition problem exists. Active column is present. Sum of active column has one digit.	Write sum of active column. Mark active column as completed.
C5: Addition problem exists. Active column is present. Sum of active column has two digits. At least one uncompleted column is present.	Write rightmost digit of active column sum. Carry leftmost digit of active column sum (i.e., write digit above next left column). Mark active column as completed.
C6: Addition problem exists. Active column is completed. At least one uncompleted column is present.	Find next left column. Mark column as active.
C7: Addition problem exists. Active column is present. Sum of active column has two digits. No uncompleted columns are present.	Write all digits of active column sum.
C8: Addition problem exists. Active column is completed. No uncompleted columns are present.	Declare problem solved.

The preliminary interview also established that Molly knew the standard algorithms for written carrying. Her knowledge of carrying can be represented in the form of a production system, PS CARRY, shown in Table 7.2. In this procedure, the rightmost column is identified first (C1), and its sum found (C2). This sum is then tested (C3). If it has one digit, the sum is written down and the column treated as completed (C4). If there are two digits, the rightmost digit is written and the left one carried (C5). Productions C6–C8 allow the system to cycle through this process until all columns are completed. As can be seen, the productions in the system perform the standard written carrying algorithm, in which ''carry'' digits are identified and moved leftward into the next column. However, no value is assigned to the carry digit—a fact that caused difficulty for Molly when she attempted to map written and block procedures for addition.

Molly's Learning Attempt: A New Procedure for Adding with Blocks

Comparison of PS CARRY and PS ADDBLOCKS–1 shows that they map to one another at only the most global level—that is, they produce the same answer. Molly made it clear in the preliminary interview that she commanded this ''results map.'' At several points in the preliminary learning segment shown in Table 7.3, she used a failure to get the same answer as a reason to reject the new blocks procedure she was attempting to build. In this learning segment, Molly was asked to ''show something that looks like carrying with the blocks.'' As we study her response, it is quite evident that Molly adopted this goal wholeheartedly. What she attempted to do was to create a new blocks procedure that would match her written carrying procedure. This was necessary because there is nothing in her original production system, PS ADDBLOCKS–1, that corresponds to carrying. Furthermore, PS ADDBLOCKS–1 makes sets and counts combined sets from largest-to-smallest block denominations, whereas PS CARRY processes columns from right (smallest value) to left (largest value). The mismatch is sufficiently large that Molly appeared to begin essentially ''from scratch'' rather than modifying her original blocks procedure, although she clearly drew on the same declarative knowledge structures that played a role in the original ADDBLOCKS procedure.

Table 7.4 shows Molly's new production system, PS ADDBLOCKS–2, for adding with blocks. The individual production rules have been numbered to highlight their correspondence with PS CARRY (Table 7.2). No productions corresponding to C6–C8 are shown because Molly never moved beyond adding and carrying from the ones blocks.

Molly constructed the PS ADDBLOCKS–2 procedure in her first try at showing carrying with blocks (Table 7.3, lines 1–8). Then she used it a second time (lines 9–12) but was concerned over the fact that it did not yield the same answer as the written routine. Finally, in the third try (lines 13–17), Molly rejected it

TABLE 7.3
Protocol for Molly Mapping Blocks to Writing

---

1. E: Let's do this. 54 plus 27. Let me just show you a thing to do. (Puts 5 tens together on left and 4 ones together on right, then puts 2 tens in same column as the 5 tens, and 7 ones in the same column as the ones.) Now, if you think of them as sort of living in these columns—that's the tens, that's the ones—could you show me something that looks like carry with the blocks?

2. S: Hmmm. (Pauses. Puts ones together.)

3. S: (Counts the ones.) 11.

4. E: Mm-hmm.

5. S: (Counts 9 of the 11 blocks and pushes them away from the other 2.)

6. E: Tell me what you're thinking.

7. S: I'm thinking of doing—wait (counts 9 blocks), there are 9 here (pulls two blocks over to tens side and puts one block in each pile of tens).

8. S: I put a block in each pile (laughs), each of these blocks—oh! 10—(looks at E; takes 2 tens bars from the extra blocks and removes the 2 ones blocks) 'cause the blocks count 10.

9. E: Start over again. I think you have the right idea. Let's see if you do not get lost. There's the original. Now. (Sets up 54 + 27 in blocks.)

10. S: You put these together—get 11. (Pushes ones together.)

11. S: And this is the ones column—11 (laughs) in the ones column—and you take 2 out, so you have 9 (separates 2 ones blocks from the rest) so these (2 ones blocks) count as 10. (Trades the 2 ones for 2 tens and leaves 9 ones in the ones column. Counts remaining blocks.)

12. E: Does that give you the right answer?

13. S: No. (Laughs.)

14. E: Do it over here (on paper) and say it out loud to yourself and then go back and do it in the blocks.

15. S: 7 plus 4 is 11, carry the 1, then 5 plus 2 plus 1 is 8. (Points to paper. Laughs.)

16. E: All right. Now think about it. You just did it exactly right, and you said all the right things. Just try it once more.

17. S: Um, well, there were 11 here. (Points to 11 ones blocks.) I had to take 2 out. (Takes 2 ones blocks out of ones pile.) And then that's 70 here (looks at tens blocks). That's 79. This is 70 here (points to tens blocks) and this is 9 (points to ones blocks), 79, 80, and 81. (Looks at E.) *But I can't do the carrying.*

TABLE 7.4
Production System for Molly's Knowledge of Carrying with Blocks

PS ADDBLOCKS-2

	Condition	Action
AB1a:	Addition problem exists.	Make block displays to represent each addend.
AB1b:	Addition problem exists. Two block displays are present.	Find smallest block shape in both displays and combine. Mark block shape as active.
AB2:	Addition problem exists. Active shape is present.	Count blocks in active shape.
AB3:	Addition problem exists. Active shape is present and counted.	Test active display for total number of blocks.
AB4:	Addition problem exists. Active shape is counted. Count is ≤ 9.	Declare active shape completed.
AB5a:	Addition problem exists. Active shape is counted. Count is > 9. At least one uncounted shape is present.	Keep 9 blocks in active shape. Move extra blocks into next block-shape pile. Declare active shape completed.
AB5b:	Addition problem exists. Extra blocks are in next block-shape pile.	Convert extra blocks to shape of next block-shape pile.

and returned to her old system (Table 7.1), saying, "But I can't do the carrying."

Consider what kind of reasoning and knowledge Molly must have used in constructing and then eventually rejecting PS ADDBLOCKS–2. She began by making block sets for each addend (AB1a), thus beginning to apply the schema for addition shown in the left side of Figure 7.5. How did Molly know that this "block-defined" definition of addition as combining sets actually mapped to the addition-facts "look-up" definition that was implicit in her written procedure? She could not know by inspecting the actual steps in the procedure, for there was nothing corresponding to combining and counting objects in the written procedure. Yet she was able to map "getting the sum" in look-up memory (C2) to "counting the blocks in a combined set" (AB2). It seems likely that Molly had constructed this mapping at some previous time (the speed of performance on this occasion was too great for the construction to have been made during our observational period). If this is so, then presumably she had a knowledge struc-

ture of the form shown in the right side of Figure 7.5. The look-up method for
addition requires that a table be entered and then read. The two methods, Count
and Lookup, are recognized in the schema as *equivalent* because they operate on
the same input (addends A and B) and yield the same output (the sum). The
variables in an addition problem are thus bindable to either the Count or the
Lookup branch of the ADD schema.

Production AB1b matches the first production (C1) of PS CARRY. This
mapping reveals Molly's understanding of a basic principle of addition, which
we call *partitioning*. Molly clearly knew that to add numbers it is permissible to
partition the numbers into any convenient smaller quantities, find partial sums,
and then add up the partial sums. This principle of partitioning is, in fact, what
permits column-by-column processing in multidigit numbers. In Molly's case,
she had to know this principle in order to: (a) recognize the equivalence of right-
to-left and left-to-right procedures, and thus to use both of them interchangeably;
(b) be indifferent to whether all the block shapes are combined at one time (as in
her original procedure) or only successively (as in the new procedure). The
partitioning principle plus the correspondence between the smallest shape and the
rightmost column (as represented in Figure 7.4) are knowledge that clearly
underlay this part of Molly's new procedure construction.

Molly was next confronted with a more complex reconstruction task, one for
which she was less well prepared. She counted 11 ones blocks in the combined
sets. Had Molly not been deliberately attempting to match her written algorithm,
we would have expected her simply to move on to counting the next block
denomination because her previous performance had made it clear that she had
no rule demanding canonical block displays. However, her written carry procedure next called for a test and contingent actions (C3–5, Table 7.2). The
matching blocks rules are AB3–5 (Table 7.4). What Molly appeared to do here
was to map the condition of C4, *sum has 1 digit,* to having nine or fewer blocks;
and the condition of C5, *sum has 2 digits,* to having more than nine blocks. In
other words, she recognized that more than nine blocks would require more than
one digit if written. This is why she repeatedly counted out nine ones blocks from
the combined set. Building a production to match C5, she kept the nine blocks
and moved the "extras" left. Keeping nine was, for her, equivalent to writing
the rightmost digit; moving the extras to the left was equivalent to carrying the
leftmost digit.

This was, of course, an error: 10 ones should have been carried left and the
extra ones blocks allowed to remain in place. Yet exactly the same use of a
schematic knowledge structure that produced the correct mapping for AB1b and
AB2 can account for this error. Figure 7.7 shows the schema for carrying that
Molly appears to have had and to have applied in this episode. On the left, her
schema for written carrying is shown; this is a declarative structure that corresponds to PS CARRY. On the right is the representation Molly constructed for
the blocks in the course of our observations. Presumably, she constructed the

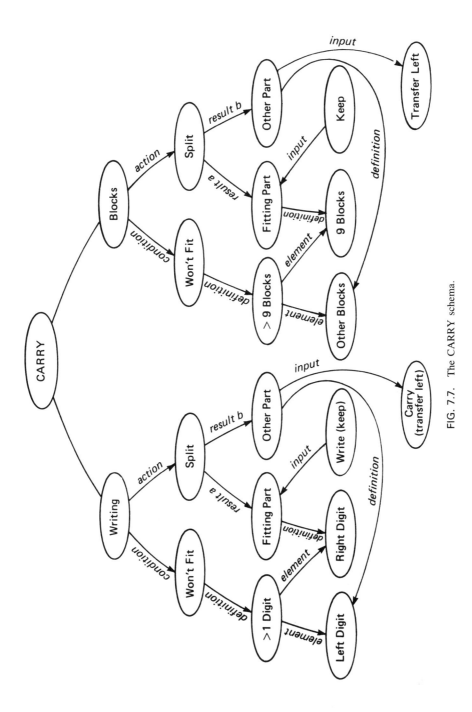

FIG. 7.7. The CARRY schema.

blocks schema by building nodes that exactly matched the already existent writing nodes.

Molly's schema for written carrying specified a *condition* (i.e., the answer to a column not fitting) and an *action* (i.e., splitting the answer). The schema specifies that an answer will not fit when it has more than one digit. In this case the rightmost digit is defined as *fitting* and is written down, whereas the left-hand digit is defined as not fitting and is carried into the next column. Molly appears to have tried to construct matching nodes for blocks. She established a "won't fit" condition and defined it as having more blocks than can be written with one digit—therefore more than nine blocks. The blocks could now be divided into the part that fit (nine blocks) and was therefore kept, and the "other" part (the other blocks), which was transferred left. Her representation of sums "fitting" or not, according to number of digits, was what led her to construct rules AB4 and AB5a.

The mapping *process* then, was perfect. Molly's error apparently derived not from a difficulty in reasoning or in finding and applying analogies, but in a less than optimal representation on the source side of the analogy. If Molly had represented a two-digit number as a quantity greater than 10, and partitioned the digits into a ones part (the right digit) to be written and a tens part (the left digit) to be carried, then her blocks schema would have also included a tens and ones partition of blocks, with the ones to be kept and the tens to be transferred over. Using such a schema, she might have constructed the following rule:

CONDITION	*ACTION*
AB5a: Addition problem exists.	Partition active shape blocks
Active shape is counted.	(10 blocks plus extra blocks).
Count is > 10.	Move 10 blocks left.
At least one uncounted shape is present.	Declare active shape completed.

With this procedure, Molly could have added a rule for trading tens blocks and produced a correct blocks representation of carrying. Given her actual procedure, however, Molly was clearly puzzled, as can be seen in the protocol (Table 7.3). She knew that she should not have ones blocks mixed in with the tens blocks, and so she exchanged the ones for tens (a one-for-one, and thus an incorrect, trade). However, she also knew that there was something wrong with this trade. Hence her laugh (Table 7.3, line 8) and the hesitation that prompted the experimenter to have her start again. On the next try, when Molly reached this point (line 11) she again showed discomfort, and this time she acknowledged that the blocks did not yield the right answer (lines 12–13).

In her final try, Molly seemed to be inspecting her new production system to find the source of the error (line 17). She ran through the whole system up through AB5a. But she did not go on to production AB5b. Instead, she counted up all of the blocks on the table, first counting the tens and then the nine ones that had been selected by rule AB5a ("This is 70 here, and this is 9"). Then she used her old counting-on routine, starting at 79 and counting in the two "extra" ones.

What made Molly finally reject her own incorrect blocks procedure (especially AB5b)? A reasonable hypothesis is that when Molly moved the two "extra" blocks left, she interpreted the result in terms of the rules of column block correspondence that are embedded in the NEXT structure shown in Figure 7.4. The NEXT structure specifies that all blocks in the tens column must be tens blocks. To make her display accord with this structure, Molly needed to construct the production rule (AB5b) that converts the extra ones to tens. However, the conversion itself called up another of Molly's schemata, TRADE (Figure 7.6). This schema specifies that the column (pile) from which blocks are taken gets smaller by *ten* blocks, and the column (pile) into which blocks are put gets larger by *one* block. It thus specifies a ten-for-one trade, not the one-for-one trade that Molly made in order to satisfy the requirements of NEXT. Molly had created a dilemma for herself. Because she had only two extra ones blocks, not ten, she could not satisfy the requirements of both TRADE and NEXT at the same time. She had encountered a contradiction that she could not resolve. She therefore "gave up" on the goal of showing carrying. Specifically, she deleted from her procedure the steps that created the dilemma: Because she could not exchange (AB5b), she avoided the step that produced the necessity of exchanging (AB5a). But this meant that she could not "carry" blocks over—that is, she could not construct an action for the Blocks side of the CARRY schema (Figure 7.7) that would match the transfer-left node on the Writing side.

This episode and our analysis of it point to several key features of the learning process. We will mention them briefly here, reserving a fuller discussion and a consideration of their implications for a theory of individual differences until after we have presented another example of learning. First, throughout the episode Molly was pursuing a "metagoal" that required the construction of new knowledge. As we have shown, her performance with the blocks clearly reflected a deliberate effort to construct a new procedure that matched written carrying. In HPM too, invention of MIN occurs because of a metagoal to construct a more efficient procedure. We will comment later on differences in metagoal setting as potential sources of individual differences in learning. Second, Molly failed in her effort to construct an analog to written carrying because of the particular schematic representation of carrying that she brought to the task. Her carrying *procedure* was flawless, but the schema underlying it provided a weak representation of the semantics of carrying (cf. Resnick, 1982). Thus the role of domain-specific, semantic knowledge in learning that emerged in HPM is even more strongly emphasized in Molly's case. At the same time, this case underlines the active interplay between schematic and procedural knowledge in learning. Molly clearly had to refer to schematic knowledge in order to decide what block productions would be analogous to writing productions. Further, the need to build new production rules sometimes forced Molly to *construct* new schemata, which then guided construction of production rules. Finally, it was the recognition of a *contradiction* (the fact that the two schemata could not both be instantiated at once) that kept Molly searching for a solution and eventually forced her to give up on the effort.

A LEARNING EPISODE FROM GENEVAN RESEARCH

The role of schema contradiction in learning can also be observed in a rather different learning episode in which no procedures were to be built. In this episode, which focused on the concept of conservation of liquid quantity, a child was asked to predict whether quantities would remain the same under various transformations and to explain apparent discrepancies between quantity and appearance. The episode is taken from Inhelder, Sinclair, and Bovet's (1974) teaching experiments in which attempts were made to induce growth in understanding by directing children's attention to contradictions between their predic-

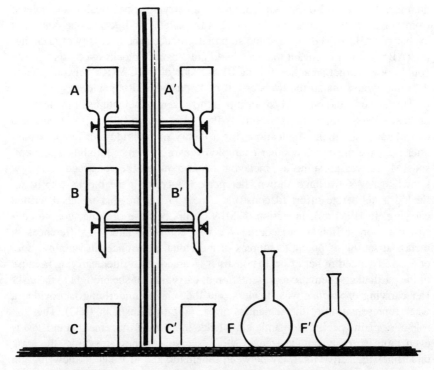

FIG. 7.8.   Apparatus for testing knowledge of liquid conservation. (From Inhelder, Sinclair, & Bovet, 1974.)

tions and the actual behavior of physical systems. Figure 7.8 shows the apparatus used. In the first phase the child, Jac, was asked to predict whether the same amount of liquid (from F filled to the top of the round portion) poured into A and A′ would produce the same amounts in C and C′. Jac predicted equality of C and C′. We can therefore attribute to him the knowledge that quantities that are equal before transfer are equal after transfer. Two schemata are involved in this knowledge. The first is a TRANSFER schema, in which the "before" container and the "after" container are both linked to the same amount of liquid. The second is an EQUAL/LIQUID–1 schema (Figure 7.9) that specifies the conditions under which two containers contain the same amount of liquid. EQUAL/LIQUID–1 specifies that the two containers have the same amount of liquid if the liquid column in each has the same height and width. Using these schemata, Jac could

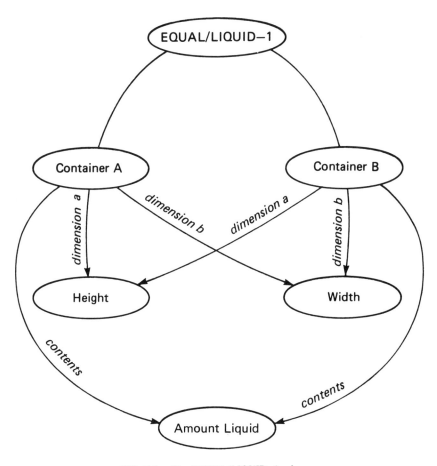

FIG. 7.9.   The EQUAL/LIQUID–1 schema.

assert first that A and A' had the same amount of liquid (by trying to and succeeding in instantiating EQUAL/LIQUID) and then that the amounts should remain equal when transferred to B and B' because (according to TRANSFER) there would be the same *amount of liquid* before and after the transfer. This prediction in turn led him to expect the heights of the water columns in the intermediate jars, B and B', to be the same—because EQUAL/LIQUID-1 requires this.

But Jac's prediction was not confirmed. When he actually watched the transfer, he expressed surprise at the heights in B and B': "Gosh, it's coming up very high (in B'), but I've poured with the same flask. . . ." He had encountered a contradiction similar to Molly's. That is, he could not meet the requirements of two schemata at once. If the heights are not equal, B and B' cannot have an equal amount of liquid according to EQUAL/LIQUID-1; but they *must* have an equal amount according to TRANSFER. Jac also said, "I poured it all!", a comment that suggests he also possessed another schema, PART-WHOLE/LIQUID, specifying that the whole can be divided into parts and all parts together make a quantity equal to the whole. This schema combines with TRANSFER to produce an implicit assertion that the total quantity should be equal, since all of the parts were transferred.

In the second phase, the interviewer tried to focus Jac's attention explicitly on this conflict. A and A' were filled to the same level from F. The liquid in A was allowed to flow into B. Jac was then asked to let enough liquid flow into B' ". . . that there's the same amount to drink in B and B'." He was then asked to predict the quantities in C and C' if B and B' were allowed to flow through, and to check his predictions. Under these conditions Jac found a further contradiction: He could not instantiate PART-WHOLE/LIQUID and EQUAL/LIQUID-1 at the same time. He said, "If I stop at the same place (i.e., if the height node is the same for container B and container B'), then I won't have enough to drink at the end. Look, I left a bit up there" (i.e., then I won't have used all the parts, so the whole will not be the same after transfer). Then he tried the opposite: "To have the same at the end, I've got to put it all in (an assertion of PART-WHOLE/LIQUID), but then it comes up to a different place" (i.e., I can't instantiate EQUAL/LIQUID-1 because the heights in the two containers are not the same).

Eventually, Jac let PART-WHOLE/LIQUID and TRANSFER prevail. He said, "Well, it must still be the same amount of lemonade; it's all there. . . ." He then had to search for a justification for not being able to instantiate EQUAL/LIQUID-1. To do this he called upon a COMPENSATION schema (Figure 7.10), which specifies that if the width of a container is narrow the effect is to "squash up" the liquid, and that this in turn has the effect of making the height of the liquid higher. Conversely, a wider width "spreads out" the liquid, which makes its height lower. His words were: "I know. It just looks as if there's more. . . . In the thin glass the lemonade is all squashed up, it has to go up; in the wide one it's spread out." The COMPENSATION schema can be

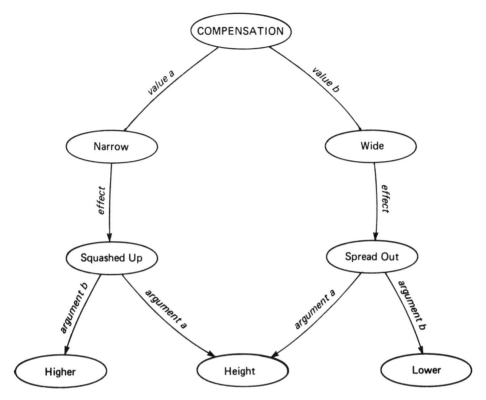

FIG. 7.10.   The COMPENSATION schema.

incorporated into EQUAL/LIQUID as shown in Figure 7.11 (EQUAL/LI-QUID–2). Now Jac could instantiate PART-WHOLE, TRANSFER, and EQUAL/LIQUID–2 simultaneously. He had resolved the contradiction by using one schema to elaborate another.

In the final phase of the study several weeks later, unequal quantities (from F and F') were poured into A and A'. New jars were used for B and B' of a size such that when the liquid flowed into them from A and A', the heights were the same. Jac was perplexed by this. This suggests that he had one more schema, SIZE/AMOUNT, which specifies that if the sizes of the containers stand in a certain relationship, then the amount of liquid in the containers stands in the same relationship. Since F > F', there should be more liquid in B than in B'. But according to his original EQUAL/LIQUID–1 schema (i.e., before COMPEN-SATION was added), equal heights imply equal amounts of liquid. Thus, at first he had a contradiction: He could not instantiate both SIZE/AMOUNT and EQUAL/LIQUID–1. His resolution was, apparently, to call again on COMPEN-SATION, and thus on the revised EQUAL/LIQUID–2 schema. This allowed him to predict that "It's still less." He then went on to confirm that this must be so, by asserting that all of the other relevant schemata could be instantiated with the same data. He said, "There's always less in this line . . ." (thus TRANS-FER is compatible) and "We haven't added any in the middle . . ." (thus PART-WHOLE/LIQUID is compatible) ". . . so it must be right."

The outcome of the total learning sequence was a knowledge structure in which several schemata were brought into relationship with one another (Figure

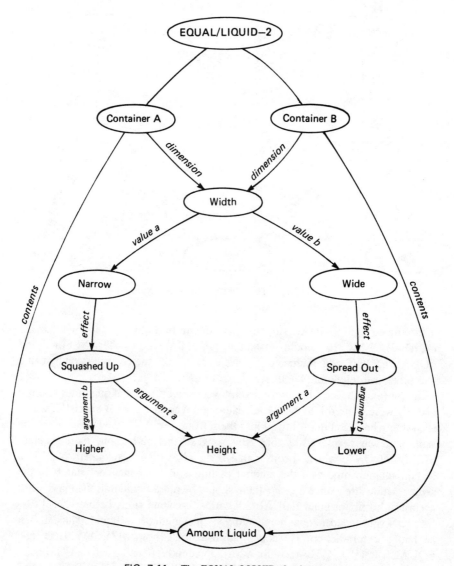

FIG. 7.11.   The EQUAL/LIQUID–2 schema.

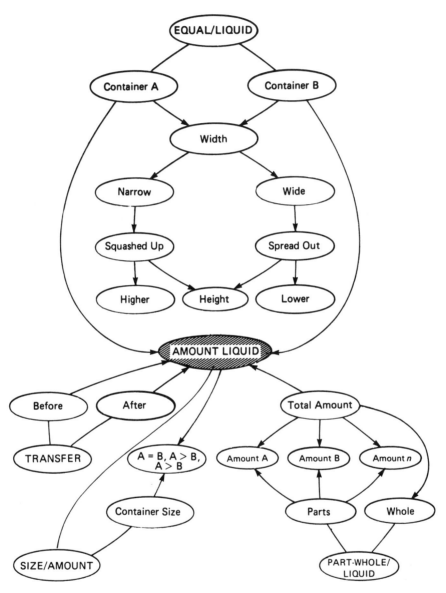

FIG. 7.12.   Combined schemata as outcome of learning liquid conservation principle.

7.12). The shared node for all of them is "amount of liquid." Thus, the question of quantity (amount) was—appropriately enough—at the heart of Jac's learning about conservation.

THE SOURCES OF INDIVIDUAL DIFFERENCES

With these three examples of learning in hand, we can now reconsider in a fresh way the question of individual differences in ability to learn. Our approach is to inspect our three examples for features that are clearly critical to the learning process and that may be present in different degrees in individuals.

It is commonplace to divide the sources of differences in learning ability into two broad classes: capacity differences and knowledge differences. A similar distinction is made in accounts of cognitive development (Chi & Rees, in press). Capacity differences are structural differences, such as size of working memory or speed of processing. Although capacity may grow with age, it is at any given point in development a fixed characteristic of an individual, setting limits on the individual's ability to process many different kinds of tasks. The speed difference in access to overlearned codes identified by Hunt (1978) and others is an example of a capacity difference. So also is the enlarged memory space that Case (1978) suggests is what allows older children to learn concepts and ideas that younger children are normally unable to grasp.

Knowledge differences are those that are acquired through learning about specific domains. Because the relevant knowledge may vary sharply from domain to domain, individuals who are likely to learn easily in one domain by virtue of prior knowledge may have no particular advantage in some other domain. Several recent analyses of the cognitive processes involved in taking intelligence tests have shown that differences in depth of knowledge may account for individual differences in test performance. For example, Curtis and Glaser (1981) have shown that people who score high on verbal aptitude tests that include analogies tend both to have larger vocabularies and to know more about the nuances of word meanings than those whose scores are low. Pellegrino, Chi, and Majetic (1978) have revealed a body of specific knowledge about number that accompanies good performance on numerical analogies. Sternberg (1977) has shown age- and ability-related differences in the kinds of analogy-solving strategies that people use, and Cooper (1980) has identified differences in spatial processing strategies. Thus, domain-specific knowledge relevant to learning also includes differences in knowledge of strategies.

Both domain-specific knowledge and capacity differences play roles in the learning episodes we have discussed in some detail. These two classes, however, do not seem to provide the complete picture. We therefore consider two other potential sources of individual differences that clearly interact with both knowledge and capacity differences but do not seem to fit well in either category. The first of these *metaprocedural knowledge*—knowledge about the general structure of procedures. This kind of knowledge is central to HPM's procedure-modification process and can also be noted in Molly's procedure-construction efforts. The second source of differences, which may be more a matter of temperament than of cognitive abilities, is degree of engagement with the learning problem at hand. We refer to these as differences in *metagoals* because they seem to produce differences in what the learner is *trying* to do at any given time.

Domain-Specific Knowledge

We begin with what is, in our examples, perhaps the most obvious source of learning power: prior knowledge about the domain itself. In each of our three examples, specific knowledge of the domain is required in order to learn something new. Jac was able to resolve the conflict between the EQUAL/LIQUID and the TRANSFER and PART-WHOLE schemata by drawing on knowledge that allowed him to assert that things do not always look the way they really are. The knowledge he drew on was embedded in his COMPENSATION schema (Figure 7.10). Without this schema, which presumably resulted from his prior experience with the squashing and spreading out of substances in containers of different shapes, he could not have constructed the unified knowledge structure that we saw at the end of his performance. Further, had he not possessed strong schemata for TRANSFER and PART-WHOLE/LIQUID, each consonant with and supporting the other, he would not have so strongly *expected* the liquids to be equal in the two containers. As a result, he would have been content to declare the liquids unequal when they reached different heights. In that case, he would have had no need even to begin the search that led to the COMPENSATION schema. Although the mechanisms of search and recognition are left unspecified in our present analysis of Jac, it is clear that he could not have learned what he did without access to each of these domain-specific schemata specifying properties of liquids.

Molly provided examples of both learning successes and learning failures as a result of specific schematic knowledge. As our analysis reveals, the ease with which she constructed the first steps in the procedural analogy clearly depended on prior knowledge about equivalences between blocks and written representations of number and arithmetic operations. Molly already knew that addition could be performed in both representations and would yield the same result. Note, however, that her particular schematic representation of written borrowing *inhibited* her capacity to complete the procedure construction she was working on: She created a contradiction between her TRADE and her CARRY schemata because her representation of CARRY led her to transfer the nonfitting "extra" blocks rather than the 10 ones blocks that would have been transferred if she had attempted to make the display canonical.

As we noted earlier, Molly's performance prior to the request to map blocks to written carrying makes it clear that the appropriate plan of action for cases with too many blocks in a column (i.e., transferring 10 of them) was *available* to

Molly. The problem seems to be *accessing* that knowledge. Why did Molly work to construct a new procedure for identifying and discarding extra blocks when she had a perfectly good one (actually a better one) already available? The answer seems to lie in the fact that she was actively trying to build an analogy to her schema for written carrying and thus did not activate block knowledge directly. She thus had no "route" to her procedure for canonicizing a block display. This interpretation is supported by an episode later in Molly's protocol where she was again asked to use blocks to model written carrying. This time, however, the effort was preceded by a discussion of written carrying in which Molly correctly identified the value of the carry mark as 10. This time Molly built a perfectly correct blocks routine—i.e., she exchanged 10 ones blocks for a tens block, which she placed in the tens pile.

Molly's immediate switch to an alternative representation of carrying, which in turn produced a successful blocks analog, strongly suggests that this representation itself was already available to her. It was not constructed during her discussion with the experimenter, but the discussion reminded her of it. This phenomenon raises the question of how individual learners choose between alternative available knowledge structures as a basis for building new knowledge. It seems that momentary events can prompt a particular representation. But in the absence of specific prompts it seems likely that the "better learned" or more practiced alternative will be chosen—in Molly's case, a digit-fitting rather than a quantity-transposition representation of carrying. From our examples, we are not able to directly address the question of how well established particular schemata are. Other evidence, however, suggests that a considerable degree of reliability and perhaps automaticity of access may be required if knowledge is to function well in new learning (cf. Lesgold & Resnick, 1982).

As we have shown, HPM's learning is also facilitated by specific prior knowledge as it constructs its more efficient addition procedure. When the program is allowed to generalize over counting objects, it is able to make a series of transitions leading it from SUM to MIN on the basis of only within-problem observation. The prior knowledge in the second version of the system, which causes it to treat sets as equivalent if they yield the same final count regardless of whether the same objects were counted (see Figure 7.3), enables the system to move quite efficiently to a new strategy in which counting-on always begins with the larger addend. Without that knowledge the program can make the transition from SUM to MIN, but the path taken involves additional complexities that slow the system's learning rate considerably.

HPM is able to treat different sets of objects as equivalent because it uses a system of tagging in which: (a) objects can receive more than one tag, and thus be described in more than one way; and (b) once a tag is assigned it becomes a new "object" on which the system can operate directly. The tags in HPM can be thought of as a way to allow an information-processing system to make use of alternative descriptions of the same object. HPM only allows for a single alternative description, but there is no intrinsic reason why a more powerful system could not maintain multiple descriptions (or "perspectives") for each concept it manipulates. The examples given by HPM suggest that the capacity to do so, and the particular knowledge available for each description, might be important sources of variance in learning capacity.

In each of our examples we have seen that the presence or absence of specific knowledge and the degree to which this knowledge is accessible influence the capacity to learn a particular piece of new knowledge. This means that people who already know more in a domain will, in general, be able to learn new things in that domain more quickly and reliably than those who know less. Cumulated over time, relatively small initial differences in knowledge could produce quite large learning ability differences. Indeed, knowledge differences of this kind may be so dominant in contributing to ability to learn in specific domains that they override other possible sources of differences in learning ability. Thus, for example, by the end of high school the main difference between those with high and with low mathematical "aptitude" may lie in the greater amount of mathematical knowledge the former have.

This leaves us with the question of where the greater amount of mathematical knowledge came from in the first place. Unless we want to argue that it is present in some form genetically, or that differences in opportunity to learn mathematics and/or motivation to engage in such learning account *entirely* for later observed differences, we are still forced to look further for individual differences that could account for the rather large differences in knowledge that are clearly present by the age of 15 or so.

Capacity Differences

One obvious possibility is to look for capacity differences of various kinds. There are several ways in which individuals might differ in basic capacity for learning. These include differences in: (a) the speed with which elementary units of processing are carried out; (b) the number of exposures needed to notice similarities or differences in stimulus conditions and thus build a performance rule, or to "strengthen" a knowledge structure or associative rule to the point where it is easily accessible; and (c) working memory capacity. On the basis of our three learning examples, we can discuss only the last—working memory capacity—in detail. However, we will first comment briefly on the two other types of capacity differences and their role in learning.

Processing Speed. Small but reliable differences in speed of elementary processes—especially access to verbal codes—have been documented for high and low performers on verbal aptitude tests (Hunt, 1978) and for individuals of different ages (Bisanz & Resnick, 1978; Bisanz, Danner, & Resnick, 1979). Hunt suggested that these small differences can cumulate over time to large differences in amounts of verbal knowledge held by individuals. Thus these differences in speed—which are presumed to be biological—can have dual impact: They make processing during a learning episode more efficient, and they provide a more extensive knowledge base for learning.

Exposure Frequency.   Although it has been less extensively and less directly studied, much the same dual effect can be hypothesized for differences in the number of exposures it takes to strengthen an association or to notice patterns of co-occurrences, similarities, or differences. Many computer simulations of learning include mechanisms for incrementally strengthening knowledge components, usually based upon the frequency with which the components are accessed (Langley, in press; Langley, Neches, Neves, & Anzai, 1981). We have discussed how HPM, for example, could increment the strength of a production rule each time it is rediscovered. This strengthening mechanism is what eventually leads HPM reliably to choose the count-on-from-larger-addend production rules. If humans have similar learning mechanisms, then differences in how much a rule's strength is incremented each time it is accessed could produce important differences in how quickly individuals learned.

HPM's procedure modification also depends on its recognizing that the conditions for one of its transformation heuristics has been met—for example, that two counts yield the same result and so there is thus a "result still available." How many exposures are required for this recognition to take place? Observation of children makes it clear that construction of counting-on, and later of MIN, takes place over long periods of practice. Hence, more than a single such exposure is clearly required. It is reasonable to assume that people will differ in the number of exposures they require before a threshold of "recognition" is passed. Such differences could well produce important individual differences in learning rates.

We may imagine that learning difficulties resulting from the need for frequent exposure to certain conditions would respond well to instructional efforts that arrange for frequent exposure and perhaps highlight relevant conditions for the learner. Individuals less dependent on such specially structured instructional stimuli could be expected to learn more easily even in an informationally "noisy" environment; they would more quickly discover regularities in the world and more quickly invent procedures that recognize these regularities. This would help to explain the often-noted finding that "low ability" individuals are more sensitive to the quality of instruction than "high ability" individuals (Cronbach & Snow, 1977).

Working Memory Capacity.   The capacity difference whose influence on learning is most directly highlighted in our examples is the limited number of places in working memory. Several investigators (Case, 1978; Kintsch, 1974) have argued that limited working memory capacity can critically limit learning.

Case has proposed a central role in cognitive development for memory capacity, suggesting that expansion of this capacity is what enables the more complex reasoning of older children. He argues that memory limitations interfere with young children's ability to learn complex things because the learning processes themselves use up critical memory capacity. Even in theories that are not aimed explicitly at accounting for individual differences, the number of "slots" in working memory turns out to have an impact on how easily a system is able to learn or to comprehend new information. An interesting case in point is Kintsch's theory of text comprehension in which the number of slots in working memory limits the number of propositions that can be carried over from one processing cycle to the next. This in turn influences the system's capacity to understand texts that are not perfectly coherent or that have complex metastructures (Kintsch & van Dijk, 1978).

Among the three learning examples under consideration in this paper, only HPM is explicit about assumptions concerning working memory. Close inspection of HPM's code makes it clear that too small a working memory would critically hamper the system's ability to construct the more efficient MIN procedure. Neches (1981b) found that only about a third of the symbols in the HPM production systems for addition were required for a system concerned with performance alone; the remaining two-thirds were necessitated by the learning mechanisms. In fact, the system could actually function more efficiently—in the sense of entering fewer propositions in working memory, matching fewer production rules, and having fewer conflicts to resolve in selecting rules to apply—with a *smaller* working memory, if it were concerned only with *performing* an already established procedure rather than inventing a new one. However, with a small working memory there is only a small chance that all of the information needed for learning will be in working memory on a given processing cycle. Thus, *learning* rates would degrade, because more trials would be needed before certain critical propositions entered working memory.

It is clear, then, that differences in working memory capacity could critically affect learning. With a larger memory, the probability of a learning event on a given trial would increase; but the processing time required to produce that event would also increase dramatically as the combinatorics of searching long-term memory for matches to production rules grew with each proposition added to the active set. In fact, an infinitely large working memory could make search so slow and produce so many conflicting rule matches that learning would occur only very slowly. These observations suggest that it is not simply size of working memory that may cause differences in learning ability, but also certain skills and strategies of *memory management*—that is, of ability to constructively constrain *what* is entered into working memory. These in turn depend on certain generalized knowledge about the structure of procedures built into HPM, which we consider next.

Metaprocedural Knowledge: The Structure of Procedures

Goal Structures As a Way of Limiting Memory Requirements.   One of the ways in which a learning system can constrain its attention is through some kind of metaknowledge of the kind of structure it is trying to build. In Miller and Kintsch's (in press) model of reading comprehension, the system knows certain principles that permit it to choose propositions for retention in working memory that are most likely to summarize the current propositions and connect with new propositions as more text is read. The program uses criteria such as connectivity, inherent interest, and type of syntactic marking in deciding which propositions to retain. The principles thus maximize the likelihood that a small working memory will contain propositions necessary for constructing a coherent representation of the text and avoid the necessity for extended search that a larger working memory would involve.

HPM constrains what is entered into working memory in much the same way, except that the principles that it uses to choose among propositions are concerned with the general structure of procedures. HPM has embedded in it rather extensive knowledge about the general structure of procedures. It analyzes procedures in terms of their *goal structures,* recognizing a hierarchy of goals in which a goal at the top of the "stack" can invoke subgoals. This knowledge is used in a number of ways to guide HPM's attention-focusing mechanisms. For example, the system "knows" that when a subordinate goal is achieved, it should automatically reactivate the next superordinate goal in the stack, and so forth. When a new subordinate goal is asserted, the system "knows" it should activate and consider propositions related to methods for achieving those goals and not propositions that are linked to other goals. The system also knows that it is important to stop trying to fulfill goals as soon as possible and to restrict processing to a single plan of action at a time in order to avoid conflicting plans. This prevents the explosion of memory size that would occur if several goals were allowed to operate in parallel.

All of these constraints prevent wasted effort being put into unnecessary processing. They help minimize memory size both by allowing the system to determine precisely what information should be brought into active memory and by helping it detect unneeded information to be dropped out of active memory as quickly as possible.

The effect of this implicit knowledge on HPM's learning ability can be illustrated by considering what happens in its absence. For example, HPM has a mechanism affecting its active memory contents, called "goal-driven associative retrieval" (Neches, 1981a). This mechanism embodies the implicit knowledge just described by searching through HPM's semantic networks only in restricted directions that are determined by the processing context of the moment. This reduces the number of propositions required to be active in working memory for learning to take place. It is possible to compare runs of HPM with and without the goal-driven associative retrieval mechanism. Empirical tests of the system indicate that producing the same learning events without that mechanism would require a working memory three to five times larger than that required when the mechanism is in place. Thus, a system without this metaprocedural knowledge could still function, but would have to accept the slowdown inherent in greatly increased active memory size.

The general characteristics of HPM's goal-structure knowledge are shared with many major artificial intelligence problem-solving systems (e.g., Newell & Simon, 1972; Sacerdoti, 1977). As far as we know, however, HPM is the first *learning system* to systematically incorporate knowledge of goal structures for procedures into the learning mechanism itself. The centrality of goal-structure knowledge to HPM's learning capacity invites the conjecture that differences in the extent and depth of this knowledge may be a factor that accounts for differences in learning ability among individuals.

All of this knowledge is implicit rather than explicit in HPM. That is, it exists as part of the system's rules for action, rather than in the form of declarative knowledge structures. Presumably, a child whose knowledge of the structure of procedures matched HPM's would be able to construct and modify procedures in accordance with principles of goal-directedness, but not describe these principles—even in very informal language. However, little is known about differences in knowledge *about* goal structures or about human ability to apply that knowledge. Research on this aspect of metaprocedural knowledge may yield riches for those interested in accounting for individual differences in learning ability.

Strategies for Transforming Procedures.   HPM also points to another kind of metaprocedural knowledge that is required for actually building new procedures. This is knowledge of permissible transformations. HPM learns through the application of a limited number of strategy transformation heuristics (*result still available,* etc.). These are a subset of a group of 21 heuristics that Neches (1981b) has shown could be used by a system like HPM. Those heuristics vary considerably, both in their sophistication and in the degree of specificity in their conditions, just as individuals might differ in the number and complexity of strategies available to them.

Consider, for example, the sample heuristics listed in Table 7.5. Some heuristics are relatively weak, such as the *composition* rule (C.1) for building units from co-occurring procedures (cf. Anderson, Kline, & Beasley, 1981; Lewis, 1978). That heuristic essentially calls for chunking together actions that are frequently performed one after the other. Other heuristics are much more powerful—for example, the *side costs* heuristic (B.1) for replacing one procedure with another when the effort associated with auxiliary operations of the first procedure is too great relative to the effort expended on the main goal of the procedure.

TABLE 7.5
Sample Heuristics for Transforming Procedures

A. Reduction to a rule: replacing a procedure with an induced rule for generating its results.

   1. *Effort difference*: IF a difference in expended effort is observed when the same goal is operating on the same input(s) at different times, THEN set up a goal to find a difference between the methods used, and try to produce the circumstances that evoked the more efficient method.

B. Replacement with another method: substituting an equivalent procedure obtained by noting analogies.

   1. *Side costs*: IF the efforts of set-up and clean-up operations are not small compared with costs of mainstep operations, THEN try to find the major factor dealt with by these operations and look for a method in which that factor is not present.

C. Unit building: grouping operations into a set accessible as a single unit.

   1. *Co-occurring procedures (composition)*: IF a procedure, P_1, is frequently followed by another procedure, P_2, and the result of P_1 is used by P_2, THEN try to merge the two as a new single procedure.

D. Deletion of unnecessary parts: eliminating redundant or extraneous operations.

   1. *Untouched results*: IF a procedure produces an output but no other procedure receives that result as input, THEN try deleting the procedure.

   2. *Over-determined tests*: IF a procedure contains two tests (T_1 and T_2) as part of a decision and it is observed that the tests agree (i.e., T_1 is observed to succeed on several occasions, with T_2 also succeeding on all of these occasions, and is observed to fail on several other occasions, with T_2 also failing on all of these occasions), THEN try deleting one of the two tests.

E. Saving partial results: retaining intermediate results that otherwise would have to be recomputed later in a procedure.

   1. *Result still available*: IF a procedure is about to be executed with a certain input but the result of that procedure with the same input is recorded in working memory, THEN try to borrow that result now and in the future.

F. Re-ordering: changing the sequence in which operations are performed.

   1. *Crowding*: IF there are a large number of items in working memory that have not been used, THEN set up a goal to change the sequence of operations.

   2. *Waiting*: IF a result is generated but many operations intervene before any use of it is made, THEN set up a goal to change the sequence of operations so that the operation producing a result and the operation using it are performed closer in time.

   3. *Non-optimal state utilization*: IF a state that appeared previously must be restored in order to satisfy the enabling conditions of a planned operation, THEN set up a goal to find the action that changed the state and to place the planned operation ahead of that action.

These two heuristics[3] entail very different degrees of knowledge about the underlying semantic structure of a procedure. The *composition* rule requires only information about temporal contiguity, whereas the *side costs* rule requires maintaining information about the reason why a particular action is incorporated into a procedure—i.e., the goal or subgoal it serves. Thus, the *composition* rule might be expected to be available as a learning strategy to more people than the *side costs* rule. Further, even if available, *side costs* may require so much additional working memory capacity that only some individuals will be able to use it.

To take another example, we can contrast three heuristics for reordering the sequence in which operations are performed: the *crowding, waiting,* and *non-optimal state utilization* strategies (F. 1, 2, 3). The first two require only relatively local information about the presence of objects in working memory. The third, however, requires access to knowledge about preconditions of operators and the goals invoked to satisfy those preconditions. Like *side costs,* a strategy such as *non-optimal state utilization* is likely to be available only to some people and usable only by those with adequate working memory capacity.

The point of these examples is that the number and power of learning heuristics available to and usable by a learning system or by a human learner may be an important source of individual differences. Neches (1981b) has shown that there could be many alternative paths from SUM to MIN, with different heuristics involved in some of those paths. The different paths require different amounts of time for learning. Similarly, we propose that human learning rates may vary with the number and type of transformation heuristics available to individuals. This, in turn, is dependent on the richness of their representation of knowledge about their own procedures.

Metagoals: Trying to Learn

The analyses of Molly and of Jac presented here allow us to make only rather general statements about their metaprocedural knowledge. In Molly's case we can clearly see that Molly had the ability to construct analogies between procedures. We have also seen that this ability depends on declarative knowledge about goal structures and about the inputs and outputs for analogous actions.

---

[3]Although neither of these two heuristics has been implemented in HPM, work by others indicates that both are quite plausible. Lewis (1978), Neves and Anderson (1981), and others have implemented programs using variants of the composition heuristic. HPM contains the effort measurement capabilities required for the *side costs* heuristic. Artificial intelligence research efforts, such as Miller's SPADE system (Miller, 1982) and Brown and VanLehn's (1982) planning nets, have shown how a program could represent the causal knowledge about components of a procedure required to determine the role those components play in the procedure. Thus, both heuristics are within the range of capabilities that could be given to an intelligent learning program.

However, we cannot tell how Molly might spontaneously use this ability to support learning in a situation in which the analogy was not specifically requested. In Jac's case, we *inferred* a search for prior knowledge that might resolve the conflict between his initial schemata—but this search cannot be observed directly, nor do we have a simulation to formally support the inference.

Although these protocols do not lend themselves to detailed specification of learning strategies or knowledge about the structure of procedures, they do highlight certain features of engagement with the learning task that may turn out to vary with individuals. Both of these children were *trying* to learn—that is, to find a solution to the problem at hand. Molly clearly accepted the task of building a blocks analogy to her written procedure and struggled with it. Jac was moved by his discovery of a schema contradiction to work on the problem of resolving it. He did not dismiss it as irrelevant or unimportant. We have documented many hours of children's engagement with tasks such as Molly's. Even with an experimenter present, encouraging work on the problem and pointing out contradictions, children do not always put out the efforts that are apparent in Molly and Jac. It seems likely that there are important differences among learners in their *tendency* to engage in the kinds of processing that produce learning. These we call differences in metagoals.

Molly and Jac both clearly expended mental effort beyond the minimum needed to satisfy the social demands of the situation. They recognized and acted on contradictions that with a little less aggressive long-term memory activation might never have been noticed. If Jac had not activated PART-WHOLE/ LIQUID, for example, the "truth" of TRANSFER might not have been so compelling for him, and the contradiction with EQUAL/LIQUID might therefore not have been noticed or acted on. If Molly had simply converted ones blocks to tens blocks without also invoking the TRADE schema, there might have been no conflict to trouble her and keep her engaged in the task. A similar willingness to go beyond immediate performance demands can be seen in HPM, whose preference for later performance efficiency leads it to engage in a variety of extra current work. As we have seen, the entire system would be simpler and engage in much less processing work if it needed only to perform its previous procedure for addition rather than also learn a new one.

This trade-off between future efficiency and current effort is, we suspect, a normal condition of learning: When one learns, one is always putting in extra current effort in the interest of later improvements in power or efficiency. This includes the extra work of keeping track of one's own procedural actions so as to be able to reflect on and modify them, or of "storing" representations of recurring events and patterns in the environment that may eventually become the basis for formulating a rule or applying a strategy transformation. It would seem reasonable to posit differences in the extent to which individuals are likely to engage in this kind of mental work. We suggest that such microdifferences in what others might call "motivation" may be worth exploring as sources of differences in learning ability. Of course, this exploration may lead back again to differences in knowledge and basic capacity, because the probability of invoking potentially conflicting schemata will depend both on the way knowledge is structured and on differences in the rate at which activation spreads. There are, in addition, a number of other mechanisms suggested by our analyses that might help relate motivation more precisely to cognitive constructs. In HPM, for example, the semantic structures built in the course of executing a procedure represent the system's memory trace for having carried out the procedure, a notion similar to the "time-line" in the developmental theory of Klahr and Wallace (1976, in press). Differences either in the probability of retaining the procedural trace, or in the degree of elaboration in its contents, would implicitly represent the system's "level of self-awareness" in examining its own actions. Obviously, such differences would have a large effect on HPM's learning capacity.

HPM also assumes parallel processing, with one set of productions (representing its learning mechanisms) inspecting the procedural trace at the same time that other productions (representing the system's performance processes) are adding new actions to the trace. Separate policies govern the selection of productions for execution from these different sets. The details provide an example of meta-procedural knowledge beyond the scope of this paper, but we can briefly say that it is possible to have policies that allow a greater number of learning productions to be applied. The resources allocated to learning in this fashion implicitly represent the system's "curiosity."

CONCLUSION

The work reported in this paper represents for us the beginning of an effort to explore individual differences by as direct as possible an inspection of learning processes. How shall we assess the current state of the effort and its future prospects? A first thing to note is that the study of individual differences in learning is only as good as the studies of learning on which it is based. We are, in other words, limited by the quality of our own analyses of learning and by the general state of cognitive learning theory.

In the matter of the role of knowledge in learning, we have been able to proceed usefully beyond simply noting that people who have a good deal of knowledge of a domain are able to perform better in that domain. In the case of Molly and Jac, we have been able to show the role of particular schemata in both inducing and resolving the cognitive conflict that appears to be at the heart of some forms of learning. It seems likely that a careful plotting of key knowledge structures for individuals will be able to tell us a great deal about which individuals are likely to learn easily the concepts and procedures that depend on those structures. Of course, in order to know which knowledge structures are key for learning, it will be necessary to have in hand detailed cognitive analyses of the domain in question. For this reason, research on individual differences in knowledge cannot be expected to advance ahead of or separately from research aimed at a more general theory of learning and performance in the domain in question.

In the case of Molly and Jac, our analyses do not yet permit us to offer more than the most general conjectures on the *processes* by which they accessed and used their schematic knowledge. We suggested, in Molly's case, that procedural knowledge (in the form of production systems) and declarative knowledge are interdependent. More specifically, we have argued that in order to recognize the analogy between steps in two different procedures, it is necessary to call on declarative knowledge that specifies the correspondences or equivalences between two domains of action. This is a plausible but not formalized argument. We did not specify the processes by which schematic knowledge was accessed, how reasoning proceeded, or exactly how the new procedure was constructed on the basis of the declarative knowledge structure. All of these processes may be ones in which individuals systematically differ. However, until we have a more explicit theory of how they function in learning, it is premature to address questions of individual differences.

In the case of HPM, which is a formalized theory of learning, we are able to address process differences much more directly. We have pointed to a number of factors that can affect the system's learning capacity. Well-known information processing concepts, such as working memory capacity and decay rates, clearly play a role in HPM's learning rate. However, our analyses show that more is not necessarily better. Overly large working memories slow and confuse the system. It seems much more important to manage the system's resources well than to give it more resources. We have concentrated on some particular aspects of this point. For example, we analyzed how particular domain-specific knowledge can facilitate learning in two accounts of children's transition from SUM to MIN. We also analyzed the role of a particular kind of general knowledge that pervades the HPM system, which we called "metaprocedural knowledge." In specifying this notion of general sophistication about procedures, which we believe may have implications for developmental research analogous to the work on "meta-memory" (e.g., Flavell & Wellman, 1977). We showed how metaprocedural knowledge in HPM guides its attention-focusing processes and its learning processes.

In moving from the general claim that intelligence lies in learning capacity to more specific claims about individual differences, we have been guided by the realization that we can really understand differences in processes only to the extent that we understand the fundamental nature of those processes. The examples of learning we have considered leave unaddressed many items on a large agenda. Still, they do show the beginnings of a capacity to specify learning mechanisms in terms that give us useful cognitive constructs for discussing individual differences in processes, including "motivational" factors not usually considered in the domain of cognition.

REFERENCES

Anderson, J. R., Kline, P. D., & Beasley, C. M. Complex learning processes. In R. E. Snow, P. A. Federico, & W. E. Montague (Eds.), *Aptitude, learning, and instruction: Cognitive process analyses* (Vol. 2). Hillsdale, NJ: Erlbaum, 1980.

Anderson, J. W., & Bower, G. H. *Human associative memory: A brief edition.* Hillsdale, NJ: Erlbaum, 1980.

Ashcraft, M. H., & Battaglia, J. Cognitive arithmetic: Evidence for retrieval and decision processes in mental addition. *Journal of Experimental Psychology: Human Learning and Memory,* 1978, *4*(5), 527–538.

Bisanz, J., & Resnick, L. B. Changes with age in two components of visual search speed. *Journal of Experimental Child Psychology,* 1978, *25,* 129–142.

Bisanz, J., Danner, F., & Resnick, L. B. Changes with age in measures of processing efficiency. *Child Development,* 1979, *50,* 132–141.

Brown, J. S., & VanLehn, K. Toward a generative theory of bugs in procedural skills. In T. P. Carpenter, J. Moser, & T. A. Romberg (Eds.), *Addition and subtraction: A cognitive perspective.* Hillsdale, NJ: Erlbaum, 1982.

Carpenter, T., & Moser, J. The development of addition and subtraction problem solving skills. In T. Carpenter, J. Moser, and T. A. Romberg (Eds.), *Addition and subtraction: A cognitive perspective.* Hillsdale, NJ: Erlbaum, 1982.

Carroll, J. B. Psychometric tests as cognitive tasks: A new "structure of intellect." In L. B. Resnick (Ed.), *The nature of intelligence.* Hillsdale, NJ: Erlbaum, 1976.

Case, R. Piaget and beyond: Toward a developmentally based theory and technology of instruction. In R. Glaser (Ed.), *Advances in instructional psychology* (Vol. 1). Hillsdale, NJ: Erlbaum, 1978.

Chi, M. T. H., & Rees, E. A learning framework for development. In M. T. H. Chi (Ed.), *Trends in memory development research* (Vol. 9). Basel, New York: Karger, in press.

Collins, A. M., & Loftus, E. F. A spreading activation theory of semantic processing. *Psychology Review,* 1975, *82,* 407–428.

Cooper, L. A. Spatial information processing: Strategies for research. In R. E. Snow, P. A. Federico, & W. E. Montague (Eds.), *Aptitude, learning, and instruction* (Vol. 1). Hillsdale, NJ: Erlbaum, 1980.

Cronbach, L. J. Two disciplines of scientific psychology. *American Psychologist,* 1957, *12,* 671–684.

Cronbach, L. J., & Snow, R. E. *Aptitudes and instructional methods: A handbook for research on interactions.* New York: Irvington, 1977.

Curtis, M. B., & Glaser, R. Changing conceptions of intelligence. *Review of Research in Education,* 1981, *9,* 111–148.

Flavell, J. H., & Wellman, H. M. Metamemory. In R. V. Kail, Jr., & J. W. Hagen (Eds.), *Perspectives on the development of memory and cognition.* Hillsdale, NJ: Erlbaum, 1977.

Fuson, K. An analysis of the counting-on solution procedure in addition. In T. P. Carpenter, J. Moser, & T. A. Romberg, (Eds.), *Addition and subtraction: A cognitive perspective.* Hillsdale, NJ: Erlbaum, 1982.

Fuson, K. C., Richards, J., & Briars, D. J. The acquisition and elaboration of the number word sequence. In C. Brainerd (Ed.), *Progress in logical development: Children's logical and mathematical cognition* (Vol. 1). New York Springer-Verlag, 1982.

Gardner, H. *The quest for mind: Piaget, Levi-Strauss, and the structuralist movement.* New York: Knopf, 1973.

Gelman, R., & Gallistel, C. R. *The child's understanding of number.* Cambridge, MA: Harvard University Press, 1978.

Ginsburg, H. *Children's arithmetic: The learning process.* New York: Van Nostrand, 1977. (a)

Ginsburg, H. The psychology of arithmetic thinking. *Journal of Children's Mathematical Behavior,* 1977, *1*(4), 1–89. (b)

Glaser, R. The future of testing: A research agenda for cognitive psychology and pychometrics. *American Psychologist,* 1981, *36,* 923–936.

Greeno, J. G., Riley, M. S., & Gelman, R. Conceptual competence and children's counting. *Cognitive Psychology,* in press.

Groen, G. J., & Parkman, J. M. A chronometric analysis of simple addition. *Psychological Review,* 1972, *79,* 329–343.

Groen, G. J., & Resnick, L. B. Can preschool children invent addition algorithms? *Journal of Educational Psychology,* 1977, *69,* 645–652.

Hunt, E. Mechanics of verbal ability. *Psychological Review,* 1978, *85,* 109–130.

Inhelder, B., Sinclair, H., & Bovet, M. *Learning and the development of cognition.* Cambridge, MA: Harvard University Press, 1974.

Kintsch, W. *The representation of meaning in memory.* Hillsdale, NJ: Erlbaum, 1974.

Kintsch, W., & van Dijk, T. Toward a model of text comprehension and production. *Psychological Review,* 1978, *85,* 363–394.

Klahr, D., & Wallace, J. G. *Cognitive development: An information processing view.* Hillsdale, NJ: Erlbaum, 1976.

Klahr, D., & Wallace, J. G. The development of rudimentary quantitative processes. In D. Klahr, P. Langley, & R. Neches (Eds.), *Production system models of learning and development.* Cambridge, Mass.: Bradford Books/MIT Press, in press.

Langley, P. A good general theory of discrimination learning. In D. Klahr, P. Langley, & R. Neches (Eds.), *Production system models of learning and development.* Cambridge, Mass.: Bradford Books/MIT Press, in press.

Langley, P., Neches, R., Neves, D., & Anzai, Y. A domain-independent framework for procedure learning. *Policy Analysis and Information Systems,* Special Issue on Knowledge Acquisition and Induction, 1981, *4*(2), 163–197.

Lesgold, A., & Resnick, L. B. How reading difficulties develop: Perspectives from a longitudinal study. In J. P. Das, R. Mulcahy, & A. E. Wall (Eds.), *Theory and research in learning disability.* New York: Plenum, 1982.

Lewis, C. H. *Production system models of practice effects.* Unpublished doctoral dissertation, Ann Arbor, University of Michigan, 1978.

Miller, M. L. A structured planning and debugging environment for elementary programming. In D. Sleeman & J. S. Brown (Eds.), *Intelligent tutoring systems.* New York: Academic, 1982.

Miller, J., & Kintsch, W. A knowledge-based model of prose comprehension: Applications to expository text. In B. Britton & J. Black (Eds.), *Understanding expository text.* Hillsdale, NJ: Erlbaum, in press.

Neches, R. Learning through incremental refinement of procedures. In D. Klahr, P. Langley, & R. Neches (Eds.) *Production system models of learning and development.* Cambridge, Mass.: Bradford Books/MIT Press, in press.

Neches, R. HPM: A computational formalism for heuristic procedure modification. In *Proceedings of the Seventh International Joint Conference on Artificial Intelligence,* 1981, 283–288. (a)

Neches, R. *Models of heuristic procedure modification.* Unpublished doctoral dissertation, Pittsburgh, Carnegie-Mellon University, 1981. (b)

Neves, D. M., & Anderson, J. R. Knowledge compilation: Mechanisms for the automatization of cognitive skills. In J. R. Anderson (Ed.), *Cognitive skills and their acquisition.* Hillsdale, NJ: Erlbaum, 1981.

Newell, A., & Simon, H. A. *Human problem solving.* Englewood Cliffs, NJ: Prentice-Hall, 1972.

Omanson, S. F. *Instruction by mapping: Its effects on understanding and skill in subtraction.* Unpublished master's thesis, University of Pittsburgh, Learning Research and Development Center, 1982.

Pellegrino, J. W., Chi, M. T. H., & Majetic, D. *Ability differences and the processing of quantitative information.* Paper presented at the meeting of the Psychonomic Society, San Antonio, TX, November, 1978.

Piaget, J. *The psychology of intelligence.* New York: Rutledge & Kegan, 1971. (Originally published, 1950.)

Resnick, L. B. The role of invention in the development of mathematical competence. In H. R. Kluwe & H. Spada (Eds.), *Developmental models of thinking.* New York: Academic, 1980.

Resnick, L. B. A developmental theory of number understanding. In H. P. Ginsburg (Ed.), *The development of mathematical thinking.* New York: Academic, 1983.

Resnick, L. B. Syntax and semantics in learning to subtract. In T. P. Carpenter, J. Moser, & T. A. Romberg, (Eds.), *Addition and subtraction: A cognitive perspective.* Hillsdale, NJ: Erlbaum, 1982.

Resnick, L. B., Greeno, J. G., & Rowland, J. *MOLLY: A model of learning from mapping instruction.* Unpublished manuscript, University of Pittsburgh, Learning Research and Development Center, 1980.

Sacerdoti, E. D. *A structure for plans and behavior.* NY: American Elsevier Press, 1977.

Steffe, L. P., & Thompson, P. W. Children's counting in arithmetic problem solving. In T. P. Carpenter, J. Moser, & T. A. Romberg, (Eds.), *Addition and subtraction: A cognitive perspective.* Hillsdale, NJ: Erlbaum, 1982.

Sternberg, R. J. *Intelligence, information processing, and analogical reasoning: The componential analysis of human abilities.* Hillsdale, NJ: Erlbaum, 1977.

Svenson, O. Analysis of time required by children for simple additions. *Acta Psychologica,* 1975, *39,* 289–302.

Svenson, O., & Broquist, S. Strategies for solving simple addition problems: A comparison of normal and subnormal children. *Scandinavian Journal of Psychology,* 1975, *16,* 143–151.

Svenson, O., Hedenborg, M., & Lingman, L. On children's heuristics for solving simple additions. *Scandinavian Journal of Educational Research,* 1976, *20,* 161–173.

8 An Analysis of Hierarchical Classification

Ellen M. Markman
Maureen A. Callanan
Stanford University

INTRODUCTION

Categorization is a basic cognitive process, involved in one way or another in almost any intellectual endeavor. All animals must classify objects in their world to some extent, but the ability to classify with originality and flexibility is a major intellectual advance, probably accomplished by few species other than man.

The primary advantage of categorization is that it provides information that goes beyond the knowledge one has about a specific object. If one knows, for example, that a given object is a cat, one can be fairly sure about whether or not it has fur, how it moves about, how it stalks its prey, how it reproduces, and even what internal organs it has. A taxonomy is particularly useful in extending information because by grouping objects into more and more general categories (e.g., Siamese cat, cat, feline, mammal, animal), it creates a rich set of deductive possibilities.

The importance of classification has been taken into account in the design of intelligence tests. Most intelligence tests contain subtasks that involve application of a category principle, recognition of similarity among items, or some other ability that is related to classification. Similarities subtests, such as those on the Wechsler tests, require analysis of the ways in which items are alike, whereas oddity tasks require analysis of the ways in which items differ. Even vocabulary and word definition tasks, though not direct tests of classification ability, reflect knowledge about how objects are classifed into more general categories. For example, just knowing the superordinate category membership of ''apple'' (that it is a fruit), guarantees full credit for that item on the vocabulary sections of the

Stanford-Binet and Wechsler tests (Terman & Merrill, 1960; Wechsler, 1949, 1967). The form of the similarities and oddity tasks varies with the age of the children tested. Children under five years of age are generally asked to pick out one picture that is different from others in an array (e.g., one cat from three dogs), or to complete sentences such as "You wear a coat and you also wear a . . . ." These tasks show that young children are expected to be able to recognize similarity and differences among objects. Older children, on the other hand, are asked questions such as, "In what way are a peach and an apple alike?" In order to succeed on these items, children must know more than that a peach is like an apple; they must be able to explicitly state the nature of the similarity.

Various differences in intellectual functioning have been shown to affect classification and concept formation. Many differences have been reported for abnormal populations. For example, schizophrenic and brain-damaged patients' performance on concept attainment tasks has sometimes been described as over-inclusive, sometimes as concrete or rigid, relative to normal subjects (Jensen, 1972; Payne, 1973). Concept formation tasks have also differentiated between long-term alcoholics (patients with a history of more than 10 years of heavy drinking) and short-term alcoholics (less than 10 years). People with a longer history of alcoholism are less successful on tasks that require them to discover a category principle over a number of trials (Parsons & Prigatano, 1977). In addition, senile patients respond differently than normal adult subjects on memory tasks that are thought to reflect category organization, such as release from proactive inhibition (Craik, 1977). Finally, mentally retarded subjects have been shown to be deficient on several measures of conceptual ability, including sorting tasks and clustering in recall (Blount, 1968; Campione & Brown, 1977; Davies, Sperber, & McCauley, 1981; Glidden & Mar, 1978). In several of the cases mentioned here, researchers have argued that the differences found may be due to processing demands of the task (Davies et al., 1981) or to failure to use conscious memory strategies (Campione & Brown, 1977), rather than to differences in the underlying representation of knowledge. Similar arguments have been raised with regard to developmental differences on classification tasks; these issues will be addressed later in the chapter.

One does not need to look to abnormal populations, however, to find differences in classification. For example, there are cross-cultural differences in the ways that classification tasks are solved. In one study, Sharp, Cole, and Lave (1979) found a tendency for Mayan adults to group objects on the basis of thematic criteria rather than taxonomic criteria, e.g., grouping a knife with a loaf of bread rather than with a fork. Sharp et al. (1979) argue that the bias toward taxonomic sorting is largely an effect of schooling.

And of course, there are striking differences between younger and older children on many types of classification tasks. There is also evidence that elderly subjects occasionally classify as younger children do. Smiley and Brown (1979) found a preference for thematic sorting in older adult subjects, and Hultsch

(1971) found that younger adults recalled more from categorized lists than did older adults.

In summary, a variety of disturbances in mental functioning appear to result in a failure to use similarity or category membership as a basis for classification. There are also cross-cultural and developmental differences in performance on classification tasks. In order to understand these individual differences, it is important to understand what intellectual ability these classification tasks are measuring.

In the standard classification task, children are presented with objects from several different categories, e.g., vehicles, animals, clothing, and people, and are instructed to put together the objects that are alike or that go together. Older children sort on the basis of taxonomic category, placing all and only the vehicles together, all and only the clothing together and so on. Younger children sort on some other basis. Sometimes, especially when geometric figures are used, young children create spatial configurations with the objects, arranging them into designs or patterns. When more meaningful objects are used, children represent causal and temporal relations among the objects as well as spatial relations. These thematic relations emphasize events rather than taxonomic similarity. For example, children might sort a man and a car together because the man is driving the car. Or they might place a boy, a coat, and a dog together because the boy will wear his coat when he takes the dog for a walk. This attention to relations between objects rather than to how objects are alike is a common finding, replicated in many studies. Inhelder and Piaget (1964), Bruner, Olver, and Greenfield (1966) and Vygotsky (1962) interpret this result as reflecting the underlying conceptual organization of the child. That is, children's performance on this task is interpreted as indicating how they organize objects into categories. Consider what it would mean if children really did organize objects into categories that correspond to the stories they create in classification tasks. A child's concept of "animal" might include a cow and grass (because the cow is eating the grass); a dog and a leash (because the dog is on the leash); a cat and a bowl of milk (because the cat is drinking the milk). Thus the child's concept would consist of cow, grass, dog, leash, cat, and milk. Casual observation of 5–year-old children should convince anyone that this is not true. The 5–year olds who participated in these classification studies certainly do not believe that grass, a leash, and milk are animals. Although children's concepts of "animal" are not fully formed (e.g., they do not believe that insects are animals), their notion of animal would not allow instances such as leash and milk. It would be impossible to communicate with children whose concepts had this structure (Fodor, 1972). Moreover, children can certainly correctly answer simple questions such as "Do animals eat?", though they would deny that a leash eats. And if explicitly asked, they would deny that these objects are animals.

To summarize, although children's concepts may be incomplete and differ from the adult form in many ways, this extreme form of thematic grouping is not characteristic of their concepts. Thus, taking these data very literally, it is just not possible that the classification task reflects how young children organize objects into categories. What, then is it measuring?

We will look to the developmental literature to try to understand what the classification tasks measure. A review of this literature should also help explain why some tasks requiring use of concepts are highly sensitive to individual differences but others are not. The review will concentrate on developmental theories and data but under the assumption that the same principles and arguments that account for age differences among children might account for other individual differences as well.

Before reviewing the literature, we will frist provide a brief analysis of what the intellectual challenge of different types of conceptual tasks might be and what would count as evidence for advanced conceptual abilities.

WHAT COUNTS AS EVIDENCE FOR HIERARCHICAL ORGANIZATION

To understand the relationship between classification and intelligence it is important to consider what might be especially intelligent about the acquisition and use of concepts. This raises the question, not just of individual differences, but of what kinds of conceptual abilities might be unique to human conceptual functioning and be unlikely to be found in lower animals.

The minimal criterion for having a concept is to treat discriminably different things as similar. On this criterion, even very unsophisticated animals will, of course, have concepts. For example, pigeons can learn to peck at circles to be rewarded with food. Because pigeons can see the differences between large and small circles, yet treat them equivalently, it could be argued that they have the concept of circle.

Concepts such as circle are perceptually defined. Perhaps the use of nonperceptual features to define categories would be limited to humans or higher organisms. Although categories that are defined by nonperceptual features may be more difficult to acquire than those defined by perceptual features, there are several reasons why this criterion fails. First, it is likely that many animals have concepts that are nonperceptually based. For example, omnivorous animals will recognize berries and small mammals as edible even though they are quite different perceptually. Language-trained chimps can even classify symbols for food as "food" (Savage-Rumbaugh, Rumbaugh, Smith & Lawson, 1980). Thus, animals can have concepts such as food or edible objects that do not have any obvious perceptual basis. Another problem with this criterion is that one could learn nonperceptual categories in a rote fashion without really understanding anything at all about the category. For example, children (or even adults— see Smith & Medin, 1981) might be able to identify many instances of furniture by simply memorizing their category membership. That is, a child could learn that tables, chairs, dressers, and couches are called "furniture" without understanding why. Thus, the nonperceptual basis of categorization fails as a criterion because it can be fulfilled in a trivial way.

It is the systematic organization of categories that we believe to be the major intellectual achievement of human conceptualization. Human categories tend to be organized into systems where the categories are related to each other in various ways rather than each concept being represented in isolation. Many categories form hierarchies that consist of more and more general levels of categorization (e.g., delicious apple, apple, fruit, food; poodle, dog, mammal, animal). Because hierarchical organization is an important and common way of organizing categories, a great deal of research has been devoted to understanding the development of this particular type of organization.

Assuming hierarchical organization is a major intellectual achievement, one needs to consider what would count as evidence that someone had represented categories hierarchically. The minimal criterion would be that the child can recognize that an object that can be seen to be at one level of categorization, e.g. a chair, is also a member of a more general category, e.g., furniture. The problem with this criterion is that it is trivially fulfilled by any concept whatsoever. Earlier it was proposed that the minimal criterion for having a concept is that discriminably different objects be treated as similar. A pigeon who can tell the difference between large and small circles yet treats them similarly, would have the concept "circle." This pigeon could be said to know that a given object is a large circle and that it is a circle and would therefore be credited with understanding inclusion on this criterion.

In the example with circles, both levels of the hierarchy are given perceptually. That is, the fact that the object is a large circle and that it is a circle can both be seen by inspecting the object. Perhaps one should require that one level of categorization be nonperceptually based. However, the nonperceptual criterion also fails to differentiate between a true understanding of inclusion and a trivial one. As mentioned earlier, animals have nonperceptually based concepts and would therefore automatically be credited with understanding class inclusion. And, as before, children may have rote memorized instances rather than genuinely understanding the hierarchical organization.

What is required is evidence that the child understands the inclusion relation and not just that the child can apply two labels to the same object. Someone who understands class inclusion should show some appreciation of what the relation entails. Inclusion is an asymmetric transitive relation. The asymmetry of the relation means that if a class A is included in a class B then all of the members of A are members of the more general class B but not vice versa. To take a concrete example, if a child understands the relation between dogs and animals, he or she should know that all dogs are animals and that not all animals are dogs. The transitivity of the relation means that if class A is included in class B and if class B is included in class C, then class A is included in class C. If someone understood the transitivity of the relation, then from all dachshunds are dogs, they should be able to conclude that all dachshunds are animals. Further, if one knows a property is true of the more general category, e.g., that all dogs bark, then one should be able to conclude that the class included also has the property, e.g., that all dachshunds bark. The converse, however, is not true. From all dogs have claws, one cannot conclude that all animals have claws.

The understanding of asymmetric and transitive relations between concepts is a type of second order relation, a relation between relations. The understanding of second order relations appears to be a major intellectual achievement in domains other than classification. Sternberg and Powell (in press) have reviewed developmental changes across a wide variety of tasks. They argue that the ability to comprehend second order relations is a developmental achievement that recurs across various cognitive domains. They postulate that it is an important component of intelligence and that it appears in various guises on many tests of and theories of intelligence. Premack (1976) has also noted the difficulty in understanding relations between relations and suggested that it may be restricted to primates.

To summarize, simple acquisition of concepts, even those that are nonperceptually based, is not sufficient to distinguish human concepts from those that no other animals possess. We suggest that what may be unique about human conceptualization is the tendency to organize concepts into systems, in particular into hierarchically related inclusion relations. Simply being able to categorize the same object in two different levels of a hierarchy is not sufficient grounds for concluding that one has a hierarchical organization. That criterion is trivially satisfied by any concept at all. What seems to be required before we can conclude that someone has a hierarchical organization is evidence for understanding that the relation between the categories is an asymmetric and a transitive one.

With these criteria in mind, we turn now to the developmental literature. Only a very few studies have directly examined children's understanding of the asymmetry and transitivity of inclusion. However, an enormous amount of research has been conducted to study the conceptual organization of young children. According to some studies, it is not until children are seven or eight years old that they show evidence of hierarchical organization. Yet, according to other studies, even infants show abilities to classify objects into taxonomic categories. Obviously, depending on the difficulty of the task one selects to measure classification abilities, performance will vary. But what we are especially concerned with is whether or not the studies provide evidence for an appreciation of inclusion. Several different types of procedures used to study classification will be briefly reviewed. We will argue that some of the tasks, for example the Piagetian class inclusion problem and object sorting tasks, are overly demanding. That is, a child could fully understand the asymmetric transitive nature of class inclusion and still fail these problems. Other tasks used to measure classification, such as habituation studies of infants or memory procedures used with preschoolers, are overly lenient. That is, a child could solve these problems without genuinely understanding inclusion.

From these studies, we will conclude that there is little evidence for infants or very young children's understanding of inclusion. Children may have only a fragmentary grasp of the asymmetry and transitivity of inclusion by four or five years of age. We will then present evidence from work contrasting collections and classes that shows that when the asymmetry of the relation is made more salient, as in the part-whole structure of collections, children become capable of dealing with hierarchical organization.

RESEARCH ON THE DEVELOPMENT OF CLASSIFICATION

The Piagetian Class Inclusion Problem

One frequent way of assessing whether children understand hierarchically organized class inclusion relations has been to ask the Piagetian class inclusion question. For this task, children are presented with a category of objects, e.g., flowers, that are divided into two mutually exclusive subsets, e.g., daisies and roses. In this case, children would be presented with more daisies than roses and asked, "Are there more daisies or more flowers here?" According to Piagetian theory, children must be able to simultaneously add the subclasses of daisies and roses to obtain the whole class flowers ($B = A + A'$) and subtract daisies from the whole class ($A = B - A'$) in order to answer the question correctly. That is, they must be able to think of daisies as *daisies*—as subtracted out from the class of flowers, while simultaneously thinking of daisies as *flowers*—as included in the class of flowers, to make the daisies-flowers comparison. This is an extremely difficult question for children and until they are about 7 or 8 years old, they incorrectly claim that there are more daisies than flowers.

In devising this task, Piaget was concerned in part with children's ability to recognize the asymmetry of class inclusion, e.g., that all daisies are flowers but not all flowers are daisies. And more generally, Inhelder and Piaget (1964) were concerned with the systematic nature of the classification, because their theory of concrete operational thinking specifies that the major developmental change from preoperational to concrete operational thinking is the acquisition of a system of reversible cognitive operations. This reversible system was thought to underlie much of cognition, including classification. Thus the class inclusion task was designed to assess whether children have the reversible system of addition and subtraction of classes.

Children must answer the question correctly before Inhelder and Piaget grant them a true understanding of classification. This, in our opinion, too stringent a criterion. First, the class inclusion question suffers from many additional task requirements, beyond what it is trying to measure. It has been criticized for its confusing language and methodology and many questions have been raised as to what it is really measuring (see Gelman & Baillargeon, in press; Trabasso, Isen, Dolecki, McLanahan, Riley, & Tucker, 1978; and Winer, 1980 for reviews and discussions of the problems). But even if the class inclusion question were a valid measure of class addition and subtraction, it still seems to be too conservative a measure of having a classification system. A child could understand the asymmetry and transitivity of class inclusion without being able to fulfill the additional requirement of simultaneously adding and subtracting classes.

Object Sorting

Another common way of assessing children's conceptual organization has been to have them sort or classify objects. Inhelder and Piaget (1964), Vygotsky (1962), and Bruner et al., (1966) have each used a variant of this task as a basis for their theories of conceptual development (see Gelman & Baillargeon, in press, for an insightful summary and comparisons of these theories). As described earlier, in the standard classification task, children are presented with an array of meaningful objects (e.g., people, animals, buildings, and plants) or geometric figures of various shapes and colors. They are asked to put together the things that "go together" or that "are the same kind of thing." Bruner and his colleagues (e.g. Olver & Hornsby, 1966) used a slightly different task: children were presented with a pair of objects and asked to say how they were alike; then another object was added and they were asked to say how the three were alike, and so on. In these tasks, the youngest children seem to sort on the basis of thematic organization. With blocks, they form designs; with meaningful materials, they construct a scene or put together objects with which they could tell a story. In the second stage, children construct what are sometimes called "complexive" sorts. These groupings are based partially on similarity, but children are not consistent in the criteria that they use within a category. For example, a child might put together a red circle and a green cirle, then add a green triangle because it is green like the circle, and so on. In the final stage, by around age 7 or 8, children sort taxonomically, as adults do.

On the one hand, a child could sort objects into categories without understanding the asymmetry and transivity of class inclusion. On the other hand, these tasks can underestimate whatever knowledge children do have of these object categories. Taxonomic principles may govern the category representations of young children, but other factors prevent this category knowledge from being revealed.

One difficulty children have with the sorting task is that they may take the spatial nature of the task too literally. Markman, Cox, and Machida (1981) argued that children may interpret the spatial arrangement of the objects to be an important part of the task, and that this may bias them to construct meaningful scenes or story-like groupings. They attempted to reduce the salience of the spatial arrangement of objects by asking children to sort objects into transparent plastic bags rather than into spatially segregated groups on a table. Children displayed more taxonomic sorting when they sorted into bags than when they sorted the identical objects on the table. Thus, the spatial demands of the task confuse children and mask some of their knowledge of categories.

Another problem children may have with the standard sorting task is that they have to cope with a very large number of objects. Children are typically faced with a scrambled array of 16 different objects, four each from four different categories. To successfully classify the objects, children must scan this bewildering array, find some of the categories salient enough to emerge from this confusion, and keep them in mind while trying to impose some order on the remainder of the objects. In a variation of the standard task—the oddity task—children see only three (or four) objects and are asked to choose the two that are the same kind of thing (Daehler, Lonardo & Bukatko, 1979; Rosch, Mervis, Gray, Johnson, & Boyes-Braem, 1976). This task is much easier and can be used with children as young as two years old.

Most traditional studies require classification at a superordinate or relatively general, nonperceptual level of categorization. When there is a clear perceptual basis for the sorting, such as color or shape, children often show an ability to classify (Bruner, et al., 1966; Melkman & Deutsch, 1977; Melkman, Tversky, & Baratz, 1981). Furthermore, Rosch and her colleagues (Mervis & Rosch, 1981; Rosch, 1978; Rosch et al., 1976) have argued that there is a basic level of categorization at which category members have the most features in common without being confusable with members of contrasting categories. There is a great deal of evidence in support of the primacy of the basic level of categorization for adults (Murphy & Smith, 1982. Rosch et al., 1976). Basic level categories also seem to be the easiest for children to learn. Children's first names for objects are basic level terms (Anglin, 1977), and artificial basic level categories are easier for children to learn than are superordinate or subordinate categories (Horton & Markman, 1980; Mervis & Crisafi, 1982). Rosch, et al. (1976) have shown that kindergarten children who fail to show evidence of categorical knowledge when they sort superordinate categories, show perfect knowledge of the categories when they sort basic level objects. On an oddity task, even 3–year olds select the categorically related pair of objects almost 100 percent of the time, when they are dealing with basic level categories.

Another problem with the standard procedure is that the children may not always be familiar with the categories used. If the category used by the experimenter in choosing objects to be sorted were not familiar to children, then it would not be surprising that they did not sort taxonomically. Given sets of objects that can be sorted into more familiar concepts, they should do better. Horton (1982) pretested children for their ability to explicitly describe the superordinate principle that united exemplars of a category. She later had children classify objects that came from categories with principles they could explicitly state compared to those they could not formulate but could recognize. She found that a given child could more successfully classify objects from the superordinate categories that were familiar to that child than from the categories that were less familiar. Mervis and Judd (cited in Mervis, 1980) have shown that children are better able to sort groups of typical category members than groups containing typical and atypical exemplars of categories. They argue that atypical members may not be part of the child's representation for that category and therefore very difficult for the child to sort correctly.

A final criticism of the classification procedure is that children's preferences for thematic sorts may conceal any categorical knowledge that they have. Smiley and Brown (1979) presented subjects of different ages with triads of items, including a standard, a thematic associate, and a taxonomic associate. None of the children in their youngest age group (mean age 4 years 3 months) were able to consistently justify their original choices; nor were they asked to justify the alternatives. However, all of the other children were asked to justify the opposite pairing after they made their original choice on an oddity task. For example, if a subject responded with the pair "cow" and "milk," they were later asked whether "cow" and "pig" could go together. Except for the youngest subjects, all children who showed a consistent preference were able to explan both types of groupings. Smiley and Brown conclude that the shift is due to differences in preference rather than capacity, because subjects were able to justify both types of groupings. It is not possible to evaluate this claim in the case of the youngest children, however.

In a study with 2– and 3–year old children, Daehler, Lonardo, and Bukatko (1979) attempted to assess the early end of the developmental trend from thematic to taxonomic sorting. They presented their subjects with an object and then asked them to "find the one that goes with this one" from an array of four objects. Daehler et al. found that children were better at matching superordinate pairs than thematically related pairs. They concluded that the thematic bias does not appear until after age 4. However, the results are not as clear-cut as they seem. Several of the superordinate pairs were also thematically related (e.g., comb-brush). Children's good performance on matching these items may be based on their thematic relations rather than on their common superordinate category membership. Another problem is that the procedure may have biased children toward perceptual or identity matching because children were trained to match identical items and there were identity matches interspersed throughout the session. Children may have interpreted the task requirements to be "always look for an object that is identical to the standard." When none was there, children would probably choose the item that is most perceptually similar to the standard, and this is less likely to be a thematically related item. These problems are not specific to this study. Children's sorting responses are strongly determined by the biases inherent in the task instructions, and experimentally derived lists of taxonomic items often contain items that are also related thematically.

In conclusion, there are many demands of the classic sorting task that may prevent children from demonstrating whatever incipient knowledge of categories they may have. To solve the classification problems successfully, a child must find the categories to be salient, explicitly represented, and readily accessible. Knowledge that is less explicitly available may be obscured by the procedure. The requirement to form spatial arrangements, the large number of objects to be sorted, the wording of the instructions, the superordinate level of categorization, and children's relative unfamiliarity with the categories all pose problems for children and may interfere with their categorical knowledge. When these demands are minimized, children's ability to classify improves. However, even when some of the confusion is cleared up, young children do not exhibit overwhelmingly mature taxonomic performance. If there is a striking thematic option, young children are likely to take it. This preference to sort objects thematically, however, cannot be taken to rule out the existence of taxonomic knowledge.

Studies of Categorization in Infants

No task used to study categorization in infants or very young children has provided evidence about the transitivity or asymmetry of inclusion. However, there is a growing body of evidence about the categorization abilities of infants and extremely young children that at first sight appears to contradict findings with older children. That is, there is evidence for categorical structure in infants that needs to be reconciled with older children's failure to indicate categorical knowledge on the classification task. The procedures used with infants require much less explicit knowledge and have fewer extraneous demands than the standard classification task.

One of the main procedures for studying categorical knowledge in infants is the habituation paradigm. In this procedure, originally used to study infant perception, a given object is shown over and over again until the infant's fixation time decreases. Once the infant has habituated to an object, a new object is shown that is either identical to the original object or different in some way. When infants look longer at the novel object than the familiar one, that is evidence that they have perceived the difference between the two objects. The logic of this design has been extended to studying concepts in infants and young children (Cohen & Younger, 1981; Faulkender, Wright, & Waldron, 1974; Ross, 1980). Instead of showing the same object over and over again, the infant is shown different objects within the same category. If infants look longer at a new object from a novel category than at a new object from the familiar category, then that is taken as evidence for the infant's perception of the category. Taking dishabituation as a measure of having the concept, there is evidence for categorization abilities in infants, at least in those older than six months. Most of this evidence, however, is for infants' ability to form categories that are defined by perceptually available features. Cohen and Younger (1981) review many studies demonstrating conceptual abilities on the part of infants, but none of these studies used materials that would qualify as nonperceptually based or superordinate categories. Stuffed animals (as contrasted with rattles) and faces were the kinds of categories used. These are most like basic or subordinate categories on Rosch et al.'s (1976) criteria. Ross (1980) and Faulkender, et al. (1974) have evidence from studies with 1– to 3–year olds that suggests some rudimentary perception of superordinate categories. Faulkender et al. habituated 3–year olds to animals, fruit, or environmental patterns. These children looked longer at an object from one of the other two categories than from the one they had been habituated on. Because these categories differ so much perceptually, it could be some more superficial perceptual feature that accounted for these findings, though by three years old, one would expect that children would have begun to work out the animal and fruit categories at least. Ross (1980) presented 12–, 18–, and 24–month old infants with the following categories: Ms, Os, men, animals, food, and furniture. Over trials, children's looking times decreased for the Ms and Os but not for the other categories. Nevertheless, for all categories, children looked longer at a new object from a novel category than at a new object from a similar category. Ross made some attempt to control for the superficial perceptual properties of the novel objects. Thus, 1– to 2–year olds showed evidence of perceiving different kinds of food, different kinds of animals, etc. as similar.

There are several ways in which these procedures might make the problem easier than the traditional classification paradigm. First, of course, single objects are viewed one at a time, and a simple response measure is taken. The child is not forced to scan a jumble of 16 objects to explicitly determine which are most similar. Also, there is always only one contrasting category.

Another main difference is that there is no competing response to the judgment of similarity. That is, for children asked to sort objects, their perception of similarity must be salient enough to dominate their perception of other relations between the objects. But in the way habituation procedures have been run, no other relations are possible. For example, children are presented with pictures of babies over and over again until they have habituated to them. In the standard way in which this procedure is run, children would then be shown either another baby or a totally unrelated object, e.g., a dresser. There is never a comparison group where a bottle or a crib or some other strong associate of baby is shown and compared to an unrelated object. Thus there is no way to assess the relative salience of similarity or category membership over other relations. Yet, this is what the classification procedure measures.

There is some preliminary evidence that children will select a salient thematic relation over a perceptually similar one when given the opportunity. Markman (in perparation) presented 2– and 3–year-old children with a standard picture, for example, a dog, and asked them to find another one like the standard from two possibilities, a different dog and another object. There were two conditions to the study. In one condition, the third object was unrelated to the standard picture. Rosch et al. (1976) had previously found that when young children were presented with two objects from the same basic level category (e.g., two dogs) and an unrelated object, they selected the two dogs as similar almost 100 percent of the time. Markman (in preparation) replicated this result. In the second condition, the distractor was thematically related to the target. In the case of the dog example, the third picture was dog food. In contrast to the earlier findings, when a thematically related object was present, it was often selected over the perceptually similar basic level object. Thus, although under some circumstances children could categorize on the basis of basic level similarity, if a competing thematic option was available, they would often select it instead.

It is not clear what would happen if thematic alternatives were given to infants. There might be a curvilinear development pattern here. Young infants may not find thematic associations salient enough to interfere with the perceptually based categorization. Some knowledge of the world and what causal, temporal events the objects participate in is necessary before thematic responses are possible. So even if infants were presented with such alternatives, it might not interfere with their performance. At an intermediate level, the thematic relations compete for attention with taxonomic ones and will often win out, even at a basic level of categorization where the perceptual similarity is high, but especially at a superordiante level where the perceptual similarity is greatly reduced. At a more mature level, the categorical similarity becomes salient enough that it will continue to be preferred to the thematic relations.

Until more studies are conducted using thematic distractors, the developmental course cannot be determined. Currently no thematic relations have been used in the studies of visual habituation or visual perference that we have seen; nor have they been used in most of the studies using sequential touching described below.

Riccuiti (1965) introduced another procedure for studying conceptual development in infants that has been further developed by Starkey (1981) and Sugarman (in press). In this procedure, young children are given objects to play with, but are not told to group them in any way. Their spontaneous manipulation of the objects is recorded. Ricciuti found that the order in which children touched the objects defined a temporal grouping and could be used to indicate that children perceived the similarity of the objects. Ricciuti used only geometric forms that differed on some dimension. Thus they were very similar perceptually. Using sequential touching as the measure, Starkey (1981) found that 9– and 12–month olds perceive several categories. By 12 months old, children actually manipulated the objects into groups. However, the stimuli that Starkey used consisted of concepts such as: red squares, red hooks, ovals, metal bottle caps, toy plastic people, etc. None of these categories is at a superordinate level of categorization. That is, none requires going much beyond a perceptual similarity. Moreover, no thematic relations were possible with these materials. Sugarman (in press) also used only objects that were highly similar perceptually. However, because Sugarman provided such rich data and intriguing interpretations of the findings, we will discuss this study in greater detail.

Sugarman (in press) argues that because the final product of classification can be achieved by different routes, it is important to observe the procedures by which infants manipulate objects. Three object manipulation tasks were presented to children ranging in age from 12 to 36 months. Children were presented with 8 objects, 4 each from pairs of categories such as plates and squares, spoons and cups, or dolls and circular rings.

In the spontaneous play task, infants were given the objects and told to play with them. All children produced at least one construction that contained at least 3 out of 4 objects from one category. There are no data reported indicating how many of the constructions children made would have qualified as graphic or thematic constructions. We do not know, for example, how many times the child placed a spoon in a cup or put the doll in the ring. It would be interesting to compare the rate of production of such constructions to the classification data reported.

The percent of constructions that sorted objects into two groups increased with age. Moreover, Sugarman argues that there is an important developmental difference in the way the two class groupings are constructed. With one exception, all of the 12– and 24–month-old infants sorted objects one category at a time. That is, they would place the dolls together before placing the rings together. The older infants were able to produce mixed groupings; that is, they would shift back and forth between categories. It should be noted however, that an extremely small percent of the two class constructions were produced in mixed order even for the oldest children. The percent increased from 0% at 12 months to 2.6% at 36 months, a statistically significant but very small difference.

Although the rate of spontaneous production of mixed groups was very low, the developmental findings were substantiated in the other two tasks used. In the elicited grouping, one object from one of the categories was placed on the table separated from one object from the other category. Then the infant was shown another object and asked where it should go. This procedure was continued with the remaining objects from the two categories. Only the older children were able to alternate placement of objects from one category to the other. In the third task, children were presented with three items from one category and one item from the other and asked to fix them up. Again, only the older children could interchange the objects.

Sugarman argues that this developmental change indicates an ability to deal with relations between relations, or the coordination of relations. To construct a single category, children have only to decide whether an object is or is not in category A. In fact, construction of a single category can be accounted for by assuming increased salience of the category after selecting one member without any explicit awareness of the equivalence of the members. But according to Sugarman, to shift back and forth between categories, the child must consider whether the object is "A or B." Apparently, Sugarman believes the disjunction implies a comparison between two similarity relations and this relating of relations is a significant achievement.

This interesting analysis is consistent with data from other sources that Sugarman (in press) reports. However, the existence of mixed categorization strategies is rather weak evidence for the coordination of relations. The data reveal that older infants are capable of simultaneously keeping both categories in mind. But this in itself is not evidence for any relating of the two categories. From the infant's point of view, the two tasks may be relatively independent of each other. The fact that two activities are conducted in alternation does not imply any conceptual link between the two. It implies the ability to shift attention from one task to another without interfering with the performance of either task. But this is not evidence that the two categories are being coordinated in any conceptual way.

For the moment, however, assume that Sugarman's analysis of children's performance is correct and that infants do show evidence of relating relations. Earlier, we argued that transitive inferences about class inclusion relations and properties is evidence for hierarchical organization of classes. Such transitive inferences are themselves a type of relation between relations. Sugarman's criterion is a weaker one; it would be necessary but not sufficient for drawing transitive inferences.

Studies of Organization in Memory

There are several different procedures for studying the effects of categorical organization on memory that, like the habituation technique with infants, are more sensitive to knowledge of categories than is explicit classification. These procedures are designed to demonstrate that the underlying organization of categories determines how people remember material. On free recall tasks, adults remember more from categorized lists than from lists of unrelated words, and they tend to cluster their responses by category even if the initial presentation of words was random. On recognition memory tasks, adults often mistakenly report that they have seen words that are taxonomically related to target words. In studies of release from proactive inhibition, recall declines as more items from the same category have to be remembered (proactive inhibition), but shifting to a new category results in a sudden increase in recall (release from proactive inhibition). The results on each of these tasks are interpreted as reflecting the strong associations that presumably exist among hierarchically related concepts in semantic memory. One's categorical knowledge can be revealed on these tasks without any explicit statement or deliberate attempt to categorize. Because category structure can influence memory relatively automatically, these memory procedures can detect knowledge of categories that might otherwise be missed (c.f. Huttenlocher & Lui, 1979, for a review). Therefore, if children have any knowledge of category relations, they should respond as adults do on these automatic and nonstrategic tasks.

Many researchers have argued that young children do not have the type of category knowledge that is tapped by these memory organization tasks. As in the object sorting literature, there are many studies that demonstrate a developmental trend on memory tasks, from thematic or perceptual organization to taxonomic or conceptual organization. The developmental shift has been found in studies of clustering in recall (Melkman & Deutsch, 1977; Melkman et al., 1981); on false recognition tasks (Heidenheimer, 1978), and on studies of release from proactive inhibition (Hoemann, DeRosa, & Andrews, 1974).

This developmental shift notion has not gone unchallenged. In several recent studies, young children have responded as if their knowledge is taxonomically organized. There may be several reasons for these discrepancies between findings, but most of the evidence supports the studies that find no developmental differences. On some of the tasks where a thematic-taxonomic shift was found, young children's thematic preferences may have prevented them from responding to the taxonomic relations that were present. When these salient thematic relations are removed, children seem to be more likely to organize information taxonomically. For example, on clustering tasks in which thematic and taxonomic lists are presented to different groups of subjects (Galbraith & Day, 1978), or in which there are no thematic choices available (Rossi & Rossi, 1965), children at all ages tend to cluster by category. Thus, without competing thematic relations, children are sensitive to taxonomic relations.

Other seemingly contradictory findings might be accounted for by the relative difficulty of the procedures used. In some cases, simplified versions of a task reveal taxonomic organization. One source of difficulty for children would be the use of superordinate categories that are unfamiliar to them. Hoemann et al. (1974) found a developmental difference in build-up and release from proactive inhibition with the categories "toys" and "kitchen utensils." "Kitchen utensils" probably is a particularly unfamiliar superordinate for young children; this may have made the shift between categories too difficult for the 4–year-olds in the Hoemann et al. study to notice. However, 3–year olds showed just as much buildup and release as did 5–year olds when they were shown pictures of "animals" and "clothing" (Esrov, Hall, & LaFever, 1974) and when they were verbally presented with exemplars of "clothing," "animals," "body parts," and "furniture" (Huttenlocher & Lui, 1979). Horton (1982) found a larger difference between the shift and control conditions when the superordinate category principles were familiar to the child than when they were unfamiliar, indicating that hierarchical knowledge for a given set of items does affect responses made on this task.

There are other ways in which tasks have been made less difficult and have erased developmental differences. For example, Goldberg, Perlmutter, and Myers (1974) found higher recall from related than unrelated lists in 2–year olds, whereas Nelson (1969) found equal recall by 5–year olds from related and unrelated lists. There are two important differences between the procedures used: Goldbert et al. used two item "lists" of physical objects; Nelson used orally presented lists of 15 words. The simplicity and concreteness of the Goldberg et al. task are clearly important factors in children's performance. Another example of discrepant findings that may have resulted from level of difficulty comes from the false recognition literature. Mansfield (1977) found a similar pattern of results in children in kindergarten, first, third, and fifth grade, and adults. At all ages, subjects showed longer latencies and made more errors to related than to unrelated probes. That is, they tended to falsely report that words such as "animal" and "toy" had been presented, when they had actually heard "horse" and "doll." On the other hand, Heidenheimer (1978) found virtually no false recognition errors to superordinate probes among 4– and 5–year-old children. There are a few crucial differences between Mansfield's and Heidenheimer's procedures. Heidenheimer used word lists and delayed the recognition task. Manfield embedded the target words in meaningful sentences and tested recognition immediately after each sentence. Mansfield's design may be more likely to elicit false recognition errors in children, because the sentences allow the children to understand each target word fully, and the immediacy of the test reduces memory demands for the target words. In cases like these, then, young children's difficulty with some versions of the tasks may have nothing to do with their category knowledge.

One task that has consistently shown no developmental differences is cued recall. In one study, Steinberg and Anderson (1975) found evidence for hierarchical knowledge in first-grade children. Children were given a list of sentences followed by various types of cues, and their task was to remember the last word in each sentence. Suppose the target word to be remembered was "apple." Children were better able to recall "apple" when they heard the superordinate word "fruit" as a cue than when they heard the cohyponym "banana." In general, superordinates of the target words cued recall more effectively than did cohyponyms of the target words. In addition, words that were predicted to be closer to the target in a semantic tree structure (e.g., "banana" vs. "hot dog") were also better cues. Similarly, Melkman et al. (1981) showed that superordinate category labels were the most effective retrieval cues for all ages tested (4,

5, and 9 years). Conceptual cues were more effective than color or form cues, even for children who, in a separate task, had shown a bias to group objects by color or form rather than by concept.

On each of these memory organization tasks, there are at least some conditions under which children have been shown to respond as adults do. However, the nature of these tasks is such that even adult-like performance does not allow us to credit children with knowledge of the asymmetry and transitivity of inclusion. Mansfield has claimed, to the contrary, that one result of her false recognition study reveals some sensitivity in children to the asymmetry of the hierarchical relation. Subjects displayed longer latencies and more false recognitions to probes that were superordinate than to those that were subordinate to the target. This finding cannot, however, be taken as strong evidence for knowledge of asymmetry because there are alternative explanations that might account for it. Children might be forming an image when presented with the sentence, and the latency and error differences may reflect the degree to which the probe word matches the image. For a concrete target word (e.g., "horse"), children's images would match both the concrete and the general word (e.g., "horse" and "animal"), whereas for a more general target word (e.g., "animal"), children are likely to form an image of a concrete object (e.g., a dog), which may match only the target and not the probe (e.g., "horse"). In any case, this task provides no direct evidence that children are aware of the asymmetry of the superordinate-subordinate relation.

In general, though, there is fairly good evidence that young children make use of some kind of taxonomic knowledge in each of the memory tasks we have discussed. As in the object classification work, some of these findings should be interpreted cautiously because taxonomic relations are often confounded with other types of relations. For example, when categorized lists of words are compared with random lists, there may be more opportunities for a child to find thematic relations among members of categorized lists, such as the relation between "shoe" and "sock" or "knife" and "fork." In addition, when children respond to an association between two category members, their responses may often be based on perceptual similarity rather than category knowledge. Children's mature performance on memory organization tasks may not be entirely due to their knowledge of categories; there may be other relations among the items that are also affecting children's responses.

To summarize: Classification tasks, the class inclusion problem, habituation in infants, and a variety of memory tasks have all been taken as measures of children's sensitivity to categorical structure. Successful classification provides evidence that children can form the relevant categories. It does not, however, provide direct evidence that children appreciate the class inclusion relation because successful solutions can be achieved without understanding the asymmetry and transitivity of inclusion. Conversely, the classification task contains many extraneous task demands that could prevent successful solution even in children who understand inclusion. Successful solution of the class inclusion problem, where children must quantitatively compare the subset to its superset, provides strong evidence for understanding inclusion. But this task has so many super-fluous task requirements that children's failure to solve it cannot be taken as evidence that they do not understand inclusion. The various habituation and memory tasks access implicit knowledge or sensitivity to categorical structure without as many additional task demands. The findings from these procedures indicate that quite young children have at least begun to acquire superordinate categories. The tasks, however, many be overly sensitive to all sorts of relations other than taxonomic ones that exist between the objects. Moreover, children's use of categorical structure in these tasks does not provide evidence that the asymmetry and transitivity of inclusion is understood. There are however, sever-al studies that have more directly assessed whether children's categories are organized hierarchically.

Hierarchical Organization of Ontological Knowledge

Some evidence that young children have categories organized hierarchically comes from extremely interesting work by Keil (1979) on the development of ontological knowledge. Ontological knowledge refers to beliefs about what the basic categories of existence are. These are very general categories such as events, abstract ideas, physical objects, living things, and nonliving things. Building on a philosophical analysis by Sommers, Keil (1979) argues that these ontological categories are organized into strict hierarchies, that is, there are no intersecting sets. One source of evidence for the hierarchical organization of ontological categories was obtained by determining what types of predication are permissible at different levels of the hierarchy. If categories are organized hier-archically, then a predicate that is applicable to a category term at one level in the hierarchy should be applicable to all terms below it. The appropriateness of a predicate depends on whether or not it makes sense to apply the predicate to the term, and not on whether or not the predicate truthfully applies. In other words, the predicate must produce a sensible and nonanomalous sentence, but it need not produce a true one. Thus "green" can be predicated of cows because, although cows are not green, we can make sense out of the sentence. In contrast, it makes no sense to say that a cow is an hour long. This is anomalous because terms denoting physical objects such as "cow" cannot take predicates such as "an hour long."

The claim for hierarchical ordering implies that predicates that are sensibly applied to a category term at one level of the hierarchy will apply to all those below it. For example, the predicate "is red" can be sensibly attributed to physical objects but not to events. In accord with the hierarchical prediction, "red" can also be sensibly applied to all of the subsets of physical objects such as artifacts, plants, animals, liquids, and so on.

The claim that ontological categories are hierarchically organized is not a trivial or vacuous one. In principle, it is certainly possible for there to be exceptions and, in fact, there do appear to be violations of this constraint (see Keil, 1979, for discussions of why they may be only apparent exceptions). For example, the predicate "is rude" applies to nonphysical entities such as "a rude remark." It also applies to people, as in a "rude person." However, it does not apply to other physical objects. For example, it is anomalous to speak of an orange being rude. But because "rude" refers to nonphysical entities high in the hierarchy (e.g., remarks) and to a physical object category low in the hierarchy (people), it should refer to the intervening physical object categories as well. Since it does not, it violates the hierarchical order.

Assuming, however, that most terms will obey the hierarchical ordering constraint, Keil (1979) investigated whether children's conceptual structure was hierarchical. Children as young as 5 years old were asked to make judgments about the appropriateness of a predicate for a term. Keil found that, as children developed, their ontological trees became more differentiated. That is, adults' ontological trees have several nodes in spots where children have only one node. For example, children allowed physical objects and events to share predicates that adults would have differentiated. Yet, despite this difference, the children's categories still appeared to be ordered in a strictly hierarchical pattern. The children seemed confused about the distinctions between abstract ideas, events, and physical objects, and had not differentiated them as clearly as adults have. But the ontological categories children have established appear to be hierarchically ordered.

There are many differences between the work on ontological categories and standard treatments of categorical knowledge. First, the level of generality of the two types of categories differs. Ontological categories consist of extremely general categories such as "physical object" and "abstract idea," whereas most studies of categories focus on more specific categories such as "vehicles," "dogs," "roses," etc. Keil (1979) points out another difference: Most studies of traditional categories specify which features of a given category are true rather than which are sensible. For example, most analyses of categorization would emphasize that birds have feathers but bats do not. In contrast, from the ontological perspective, the predicate "having feathers" can be sensibly attributed to both birds (truly) and bats (falsely), so these two predicates would not be differentiated in the ontological hierarchy. If we convert Keil's procedure to making judgments of truth rather than appropriateness of the predicate, it can be seen that the predicates are extremely general, as are the categories. For example, it is because ideas do not have color that "the idea is green" becomes anomalous. Because physical objects do have color, the sentence "the cows are green" is sensible. Thus the predicates that are truly attributed to the terms are extremely general ones such as "has color," "has weight," "has duration." In sum, ontological knowledge can be expressed as sentences attributing very general properties to extremely general categories such as "physical objects have weight."

It is difficult to know how to generalize from Keil's work to ordinary categories. On the one hand, one could argue that if children have organized their ontological knowledge hierarchically, this shows that they have the capacity for hierarchal representation. On the other hand, it may not be appropriate to generalize from the way children represent ontological knowledge to whether children are capable of representing much more differentiated categories such as poodle, dog, and mammal as class inclusion hierarchies.

Children's Understanding of the Asymmetry and Transitivity of Inclusion

A study by Harris (1975) more explicitly addressed the question of whether children appreciate the transitivity and asymmetry of class inclusion. In this study, children ranging in age from 5 to 7 years old were told, "A mib is a bird" and then were asked "Does a mib have wings?" and "Does a mib eat food?" Children almost invariably responded "yes" to these questions. This suggests that they are capable of making the simple inference that the properties of the category will transfer to a new subset or a new member of the category. It is possible, however, that children took the term "mib" to be a synonym for "bird" rather than a type of bird. Moreover, the children showed little evidence of understanding the asymmetry of inclusion. When told, for example, that a mib was a bird, a sizable proportion of children were likely to conclude that it was a robin. The results are not reported according to age, so we do not know whether these invalid inferences came mainly from the younger children. The inappropriate inferences could be prevented by specifying a property that would be incompatible with the inference. For example, when told that a mib is a *white* bird, children no longer concluded that it was a robin. However, this could be because children know that robins are not white and not because they understand the asymmetry of inclusion.

The clearest evidence that young children have some appreciation for the asymmetry of inclusion comes from a study by Smith (1979) that improved upon the methodology originally used by Inhelder and Piaget (1964) to study this question. Inhelder and Piaget (1964) asked children quantified questions such as, "Are all the roses flowers?" In their study, children denied that all the roses were flowers, noting that there were daisies too. This finding suggests that children interpreted the inclusion relation as being symmetrical (all the roses are flowers and all the flowers are roses) rather than asymmetrical. However, the details of the methodology and data are not clear in this report. The research has been extended in important ways by Smith (1979) and also by Carey (1978).

In Smith's (1979) study, children ranging in age from 4 to 6, who had passed a pretest demonstrating their understanding of "all" and "some," were questioned about three consequences of inclusion. One type of question was about class inference. Children were told "A _____ is a kind of x." They were then asked "Does a _____ have to be a y?" In one-third of the cases the conclusion was valid (where x was a subset of y), in one-third of the cases the conclusion was indeterminate (where x is a superset of y), and in one-third of the cases the conclusion was invalid (where x and y were disjoint). An example of a valid item is "A pug is a kind of dog. Does a pug have to be an animal?" Note that "pug" is unfamiliar to the children but "dog" and "animal" are familiar.

Children were also asked questions about property inferences. They were told "All xs have _____," and asked "Do all ys have to have _____?" As before, one-third of the inferences were valid, one-third were indeterminate and one-third were invalid. An example of a valid inference is "All milk has lactose. Does all chocolate milk have to have lactose?"

The 6–year-old children were able to draw these appropriate inferences from the class inclusion relation. In contrast, the 4–year olds in this study showed only minimal evidence of being able to draw the appropriate transitive inferences. For the class inference task and the property inference task, the 4–year olds were answering 64% and 66% of the questions correctly—just above chance performance. Smith suggests that the wording of the questions, asking children whether an object *had to* have a given property, may have confused them. Replication of this study with changes in the wording of questions is needed before we can assess the ability of the younger children. Based on the available data, however, 4–year olds do not seem able to draw the appropriate inferences.

Although the 4–year olds seemed unable to draw the transitive inferences from the class inclusion relation, they did seem to understand the asymmetry of inclusion. Children were asked questions using the quantifier "all" and "some," again for three types of set relations, where x is a subset of y, where x is a superset of y and where x and y are disjoint. Half of the children heard questions involving the quantifier "some" first, and a half heard questions involving the quantifier "all" first. The youngest children's ability to answer the questions correctly varied markedly as a function of the task demands. By the second half of the procedure, the youngest children were showing little signs of understanding the asymmetry of the relation. Similarly, when the questions involving the quantifier "some" were asked first, children showed little sign of understanding the asymmetry of the relation. In these "unfavorable" conditions, children sometimes responded in accord with Inhelder and Piaget's claim that children treat the inclusion relation as a symmetric one. However, on the first half of the trials for those children who answered questions about the quantifier "all" first, even the youngest children consistently honored the asymmetry of class inclusion. Though their ability to deal with asymmetry of inclusion is fragile and easily disrupted, 4–year-old children are able to appreciate the asymmetry of the relation.

There has even been some work on a chimpanzee's understanding of quantified relations (Premack, 1976). Premack taught Sarah, the linguistically trained chimpanzee, the quantifiers "all," "none," and "one." Two sets of crackers were used in training. One set consisted of 5 round crackers and nothing else, the other set consisted of 5 square crackers and nothing else. Sarah had to note that "all" of the crackers were round when presented with the round crackers. She had to note that "none" of the crackers were round when presented with the square crackers. In the first attempts to train Sarah, her error rate was very high, e.g., 12 errors out of 20 trials. The training was then modified to include another set of crackers, triangular ones, and to ask Sarah separate questions about round, square, and triangular crackers instead of always asking about round ones. With this additional training, Sarah's performance rose to 74% correct. Thus, this advantaged chimpanzee seems capable of making simple quantified inferences.

However, there is no way of knowing whether or not Sarah understood the asymmetry of the relation. Recall that the error children make in interpreting quantifiers is to deny that all roses are flowers because there are some daisies too. To be able to find the analogous error in this situation, the materials would have to consist of all round crackers plus some other round things, e.g., round cookies. With the current materials, the relation between the two classes is in fact symmetric, that is, all the crackers are round and all the round things are crackers. Because Sarah was presented with a symmetric rather than an asymmetric relation, it is not possible to tell whether she understood the asymmetry of class inclusion.

Premack (1976) noted that in this training the relations being quantified were perceptually defined. Sarah could see that the crackers were round. The materials were extended to see if Sarah could learn to quantify over conceptually defined relations. She was asked to quantify over part-whole or belonging relations. For example, she was asked to judge whether an apple wedge, apple skin, and apple stem were all parts of an apple. Sarah could successfully quantify over this conceptual relation. One might be tempted to generalize from this finding to assume that Sarah could quantify class relations on a conceptual basis. However, as we will argue next, there are striking differences between part-whole and inclusion relations, and children are capable of solving problems with part-whole relations that they fail to solve with class inclusion (c.f. Markman, 1981).

COLLECTIONS VERSUS CLASSES AS HIERARCHICAL ORGANIZATION

We turn now to describe work that has contrasted the hierarchical structure of classes with a different type of hierarchical structure—the part-whole structure of collections. The differences between collections and classes may help explain why children find class inclusion relations difficult. Collections are the referents of collective nouns, e.g., forest, pile, family, army, and are structured into part-whole hierarchies, e.g., a tree is part of a forest, a block is part of a pile, a child is part of a family, etc. We will argue that collections form a simpler hierarchy for children to deal with because the asymmetry of part-whole relations is easier to maintain than that of class inclusion.

One of the reasons that the asymmetry of collections may be easier to maintain than that of classes is that the two levels of a collection hierarchy are clearly distinct, whereas the levels of a class inclusion hierarchy are more similar and thus more confusable. For class inclusion, both levels of the hierarchy involve the same *is a* relation. A poodle *is a* dog and *is an* animal. This may contribute to the child's confusion of levels and difficulty in keeping track of the asymmetry. For part-whole structures, the relations differ at the two hierarchical levels. A boy *is a* child but is *part of* a family. An oak *is a* tree but is *part of* a forest. If there were less confusion between part and whole than between subclass and superclass, than the asymmetrical relations of collections would have greater psychological stability and would not so readily degenerate into symmetrical relations.

One might think that collections should help children appreciate transitivity, because collections are predicted to help children maintain the asymmetry of the hierarchy. This does not follow, however, because the part-whole relations of collections are not transitive. A property true of the whole will not necessarily be true of the part. For example, if we know that the family is large, it does not follow that the child in the family is large. If we know that a pile of bricks is U-shaped, it does not follow that the bricks in the pile are U-shaped. Because the two levels of the collection hierarchy are defined by different relations, transitivity is violated, but the asymmetry should be simpler for children to establish and maintain.

Before describing the results of studies comparing collections to classes, we will describe further the ways in which these two types of hierarchies differ.

How Membership is Determined.   Membership in a class can be determined by evaluating an object against the defining criteria of the class. To know whether an object is a toy block, for example, one must examine it for its size, shape, material, or function, etc. To know whether an object is a member of a collection, however, one needs to know something about its relationship to the other possible members of the collection. To determine whether a block is part of a pile of blocks, for example, one must examine its relation to other blocks in the pile. Although spatial proximity is not necessary for membership in a family, a team, or a club, some type of relationship is still required.

The Nature of Their Part-Whole Relation.   Collections have more literal part-whole relations than do classes. A dog, for example, is a kind of (or type of or example of) an animal, not part of an animal. In contrast, children are parts of families, not kinds of (or types of or examples of) families.

Internal Structure and the Nature of the Whole Formed.   The internal structure of collections results in their greater psychological coherence compared to classes. Collections have an internal organization that results in a coherent structure. A random set of people does not make a family. To be a family, the people must be related to each other. Intuitively it seems fairly natural to consider a family, a pile, or a crowd as a single thing. English captures this intuition in that collective nouns are singular in form.

What is so interesting about collections is that, unlike objects, they are readily conceptualized as a multiplicity of objects rather than a single entity, yet we have the ability to think of them as a single aggregate as well. It is not obvious whether the more natural level of organization is trees or forest, soldiers or army, ships or fleet. These levels do not contrast in naturalness to the same extent as person parts vs. person. The parts of a collection—e.g., the trees, the soldiers, or the ships—can be readily perceived without literally segmenting the perceptual array. Collections impose singularity on an array that can be easily seen as consisting of discrete objects. In so doing, collections reveal that the principles that unify an array are not entirely perceptual. A cognitive act can give objectlike properties to highly individualized discrete elements.

It may seem surprising to argue that by being relational, collections could simplify hierarchical organization. Having to take relations into account could just as well complicate as simplify the problem. But noticing relations may not necessarily be an additional requirement. It may be that having to ignore relations rather than notice them is what causes difficulty. In common, everyday situations, objects are found in spatial, temporal, and causal contexts. To treat an object solely as a member of a class requires abstraction away from this contextual information to consider only what is relevant for the category. To treat an object as a member of a collection involves noticing relations that exist between the objects. In this regard, collections are similar to events or themes that also have relational organizations (see Mandler, 1979; Nelson, in press). These eventlike meaningful structures might be a more spontaneous, natural way of organizing information (see Mandler, 1979 and Markman, 1981 for related arguments). Probably little time is spent cataloging objects, in trying to generate the taxonomies to which objects belong. Because stories have relational organizations, there are few cross-cultural or developmental differences in the principles people use to understand stories (Mandler, Scribner, Cole, & DeForest, 1980). In marked contrast, many cross-cultural and developmental differences are found in the use of taxonomic organization. Thus the relational structure of collections does not necessarily have to be more difficult for children to understand.

To summarize, collections and classes are both hierarchically organized concepts, but they differ in their structural principles. The part-whole structure of collections is a type of relational structure that confers psychological coherence on the higher order aggregate formed and may thereby enhance the asymmetry of the relation. If this analysis is correct, then organizing items into collections should help children solve problems that require dealing with two levels of a hierarchy at the same time.

The Piagetian Class Inclusion Problem

Some evidence for the greater coherence of collections over classes comes from work on the Piagetian class inclusion problem described earlier, where children are asked to make a quantitative comparison between a superordinate set and the larger of its subordinate sets (Inhelder & Piaget, 1964). For example, a child might be shown pictures of five boys and three girls and asked, "Are there more boys or more children?" Although children are asked to make a part-whole comparison (boys vs. children) they make part-part (boys vs. girls) comparisons instead. To answer the class inclusion question correctly, children must maintain the whole class in mind while simultaneously attending to its subclasses. This division of the superordinate class into subordinate classes weakens the psychological integrity of the superordinate class. If collections have greater psychological integrity they should be less vulnerable to this weakening.

In several studies, children have consistently revealed a superior ability to make part-whole comparisons with collections than with classes (Markman, 1973: Markman & Seibert, 1976). In each of the studies, the objects children viewed and the questions they were asked in the two conditions were identical. The only difference in the two conditions was in the description given the higher level of the hierarchy. For example, for the "boys-children" comparison in the class condition, children were told, "Here are kindergarten children. These are the boys and these are the girls and these are the children." They were then asked: "Who would have a bigger birthday party, someone who invited the boys or someone who invited the children?" As usual, young children often answered incorrectly, claiming that there were more boys. The collection version of this question was identical except that "kindergarten children" was changed to "kindergarten class" (note *class* is a collection term). So the question became "Who would have a bigger birthday party, someone who invited the boys or someone who invited the class?" With this change or just one word in the question children were able to solve the part-whole comparison that they usually find so difficult.

An alternative explanation for these findings has been proposed and tested by Dean, Chabaud, and Bridges (1981). They point out that collective nouns in English often connote large numbers of objects. For example, terms like "bunch," "pile," and "army" by definition refer to large numbers of objects. If children are sensitive to this aspect of collections, Dean et al. argue, it may provide them with a strategy for answering the collection question that does not require knowledge of the logic of part-whole relations. In other words, it may be that children think collective nouns mean "a lot" of something, and that in the class inclusion task, they choose the collective term for this reason. If Dean et al. are right, this would mean that the collection advantage of the class inclusion task would be an artifact of the procedure—collections always label the most numerous set of objects (the whole array), and the correct answer is always to choose the collection. Under the large number interpretation, though, children should choose the referent of a collective noun, even when it is not the correct answer. If, for example, the smaller subset of objects is labeled as a "family" or a "bunch," children who are responding on the basis of the semantics of the collective terms should incorrectly respond that the small subset has more objects. Dean et al. set out to test this hypothesis by comparing children's responses to standard collective whole questions with their answers to class inclusion questions in which the smallest subpart was labeled as a collection. They found evidence that children will incorrectly choose the least numerous subset when it is labeled as a collection.

Although it is possible that children do have some sensitivity to the large number aspect of the semantics of collective nouns, we have evidence that the large number explanation cannot account for the results. Due to a number of problems in the procedure used by Dean et al., children in their study probably become very confused by the questions asked of them. In particular, children always viewed the same array of objects, and the same collective noun was used to refer to different parts of the array from one question to the next. For example, a child might be asked one question about green and brown frogs where they would be told to suppose that the green and brown frogs were a family. On later questions, the child might be told to suppose that the green frogs are a family, but the brown frogs are not a family. This continual shifting of referents for the collective nouns was likely to confuse the children. In addition, the wording of the question in the example just given suggests another problem. The class inclusion question was worded in a hypothetical manner; children were asked, for example, to "suppose" that one group of frogs were a family, and then asked "Do you think that there are more frogs or more in the family?" This departure from the standard wording of the class inclusion problem was likely to encourage the children to answer the question on the basis of their knowledge of the meaning of the terms, rather than on the basis of the array of objects in front of them.

There is one final problem with the Dean et al. procedure. To ensure that the children would know which group of objects was currently being labeled with the collective noun, they were tested repeatedly. For example, they were asked, "Which one is the family?" Children who answered incorrectly were given feedback. This procedure may have made the collective referent very salient to the children and biased them to give collective responses.

Children in the Dean et al. study may have been biased to make collective responses, either by their confusion, or by the experimenter's repeated emphasis on the collective array. Particularly when children are confused about what they are being asked to do, the large number aspect of collections is likely to provide them with a strategy for answering the question. We have designed a new test of the large number hypothesis that elminiates these problems (Callanan & Markman, in preparation). In this study, children were divided into four groups. One group was asked to compare the collective whole to the larger of its subparts, and another group was asked the analogous class inclusion questions. A third group was asked to compare the whole array to the smaller subpart, which was labeled as a collection, and a fourth group was asked analogous questions without any collective nouns. The children were asked 5 questions about 5 different arrays. The results of this study contradict those of Dean et al. We replicated the standard class-collection difference, as did Dean et al. That is, children were more likely to choose the collective whole than to choose the whole array labeled with a class term. However, children almost never chose the least numerous part of the array when it was labeled as a collection. For example, children who were shown an array of trees labeled as a forest of oak trees and some Christmas trees, were not likely to say that there were more in the forest than there were trees. Thus, these results are counter to those predicted by the large number hypothesis.

In the light of these results, the large number hypothesis does not appear to be a viable alternative hypothesis for the collection advantage on the Piagetian class inclusion problem. When children are not confused by shifting labels and hypothetically worded questions, they do not show a bias to choose small arrays labeled with collective nouns. Moreover, the large number hypothesis would have no force in explaining other collection effects, which will be discussed in the next sections. Collections have been shown to help children on very different sorts of tasks, tasks for which the large number hypothesis is not relevant.

Empirical Vs. Logical Solutions to Part-Whole Comparison Problems

In the studies of part-whole comparisons just described, children unable to solve the problems with classes were able to solve them with collections. In the studies to be reported below (Markman, 1978), all children who participated were capable of correctly solving the Piagetian class inclusion problem. These studies addressed the question of whether the children had an explicit understanding of the logic of the solution rather than whether they had the ability to solve the problem.

Given a part-whole relation, it follows logically that the whole is larger than one of its parts. However, children who correctly answer the Piagetian class inclusion question could do so on empirical rather than logical grounds. They could take the greater numerosity of the superordinate set as compared to its subordinate set to be an empirical fact about the classes rather than a logical consequence of the inclusion relation. Given the hypothesized abstractness of the part-whole relation of class inclusion, children might be expected to have difficulty examining the relation in order to assess its logical consequences.

There are several ways of determining whether children understood the logic of the problem. First, when empirical means of judging the relative numerosity of the classes are withheld, the children should still be able to answer the question. Second, children should realize that no addition or subtraction of objects could result in the subordinate set having more members than its superordinate set. Third, if a new unfamiliar class is said to be subordinated to another class, then children should be willing to make the part-whole comparison without any additional information about the classes. A child who does not solve the part-whole comparison problems in these situations can be said to be treating the answers as empirical rather than logical consequences of the classes.

The first study reported in Markman (1978) established that when children initially solve the class inclusion problem, they do so on empirical rather than logical grounds. Children from grades two through six participated in the study, once it was established that they could consistently solve the class inclusion problems. Children under the age of 10 or 11 did poorly on class inclusion problems when empirical means of quantification were not available, and they often allowed for the possibility that a subordinate class could be made larger than its superordinate class. Thus, children who could consistently solve the class problem treated the quantitative relationship between the subordinate classes as an empirical fact.

If children do not appreciate the logical status of part-whole comparisons on classes, a comparison between classes and collections becomes of interest. The more literal part-whole relation that characterizes collections should promote an explicit appreciation of the logic of the problem. This hypothesis was tested in a replication of the first study that included a condition where children heard objects described as collections. As before, children from grades two through six participated and only children who demonstrated competence in solving standard class inclusion problems were included in the study. The findings from the first study were replicated. Children failed to appreciate the logic of the class inclusion problems. In marked contrast, the collection questions produced significantly superior performance. Though the materials used and the questions asked were identical in all respects except for the collection-class difference, children solving collection problems better appreciated that empirical confirmation of the part-whole comparison is not needed.

Cardinal Number

In his work on number, Piaget argued for the importance of the relation between classification and an understanding of number (Piaget, 1965). In fact, the class inclusion problem was discussed at length as part of the study of the child's conception of number. For Piaget, number requires integrating the logic of classes and the logic of asymmetrical relations: "Number is at the same time a class and an asymmetrical relation, the units of which it is composed being simultaneously added because they are equivalent, and seriated because they are different from one another. . . . Since each number is a whole, born of the union of equivalent and distinct terms, it cannot be constituted without inclusion and seriation. [p. 184]." The work we are about to describe, emphasizes a different way in which number and classes are related. The number studies we will discuss provide more evidence that children can think of a collection as a coherent whole more easily than they can do so for a class. Although these studies do not provide a direct test of how collections differ from classes in terms of hierarchical organization, they are relevant to the analysis of the structure of collections. In these studies, children were not explicitly asked to conceptualize two levels of a hierarchy as in class inclusion problems. However, we will argue that dealing with cardinal number implicitly requires a part-whole analysis and that children should be better able to solve number problems when they conceptualize the objects as organized into the part-whole structure of collections.

The cardinal number of a given set of items is not a property of the individual items themselves. Number is a property of the set taken as a whole and not a property of the elements that compose the set. To see why, consider the following syllogism: "Men are numerous. John is a man. Therefore, John is numerous." The syllogism is absurd because numerosity does not distribute over each element of a set but is a characteristic of sets themselves. To take another example, "There are five books" does not imply that any one of the books is five. "Five" applies only to the group, not the individuals in it. Of course, one cannot ignore individual members when calculating the numerical value of a set. Individuals must be counted or otherwise enumerated; that is, the "parts" must be taken into account. But it is not enough just to focus on the individuals; one must also consider the set taken as a whole. Because collections should promote conceptualization of individual objects as aggregates and because cardinal number applies to aggregates, not individuals, collections should facilitate numerical reasoning about discrete objects. There are many well-known problems that young children have in dealing with cardinal number (e.g., number conservation). Young children should be better able to solve these problems when the objects are thought of as collections rather than classes. This hypothesis was investigated in the following studies (Markman, 1979), which focused on different aspects of a full appreciation of cardinal number.

Number Conservation—Understanding the Irrevelance of a Length Transformation. In the standard conservation task (Piaget, 1965) two equal rows of pennies, or other items, are lined up in one-to-one correspondence. A 4- to 5-year-old child will usually claim that the rows are equal. One of the rows is spread out in front of the child who then typically judges that the lengthened row now has more pennies, though no pennies have been added or subtracted from either row. There are several ways in which the spreading of the pennies could prevent children from judging that the rows still have the same number of objects. First, it could draw the child's attention to individual pennies rather than the aggregate of pennies as the individual coins are moved about. Second, the one-to-one correspondence between rows has been disrupted, forcing the child to rely on more abstract notions of numerical equality (Gelman & Gallistel, 1978). Third, other quantitative dimensions—length and density—have been changed, although number remains invariant. A child msut correctly interpret the original judgment in terms of number and must attend to number per se throughout the physical transformation in order to override these other misleading factors. Collection labels, by making it easier for children to think about the aggregate and thus about number, might help them to conserve.

This hypothesis was tested by having 4–year-old children solve conservation problems where the objects were given either class or collection labels. Half of the children received class questions and half received collection questions. Each child was given four conservation problems. The only difference between conditions was that a collection label (e.g., *army*) was substituted for a class label (*soldiers*) for the rows. For example, a child in the class condition saw two rows of soldiers lined up in one-to-one correspondence and heard: "These are your soldiers and these are my soldiers. What are more: my soldiers, your soldiers, or are they both the same?" A child in the collection condition saw the identical two rows and heard: "This is your army and this is my army. What's more: my army, your army, or are they both the same?" Then in both conditions, the experimenter spread out one of the rows and repeated the question.

The children in the two conditions were presented with identical perceptual information and asked virtually identical questions. Yet, simply relabeling the objects as collections helped children to conserve. Children hearing the objects described as classes correctly answered an average of only 1.46 out of 4 problems. Children hearing objects described as collections correctly answered an average of 3.18 problems.

Understanding the Relevance of Addition and Subtraction.   The study to be reported next addressed whether children who have heard objects described as collections would be more likely to realize that the addition or subtraction of an object does in fact change the number.

After a child has seen someone add or subtract an object from one row, that child will strongly tend to judge that two initially equal rows differ. Even in the standard conservation task, children judge that the rows are different though the rows are in fact the same. The conservation procedure leads children to erroneously respond "different"—because: (a) Children make an initial judgment that the two quantities are equal, witness a change, and then are requestioned. These demand characteristics call for a "different" response (Hall & Kingsley, 1968; McGarrigle & Donaldson, 1975; (b) there are misleading perceptual differences that the child must resist in order to judge the rows to be equivalent; (c) the rows do in fact differ on other quantitative dimensions, e.g., length. All of these factors would lead a child to judge that the two rows are not equal. When an object is added or subtracted from a row, all of these factors remain and so still call for a judgment of difference. Now, however, "different" is the correct answer, so children could respond correctly without attending to number per se. One way to determine whether or not children base a judgment on number is to examine their justifications for their responses. Though children hearing arrays described as collections are predicted to be more sensitive to numerical change, this difference may appear only when their justifications are taken into account.

This hypothesis was tested by having children solve addition and subtraction problems where the objects were given either class or collection labels. Four-year-olds participated in the study. Half were in the class condition and half in the collection condition. The procedure in this study was identical to the conservation procedure in the previous study except that instead of lengthening a row the experimenter added or subtracted an object from a row.

As expected, after witnessing an addition or subtraction, children almost always judged that the two rows were no longer equivalent. The mean number correct for children hearing class descriptions was 3.14 out of 4 compared to 3.55 for children hearing collection descriptions.

The fact that children in the collection condition are so willing to say the rows are different rules out an alternative explanation for the results of the conservation study. Children were not better able to conserve because of any type of "same" bias that a collection term might have introduced. Children hearing collection labels are quite ready to respond "different" when it is appropriate.

The children's justifications for their judgments were scored as to whether or not they were basing their answers on numerically relevant information. The modal justification for correct answers was to say that an item had been added or subtracted. The main difference in the justification between the two conditions was that collection children mentioned number relatively more often whereas class children gave relatively more irrelevant explanations. Overall, collection children were significantly more likely to base their judgments on numerically relevant information.

The Cardinality Principle.   Three–and 4–year-old children are generally able to count an array of five toys. However, when they are then asked "How many toys are there?" they often count again rather than answering "five." This is a reflection of their difficulty with the cardinality principle, the failure to appreciate that the last number counted becomes the cardinal number of the set (Gelman & Gallistel, 1978; Schaeffer, Eggleston, & Scott, 1974). If part of the child's problem with the cardinality principle is a difficulty in thinking of the individual items as a set to which cardinal number applies, then helping the child think of the arrays as collections might promote correct use of this principle.

Three– and 4–year olds participated in a study designed to test this hypothesis. Half of the children were assigned to the class condition and half to the collection condition. In both conditions children viewed some objects, were instructed to count the objects, and then were asked how many objects there were.

When children heard a class description, e.g., "Here are some pigs. count the pigs," they counted "One, two, three, four, five." When they were then asked "How many pigs are there?", they tended to count again, "One, two, three, four, five." In marked contrast, when children in the collection condition heard, e.g., "Here is a pig family, count the pigs in the family," they counted. But when asked "How many pigs are in the family?", they very often responded, "Five" without recounting.

In summary, we have argued that number is a property of a set of objects and not of objects themselves. If thinking about individuals as collections helps children focus on the aggregate as well as the individual, it should also facilitate numerical reasoning. As predicted, thinking of objects as collections helped children solve numerical problems they otherwise would have failed. It helped them conserve number in the face of an irrelevant change. It helped them access and verbalize a numerically relevant basis for their judgments of equality and of difference, and it promoted their use of the cardinality principle.

This is, of course, by no means the frist demonstration that children's performance can be improved during an experimental session. However, when training, feedback, modeling, or other types of practice are used, it is less surprising that children improve. Or when the problems are modified so as to simplify the task demands, improvement would be expected. In the present work, however, there is no obvious way in which the problems, such as conservation task, for example, would be simplified by relabeling trees as a forest, or soldiers as an army. There is certainly no way in which the procedure trained children or induced any abilities or knowledge that they did not already possess before they participated in the studies. To take the clearest case, consider the study on the cardinality principle where after children counted an array of objects they were asked how many objects there were. Children hearing the objects described as classes tended to count again, whereas children hearing the objects described as collections correctly gave the cardinal number. Relabeling trees as forest could not possibly have taught children that the last number in a count series becomes the cardinal number of the set. They must have already possessed this principle, yet have been prevented from accessing it. The general point that young children's abilities may be underestimated by traditional procedures had been forcefully argued by Gelman and her colleagues (Gelman, 1978; Gelman & Gallistel, 1978).

Learning Hierarchial Relations

Children must eventually learn hierarchically organized class inclusion relations, e.g., that chairs are furniture, that poodles are dogs, that oaks are trees. In first learning terms, children learn common labels for objects, often at the basic level (Anglin, 1977; Brown, 1958; Rosch et al., 1976). Once these labels are learned, the child must cope with the fact that now the car will also be labeled "vehicle" and the dog, "animal," etc. As Macnamara (1982) pointed out, children must learn how one object can have multiple labels and figure out what the relations between them are. Many options are possible, including that the terms be synonomous, overlapping, or hierarchical. If the terms are taken to be hierarchical, one might suppose that class inclusion would be a likely hypothesis, especially for older children, because class terms are far more frequent in the language and children must have encountered many more of them. Though collective nouns are scarce relative to class terms, it still could be that the collection hierarchy is easier for children to construct. When children are relatively free to impose their own structure on a novel hierachy, they might prefer a collection to a class organization.

This hypothesis was tested by contriving a situation where children were presented with only minimal information about a hierarchical relation (Markman, Horton, & McLanahan, 1980). This study was designed to see how children would interpret the relations when given relative freedom. In actuality the relations were novel class inclusion hierarchies, analogous to the relations between oaks, pines, and trees. Ostensive devinition (pointing and labeling) was used to achieve a minimal specification of the relationship. To illustrate, imagine that oaks and pines are lined in a row in front of the child. As the experimenter points to the oaks, he says "These are oaks;" as he points to the pines he says "These are pines;" and as he points to the trees he says "These are trees." When he describes trees in the plural, "These are trees," it means that each individual tree is a tree. Thus the use of the plural establishes the class inclusion relation. The singular would have to be used in order to establish a collection, e.g., "This is a forest." Though the ostensive definition provides only minimal information, it does establish that the objects presented form a class inclusion hierarchy.

Suppose children misinterpret the class inclusion relation as a collection hierarchy. What errors should they make? They should erroneously believe that several of the items together form an instance of the concept at the higher level of the hierarchy (trees in the example) and should not believe that any single item is an instance. To see why, consider what the correct response would be had children actually learned a collection, e.g., "forest." If asked to point to the forest, the child should point to many trees but should deny that a pine or any other single tree is itself a forest.

Children from 6 to 17 years old participated in the study. Each child learned four novel categories, one at a time, each composed of two subcategories. All of the category exemplars were small construction paper figures of novel shapes or novel animate figures. Nonsense syllables were used as names for the novel figures.

The results of this study revealed that children, until a surprisingly late age, tend to misinterpret class inclusion relations as collections when only minimal information is provided. When novel class inclusion relations were taught by ostensive definition, children as old as 14 often mistakenly interpreted the relations as collections. When asked what would be analogous to "Show me a pine," children correctly picked up a single pine. When the experimenter, while pointing to a pine, asked "Is this a pine?" children responded correctly. The errors occurred almost exclusively on the upper level of the hierarchy. When asked "Show me a tree" children scooped up a handful rather than just one. When the experimenter, while pointing to a tree asked "Is this a tree?" children often said "No." This is exactly as one would expect if children were answering questions about a collection.

Because collections form more stable hierarchies, it may be easier for children to keep the two levels of the hierarchy distinct. At least in the somewhat artificial conditions of the present study, children apparently found it simpler to impose a collection structure on a novel hierarchy than to correctly interpret it as inclusion. This is true despite the fact that children must certainly have more experience learning inclusion relations, because collective nouns are relatively rare. Because this was an unusual way to learn novel concepts, collection errors may be unlikely in natural situations. However, there is some anecdotal (Valentine, 1942) and experimental (Macnamara, 1982) evidence suggesting that such errors may be found in a naturalistic context. We have conducted a more controlled study to further investigate this possibility (Callahan & Markman, 1982). We questioned 2– and 3–year-old children about five categories: toys (balls and dolls), animals (horses and cows), drinks (milk and juice), children (boys and girls), and cars (racing cars and Volkswagens). In general there was a very low error rate in part because these category terms were pretested to ensure that children knew them (in the plural). However, there was a significant tendency for children to interpret the terms as collections. Children agree, for example, that a set of toys is toys, but deny that a single toy (a doll for example) is itself a toy, and they pick up several toys when asked for one. We were able to rule out a possible alternative explanation for these findings. Children might pick the best label for a given array and then reject any other label. If so, they would deny that a doll is a toy because "doll" is a better label than "toy." To test this hypothesis, we asked children whether the superordinate label applied to a plural but homogeneous set of objects. For example, children were asked "Are these toys?" for two dolls. If this alternative hypothesis were correct then children should deny that the dolls were toys because the best label for the two dolls as with a single doll would be "dolls" not "toys." The results argue against this hypothesis and support the collection interpretation. Children accepted the higher level labels (e.g., "toys") for groups of homogeneous objects (e.g., dolls) but not for a single object. These findings suggest that in first acquiring superordinate terms, young children distort some class inclusion relations into collections. Thus, even in naturally occurring contexts, very young children may find it simpler to impose a collection structure on what are actually inclusion hierarchies they are trying to learn.

CONCLUSION

The ability to form categories of objects is common to virtually all animals. What may be unique about humans is their ability to organize categories into systems. Hierarchially organized class inclusion is one particularly important type of organizational system. There are a variety of tasks that have been used to assess children's ability to categorize objects and their understanding of class inclusion. Some of these tasks, such as the Piagetian class inclusion problem and the object sorting tasks, require very explicit awareness of the category structure. They are insensitive to incipient categories or to those that may not be salient enough to compete with alternative organizations. On other more implicit measures, children seemed to have formed superordinate categories, but these implicit measures may be overly sensitive to associations between items rather than to class inclusion alone.

In our review of studies using different measures of classification, it has become clear that category knowledge is not an all or none acquisition. As one might expect, the subtler measures reveal category knowledge in younger children. However, we suggested that in order to find evidence of hierarchically organized systems of concepts, measures should focus more on whether or not children appreciate the asymmetry and transitivity of inclusion. The few studies that have used such measures indicate that by the time children are four years old, they have at least begun to understand inclusion. Yet their understanding is still fragile and they find the asymmetry difficult to maintain.

The comparison of collections and classes supports the idea that one of the main problems with class inclusion is keeping track of the asymmetry. Children are better able to handle asymmetrical relations for collections than for classes. The part-whole organization of collections allows for easier representation of the top level of the hierarchy, compared to classes, and the greater distinction between the levels makes the asymmetry more apparent.

These findings suggest that preschool children may have represented class inclusion relations but that their understanding of the relation is still rudimentary. The categorical organization is not yet readily accessed or easily manipulated. Similar conclusions have recently been reached by Carey (1981) and Gelman and Baillargeon (in press).

At some point the taxonomic organization becomes explicit and readily accessible for adults. Under some circumstances it may even become the dominant or preferred mode of organization. We still do not fully understand what developmental changes in taxonomic organization actually occur or how they take place.

Early theorizing about this problem suggests that the formation of categories, especially more general ones, requires abstraction away from individuals. Concepts are grounded in experience, but one must abstract away from the idosyncratic details of a given experience to form rules that define categories (Bruner, Goodnow, & Austin, 1956). Current research has discovered that concept acquisition may be less abstract than the earlier theories proposed. Concepts may be organized around prototypes or exemplars and how concepts are acquired depends on their categorical structure and level of generality (e.g., Rosch et al., 1976; Kossan, 1978; Horton & Markman, 1980). Yet on these later accounts, abstraction away from individuals to form a representation of the category is still required, even if an abstract rule is not part of the representation.

Until recently, there had not been much analysis of the way in which the initial experimental base is built up. Recently, many investigators have begun to characterize experientially based, meaningful knowledge. Though different in many respects, theoretical notions of scripts (Schank & Abelson, 1977), and story grammars (Rumelhart, 1975) share an emphasis on characterizing knowledge that has a causal, temporal, thematic, or spatial structure. Developmental accounts of the abstraction process are now beginning to incorporate a more complete description of these experiential bases (Nelson, 1978, in press). With a more elaborated set of principles to describe the original knowledge base, we may be in a better position to understand the abstraction process by which taxonomic organizations are eventually formed.

There is also evidence that taxonomic organization develops as a function of education. Cross-cultural comparisons show differences between schooled and unschooled populations in whether or not taxonomic organization is used (Sharp et al., 1979). This finding about the role of education raises the question of the utility of taxonomic organization. Why should it become more salient or more prevalent in school?

The question of schooling is in turn a question about knowledge and the dissemination of knowledge. A major purpose of categorization must be to provide knowledge that goes beyond the information one has about an individual—to provide a rich deductive network. For the purpose of scientific understanding one wants to be able to view an object not just as an individual but as a member of a more general category. Categories are used to establish and express the lawlike generalizations of scientific knowledge.

Taxonomic organizations are likely to be especially useful for organizing large amounts of information. Because hierarchically organized class inclusion is transitive, it could be an efficient means of keeping track of information. One can move up or down the hierarchy, deleting and supplying details as necessary. One has ready access to properties of an object based on all of the more general categories to which it belongs. As a consequence it could be very useful for domains where a culture or an individual has many distinctions to encode. In western societies, for example, there are enormous number of artifacts (tools, vehicles, machines) that require systematic organization. In those domains where we have little knowledge, a much less elaborated system, or even knowledge of isolated objects would be sufficient.

During school, when educators attempt to impart knowledge of the culture to children, if taxonomic systems are used and practiced more, perhaps even explicitly taught and described, children will find them more salient. Another way in which schooling could help is that children may for the first time find the categorical structure effectively used as a means of organizing knowledge rather than just as an alternative label for something. Prior to entering school, children may well know that oaks and pines are trees. But it may only be after schooling that they discover there are general properties of trees that apply to oaks and pines and any other tree they will ever learn about. They also discover that there are unique properties of oaks and pines, and for any new tree they hear about they must discover its unique characteristics. So, though children know that oaks are trees, that hierarchical information serves little purpose until children begin to acquire substantial knowledge about a domain. As more and more information must be learned, there may be greater pressure to systematize knowledge in this way.

ACKNOWLEDGMENTS

This research was supported in part by Public Health Service Grant MH 28154 to Markman. We thank Gregory Murphy, Robert Sternberg, and Barbara Tversky for their helpful comments on an earlier draft of this chapter.

REFERENCES

Anglin, J. *Word, object, and conceptual development.* New York: Norton, 1977.
Blount, W. R. Concept usage research with the mentally retarded. *Pshchological Bulletin,* 1968, *69,* 281–294.
Brown, R. *Words and things.* New York: Free Press, 1958.
Bruner, J. S., Goodnow, J. J., & Austin, G. A. *A study of thinking.* New York: Wiley, 1956.
Bruner, J. S., Olver, R., & Greenfield, P. *Studies in cognitive growth.* New York: Wiley, 1966.
Callanan, M. A. & Markman, E. M. *Why collective nouns help children to solve the class inclusion problem: A test of the large number hypothesis.* Manuscript in preparation.
Callanan, M. A. & Markman, E. M. Principles of organization in young children's natural language hierarchies. *Child Development,* 1982, *53,* 1093–1101.
Campione, J. C. & Brown, A. L. Memory and metamemory development in educable retarded children. In R. V. Kail & J. W. Hagen (Eds.), *Perspectives on the development of memory and cognition.* Hillsdale, N.J.: Lawrence Erlbaum Associates, 1977.
Carey, S. The child as word learner. In M. Halle, J. Bresnan, & G. Miller (Eds.), *Linguistic theory and psychological reality.* Cambridge, Mass.: MIT Press, 1978.
Carey, S. *The child's concept of animal.* Paper presented at the Psychonomics Society, San Antonio, Texas, October 1978.
Carey, S. *Are children fundamentally different kinds of thinkers and learners than adults?* Preliminary draft of paper prepared for NIE-LRDC Conference, Pittsburgh, October 1981.
Cohen, L. B. & Younger, B. A. *Perceptual categorization in the infant.* Paper presented at the Eleventh Annual Jean Piaget Symposium, Philadelphia, May 1981.
Craik, F. I. M. Age differences in human memory. In J. E. Birren & K. W. Schaie (Eds.), *Handbook of the psychology of aging.* New York: Van Nostrand Reinhold, 1977.
Daehler, M. W., Lonardo, R., & Bukatko, D. Matching and equivalence judgments in very young children. *Child Development,* 1979, *50,* 170–179.

Davies, D., Sperber, R. D., & McCauley, C. Intelligence-related differences in semantic processing speed. *Journal of Experimental Child Psychology,* 1981, *31,* 387–402.

Dean, A. L., Chabaud, S., & Bridges, E. Classes, collections, and distinctive features: Alternative strategies for solving inclusion problems. *Cognitive Psychology,* 1981, *13,* 84–112.

Esrov, L. V., Hall, J. W., & LaFever, D. K. Preschooler's conceptual and acoustic encoding as evidenced by release from PI. *Bulletin of the Psychonomic Society,* 1974, *4,* 89–90.

Faulkender, P. J., Wright, J. C., & Waldron, A. Generalized habituation of concept stimuli. *Child Development,* 1974, *45,* 1002–1010.

Fodor, J. Some reflections on L. S. Vygotsky's "Thought and Language." *Cognition,* 1972, *1,* 83–95.

Galbraith, R. C. & Day, R. D. Developmental changes in clustering criteria? A closer look at Denney and Ziobrowski, *Child Development,* 1978, *49,* 889–891.

Gelman, R. Cognitive development. In M. R. Rosenzweig & L. W. Porter (Eds.), *Annual Review of Psychology* (Vol. 29). Palo Alto, Calif.: Annual Reviews Inc., 1978.

Gelman, R. & Baillargeon, R. A review of some Piagetian concepts. In J. H. Flavell & E. M. Markman (Eds.), *Cognitive development,* Vol. 2 of P. H. Mussen (General Ed.), *Handbook of child psychology.* New York: Wiley, in press.

Gelman, R., & Gallistel, C. R. *The child's understanding of number.* Cambridge, Mass.: Harvard University Press, 1978.

Glidden, L. J. & Mar, H. H. Availability and accessibility of information in the semantic memory of retarded and nonretarded adolescents. *Journal of Experimental Child Psychology,* 1978, *25,* 33–40.

Goldberg, S., Perlmutter, M., & Myers, N. Recall of related and unrelated lists by 2–year-olds. *Journal of Experimental Child Psychology,* 1974, *18,* 1–8.

Hall, V. E. & Kingsley, R. Conservation and equilibration theory. *The Journal of Genetic Psychology,* 1968, *113,* 195–213.

Harris, P. Inferences and semantic development. *Journal of Child Language,* 1975, *2,* 143–152.

Heidenheimer, P. A comparison of the roles of exemplar, action, coordinate, and superordinate relations in the semantic processing of 4– and 5–year-old children. *Journal of Experimental Child Psychology,* 1978, *25,* 143–159.

Hoemann, H. W., DeRosa, D. V., & Andrews, C. E. Categorical encoding in short-term memory by 4– to 11–year-old children. *Bulletin of the Psychonomic Society,* 1974, *3,* 63–65.

Horton, M. S. *Category familiarity and taxonomic organization in young children.* Unpublished doctoral dissertation, Stanford University, 1982.

Horton, M. S. & Markman, E. M. Developmental differences in the acquisition of basic and superordinate categories. *Child Development,* 1980, *51,* 708–719.

Hultsch, D. F. Adult age differences in free classification and free recall. *Developmental Psychology,* 1971, *4,* 338–342.

Huttenlocher, J. & Lui, F. The semantic organization of some simple nouns and verbs. *Journal of Verbal Learning and Verbal Behavior,* 1979, *18,* 141–162.

Inhelder, B. & Piaget, J. *The early growth of logic in the child.* New York: W. W. Norton, 1964.

Jensen, A. R. Individual differences in concept learning. In H. Butcher, & D. Lomax (Eds.), *Readings in human intelligence.* London: Methuen, 1972.

Keil, F. C. *Semantic and conceptual development: An ontological perspective.* Cambridge, Mass.: Harvard University Press, 1979.

Kossan, N. E. *Structure and strategy in concept acquisition.* Unpublished doctoral dissertation, Stanford University, 1978.

Macnamara, J. *Names for things: A study of human learning.* Cambridge, Mass.: MIT Press, 1982.

Mandler, J. M. Categorical and schematic organization in memory. In C. R. Puff (Ed.), *Memory organization and structure.* New York: Academic Press, 1979.

Mandler, J. M., Scribner, S., Cole, M., & DeForest, M. Cross-cultural invariance in story recall. *Child Development,* 1980, *51,* 19–26.

Mansfield, A. F. Semantic organization in the young child: Evidence for the development of semantic feature systems. *Journal of Experimental Child Psychology,* 1977, *23,* 57–77.

Markman, E. M. Facilitation of part-whole comparisons by use of the collective noun "family." *Child Development,* 1973, *44,* 837–840.

Markman, E. M. Empirical versus logical solutions to part-whole comparison problems concerning classes and collections. *Child Development,* 1978, *49,* 168–177.

Markman, E. M. Classes and collections: Conceptual organization and numerical abilities. *Cognitive Psychology,* 1979, *11,* 395–411.

Markman, E. M. Two different principles of conceptual organization. In M. E. Lamb & A. L. Brown (Eds.), *Advances in developmental psychology* (Vol. 1). Hillside, N.J.: Lawrence Erlbaum Associates, 1981.

Markman, E. M. *The role of language in inducing taxonomic organization.* In preparation.

Markman, E. M., Cox, B., & Machida, S. The standard object sorting task as a measure of conceptual organization. *Developmental Psychology,* 1981, *17,* 115–117.

Markman, E. M., Horton, M. S., & McLanahan, A. G. Classes and collections: Principles of organization in the learning of hierarchical relations. *Cognition,* 1980, *8,* 227–241.

Markman, E. & Seibert, J. Classes and collections: Internal organization and resulting holistic properties. *Cognitive Psychology,* 1976, *8,* 561–577.

McGarrigle, J. & Donaldson, M. Conservation accidents. *Cognition,* 1975, *3,* 341–350.

Melkman, R. & Deutsch, H. Memory functioning as related to developmental changes in bases of organization. *Journal of Experimental Child Psychology,* 1977, *23,* 84–97.

Melkman, R., Tversky, B., & Baratz, D. Developmental trends in the use of perceptual and conceptual attributes in grouping, clustering and retrieval. *Journal of Experimental Child Psychology,* 1981, *31,* 470–486.

Mervis, C. B. Category structure and the development of categorization. In R. Spiro, B. Bruce, & W. Brewer (Eds.), *Theoretical issues in reading comprehension.* Hillsdale, N.J.: Lawrence Erlbaum Associates, 1980.

Mervis, C. B. & Crisafi, M. A. Order of acquistion of subordinate, basic, and superordinate level categories. *Child Development,* 1982, *53,* 258–266.

Mervis, C. B. & Rosch, E. Categorization of natural objects. In M. R. Rosenzweig & L. W. Porter (Eds.), *Annual Review of Psychology,* (Vol. 32). Palo Alto, Calif.: Annual Reviews Inc., 1981.

Murphy, G. L. & Smith, E. E. Basic-level superiority in picture categorization. *Journal of Verbal Learning and Verbal Behavior,* 1982, *21,* 1–20.

Nelson, K. The organization of free recall by young children. *Journal of Experimental Child Psychology,* 1969, *8,* 284–295.

Nelson, K. How children represent knowledge of their world in and out of language: A preliminary report. In R. S. Siegler (Ed.), *Children's thinking: What develops?* Hillsdale, N.J.: Lawrence Erlbaum Associates, 1978.

Nelson, K. The derivation of concepts and categories from event representations. In E. Scholnick (Ed.), *New trends in conceptual representation: Challenges to Piaget's theory.* Hillsdale, N.J.: Lawrence Erlbaum Associates, in press.

Olver, R. R. & Hornsby, J. R. On equivalence. In J. Bruner, R. Olver, & P. Greenfield (Eds.), *Studies in cognitive growth.* New York: Wiley, 1966.

Parsons, O. A. & Prigatano, G. P. Memory functioning in alcoholics. In I. M. Birnbaum & E. S. Parker (Eds.), *Alcohol and human memory.* Hillsdale, N.J.: Lawrence Erlbaum Associates, 1977.

Payne, R. W. Cognitive abnormalities. In H. J. Eysenck (Ed.), *Handbook of abnormal psychology.* London: Pitman, 1973.

Piaget, J. *The child's conception of number.* New York: Norton, 1965.

Premack, D. *Intelligence in ape and man.* Hillsdale, N.J.: Lawrence Erlbaum Associates, 1976.

Riccuiti, H. Object grouping and selective ordering behavior in infants 12 to 24 months old. *Merrill-Palmer Quarterly,* 1965, *11,* 129–148.

Rosch, E. H. Principles of categorization. In E. H. Rosch & B. B. Lloyd (Eds.) *Cognition and categorization*. Hillsdale, N.J.: Lawrence Erlbaum Associates, 1978.

Rosch, E. & Mervis, C. M. Children's sorting: A reinterpretation based on the nature of abstraction in natural categories. In R. C. Smart & M. S. Smart (Eds.), *Readings in child development and relationships* (2nd ed.). New York: Macmillan, 1977.

Rosch, E. H., Mervis, C. B., Gray, W., Johnson, D., & Boyes-Braem, P. Basic objects in natural categories. *Cognitive Psychology*, 1976, *3*, 382–439.

Ross, G. Categorization in 1- to 2-year-olds. *Developmental Psychology*, 1980, *16*, 391–396.

Rossi, E. & Rossi, S. Concept utilization, serial order and recall in nursery-school children. *Child Development*, 1965, *36*, 771–778.

Rumelhart, D. E. Notes on a schema for stories. In D. G. Bobrow & A. M. Collins (Eds.), *Representation and understanding: Studies in cognitive science*. New York: Academic Press, 1975.

Savage-Rumbaugh, E. S., Rumbaugh, D. M., Smith, S. T., & Lawson, J. Reference: The linguistic essential. *Science*, 1980, *210*, 922–925.

Schaeffer, B., Eggleston, V. H., & Scott, J. L. Number development in young children. *Cognitive Psychology*, 1974, *6*, 357–379.

Schank, R. & Abelson, R. *Scripts, plans, goals and understanding: An inquiry into human knowledge structures*. Hillsdale, N.J.: Lawrence Erlbaum Associates, 1977.

Sharp, D., Cole, M., & Lave, C. Education and cognitive development: the evidence from experimental research. *Monographs of the Society for Research in Child Development*, 1979, *44*, (1–2, Serial No. 178).

Smiley, S. S. & Brown, A. L. Conceptual preference for thematic or taxonomic relations: A nonmonotonic age trend from preschool to old age. *Journal of Experimental Child Psychology*, 1979, *28*, 249–257.

Smith, C. L. Children's understanding of natural language hierarchies. *Journal of Experimental Child Psychology*, 1979, *27*, 437–458.

Smith, E. E., & Medin, D. L. *Categories and concepts*. Cambridge: Mass.: Harvard University Press, 1981.

Starkey, D. The origins of concept formation: object sorting and object preference in early infancy. *Child Development*, 1981, *52*, 489–497.

Steinberg, E. R. & Anderson, R. C. Hierarchical semantic organization in 6-year-olds. *Journal of Experimental Child Psychology*, 1975, *19*, 544–553.

Sternberg, R. J. & Powell, J. S. The development of intelligence. In J. H. Flavell & E. M. Markman (Eds.), *Cognitive psychology*, Vol. 2 of P. H. Mussen (General Ed.), *Handbook of child psychology*. New York: Wiley, in press.

Sugarman, S. Developmental change in early representational intelligence: Evidence from spatial classification strategies and related verbal expressions. *Cognitive Psychology*, in press.

Terman, L. M. & Merrill, M. A. *Stanford-Binet intelligence scale manual for the third revision (Form L-M)*, Boston: Houghton-Mifflin Co., 1960.

Trabasso, T., Isen, A. I., Dolecki, P., McLanahan, A. G., Riley, C. A., & Tucker, T. How do children solve class-inclusion problems? In R. S. Siegler (Ed.), *Children's thinking: What develops?* Hillsdale, N.J.: Lawrence Erlbaum Associates, 1978.

Valentine, C. W. *The psychology of early childhood*. London: Methuen, 1942.

Vygotsky, L. S. *Thought and language*. Cambridge, Mass.: MIT Press, 1962.

Wechsler, D. *Wechsler intelligence scale for children (WISC) manual*. New York: Psychological Corporation, 1949.

Wechsler, D. *Wechsler preschool and primary scale of intelligence (WPPSI) manual*. New York: Psychological Corporation, 1967.

Winer, G. A. Class-inclusion reasoning in children: A review of the empirical literature. *Child Development*, 1980, *51*, 309–328.

9

Why Some People Are Better Readers Than Others: A Process and Storage Account

Meredyth Daneman
University of Waterloo

This chapter considers why some people are better readers than others. It presents a theory of reading that takes into account the processing characteristics of the reader and how these might interact with characteristics of the text being read.

I begin by delimiting the scope of the theory. I then present evidence for the current theory by contrasting the relative limitations of recent theories of reading skill with the greater success of this one. Finally, I discuss some of the dividends of the current theoretical approach and methodology.

SCOPE OF THE THEORY

This chapter does not represent a comprehensive theory of individual differences in reading comprehension. No attempt is made to provide an exhaustive specification of the loci of individual differences in reading. Rather, the focus is on certain differences that are theoretically interesting from an information-processing standpoint. In particular, I will consider differences in memory capacities that store information and differences in the processes that manipulate the information.

This chapter is not a comprehensive theory of individual differences in a second sense. The focus is mainly on accounting for individual differences within a fairly circumscribed population, namely a population of university students. However, this narrow focusing should not be regarded as a deficiency in the theory. In fact, it is of theoretical interest that within this restricted population, there is still quite a wide range of skill differences. Presumably, the theory can be extended to other groups such as extremely poor readers or children who have recently learned to read, and I will suggest later how this extension might occur. Nevertheless, some aspects of the theory may be less generalizable to other populations. For example, I will argue that people who are poor readers are also poor listeners; in other words, visual encoding processes do not seem to be the bottleneck in reading. My claims may be less cogent when applied to populations other than adult university students, such as certain types of dyslexic populations.

One positive by-product of studying a population of normal adults is that studying individual differences in reading is not only similar to studying differences in listening but is tantamount to studying differences in intelligence and academic achievement (Snow, 1978). Reading comprehension is highly correlated with scores on general tests of intelligence and with performance on school subjects as diverse as literature and science (Bloom, 1976; Perfetti, 1976). These correlations are typically .60 or larger. This level of relationship is not surprising, given that in school, a large proportion of knowledge is acquired through reading. More importantly, reading comprehension seems to be the major common denominator in most of school learning. Reading comprehension accounts for part of the high correlations in performance on different school subject areas. For example, the .40 correlation between achievement in science and literature approaches zero when the effects of reading comprehension are partialled out (Bloom, 1976). Hence, this approach to a theory of individual differences in reading comprehension, together with a theory of how to optimize the instruction of reading, could influence much of school learning.

The close correlation between reading and intelligence has prompted some researchers to partial out the effects of intelligence before studying individual differences in reading (Belmont & Birch, 1966; Cummings & Faw, 1976; Perfetti & Lesgold, 1977). Although such an approach may isolate some effects unique to reading, it probably tells us less about the more common and perhaps more interesting sources of reading difference that also happen to be sources of difference in general intelligence.

EVIDENCE FOR THE THEORY

The major tenet of the theory is that individual reader differences influence the integration processes of reading comprehension and that one crucial source of reader difference is processing efficiency in working memory. Poor readers may be less efficient at the processes that manipulate verbal material, processes such as retrieving letter or name codes from semantic memory. They may also be less efficient at other semantic computations. These deficiencies have implications for the way in which readers allocate their working memory resources. Slower and less efficient processes may consume more of the available capacity and so lessen the amount of additional capacity for storing and maintaining information in working memory. If working memory has less information, subsequent processing will not be optimal. Without the relevant information accessible in working memory, poor readers will be less able to integrate successive elements of a text.

The present theory of the functional role of working memory in reading provides a useful framework for evaluating and reinterpreting recent research on individual differences in comprehension. The research has generally focused on two classes of variables. One has been the differences in the capacities of the memories that store information; the second has been the differences in the processes that manipulate information. A major contribution of my approach is that it melds the two kinds of differences by showing how differences in measured or functional working memory capacity reflect differences in processing efficiency.

I will first discuss the relevant research on individual differences in memory capacity and processes. Then I will present my own research, done in collaboration with Patricia A. Carpenter, which shows how processing efficiency in working memory is related to the reading comprehension processes.

Differences in Short-Term Memory Capacity

The bottleneck to the information processing system is often assumed to be in short-term memory, that part of memory that stores recently processed information (Miller, 1956; Simon, 1974). The limits of short-term memory have been conceptualized as between three and seven items or chunks of information (Broadbent, 1975; Chase & Ericsson, 1981; Miller, 1956) or as a finite reserve of attentional or energy resources that can be allocated at any one time to the attending to information (Kahneman, 1973). Information is lost from short-term memory by decaying over time or by being displaced when additional incoming information exceeds capacity (Brown, 1958; Collins & Loftus, 1975; Peterson & Peterson, 1959; Reitman, 1974). Many theorists have suggested that short-term memory capacity plays a crucial role in reading comprehension and is hence a potentially important source of individual differences (Kintsch & van Dijk, 1978; Kintsch & Vipond, 1979; Norman, 1972). However, attempts to find short-term memory differences between good and poor readers have generally been unsuccessful. The usual paradigm has been to assess short-term memory with a digit span or word span test and to relate readers' performance on these tests to their performance on a general standardized test of reading comprehension. I will argue that the negative results can be attributed to both sides of the equation: the tests used to assess short-term memory and the tests used to assess reading comprehension.

Short-term memory has been assessed with a variety of span measures and in all cases the measures have failed to differentiate good from poor readers. Studies using digit and probe digit span have found no systematic differences between good and poor readers (Guyer & Friedman, 1975; Hunt, Frost, & Lunneborg, 1973; Perfetti & Goldman, 1976). Studies using letter strings or similar sounding words as predictors of reading comprehension have at best found very weak relationships (Farnham-Diggory & Gregg, 1975; Rizzo, 1939). Studies that have compared scanning rates in short-term memory by using the Sternberg (S. Sternberg, 1969) memory scanning task, have also found no relationship between speed of scanning and reading comprehension (Chiang & Atkinson, 1976).

The main conclusion to be drawn from the fairly large body of research is that, with the exception of severely retarded individuals, poor readers do not have a deficit in short-term memory capacity. This finding is not surprising, given recent developmental research, which shows that short-term memory capacity is similar in children over five years of age and adults (Case, 1978; Chi, 1976; Dempster, 1981; Huttenlocher & Burke, 1976). I will argue that the source of individual differences in memory capacity does not reside in the passive storage capacity or number of "slots" in short-term memory, as tapped by digit span or word span tests. Rather, individuals differ in *functional* capacity; that is, they differ in the processes or procedures they have for maximally utilizing their capacities.

Understanding the role of memory capacity in reading comprehension requires a reformulation of its function and the construction of a measure of working memory that is motivated by this theory. In other words, I contend that digit span and word span tests can be dismissed as tests of *functional* working memory on theoretical grounds, and I will propose a new measure that taps functional working memory capacity.

If the first flaw of the traditional research is that the theory underlying tests of short-term memory is inadequate, the second flaw is that the theory behind the general tests of reading comprehension is not specified at all. One good way of developing a theory of individual differences is to develop a theory of component processes involved in performing the reading task (Carroll, 1978). The productiveness of this approach has been very convincingly demonstrated by Sternberg for intellectual tasks such as reasoning by analogy (Sternberg, 1977, 1979, 1980). Of course, reading tasks may not lend themselves to an anlysis of component processes as easily as Sternberg's verbal analogies (Rosenshine, 1980). Nevertheless, an information-processing model of reader differences needs to analyze components of the task, because the requirements and characteristics of a reading task are distinctly related to how the reader will process that text, and many reading processes are potential individual-differences variables. In other words, a detailed analysis of the reading processes should be accompanied by a detailed analysis of the reading task. My research will show how the study of individual differences in reading benefits from the construction of theoretically motivated tests of reading comprehension.

Differences in Processing

Research on processing variables that differentiate good from poor readers has been more promising than research on short-term memory capacity differences. The most extensive investigations of individual differences in processes have focused on quantitative or speed differences, with the hypothesis that good readers might simply be faster at some processes than poor readers. The general finding has been that good readers and highly verbal subjects are faster than poor readers and low verbal subjects at retrieving a name as well as semantic or phonological information associated with that name. The most commonly used task to study the speed of retrieving verbal information compares the time to retrieve and match letter or name codes from memory with the time to match physical or visual codes (Posner, Boies, Eichelman, & Taylor, 1969). The difference in time to say that two letters have the same name (A a) versus the time to say that two letters have the same physical form (A A) is greater for poorer readers (Hunt, Lunneborg, & Lewis, 1975). Poor readers are also slower at other semantic matching tasks such as responding ''same'' if two words are synonyms or homonyms (Jackson & McClelland, 1979). However, poor readers are not slower at matching dot patterns, suggesting that the processing speed deficit is localized to visual displays with verbal content. The theory is that deficits in comprehension can be caused by taking more time to encode and retrieve a word meaning. The poor reader would be at a disadvantage because the time devoted to retrieval could not be used for other higher level processes and the additional lapsed time would allow important information to decay from working memory (Lesgold & Perfetti, 1978; Perfetti & Lesgold, 1977).

It is important to note that the speed of visual encoding and lexical access typically accounts for only 10% of the variance in the reading comprehension performance of good and poor readers. Thus, although speed of lexical access may be a factor in reading, the correlation suggests that it is not the most important factor. My theory states that poor readers may be slower or less efficient at many different processes—encoding and retrieving words being only two of those processes. However, it is the reader's level of efficiency at all the processes that is related to comprehension performance.

Speed may not be the only source of individual differences in the efficiency of lexical retrieval processes. It has long been known that better readers also know more words than poorer readers (Anderson & Freebody, 1979). Thus sheer vocabulary may be an important source of individual differences. But in spite of the persistent correlation between vocabulary and reading skill, the relation of vocabulary to comprehension is unclear. Simply trying to increase vocabulary does not automatically improve comprehension. For example, Tuinman & Brady (1973) found that pretraining on vocabulary items from passages to be read did not increase elementary school children's comprehension scores for those passages. Although knowledge of the word meanings of a text may be a necessary condition for comprehending that text, it may not be sufficient to improve comprehension. The reader must be able to interrelate the underlying conceptual structures after the individual word meanings are retrieved. This additional step is central to Sternberg, Powell, & Kaye's (in press) exciting new theory of the relationship between vocabulary and learning from context and their role in verbal comprehension. The kinds of reading tasks Pat Carpenter and I have studied reflect our belief that reading is to a large extent an integrative process; readers have to relate successive word concepts in the text if they are to develop a coherent representation for that text.

Differences in Processing Efficiency in Working Memory

The Theory.   Our research on individual differences in reading has highlighted the need to view short-term memory as an active part of the human information-processing system (Daneman & Carpenter, 1980; in press). To differentiate the current theory from the more classical "slot" conception, we use the term *working memory*. Working memory has processing and storage functions that compete for a limited capacity (Baddeley & Hitch, 1974; Case, 1978). More demanding processes consume more of the available capacity, decreasing the amount of additional information that can be stored and maintained in working memory. More demanding processes may also generate intermediate products that interfere with stored information. In either case, with less information in working memory, subsequent processing will suffer. This should be particularly evident when subsequent processing involves integrating information with information read earlier in the text. For example, if a reader encounters a pronoun but the antecedent referent noun is no longer in working memory, the reader will have to search long-term memory, make an inference, or fail to compute the pronominal referent at that point. Similarly, if the reader encounters a semantically or syntactically inconsistent phrase because of an earlier comprehension error, but the misinterpreted information is no longer in working memory, the reader will have fewer clues to assist him in monitoring and revising his errors.

The conjoint effective use of the processing and storage resources of working memory might be the source of individual differences in reading comprehension. The poor reader's processes might be less efficient (that is, more demanding on the reader), and this reduced efficiency would effectively lessen the amount of additional information the reader could store and maintain. Not only would a reader with inefficient processes be less likely to have the relevant information still active in working memory; he may also be less able to retrieve it from long-term memory. Successful retrieval depends on initially coding material in a form that can be meaningfully associated with knowledge structures in long-term memory and maintaining some retrieval cue in working memory that would serve to reinstate the coding operations (Chase & Ericsson, 1981). Readers with small working memory capacities may do less high level coding because they devote so much capacity to lower level processes.

If the source of individual differences lies in the conjoint effective use of processes and storage, working memory capacity must be assessed by a test that measures the use of both types of resources. If the test makes heavy processing demands and interferes with storage, the poor reader's inefficient processes would be functionally equivalent to a smaller storage capacity. Within this framework, traditional digit span and word span measures have failed to predict individual differences because they do not require the execution of demanding processes in working memory. The word span test, for example, involves simple processes such as rehearsal and access of common lexical items. As a result, it taps only passive storage resources that may not differ very much among adults.

The Test of Working Memory.   To measure the conjoint capacity for the processing and storage functions of working memory, we devised a test that taxed both functions. We called it the reading span test (Daneman & Carpenter, 1980). The processing and storage components of the reading span test involved the usual demands of sentence comprehension, such as word encoding, lexical access, and interclause integration. An additional component required the subject to maintain and retrieve the final words of a series of sentences. The administration of the reading span test was somewhat similar to that of the traditional digit span test. The subject was given a set of unrelated sentences one at a time to read aloud; at the end of the set, he or she attempted to recall the final word of each sentence in the set. For example, one set of three sentences was:

(1) *He had patronized her when she was a schoolgirl and teased her when she was a student.*
(2) *He had an odd elongated skull which sat on his shoulders like a pear on a dish.*
(3) *The products of digital electronics will play an important role in your future.*

After reading these sentences aloud, the subject was required to recall *student, dish,* and *future.* The number of sentences in a set was incremented from trial to trial and reading span was defined as the maximum number of sentences the subject could read aloud while maintaining perfect recall of final words. The theory was that poor readers devote more processing capacity to comprehending the sentences and consequently should be able to store and produce fewer final words.

The observed scores on the reading span test have shown performance limitations consistent with those postulated for working memory. Moreover, performance on the test also supports our contention that adults differ considerably from each other in their processing capacity. The test has been administered to well over 200 university students. For this population, individual subjects' scores on silent and oral versions of the reading span test and on a listening span test ranged from 1.5–5 words. Moreover, fewer than 10% of these university students were performing at the highest level, a span of 5. Thus, even within a circumscribed population of bright university students, the span test successfully discriminated a fairly wide range of individual differences in functional capacity, with a distinct upper limit on even the best of them.

Of primary importance, of course, is that the reading span test successfully predicts performance on a variety of reading tasks; the more traditional short-term memory tests have failed to do so. Reading span correlated with performance on a general test of reading comprehension—the Verbal Scholastic Aptitude Test (SAT)—with correlations ranging from .46 to .59 (Daneman & Carpenter, 1980; in press). Masson & Miller (in press) found a similar relationship between our reading span measure and another standardized test of reading comprehension, the Nelson-Denny ($r = .53$). However, global tests of comprehension are deficient from a theoretical point of view. Because such scores reflect a variety of skills, they are difficult to relate to any particular process. For this reason, Pat Carpenter and I have developed more specific tests of comprehension to relate to our measure of working memory capacity. As expected, reading span was even more highly correlated with these measures than with standard tests.

The Tests of Reading Comprehension.   The construction of the tests was motivated by our view that working memory capacity may play a particularly important role in the processes that integrate elements of a text. During integration, the reader represents the current chunk of text in working memory and computes its relation to previous ideas represented from the text or retrieved from semantic memory. The present theory suggests that this goal should be more easily accomplished if the preceding relevant information is accessible to working memory. Moreover, readers who make more efficient use of their working memories (those with large spans) should be the ones more likely to have the preceding information currently available. To test the relationship between reading span and integration, we constructed specific tests of comprehension that required readers to retrieve information mentioned earlier in the passage and relate it to the current information.

One specific integration process is establishing conference or relating propositions that share arguments. One test of this is to have readers compute the referent for a pronoun they have just read. Given that the computing of anaphoric reference is a major component of understanding a coherent text, general tests of reading comprehension probably do tap these processes, albeit implicitly. It is interesting to note that some general tests even tap referential processes explicitly. As many as 15% of the questions on the widely used Davis Test Series 2 (Davis & Davis, 1962) directly interrogate reference, particularly pronominal reference. A typical Davis Test pronoun reference question singles out a pronoun that occurred in the prose passage and asks the reader to which of five alternatives the pronoun referred. So, for example, one test passage in Form 2B begins as follows: "When Robert Oppenheimer, who supervised the making of the first atomic bomb, was asked by a committee of Congress whether there was any defense against it, his reply was ' Certainly.' [p. 9]" At the end of the passage, readers are given a pronoun question about this sentence. They are asked whether '*It*' *refers to* a) *making,* b) *bomb,* c) *committee,* d) *Congress,* e) *defense.* This question is a fairly good example of one that taps a reader's ability to determine the interrelationships among all the arguments and propositions of a sentence.

We assessed the reader's ability to compute pronominal reference by interrogating the reader about a pronoun mentioned in the last sentence of a passage just read. Passages were constructed so that the number of sentences intervening between the pronoun and its antecedent referent noun varied from 1 to 7. Reading span correlated with accuracy in computing pronominal reference, with correlations ranging from .84 to .90 (Daneman & Carpenter, 1980). Readers with small spans were less accurate than readers with large spans at computing pronominal reference. Moreover, readers with small spans were less likely to compute a pronoun's referent when a large number of sentences intervened between pronoun and referent. By contrast, large span readers could always compute the referent even at the longer distances. Presumably, associating a pronoun with its referent noun is easier if the referent noun is still active in working memory; hence, the working memory capacity of the reader influences the duration that the piece of information remains in working memory. A writer uses a pronoun rather than a noun when he assumes that the referential concept is active or "foregounded" (Chafe, 1972). Chafe has suggested that the foregrounding is attenuated after two sentence boundaries, although he admitted that this criterion is arbitrary and that he was unable to formalize the upper limit. Our analysis of working memory capacity suggests that the boundary will vary for different readers, with large span readers able to keep a concept foregrounded for a longer period of time.

Monitoring and revising one's comprehension errors is another skill that involves the integration of successive ideas in a text. We examined these integration skills by assessing the reader's ability to detect and recover from apparent inconsistencies, as in: *The violinist stepped onto the podium and turned majestically to face the audience. He took a bow that was very gracefully propped on the music stand.* Most readers initially interpret the ambiguous word *bow* as "a bend at the waist" because this is the meaning more strongly primed by the preceding sentence. However, "bend at the waist" is inconsistent with the subsequent disambiguating phrase, *propped on the music stand,* and a resolution of the inconsistency requires a reinterpretation of *bow* to mean "violin part." When probed after reading such passages, readers with small spans were less accurate than readers with large spans in answering questions like "What did the violinist take?" (Daneman & Carpenter, in press). Small span readers would frequently say "He bowed to the audience," indicating that they had not resolved the inconsistency. By contrast, large span readers would more often say "He took a violin bow off the music stand," indicating that they had detected the inconsistency and recovered the correct interpretation. Our theory is that recovery of the correct interpretation is easier if readers have in working memory some representation of the orthographic properties of the misinterpreted word. Since the orthographic information B-O-W is the only common link between the two meanings, "bend at the waist" and "violin part," it is a useful retrieval route to the alternate meaning. Readers with small spans may have devoted so much capacity to the processes of reading that they were less likely to have accessible in working memory a verbatim representation of the earlier phrase containing the ambiguous word.

Recovery from an inconsistency also depends on whether the verbatim wording has been purged from working memory by an intervening sentence boundary. We demonstrated this by contrasting the following two versions of the *bow* passage: (1) *He took a bow that was very gracefully propped on the music stand.* (2) *He took a bow. It was very gracefully propped on the music stand.* In case (2) a sentence boundary intervened between the ambiguous word and the disambiguating phrase. Readers with small spans were less able to integrate information across a sentence boundary. By contrast, readers with large spans answered as many questions correctly when a sentence boundary intervened as when it did not. These results may be explained in terms of the accessibility of the earlier read verbatim wording. A sentence boundary causes a marked decline in verbatim memory for recently comprehended text (Jarvella, 1971; Perfetti & Lesgold, 1977). Eye fixation and reading time studies have shown that readers pause at the ends of sentences, possibly to do additional integration processes (Dee-Lucas, Just, Carpenter, & Daneman, 1982; Just & Carpenter, 1980; Mitchell & Green, 1978). These additional processes may stress the limits of working memory capacity and contribute to the purging of verbatim wording. Presumably, readers with small spans were more prone to losing the verbatim wording at sentence boundaries and this is why they were less able to recover from inconsistencies when the text required the integration of information across a sentence boundary.

When reading lengthy texts, readers may have to integrate information over much longer distances than six or seven sentences; in these cases, it is no longer plausible that earlier read information is still active in working memory, even for the best readers. However, better readers may not simply have information active in working memory for a longer duration, but they may have better access to the information that they have read, so that they can retrieve it more efficiently. Indeed, another study showed that readers with larger spans were much better at retrieving information that had been presented much earlier in a lengthy passage and was presumably no longer in working memory (Daneman, 1981). Subjects read a 25–page detective story presented paragraph by paragraph on a computer terminal. They were instructed to search for potential suspects in a crime as they were reading. Embedded in the story were clues associated with a particular character and then later evidence which, if linked back to the appropriate clues, would potentially incriminate that character. So, for example, at one point in the story subjects read about the suspicious behavior of one of the characters, Jack Sinclair, who was seen concealing an axe and sack. Then, later in the story, subjects read about the postmortem revealing that the victim's head was severed by an axelike instrument. If they remembered the earlier association of Jack Sinclair and an axe, readers could infer that he was a potential murderer. Unlike the previous two tasks where the dependent measure was accuracy of recall, this task attempted to tap integration processes as they occurred during the course of reading the story. Instead of providing subjects with specific questions at the end of the passage, the task was more unstructured. Subjects had to decide for themselves when and how often to halt the computer presentation of the story and name potential suspects.

Readers with small spans were less able to detect potential criminals. Reading span correlated very highly with the accuracy with which readers could integrate evidence with previous clues, $r = .92$. Moreover, readers with small spans had particular difficulty detecting a potential criminal if five or more paragraphs intervened between the clues associated with the character and later evidence that could be linked to these clues. By contrast, readers with intermediate or large reading spans were as likely to detect suspects when the clue-evidence distance was long as when it was short. In this detective task, the units of text were very long: The distance between a clue and later evidence could be as much as 70 or 80 sentences. Although it is possible that in the pronoun task good readers could keep the antecedent referent active in working memory for six or seven sentences, it is less plausible that even the best readers could maintain clues about characters for 70 to 80 sentences. The superiority of the better readers at integrating information over these very large distances may be explained in terms of the probability that the prior information has been consolidated into long-term memory, and the probability that some retrieval cue has been maintained in working memory to reinstate the information when needed (Daneman, Carpenter, & Just, 1982). The larger processing capacity of the good reader might allow him more opportunities to integrate a particular piece of information into his growing representation of the text. The information would be available during more subsequent processing so that later information could be related to it. Consequently, the integration processes would provide more retrieval routes for later accessing the information from long-term memory.

Summary and Comments.   Our research has shown a strong relationship between processing efficiency in working memory and the ability to integrate text. Readers with larger working memory capacities are better able to compute the referent of a pronoun mentioned earlier, to detect and revise their comprehension errors, and to make inferences based on information read earlier. Furthermore, our research has shown that the processing capabilities of the reader interact with structural characteristics of the text being read. Our studies have varied two aspects of text structure: the distance between the two types of information to be integrated and the location of intervening sentence boundaries. We have shown that the effects of these textual cues on integration vary as a function of the reader's processing capacity. Distance and sentence boundary placement are only two organizational aspects of a text structure. One might expect similar patterns of interactions for other aspects.

The interaction of reader and text characteristics may have important implications for the teaching of reading. The fact that different kinds of texts are easier for different readers is related to the aptitude-treatment interaction. This is a term used in educational research to refer to the finding that instructional approaches are most effective when tailored to the particular aptitudes of the targeted learners (Cronbach & Snow, 1968). If we can characterize the aptitude-treatment interaction in reading, then our research on the cognitive processes of reading may be applied to reading instruction.

A valuable contribution of the research is that it offers a useful and theoretically interesting measure of processing efficiency in working memory, namely the reading span test. The reading span measure has consistently accounted for large proportions of the variance between good and poor readers. It has accounted for 25% to 35% of the variance in Verbal SAT scores and for 53% to 85% on tests of integration. This predictive value of the reading span measure contrasts rather dramatically with the limited predictive value of the other measures: Measures of pure storage capacity such as digit span and word span have failed to predict reading skill, and measures of the speed of basic processes have only accounted for about 10% of the individual-differences variance.

I think that reading span test is a good predictor of comprehension because it is a measure of overall efficiency. It taps efficiency at all processes involved in sentence comprehension, not just basic lexical access processes. Presumably, poor readers may be less efficient at many processes, but it is their general level of efficiency at all the reading processes that will determine how much information they can maintain in working memory to use for comprehending text. One merit of the reading span test, then, is that it captures many of the processes in normal reading. However, this is not its only merit. Although in some sense the reading span test is a mini-reading test, in another sense it is quite different from normal reading. It requires readers to develop strategies for identifying, tagging, and maintaining a faithful representation of the final word of a sentence, a word that is often only tangentially related to the sentence meaning. This task has proved to be quite novel and difficult, and novel or "nonentrenched" tasks (Sternberg, 1981) tend to be very good discriminators of ability differences. The reading span test may be a good predictor of reading skill because it has this component of novelty.

BY-PRODUCTS OF THE THEORY

I began by intimating that the theory and methodology described in this chapter can be applied to other intellectual skills such as listening comprehension, and to other populations such as children. Let me now indicate how this is so.

Reading and Listening

So far, I have talked about overall processing efficiency at manipulating verbal information as an important locus of individual differences in reading. Except for visual encoding, these processes are not unique to reading; they are also used in listening. Consequently, one might expect that listening and reading comprehension would be highly correlated. Indeed, our research indicates that this is true (Daneman & Carpenter, 1980). Subjects who understand prose when they hear it are also more likely to understand that prose when they read it. Moreover, efficiency at processing oral language in working memory is also related to comprehension skill. Subjects were given a listening span test, modeled after the reading span test, and listening span correlated very highly with both listening comprehension and reading comprehension tasks. Hence, it seems that the processes shared between listening and reading account for a large proportion of the variance in reading performance. A similar conclusion can be drawn from the Jackson & McClelland (1979) study cited earlier on semantic matching tasks. They found that listening accounted for 50% of the variance in reading compared to 10% for the name-letter matching task. Moreover, the listening comprehension score and the speed of the more visual, letter-matching task were not correlated. This suggests that the two components may be somewhat separable in their contribution to reading skill. Reading seems to depend on a set of language processes that are common in both listening and reading. Encoding skills may account for relatively little of the variance once readers get beyond the beginning stages of reading. After that, other aspects of semantic processing seem to be a larger source of individual differences.

The close relationship between individual differences in reading and listening ability also has implications for reading instruction. If, indeed, students who are poor readers are also poor listeners, classroom instruction should be tailored to the training of parallel listening skills. Existing reading comprehension programs do not capitalize on this relationship. Typically, books on reading instruction devote only two or three pages to listening instruction and even these tend to emphasize the differences between listening and reading rather than the commonalities.

Individual and Developmental Differences

A very exciting bonus of this individual-differences approach is that the theory and methodology can be readily adapted to the study of developmental differences in reading. We have found suggestive evidence that processing efficiency in working memory appears to increase as a child learns to read and that this affects performance measures such as reading fluency, question-answering, and inconsistency detection (Daneman & Carpenter, 1981).

Children in grades 2 to 6 were given two tests of working memory: a reading span test and a listening span test. These tests were like the adult versions except that they involved simpler sentences (e.g., (1) *Snow falls in the winter* and (2) *People send letters in the mail*). Children's working memory spans for sentence-final words varied from 2 to 4, a range very similar to the one reported earlier for adults. Working memory span correlated better with reading fluency and question-answering (correlations ranging from .60 to .70) than did age or years of schooling with these same measures of reading performance (correlations ranging from .35 to .64). Moreover, the correlations between span and reading were still significant when the effects of age or grade were partialled out, whereas the correlations between age or grade and reading were not significant when span was partialled out. Thus, working memory seems to be a better index of reading skill than chronological age or school grade.

The reader's working memory span served as the basis for all the developmental comparisons in our study. This approach to the development of reading skills differs from the more traditional approach that compares children of different ages or school grades. In the more traditional approach, researchers have chiefly been concerned with comparing the behavior of children at different stages of development. As a result, they have paid less attention to other, equally essential ingredients of a developmental model—the mechanisms that might account for the transition from one developmental stage to the next (Klahr & Wallace, 1976). Presumably, implicit in this traditional approach is the view that experience and formal education or possibly maturation are the mechanisms of development. However, more detailed specifications of the mechanisms have been typically lacking. A problem encountered by this kind of research is that there are always large individual differences in skill among the children of a particular age or grade (cf. Ballantine, 1951). Hence, although experience may indeed be related to chronological age, the relationship is far from perfect. By dividing children on the basis of working memory capacity, we were proposing that working memory is an important mechanism for development, and one that may be a better index of experience and proficiency at reading than either chronological age or years of schooling.

The role of working memory in detecting and recovering from inconsistencies was studied by having children read garden path texts (like the *bow* passage described earlier) while the sequence and duration of their eye fixations were recorded. The analysis showed that children with larger spans were more successful at detecting a later semantic or syntactic inconsistency if they had misinterpreted a word. The evidence for this finding was in the longer time these readers spent on the inconsistency and in their attempts to recover from it by making regressive eye fixations. The children with small spans gave evidence of detecting inconsistencies only if the discrepant elements were adjacent in the text. Otherwise, their eye fixation durations did not increase and they did not attempt to resolve the inconsistencies. The development of strategies to monitor and repair comprehension errors has frequently been considered as evidence for the development of "metacognitive" or "metalinguistic awareness" (Clay, 1973; Levelt, Sinclair, & Jarvella, 1979; Markman, 1979; Myers & Paris, 1978). However, little attempt has been made to account for the mechanisms responsible for the development of such skills. The interesting implication that emerges from our study is that the type and sophistication of spontaneous attempts to correct reading errors may best be understood in terms of the interaction of these attempts with the information-processing characteristics of the reader.

The other interesting implication from this research is that it is very productive to dovetail investigations of developmental and individual differences. Developmental (or age-related) differences in reading comprehension may be a very special case of individual differences. Consequently, similar mechanisms may be responsible for both kinds of differences. If this is so, it may be useful to study the two in conjunction. By identifying aspects of cognitive processing that show development, we may have potential leads to significant sources of individual differences. Similarly, by identifying aspects of cognitive processing that show individual differences among adults, we may have leads to sources of developmental differences. Working memory capacity seems to be one such aspect that accounts for developmental and individual differences in reading skill. By promoting an approach that conmbines the study of both kinds of differences, I am suggesting that there is a very special connection between developmental and individual differences. This is a connection that is all too often neither recognized nor pursued.

ACKNOWLEDGMENTS

Preparation of this chapter was supported in part by Grant A8256 from the Natural Sciences Research Council of Canada. Patricia Carpenter collaborated in much of the research reported here and her contributions are very gratefully acknowledged. I am also indebted to Marcel Just for many useful discussions on many issues.

REFERENCES

Anderson, R. C. & Freebody, P. *Vocabulary knowledge.* (Tech. Rep. No. 136). Champaign, Illinois: Center for the Study of Reading, University of Illinois, 1979.

Baddeley, A. D. & Hitch, G. Working memory. In G. H. Bower (Ed.), *The psychology of learning and motivation* (Vol. 8). New York: Academic Press, 1974.

Ballantine, F. A. Age changes in measures of eye-movements in silent reading. In *Studies in the psychology of reading.* University of Michigan Monographs in Education, No. 4. Ann Arbor: University of Michigan Press, 1951, 65–111.

Belmont, L. & Birch, H. The intellectual profile of retarded readers. *Perceptual and Motor Skills,* 1966, *22,* 787–816.

Bloom, B. S. *Human characteristics and school learning.* New York: McGraw-Hill, 1976.

Broadbent, D. A. The magical number seven after fifteen years. In A. Kennedy & A. Wilkes (Eds.), *Studies in long-term memory.* New York: Wiley, 1975.

Brown, J. Some tests of the decay theory of immediate memory. *Quarterly Journal of Experimental Psychology,* 1958, *10,* 12–21.

Carroll, J. B. How shall we study individual differences in cognitive abilities?—Methodological and theoretical perspectives. *Intelligence,* 1978, *2,* 87–115.

Case, R. Intellectual development from birth to adulthood: A neo-piagetian interpretation. In R. Siegler (Ed.), *Children's thinking: What develops?* Hillsdale, N.J.: Lawrence Erlbaum Associates, 1978.

Chafe, W. L. Discourse structure and human knowledge. In R. O. Freedle & J. B. Carroll (Eds.), *Language comprehension and the acquistion of knowledge.* Washington, D.C.: Winston & Sons, 1972.

Chase, W. G. & Ericsson, K.A. Skilled memory. In J. R. Anderson (Ed.), *Cognitive skills and their acquisition.* Hillsdale, N.J.: Lawrence Erlbaum Associates, 1981.

Chi, M. T. H. Short-term memory limitations in children: Capacity or processing deficits? *Memory and Cognition,* 1976, *4,* 559–580.

Chiang, A. & Atkinson, R. C. Individual differences and interrelationships among a select set of cognitive skills. *Memory and Cognition,* 1976, *4,* 661–672.

Clay, M. M. *Reading: The patterning of complex behavior.* Auckland, New Zealand: Heinemann Educational Books, 1973.

Collins, A. M. & Loftus, E. F. A spreading activation theory of semantic processing. *Psychological Review,* 1975, *82,* 407–428.

Cronbach, L. J. & Snow, R. E. *Project on individual differences in learning ability as a function of instructional variables* (U.S. Office of Education, Annual Report No. 2). Stanford, Calif.: School of Education, Stanford University, 1968.

Cummings, E. M. & Faw, T. T. Short-term memory and equivalance judgments in normal and retarded readers. *Child Development,* 1976, *47,* 286–289.

Daneman, M. *Individual differences in working memory and text integration.* Pittsburgh, Penna: Carnegie-Mellon Unviersity, 1981.

Daneman, M. & Carpenter, P. A. Individual differences in working memory and reading. *Journal of Verbal Learning and Verbal Behavior,* 1980, *19,* 450–466.

Daneman, M. & Carpenter, P. A. *Developmental differences in reading and detecting semantic inconsistencies.* Pittsburgh, Penna: Carnegie-Mellon University, 1981.

Daneman, M. & Carpenter, P. A. Individual differences in integrating information between and within sentences. *Journal of Experimental Psychology: Learning, Memory, and Cognition,* in press.

Daneman, M., Carpenter, P. A., & Just, M. A. Cognitive processes and reading skills. In B. Hutson (Ed.), *Advances in reading/language research* (Vol. 1). Greenwich, Conn.: JAI Press, Inc., 1982.

Davis, F. B. & Davis, C. C. *Davis Reading Test Manual.* New York: The Psychological Corporation, 1962.

Dee-Lucas, D., Just, M. A., Carpenter, P. A., & Daneman, M. What eye fixations tell us about the time course of text integration. In R. Groner, & P. Fraisse (Eds.), *Cognition and eye movements.* Amsterdam: North Holland and Berlin: Deutscher Verlag der Wissenschaften, 1982.

Dempster, F. N. Memory span: Sources of individual and developmental differences. *Psychological Bulletin,* 1981, *89,* 63–100.

Farnham-Diggory, S. & Gregg, L. W. Short-term function in young readers. *Journal of Experimental Child Psychology*, 1975, *19*, 279–298.

Guyer, B. L. & Friedman, M. P. Hemispheric processing and cognitive styles in learning-disabled and normal children. *Child Development*, 1975, *46*, 658–668.

Hunt, E., Frost, N., & Lunneborg, C. Individual differences in cognition: A new approach to intelligence. In G. H. Bower (Ed.), *The psychology of learning and motivation: Advances in research and theory* (Vol. 7). New York: Academic Press, 1973.

Hunt, E., Lunneborg, C., & Lewis, J. What does it mean to be high verbal? *Cognitive Psychology*, 1975, *7*, 194–227.

Huttenlocher, J. & Burke, D. Why does memory span increase with age? *Journal of Verbal Learning and Verbal Behavior*, 1976, *8*, 1–31.

Jackson, M. D. & McClelland, J. L. Processing determinants of reading speed. *Journal of Experimental Psychology: General*, 1979, *108*, 151–181.

Jarvella, R. J. Syntactic processing of connected speech. *Journal of Verbal Learning and Verbal Behavior*, 1971, *10*, 409–416.

Just, M. A. & Carpenter, P. A. A theory of reading: From eye fixations to comprehension. *Psychological Review*, 1980, *87*, 329–354.

Kahneman, D. *Attention and effort*. Englewood Cliff, N.J.: Prentice-Hall, 1973.

Kintsch, W. & van Dijk, T. A. Toward a model of text comprehension and production. *Psychological Review*, 1978, *85*, 363–394.

Kintsch, W. & Vipond, D. Reading comprehension and readability in educational practice and psychological theory. In L. G. Nilsson (Ed.), *Perspectives on memory research*. Hillsdale, N.J.: Lawrence Erlbaum Associates, 1979.

Klahr, D. & Wallace, J. G. *Cognitive development: An information-processing view*. Hillsdale, N.J.: Lawrence Erlbaum Associates, 1976.

Lesgold, A. M. & Perfetti, C. A. Interactive processing in reading comprehension. *Discourse Processes*, 1978, *1*, 323–336.

Levelt, W. J. M., Sinclair, A., & Jarvella, R. J. Causes and functions of linguistic awareness in language acquisition: Some introductory remarks. In A. Sinclair, R. J. Jarvella, & W. J. M. Levelt (Eds.), *The child's concept of language*. Berlin: Springer-Verlag, 1978.

Markman, E. M. Realizing that you don't understand: Elementary school children's awareness of inconsistencies. *Child Development*, 1979, *50*, 643–655.

Masson, M. E. J. & Miller, J. A. Working memory and individual differences in comprehension and memory of text. *Journal of Educational Psychology*, in press.

Miller, G. A. The magical number seven, plus or minus two: Some limits on our capacity for processing information. *Psychological Review*, 1956, *63*, 81–97.

Mitchell, D. C. & Green, D. W. The effects of context and content on immediate processing in reading. *Quarterly Journal of Experimental Psychology*, 1978, *30*, 609–636.

Myers II, M. & Paris, S. G. Chidren's metacognitive knowledge about reading. *Journal of Educational Psychology*, 1978, *70*, 680–690.

Norman, D. The role of memory in the understanding of language. In J. F. Kavanagh & I. G. Mattingly (Eds.), *Language by ear and by ear*. Cambridge, Mass.: The MIT Press, 1972.

Perfetti, C. A. Language comprehension and the deverbalization of intelligence. In L. B. Resnick (Ed.), *The nature of intelligence*. Hillsdale, N.J.: Lawrence Erlbaum Associates, 1976.

Perfetti, C. A. & Goldman, S. R. Discourse memory and reading comprehension skill. *Journal of Verbal Learning and Verbal Behavior*, 1976, *14*, 33–42.

Perfetti, C. A. & Lesgold, A. M. Discourse comprehension and sources of individual differences. In M. A. Just & P. A. Carpenter (Eds.), *Cognitive processes in comprehension*. Hillsdale, N.J.: Lawrence Erlbaum Associates, 1977.

Peterson, L. R. & Peterson, M. J. Short-term retention of individual verbal items. *Journal of Experimental Psychology*, 1959, *58*, 193–198.

Posner, M., Boies, S., Eichelman, W., & Taylor, R. Retention of visual and name codes of single letters. *Journal of Experimental Psychology Monographs*, 1969, *79*, (1, pt. 2).

Reitman, J. S. Without surreptitious rehearsal, information in short-term memory decays. *Journal of Verbal Learning and Verbal Behavior*, 1974, *13*, 365–377.

Rizzo, N. D. Studies in visual and auditory memory span with specific reference to reading disability. *Journal of Experimental Education*, 1939, *8*, 208–244.

Rosenshine, B. V. Skill hierarchies in reading comprehension. In R. J. Spiro, B. C. Bruce, & W. F. Brewer (Eds.), *Theoretical issues in reading comprehension: Perspectives from cognitive psychology, linguistics, artificial intelligence and education.* Hillsdale, N.J.: Lawrence Erlbaum Associates, 1980.

Simon, H. A. How big is a chunk? *Science*, 1974, *183*, 482–488.

Snow, R. E. Theory and method for research on aptitude processes. *Intelligence*, 1978, *2*, 225–278.

Sternberg, R. J. *Intelligence, information processing, and analogical reasoning: The componential analysis of human abilities.* Hillsdale, N.J.: Lawrence Erlbaum Associates, 1977.

Sternberg, R. J. The nature of mental abilities. *American Psychologist*, 1979, *34*, 214–230.

Sternberg, R. J. Sketch of a componential subtheory of human intelligence. *Behavioral and Brain Sciences*, 1980, *3*, 573–614.

Sternberg, R. J. Intelligence and nonentrenchment. *Journal of Educational Psychology*, 1981, *73*, 1–16.

Sternberg, R. J., Powell, J. S., & Kaye, D. B. The nature of verbal comprehension. *Poetics*, in press.

Sternberg, S. Memory-scanning: Mental processing revealed by reaction time experiments. *American Scientist*, 1969, *57*, 421–457.

Tuinman, J. & Brady, M. *How does vocabulary account for variance on reading comprehension tests? A preliminary to an instructional analysis.* Paper presented at the National Reading Conference, Houston, Texas, December 1973.

Author Index

Numbers in *italic* indicate pages with bibliographic information.

A

Abelson, R., 111, *146,* 207, *230,* 361, *365*
Abrahamson, 190, 191, *196*
Achenbach, T., 174, *195*
Adams, M. J., 113, *143*
Adkins, D. C., 106, *143*
Agunanne, B. A., 174, *195*
Alderton, D. L., 169, 182, 184, 188, 191, *195*
Allison, R. B., Jr., 48, 75, 78, 80, *100*
Anastasi, A., 74, *100*
Anderson, J. R., 99, *100,* 125, 130, *143,* 218, *230, 271,* 316, 318, *322, 323*
Anderson, J. W., 284, *322*
Anderson, R. C., 341, 371, *382, 365*
Andrews, C. E., 340, *363*
Anglin, J. M., 178, *195,* 333, 357, *362*
Anzai, Y., 313, *323*
Ashcraft, M. H., 278, *322*
Atkinson, R. C., 21, 23, *43,* 370, *382*
Austin, G. A., 360, *362*

B

Baddeley, A. D., 372, *382*
Baillargeon, R., 332, 360, *363*
Ballantine, F. A., 380, *382*

Banerji, R., 214, *230*
Baratz, D., 333, 340, 341, *364*
Barnes, G. M., 162, 163, *195, 197*
Bartlett, S., 6, 9, *43*
Battaglia, J., 278, *322*
Beasley, C. M., 99, *100,* 316, *322*
Belmont, L., 368, *382*
Benbow, C. P., 8, *42*
Berger, P. L., 7, *42*
Bernstein, M., 108, *146*
Bethell-Fox, C. E., 164, *195*
Bickel, R. N., 42, *44*
Billeter, J., 174, 177, 178, *196*
Billman, D. O., 199, 201, 216, 217, *229*
Binet, A., 3, *42*
Birch, H., 368, *382*
Bisanz, J., 172, 173, *195,* 312, *322*
Block, J., 10, *42*
Bloom, B. S., 368, *382*
Blount, W. R., 326, *362*
Blum, J. M., 1, 3, *42*
Bobbitt, B. L., 1, 19, 22, 23, 25, 29, 31, 39, 40, *42, 44*
Bobrow, D. G., 236, 243, *272*
Boies, S. J., 22, 24, *44,* 371, *384*
Bovet, M., 277, 303, *323*
Bower, G. H., 284, *322*

Bowles, S., 4, 6, 9, 41, *42*
Brady, M., 371, *384*
Braine, M. D. S., 106, 116, 133, *143*
Brainerd, C. J., 11, 12, *42*
Bramel, D., 5, 34, 37, *42*
Braverman, H., 4, 6, 34, 37, *42*
Briars, D. J., 278, *322*
Bridges, E., 350, *363*
Broadbent, D. A., 369, *382*
Broca, P., 35, *42*
Broquist, S., 278, *324*
Brown, A. L., 37, *42*, 326, 334, *362, 365*
Brown, J., 121, 122, *143, 144,* 266, *272,*
    318, *322,* 369, *382*
Brown, R., 357, *362*
Bruner, J. S., 151, *195,* 327, 332, 333, 360,
    362
Buchanan, B., 225, *229*
Bukatko, D., 333, 334, *362*
Bundy, A., 254, *272*
Burke, D., 370, *383*
Burton, R. R., 121, *143,* 266, *272*

C

California Assessment Program, 232, *272*
Callanan, M. A., 351, 359, *362*
Campbell, D. T., 7, 23, *42*
Campione, J. C., 326, *362*
Caramazza, A., 14, *44*
Carbonell, J. G., 208, 228, *229*
Carey, S., 345, 360, *362*
Carpenter, P. A., 372, 373, 374, 375, 376,
    377, 379, 380, *382, 383*
Carpenter, R. L., 174, *195*
Carpenter, T., 278, *322*
Carroll, J. D., 17, 18, 21, 35, *42,* 50, 64, 93,
    97, *100, 102,* 275, 276, *322,* 370, *382*
Carter, P., 190, *196*
Case, R., 309, 313, *322,* 370, 372, *382*
Cattell, R. B., 48, *100*
Cavanaugh, J. C., 40, *42*
Chandler, J. P., 136, *143*
Chase, W. G., 190, *195*
Chabaud, S., 350, *363*
Chafe, W. L., 375, *382*
Chase, W. G., 369, 373, *382*
Chi, M. T. H., 21, 23, 24, *42, 43,* 99, *100,*
    201, 226, *229,* 309, *323, 324,* 370, *382*
Chiang, A., 21, 23, *43,* 370, *382*
Chomsky, N., 112, *143*

Christensen, P. R., 105, 106, *144*
Church, J., 111, *144*
Clark, H. H., 109, 112, *144*
Clay, M. M., 381, *382*
Clement, J., 212, 217, 228, *229,* 237, *272*
Cohen, L. B., 335, 336, *362*
Cohen, L. J., 113, 138, 142, *144*
Cole, M., 8, 38, *45,* 326, 360, *365*
Collins, A., 107, *144,* 284, *322,* 369, *382*
Collins, J., 98, *102*
Comrey, A. L., 105, 106, *144*
Conrad, F. G., 134, 137, *146*
Conway, B. E., 108, *146*
Cooper, L. A., 309, *322*
Copeland, A. P., 37, *43*
Corballis, M. C., 98, *100*
Corcoran, M., 6, 9, *43*
Cordes, C., 41, *43*
Cox, B., 332, *364*
Cox, J. R., 114, *145*
Craik, F. I. M., 326, *362*
Crisafi, M. A., 333, *364*
Cronbach, L. J., 16, *43,* 49, 53, 64, 75, 76,
    80, 86, 97, 98, *100,* 276, 313, *322,* 378,
    382
Crouse, J., 6, 9, *43*
Cummings, E. M., 368, *382*
Curtis, M. B., 309, *322*

D

Daehler, M. W., 333, 334, *362*
Daneman, M., 372, 373, 374, 375, 376, 377,
    379, 380, *382, 383*
Danner, F., 312, *322*
Davidson, D., 110, *144*
Davies, D., 326, *363*
Davis, C. C., 375, *383*
Davis, E., 174, *195*
Davis, F. B., 375, *383*
Davis, R., 149, *195,* 225, *229*
Day, M. C., 173, *197*
Day, R. D., 340, *363*
Dean, A. L., 350, *363*
Dee-Lucas, D., 376, *383*
de Kleer, J., 121, 122, *144*
Dempster, F. N., 370, *383*
Dennett, D. C., 110, *144*
DeRosa, D. V., 340, *363*
Deutsch, H., 333, 340, *364*
Dolecki, P., 332, *365*

Donaldson, M., 355, *364*
Downing, C. J., 178, *197*
Duncker, K., 205, 214, 215, *229*

E

Eaglesfield, D., 6, 9, *43*
Egan, D. E., 149, *195*
Eggleston, V. H., 356, *365*
Eichelman, W., 22, *44*, 371, *384*
Ennis, R. H., 13, *43*
Erickson, J. R., 112, *144*
Ericsson, K. A., 369, 373, *382*
Ernest, G. W., 214, *230*
Esrov, L. V., 340, *363*
Evans, J. St. B. T., 119, 121, *144*
Evans, T. G., 161, *195*
Eysenck, H. J., 65, 67, *100*

F

Farnham-Diggory, S., 4, 39, 40, *43,* 370, *383*
Faulkender, P. J., 335, 336, *363*
Faw, T. T., 368, *382*
Feather, N. T., 114, *144*
Feigenbaum, E. A., 225, *229*
Feltovich, P., 99, *101,* 201, 226, *229*
Ferguson, G. A., 49, 74, 75, *100*
Figueroa, R. A., 94, *101*
Fillenbaum, S., 114, *144*
Fiske, D. W., 23, *42*
Flavell, J. H., 13, *43,* 321, *322*
Fleishman, E. A., 97, *100*
Fodor, J., 109, *144,* 327, *363*
Fong, G. T., 221, *230*
Ford, M. E., 1, 24, 25, 29, 31, 40, *43*
Ford, W. W., 231, *273*
Fox, L. H., 5, *45*
Frederiksen, J. R., 55, *100*
Freebody, P., 371, *382*
French, L. A., 37, *42*
Frick, F., 114, 120, *145*
Friedman, M. P., 370, *383*
Friend, R., 5, 34, 37, *42*
Frost, N., 370, *383*
Fuson, K., 278, 283, *322*

G

Galambos, J. A., 108, *144*
Galbraith, R. C., 340, *363*

Gallagher, J. M., 174, *195*
Gallistel, C. R., 279, 284, 287, *322,* 355, 356, 357, *363*
Galton, F., 3, 34, *43*
Gardner, H., 160, 169, 170, 181, 182, 190, 191, 192, *197,* 276, *322*
Garrett, H. E., 75, *100*
Gellatly, A., 131, *144*
Gelman, R., 279, 284, 287, *322, 323,* 332, 355, 356, 357, 360, *363*
Gentile, J. R., 174, *195*
Gentner, D., 200, 202, 203, 210, 212, 216, 217, *229*
Gentner, D. R., 151, *196,* 216, 217, *229*
Gentzen, G., 123, *144*
Gick, M. L., 199, 202, 205, 206, 207, 210, 213, 214, 215, 216, 219, *229*
Ginsburg, H., 278, 279, 283, *322*
Gintis, H., 4, 6, 9, 41, *42*
Glaser, R., 17, *44,* 55, 75, 99, *100, 102,* 107, 119, *146,* 149, 150, 151, 158, 159, 160, 161, 162, 165, 166, 173, 179, 180, 181, 189, 194, *196,* 201, 226, *229,* 275, 309, *322, 323*
Glidden, L. J., 326, *363*
Goddard, H. H., 3, *43*
Goldberg, S., 341, *363*
Goldman, A. I., 108, *144*
Goldman, S. R., 168, 169, 170, 174, 175, 176, 177, 182, 184, 185, 186, 187, 188, 191, *195, 196,* 370, *384*
Goodnow, J. J., 360, *362*
Gorden, R. L., 114, *144*
Gordon, P. C., 201, *229*
Gould, S. J., 1, 3, 5, 38, *43*
Green, D. W., 376, *383*
Green, R. F., 105, 106, *144*
Greenfield, P., 327, 332, 333, *362*
Greeno, J. G., 110, 115, 125, *143, 144,* 149, *195,* 233, 234, 237, 244, 253, 255, *271, 272, 273,* 279, 287, 291, *323, 324*
Gregg, L. W., 370, *383*
Griggs, R. A., 114, *145*
Groen, G. J., 266, *272, 273,* 278, 279, 284, 287, *323*
Gruber, H. E., 11, *43*
Grudin, J., 162, *195*
Guilford, J. P., 48, 64, *100,* 105, 106, *144*
Gulliksen, H. A., 76, *100*
Guttman, L., 49, 50, 51, 54, 56, 57, 58, 59, 64, 93, 94, *101, 102*

Guyer, B. L., 370, *383*
Guyote, M. J., 112, *145*

H

Hall, J. W., 340, *363*
Hall, V. E., 355, *363*
Harman, H. H., 65, 67, *101*
Hagen, E., 164, *197*
Harris, P., 345, *363*
Harris, R. J., 110, *145*
Hayes, J. R., 237, 244, 250, *272, 273*
Haynes, J. R., 64, *101*
Hedenborg, M., 278, *324*
Heidenheimer, P. A., 340, 341, *363*
Heller, J., 163, 185, 186, 187, *195,* 237, 244, 272
Hempel, W. E., Jr., 97, *100*
Henkin, L. A., 122, *145*
Henle, M., 120, *145*

Henley, N. M., 190, *195*
Hesse, M. B., 202, 208, 211, 223, *229*
Hinsley, D., 232, 244, 245, 250, *272*
Hitch, G., 372, *382*
Hoemann, H. W., 340, *363*
Hogaboam, T. W., 21, 29, *43*
Hollon, S. D., 37, *44*
Holyoak, K. J., 199, 201, 202, 205, 206, 207, 210, 213, 214, 215, 216, 217, 219, *229*
Holzinger, K. J., 65, 67, *101*
Holzman, T. G., 164, *195*
Horn, J. L., 35, *42,* 48, *101*
Hornsby, J. R., 332, *364*
Horton, M. S., 333, 341, 358, 361, *363, 364*
Hultsch, D. F., 326, *363*
Humphreys, L. G., 49, 54, 59, 64, *101*
Hunt, E., 17, 18, 21, *43,* 233, 270, *272,* 309, 312, *323,* 370, 371, *383*
Huttenlocher, J., 112, *145,* 340, 341, *363,* 370, *383*

I

Ingram, A. L., 162, 179, 180, *196*
Inhelder, B., 178, *195*, 277, 303, *323*, 327, 332, 345, 350, *363*
Isen, A. I., 332, *365*

J

Jackson, G., 6, 9, *43*
Jackson, M. D., 371, 379, *383*
James, W., 111, *145*
Janis, I. L., 114, 120, *145*
Jarvella, R. J., 376, 381, *383*
Jaskowski, S., 123, *145*
Jencks, C., 6, 9, *43*
Jensen, A. R., 5, 7, 35, *43*, 93, 94, 95, *101*, 326, *363*
Jepson, C., 113, *145*
Johnson, M., 201, *230*
Johnson-Laird, P. N., 106, 112, 116, 121, 122, 133, *145*
Jones, M. B., 97, 98, *101*
Jöreskog, K. G., 98, *101*
Junn, E. N., 199, 201, 216, 217, *229*
Just, M. A., 376, 377, *382, 383*

K

Kadane, J., 258, 260, 267, 268, *272*
Kahneman, D., 121, 122, *145*, 369, *383*
Kail, R. V., 190, *196*
Kamin, L. J., 3, *43*
Karier, C., 34, 41, *43*
Keating, D. P., 1, 5, 7, 8, 9, 11, 12, 13, 14, 15, 17, 18, 20, 21, 22, 23, 24, 25, 27, 29, 30, 31, 32, 36, 39, 40, 42, *43, 44, 45*
Keenan, J. M., 131, *145*
Keil, F. C., 343, 344, *363*
Kendall, P. W., 37, *44*
Keniston, A. H., 1, 23, 30, 39, *44*
Ketron, J. L., 108, *146*
Kingsley, R., 355, *363*
Kintsch, W., 131, *145*, 204, *230*, 314, 315, *323*, 369, *383*
Kintuk, 313
Klahr, D., 39, *44*, 320, *323*, 380, *383*
Klees, S. J., 42, *44*
Klein, G. A., 224, 228, *230*
Klein, R. M., 24, *44*

Kline, P., 99, *100*, 125, *143*, 233, *271*, 316, *322*
Korth, B., 50, *101*
Kossan, N. E., 361, *363*
Kozminsky, E., 131, *145*
Krantz, D. H., 113, *145*, 221, *230*
Kruskal, J. B., 51, 65, *101*
Kuhn, D., 14, *44*
Kyllonen, P. C., 50, 61, 95, 99, *101*

L

La Fever, D. K., 340, *363*
Lakoff, G., 109, *145*, 201, *230*
Langley, P., 287, 313, *323*
Larkin, J., 201, 225, 226, *230*, 234, 254, 258, 260, 267, 268, *272*
Lave, C., 8, 38, *45*, 326, 360, *365*
Lederberg, J., 225, *229*
Lefford, A., 114, 120, *145*
Legrenzi, P., 114, *145*
Leiman, J., 58, *102*
Leirer, V. O., 114, *146*
Lesgold, A., 99, *101*, 311, *323*, 368, 371, 376, *383, 384*
Levelt, W. J. M., 381, *383*
Levinson, P. J., 174, *195*
Lewis, C., 254, *272*, 316, 318, *323*
Lewis, J., 233, *272*, 371, *383*
Lingman, L., 278, *324*
List, J. A., 1, 29, 32, *44*
Lochhead, J., 237, *272*
Loftus, E. F., 237, 244, *272*, 284, *322*, 369, *382*
Lohman, D. F., 49, 56, 59, 62, 63, 64, 94, 95, 97, 99, *101, 102*, 164, *195*
Lonardo, R., 333, 334, *362*
Lord, C. A., 36, *44*
Luce, R. D., 191, *195*
Luckmann, T., 7, *42*
Lui, F., 340, 341, *363*
Lund, N. J., 174, *195*
Lunneborg, C., 233, *272*, 370, 371, *383*
Lunzer, E. A., 174, *195*
Lyerly, S. B., 106, *143*
Lyon, D. R., 18, 19, *44*, 155, *196*

M

Machida, S., 332, *364*
Mackie, J. L., 208, *230*

Macnamara, J., 358, 359, *363*
Maier, N., 214, 220, *230*
Majetic, D., 309, *323, 324*
Mandler, J. M., 349, *363*
Manis, F. R., 1, 23, 24, 29, 30, 39, 40, *44*
Mansfield, A. F., 341, *364*
Mar, H. H., 326, *363*
Marcus, S. L., 112, 113, 114, 133, *145, 146*
Markman, E. M., 332, 333, 337, 347, 349, 350, 351, 352, 353, 354, 358, 359, 361, *362, 363, 364*, 381, *383*
Marshalek, B., 49, 50, 56, 59, 61, 62, 63, 64, 94, 99, *101, 102*
Masson, M. E. J., 374, *383*
Matz, M., 254, *272*
Maxwell, S. E., 21, *42*
Mayer, R. E., 238, 250, 255, 258, 260, 264, 267, 268, *272, 273*
McCauley, C., 326, *363*
McClelland, J. L., 371, 379, *383*
McClelland, K., 6, 9, *43*
McDermott, J., 201, 225, 226, *230*, 234, 254, 272
McGarrigle, J., 355, *364*
McKoon, G., 131, *145*
McLanahan, A. G., 332, 358, *364, 365*
Medin, D. L., 327, 345, *365*
Melkman, R., 333, 340, *364*
Merrill, M. A., 326, *365*
Merriman, W. E., 1, 29, 32, *44*
Mervis, C. B., 333, 334, *364*
Meyer, B. J. F., 131, *145*
Michael, M., 120, *145*
Miller, G. A., 201, *230*, 369, *383*
Miller, J., 315, *323*, 374, *383*
Miller, M. L., 318, *323*
Mitchell, D. C., 376, *383*
Montangero, J., 174, 177, 178, *196*
Moore, J., 201, *230*
Moore, R. C., 118, *145*
Morgan, J. J. B., 114, 119, 120, *145*
Morrison, F. J., 1, 24, 29, 36, *44*
Morton, J. T., 114, 119, 120, *145*
Moser, J., 278, *322*
Mueser, P., 6, 9, *43*
Mulaik, S. A., 50, 98, *102*
Mulholland, T. M., 158, 159, 160, 161, 165, 166, 173, 179, 180, 181, *196*
Mumaw, R. J., 190, *196*
Murphy, G. L., 333, *364*

Myers II, M., 381, *383*
Myers, N., 341, *363*

N

Neches, R., 279, 281, 313, 314, 315, 316, 318, *323*
Neisser, V., 16, *44*
Nelson, B., 4, 39, 40, *43*
Nelson, K., 178, 179, *196*, 341, 349, 361, *364*
Neves, D., 125, *143*, 233, *271*, 313, 318, *323*
Newell, A., 17, 21, *44*, 106, 115, 116, 117, 118, 130, *145, 146*, 201, 225, *230*, 255, *273*, 316, *323*
Nicholas, D. W., 110, *147*
Nigro, G., 157, 174, 175, 177, 185, *197*
Nisbett, R., 107, 113, *145, 146*, 221, *230*
Norman, D., 151, *196*, 369, *383*

O

Olneck, M., 6, 9, *43*
Oliver, R., 327, 332, 333, *362, 364*
Omanson, S. F., 288, *323*
Oppenheimer, J. R., 151, *196*, 201, *230*
Osherson, D. N., 13, *44*, 106, 112, 116, 133, *146*

P

Pachella, R. G., 158, *196*
Paige, J. M., 243, *273*
Papagiannis, G. J., 42, *44*
Paris, S. G., 381, *383*
Parkman, J. M., 266, *272, 278, 323*
Parseghian, P. E., 168, 169, 174, 175, 176, 177, 179, 185, 186, 187, 188, i89, *195, 196*
Parsons, O. A., 326, *364*
Payne, R. W., 326, *364*
Pellegrino, J. W., 17, 18, 19, 21, 29, *43, 44*, 55, *102*, 107, 119, *146*, 149, 150, 151, 155, 158, 159, 160, 161, 162, 165, 166, 168, 169, 170, 173, 174, 175, 176, 177, 179, 180, 181, 182, 184, 185, 186, 187, 188, 189, 190, 191, 194, *195, 196*, 309, *323, 324*
Perfetti, C. A., 368, 370, 371, 376, *383, 384*
Perlmutter, M., 40, *42*, 341, *363*

Peterson, L. R., 369, *384*
Peterson, M. J., 369, *384*
Piaget, J., 11, 12, 21, *44*, 174, 177, 178,
   195, 196, 276, *324*, 327, 332, 345, 350,
   353, 354, *363, 364*
Pollard, P., 121, *146*
Polya, G., 151, *196*
Posner, M., 22, 24, *44*, 371, *384*
Poulantzas, N., 34, 37, 38, *44*
Powell, J. S., 99, *103*, 330, *365*
Premack, D., 330, 346, 347, *364*
Prigatano, G. P., 326, *364*
Pruzansky, S., 50, *102*
Pufall, P. B., 131, *146*
Pylyshyn, Z. W., 109, 122, *144, 146*

R

Raaheim, K., 214, *230*
Raven, J. C., 22, *45*, 149, *196*
Reed, S. K., 214, *230*
Rees, E., 99, *100*
Reitman, J. S., 369, *384*
Resnick, L. B., 231, 266, *273*, 277, 278, 279,
   284, 287, 288, 291, 302, 311, 312, *322,
   323, 324*
Revlin, R., 114, *146*
Revlis, R., 112, *146*
Riccuiti, H., 337, *364*
Richards, D. D., 15, *45*
Richards, J., 278, *322*
Rifkin, B., 160, 171, 172, 173, 174, 185, *197*
Riley, C. A., 332, *365*
Riley, M. S., 237, 244, *273*, 279, 287, *323*
Rips, L. J., 106, 108, 112, 113, 114, 116,
   120, 124, 133, 134, 136, 137, *144, 145,
   146*
Rizzo, N. D., 370, *384*
Robinson, C. S., 244, 250, *272, 273*
Rosch, E., 333, 336, 337, 357, 361, *364, 365*
Rose, A. M., 52, *102*
Rosenshine, B. V., 370, *384*
Ross, G., 334, 336, *365*
Ross, L., 107, *146*
Rossi, E., 340, *365*
Rossi, S., 340, *365*
Rowland, J., 291, *324*
Rumelhart, D. E., 190, 191, *196*, 202, *230*,
   361, *365*

S

Sacerdoti, E. D., 316, *324*
Sallis, R., 168, 174, 175, 176, 177, 185, 186,
   187, *195*
Sattath, S., 50, *102*
Savage-Rumbaugh, E. S., 328, *365*
Scarr, S., 4, 8, 10, *45*
Schaeffer, B., 356, *365*
Schaefer, R. A., 14, *44*
Schank, R. C., 7, 19, *45*, 111, *146*, 207, *230*,
   361, *365*
Schlesinger, I. M., 58, *102*
Schmid, J., 58, *102*
Schustack, M., 218, *230*
Schwartz, J., 6, 9, *43*
Scott, J. L.
Seery, J. B., 65, *101*
Seibert, J., 350, *364*
Sharp, D., 8, 38, *45*, 326, 360, *365*
Shepard, R. N., 51, *102*
Shortliffe, E., 225, *229*
Siegler, R. S., 11, 15, 19, 39, 40, *45*
Sigel, I. E., 10, 11, 14, 15, 16, 34, *45*
Simon, D., 201, 225, 226, *230*, 234, 254, *272*
Simon, H. A., 115, 116, 118, 130, *146*, 190,
   196, 201, 225, 226, *230*, 232, 234, 237,
   243, 244, 245, 250, 254, 255, 266, *272,
   273*, 316, *323*, 369, *384*
Sinclair, A., 381, *383*
Sinclair, H., 277, 303, *323*
Siojo, L. T., 149, *195*
Smiley, S. S., 326, 334, *365*
Smith, C. L., 345, *365*
Smith, E. E., 327, 333, 345, *364, 365*
Snow, R., 47, 48, 49, 50, 55, 56, 58, 59, 61,
   62, 63, 64, 75, 76, 79, 80, 86, 88, 94, 95,
   97, 98, 99, *100, 101, 102*, 164, *195*, 313,
   322, 368, 378, *382, 384*
Soloway, E., 237, *272*
Spearman, C., 48, 94, *102*, 149, 151, *196*
Spender, S., 227, *230*
Sperber, R. D., 326, *363*
Stake, R. E., 48, 75, 82, 83, 84, *102*
Stanley, J. C., 5, 7, 8, 22, 30, *42, 45*
Starkey, D., 337, *365*
Staudenmayer, H., 112, 114, *146, 147*
Steedman, M., 112, 122, *145*
Steffe, L. P., 278, *324*
Steinberg, E. R., 341, *365*

Sternberg, R. J., 3, 5, 10, 18, 19, 20, 33, *45*, 47, 49, 54, 55, 94, 95, 99, *103*, 106, 108, 112, 119, *145, 146*, 149, 151, 152, 153, 157, 158, 160, 161, 162, 163, 165, 169, 170; 171, 172, 173, 174, 175, 177, 179, 180, 181, 182, 185, 190, 191, 192, *196, 197*, 201, 202, 214, 223, 224, 225, *230*, 233, 270, *273*, 275, 309, *324*, 330, *365*, 370, 372, 379, *384*

Sternberg, S., 22, 27, *45*, 156, *197*, 370, *384*

Stevens, A. L., 151, *196*

Stich, S. P., 110, 113, 138, *146, 147*

Stone, B., 173, *197*

Streby, W. J., 131, *145*

Stubbs, M. E., 120, *146*

Sugarman, S., 337, 338, 339, *365*

Suppes, P., 237, 244, *272*

Svenson, O., 278, *324*

T

Taplin, J. E., 112, *147*

Taylor, R., 22, *44*, 371, *384*

Tedesco-Stratton, L., 174, *195*

Teman, L. M., 3, 4, *45*, 326, *365*

Thistlethwaithe, D., 114, *147*

Thomason, R. H., 123, *147*

Thompson, P. W., 278, *324*

Thomson, G. H., 49, *103*

Thorndike, R. L., 164, *197*

Thouless, R. H., 114, *147*

Thurstone, L. L., 6, *45*, 48, 51, 65, 66, 68, 71, 72, 73, 74, 89, *103*, 105, *147*, 270, *273*

Thurstone, T. G., 51, 65, 71, 72, 73, 74, *103*

Trabasso, T., 13, 14, *95*, 110, *147*, 332, *365*

Tucker, T., 332, *365*

Tuinman, J., 371, *384*

Tversky, A., 50, *102*, 121, 122, *145*, 208, 211, 213, *230*

Tversky, B., 333, 340, 341, *364*

U

Ullman, S., 109, *147*

V

Valentine, C. W., 359, *365*

van Dijk, T. A., 204, *230*, 314, *323*, 369, *383*

Van Lehn, K., 318, *322*

Varella, J. A., 64, *103*

Vernon, P. E., 48, 59, *103*

Vipond, D., 369, *383*

Voneche, J. J., 11, *43*

Vygotsky, L. S., 16, 21, 32, 34, 36, 37, *45*, 327, 332, *365*

W

Waldron, A., 335, 336, *363*

Wallace, J. G., 320, *323*, 380, *383*

Wang, Y., 99, *101*

Ward, S., 6, 9, *43*

Warren, W. H., 110, *147*

Wason, P. C., 112, 114, 131, *145, 147*

Waterman, D. A., 244, 250, *272*

Webb, D., 62, *102*

Wechsler, D., 326, *365*

Weitzengfeld, J., 224, 228, *230*

Wellman, H. M., 321, *322*

Wertsch, J. V., 16, 37, 38, *45*

Wescourt, L., 98, *102*

Wherry, R. J., 58, *103*

Whitely, S. E., 162, 163, 168, 170, 182, 184, 191, *195, 197*

Williams, J., 6, 9, *43*

Winer, B. J., 59, *103*

Winer, G. A., 332, *365*

Winston, P. H., 201, 202, 203, 208, *230*

Wish, M., 51, *101*

Woltz, D. J., 95, 99, *101*

Woods, S. S., 266, *273*

Wright, J. C., 335, 336, *363*

Wright, R. J., 174, *195*

Y,Z

Yalow, E., 62, *102*

Young, F. W., 65, *101*

Younger, B. A., 335, 336, *362*

Zimmerman, W. S., 67, *103*

Subject Index

A

Abilities, *see also* Learning ability, and Mathematical ability
  crystallized, 48, 58–59, 62–64, 66–70, 76–87, 91–93
  fluid, 48, 58–59, 62–63, 71–73, 76–87, 91–93
  general factor (g), 5, 8, 58–63, 66–87, 91–97
  perceptual speed, 62–64
  visualization, 58–59, 62–63, 66–68, 76–87, 91–93
Analogical thinking, 199–229
  centrality of, 200–202
  dimensions of analogy, 211–212
    completeness, 212
    similarity, 203–204, 211–212
  mapping, 200, 202–213
    horizontal relations, 202–203
    representation of relations, 204–208
    taxonomy of relations, 210–211
    vertical relations, 203
  mechanisms of transfer, 212–213
  memory retrieval, 226–228
  noticing vs. applying analogy, 217–221
  problem solving expertise, 225–226
  schema induction, 208–210, 212–213
    and analogical transfer, 221–223
  training of, 228–229
Analogy solution, 151–169 *see also* deductive reasoning

cognitive components of, 151–169
  application, 152–156
  encoding, 20, 152–156
  evaluation, 152–156
  mapping, 152–156
  inference, 152–156
latency models of, 153–164
  chronometric methods of testing, 156–159
process outcome models, 164–169
  multicomponent latent trait modeling, 168–169
ANDS model, *see* deductive reasoning
Artificial intelligence, 277–288, 316

C

California Test of Mental Maturity, 24
Cardinal number, 353–357
  cardinality principle, 356–357
  number conservation, 354–355
  understanding addition and subtraction, 355–356
Choice reaction time task, 22–23
Classification solution, 169–171 *see also* inductive reasoning
  latency models, 169–170
  process outcome models, 170–171
cognitive components approach, 17–20, 149
  evaluation of, 33–36
cognitive correlates approach, 17–18, 21–33
  evaluation of, 33–36
Componential analysis, 17–18

389

Correlational structure, 50–64
 types of, 56–64
  circumplex, 56–58
  factors, 58
  hierarchical factor models, 58–59
  radex, 56–58
  radex and hierarchical factor models, 59–64
  simplex, 56–58

D

Davis Test Series 2 (reading test), 375
Deductive reasoning, 105–106, 123–143 *see also* Individual differences, deductive reasoning
 ANDS model, 123–143
  argument evaluation, 134–136
  inference rules, 128–131, 134–143
  working memory, 125–128, 142–143
  memory for proofs, 131–133

F,G

Factor Analysis, 5–6, 48–50, 105–106, 275–276
Fluid-crystallized distinction, 98–99
g, see Abilities, general factor

H

Hierarchical classification, 325–362
 class inclusion, 328–331
  asymmetry of, 329–331
 development of, 331–347
  categorization in infants, 335–339
  memory organization, 339–343
  ontological knowledge, 343–345
  transitive inferences, 345–347
  understanding of asymmetry, 345–347
 learning hierarchical relations, 357–359
 taxonomic organization, 325–327, 330, 332–335, 339–342
  versus thematic organization, 326–327, 332, 337–338
HPM (computer program), 279–291, 311–321

I

Individual differences, *see also* Intelligence, approaches to
 in deductive reasoning, 137–143
 in inductive reasoning, 179–189, 193–194
  adolescents and children, 185–189, 194
  adults, 179–185, 194

 in learning ability, 309–320
  capacity differences, 312–314
  in domain specific knowledge, 310–312
  in metagoals, 318–320
  in metaprocedural knowledge, 315–318
  in reading comprehension, 367–368, 374, 380–381
  in reasoning, 137–142
  measurement of, 3–11
Inductive reasoning, 105–106, 149–194 *see also* Individual differences, inductive reasoning
 developmental changes, 171–179
  nonverbal analogies, 171–174
  verbal analogies, 174–178
  verbal classification, 178–179
 tests of, 149–151
 unities in, 189–193
Information processing, 16–18
Intelligence,
 approaches to,
  componential, 16–36
  Piagetian, 11–16
  psychometric, 3–11, 14–17, 232–233
  tests of, 3–11
Intelligence research,
 new directions in, 36–42
  development, 36–42
  social change, 40–42

K,L

KYST (computer program), 65–67, 71
Learning ability, 48, 275–321 *see also* Individual differences, learning ability
 learning capacity, 283–288, 321
 role of knowledge,
  domain-specific knowledge, 277, 284–309, 320–321
  metaprocedural knowledge, 279–288, 321
  schematic knowledge, 288–309
  production rules, 289–303
Letter comparison (Posner task), 22–33, 371
Lexical retrieval, 371–372
Listening span test, 379–381
Long-term memory retrieval, 25–29, 372–373, 377–378

M

Mathematical ability, 231–271
 approaches to,
  cognitive, 233–234
  psychometric, 232–233

propositions, 236–242, 250–251
  assignment, 239–242
  errors, 239–242, 250–251
  question, 239–242
  relation, 239–242
  role of knowledge, 234–271
    algorithmic knowledge, 265–269, 271
    factual knowledge, 236–242, 270
    linguistic knowledge, 236–242, 270
    schematic knowledge, 242–253, 270
    strategic knowledge, 253–265, 271
  stages in problem solving, 234–271
    planning, 253–265
    problem execution, 265–269
    translation, 236–242
    understanding, 242–253
Memory scanning (S. Sternberg task), 22–24,
  27
MIN procedure, 278–288, 302, 311, 318
Motivation, 319–320
Multidimensional scaling, 48–99
  applied to,
    the Allison matrix, 76–82
    the Stake matrix, 82–88
    Thurstone's primary mental abilities ma-
      trix, 71–75
    the Thurstone and Thurstone matrix,
      71–75
  nonmetric approach, 49, 51
    versus metric approach, 51
  task intercorrelations, 51

O,P

Object sorting, 332–335
Part-whole relations, 305–307, 310, 347–349,
  352–353
Piagetian class inclusion problem, 331–332,
  350–352

R

Radex model, 49, 56–99, see also Multidimensional scaling
  complexity continuum, 93–98
    complexity in ability tests, 93–97
    complexity in learning, 97–98
    radex map, 91–93
Raven Progressive Matrices test, 22–24,
  27–29, 91–92
Reading comprehension, 367–381, see also
  Individual differences, reading comprehension, Working memory

developmental differences, 380–381
integration of text, 374–378
  monitoring errors, 375–376
  pronominal reference, 374–375
  revising errors, 375–376
and listening comprehension, 368, 379–
  380
Reading span test, 373–381
Reasoning, 105–122, 143, see also Deductive
  reasoning, Inductive reasoning, Individual
  differences, reasoning
  criteria for a theory of, 107–113
    centrality, 107–111
    generality, 112–113
    generativity, 111–112
  and fact retrieval, 119–122
  and problem solving, 115–119

S

Short-term memory, 369–372, see also Working memory
  capacity differences, 369–371
Simple reaction time task, 22–23
Speed-accuracy tradeoff, 164
Strategies,
  isolate strategy, 257–261
  reduce strategy, 256–257, 259–261
  strategy transformation heuristics, 279–288,
    316–318
STUDENT (computer program), 236–237,
  243
SUM procedure, 278–281, 286–287

T,V,W

Task similarity, 51–56, 90–91
  invariant similarity, 52–53
  response sampling, 54–56, 90
  sample similarity, 53–54
  scoring system similarity, 52
  sign similarity, 53–54
  summary score similarity, 52
  variant similarity, 52–53
Verbal Scholastic Aptitude Test (SAT), 374,
  378
Visual search task, 23–24
Working memory, 312–314, 321, 368–381
  capacity, 312–314, 321, 368–370, 372–
    381
  processing functions, 368–369, 372–381
  storage functions, 368–369, 372–373

THE LIBRARY
ST. MARY'S COLLEGE OF MARYLAND
ST. MARY'S CITY, MARYLAND 20686